PRAISE FOR *The Penguin Book of the Sonnet*

"Thanks t̶ ... ium of the
sonnet in ... nerosity—a
treasure-tr̶ ... a

—F ... ive

I

t

"As Phillis ... g a move-
ment that ... g. She has
undertaken ... knowledge
from early ... elegance of
style, leadin ... It is a kind
of twenty- ...

—N ... h,

a ... sity

o

"Edited by ... mplary in-
troduction ... ry. Levin's
prose and ... iveness the
sonnet tran ...

— ... m for

PENGUIN BOOKS

THE PENGUIN BOOK OF THE SONNET

Phillis Levin is a poet whose work has appeared in many publications and anthologies, including *The New Yorker*, *Grand Street*, *The Paris Review*, *The Atlantic*, *The Nation*, *The New Republic*, and *The Best American Poetry*. She is the author of *Temples and Fields* (which received the Norma Farber First Book Award from the Poetry Society of America), *The Afterimage*, and *Mercury*. Phillis Levin is also the recipient of an Amy Lowell Poetry Travelling Scholarship, an Ingram Merrill Grant, and a Fulbright Fellowship to Slovenia, and has been a fellow of the Bogliasco Foundation at the Liguria Study Center for the Arts and Humanities in Italy. Educated at Sarah Lawrence College and Johns Hopkins University, she has taught at the University of Maryland, College Park, and the Unterberg Poetry Center of the Ninety-second Street Y in New York City. She lives in New York City and is currently professor of English and Poet-in-Residence at Hofstra University.

The Penguin Book of the Sonnet

500 YEARS OF A CLASSIC TRADITION IN ENGLISH

❖

EDITED BY

Phillis Levin

PENGUIN BOOKS

PENGUIN BOOKS

Published by the Penguin Group
Penguin Putnam Inc., 375 Hudson Street,
New York, New York 10014, U.S.A.
Penguin Books Ltd, 80 Strand,
London WC2R 0RL, England
Penguin Books Australia Ltd, 250 Camberwell Road, Camberwell,
Victoria 3124, Australia
Penguin Books Canada Ltd, 10 Alcorn Avenue,
Toronto, Ontario, Canada M4V 3B2
Penguin Books India (P) Ltd, 11 Community Centre, Panchsheel
Park, New Delhi – 110 017, India
Penguin Books (N.Z.) Ltd, Cnr Rosedale and Airborne Roads,
Albany, Auckland, New Zealand
Penguin Books (South Africa) (Pty) Ltd, 24 Sturdee Avenue,
Rosebank, Johannesburg 2196, South Africa

Penguin Books Ltd, Registered Offices:
Harmondsworth, Middlesex, England

First published in Penguin Books 2001

3 5 7 9 10 8 6 4 2

Pages 440–448 constitute an extension of this copyright page.

LIBRARY OF CONGRESS CATALOGING-IN-PUBLICATION DATA
The Penguin book of the sonnet : 500 years of a classic tradition in English /
edited by Phillis Levin.
p.   cm.
Includes bibliographical references (p.) and indexes.
ISBN 0-14-058929-5
1. Sonnets, English.   I Title: Book of the sonnet.   II. Levin, Phillis, 1954–
PR1195.S5 P38 2001
821'.04208—dc21   00-062350

Printed in the United States of America
Set in Bembo
Designed by Suvi Asch

ACKNOWLEDGMENTS

I would like to express my gratitude to a number of people who, directly or indirectly, encouraged me to edit this anthology: Peter Mandelstam, whose enthusiasm for the project got me going; acquisitions editor Dawn Drzal; and my agent, Kathleen Anderson, who believed in this anthology from the start. In 1991, my colleague Professor John Auchard supported my proposal to teach an honors seminar on the sonnet at the University of Maryland, College Park; the creative and critical response of my students in that course, and in other seminars that followed, clarified the need for a new anthology, especially after the volume edited by Bender and Squier went out of print. I owe a debt to Robert M. Bender and Charles L. Squier for the excellent work they did; I am equally grateful to Robert Nye, whose sonnet anthology published in England is also out of print, and whose fine selections informed some of my decisions.

For crucial advice at different stages of the editing process, I would like to thank Robert Carl, Patricia Carlin, Dana Gioia, Johanna Keller, Kate Light, Amy Nussbaum Mack, James McCorkle, Glenn W. Most, Robert Nussbaum, Elfie Raymond, Matthew Rohrer, and Christopher Ricks. I am particularly indebted to the scholarship of Maurice Evans, Anne Ferry, Joel Fineman, John Fuller, Stephen Greenblatt, Jane Hedley, S. K. Heninger, Jr., Louis Martz, Paul Oppenheimer, Barbara Hernnstein Smith, Michael R. G. Spiller, and Helen Vendler.

I would like to express my profound gratitude to the Bogliasco Foundation, the Liguria Study Center for the Arts and Humanities, for their unstinting support and hospitality during the time I worked on the Introduction to this anthology. I would also like to thank the staff of the Harold Acton Library of the British Institute of Florence, Mark Roberts in particular, and the following faculty members affiliated with the British Institute, whose lectures on Florentine art and architecture, and on Italian history and literature, proved enlightening: Dott. Marcello Bellini, Dott. Alessandro Gentili, Dr. Adrian S. Hoch (also of New York University), and Dr. Kevin Murphy. My special thanks go to the staff of the Sarah Lawrence College Program in Florence, especially Dr. Cristina Anzilotti, director, and art historian Dott. Cristina Frulli. Thanks are also due to the faculty and staff at Italiaidea in Rome.

To the trustees of the Louise Bogan Charitable Trust, I would like to express my sincere thanks for a grant that helped defray some of my permissions costs.

Adam Madonia helped valiantly and extensively with monolithic practical matters; for meticulous work at all hours I would like to thank him and Hugh

McGowan, as well as Jaymie ScottodiSantolo and Kazim Ali. I would also like to thank Jason Zuzga for his help, and David Vaughn for his computer expertise. I am grateful to Peter Thurrell for his help, faith, and support.

I am immensely grateful to Elizabeth Macklin for her editorial help in both New York and Rome, where she appeared as the ideal reader just when I needed her most. My thanks also go to Rosanna Warren and to Stephen Scully for their valuable critical comments on the Introduction. I must also thank again my friend and mentor, philosopher Elfie Raymond, whose haiku compresses truth even more completely than the sonnet: "Form is the law of life: in every human soul resides the measure."

My deep appreciation and gratitude go to Caroline Burton Michahelles for her extraordinary generosity, which has made it possible for some of these poems to be included. Finally, I would like to thank my editor, Caroline White, of Viking Penguin, for her steady encouragement and guidance, and her remarkable skill and insight; her editorial assistant, Zelimir Galjanic; my permissions editor, Fred Courtright, whose love of poetry matches his knowledge of copyright law; and my assistant, Jason Schneiderman, who has been invaluable at every stage of the process, every step of the way. Special thanks go to him for his design of the Appendix.

CONTENTS

CONTENTS

CONTENTS

CONTENTS

CONTENTS

CONTENTS

CONTENTS

CONTENTS

CONTENTS

CONTENTS

CONTENTS

CONTENTS

CONTENTS

❖   ❖   ❖

INTRODUCTION

The sonnet is a monument of praise, a field of play, a chamber of sudden change. In its limited space it has logged, from the start, the awakening of a rational being to an overwhelming force in the self or the world. Its legacy of fourteen lines offers myriad challenges and opportunities, ranging from the technical to the spiritual. As a highly focused form, the sonnet attracts contradictory artistic impulses: in choosing and succumbing to the form, the poet agrees to follow the rules of the sonnet, but that willing surrender releases creative energy. The earliest sonnets record the unceasing conflict between the law of reason and the law of love, the need to solve a problem that cannot be resolved by an act of will, yet finds its fulfillment, if not its solution, only in the poem. Thematically and structurally, this tension plays itself out in the relationship between a fixed formal pattern and the endless flow of feeling. The poet experiences the illusion of control and the illusion of freedom, and from the meeting of those illusions creates the reality of the poem.

What makes the sonnet so compelling for both reader and writer? Not only is it one of the only poetic forms with a predetermined length and a specific—though flexible—set of possibilities for arranging patterns of meaning and sound, but it is also a blueprint for building a structure that remains open to the unknown, ready to lodge an unexpected guest. The sonnet inscribes in its form an instruction manual for its own creation and interpretation: it is a portrait of the mind in action, a miniguide to the progress of an emotion that tells us when to anticipate an irreversible turn. People are drawn to watching an Olympic athlete going through a certain set of motions known in advance, but executed differently each time. The same moves are never performed by one person exactly the same way each time, and the difference between the performances of two individuals can be dramatic. But when it comes to poetry, people are often surprised to discover the extraordinary range of difference in the treatment of a particular form. As with any established pattern—from figure skating to break dancing—the results can be tedious or sublime.

The easiest thing to say about a sonnet is that it is a fourteen-line poem with a particular rhyme scheme and a particular mode of organizing and amplifying patterns of image and thought; and that, if written in English, the meter of each line usually will be iambic pentameter. Taken as a whole, these fourteen lines compose a single stanza, called a quatorzain, the name given to any fourteen-line form. But though a sonnet typically has fourteen lines, fourteen lines do not guarantee a sonnet: it is the behavior of those lines in relation to each other—their choreography—that identifies the form. There are two basic types of sonnets, the Italian (Petrarchan) and the English (Shakespearean); at least that is what we say in retrospect. In truth, by the time Petrarch and Shakespeare met the sonnet, each in his own era, its form was already prevalent, an excessively imitated fashion. Their names are thereby associated with specific patterns that they perfected but did not themselves invent. But each poet brought the sonnet to its peak in his own native language, in terms of consolidating its structural integrity and affirming its expressive power.

In Italian, the word *stanza* means "room." It may help to conceptualize the sonnet as a room (or stage) that can be divided in a number of different ways to serve many functions. Since its overall dimensions and circumference do not change, whatever occurs within that space will always be determined to some degree by its size and haunted by the presence of its former occupants. Even if we rearrange, replace, or remove some of the furniture, the marks will still be there to remind us of how things were positioned in the past. The English sonnet, whose mode of organization differs greatly from the Italian form that gave birth to it, still carries the traces of its ancestry—not only in the number of lines determining the form, but also in the place where the Italian sonnet registers a change that can feel seismic in so small a space.

In any language, the sonnet has an undeniably recognizable shape, easy to see at a distance. This visual impression results not only from its fourteen lines, but also from the average number of syllables per line, which is also quite consistent, and varies only by a syllable or two from one language to another. Each line's metrical structure affects how long it takes to say the line and with how much breath, and to some degree how much space (as well as time) the line occupies. Nonetheless, this predetermined length—its most obvious, superficial characteristic—is not its most important quality. Sometimes the sonnet looks like a little rectangular box ("I am a little world made cunningly," Donne says); sometimes we see a bipartite structure with a white space, a gap, separating the first eight lines (the octave) from the second six (the sestet). Sometimes we see a form subdivided into two quatrains or four-line units, followed by two tercets (units of three lines); or we see a series of three quatrains, and then a single couplet (two lines) standing alone. But the quintessential feature of its design is not as apparent. Whatever its outward appearance, by virtue of its infrastructure the sonnet is asymmetrical. The dynamic property of its structure depends on an uneven distribution of lines, of the weight they carry. It is top-heavy, fundamentally. Opposition resides in its form the way load and support contend in a great building.

Being dialectical, the sonnet is divided by nature: its patterns of division multiply perspective and meaning. But that does not mean the eye will always find the dividing point. We may locate these divisions sonically, by noting the arrangement of lines into units that follow a particular rhyme scheme. Though the variety of rhyme schemes is limited, the possibilities are surprisingly varied. And the arrangement of lines into patterns of sound serves a function we could call architectural, for these various acoustical partitions accentuate the element that gives the sonnet its unique force and character: the *volta,* the "turn" that introduces into the poem a possibility for transformation, like a moment of grace.

The *volta,* the sonnet's turn, promotes innovative approaches because whatever has occurred thus far, a poet is compelled, by inhabiting the form, to make a sudden leap at a particular point, to move into another part of the terrain. Reading sonnets, one constantly confronts the infinite variety of moves a poet can make to negotiate a "turn." Though a poet will sometimes seem to ignore the *volta,* its absence can take on meaning, as well—that is, if the poem already feels like a sonnet. We could say that for the sonnet, the *volta* is the seat of its soul. And the reader's experience of this turn (like a key change) reconfigures the experience of all the lines that both precede and follow it. The *volta* foregrounds the paradigm, making us particularly conscious of the rhyme scheme; likewise, the poet's anticipation of the *volta* guides every move he or she will make. The moment a pebble is dropped into a pond, evidence of that action resonates outward, and at the same time continues to draw the eye back to the point from which all succeeding motions ensue.

The phenomenon we call the sonnet tradition has resulted in some of the greatest lyric poetry, crossing boundaries of time, style, religion, race, nationality, and ethnic identity. One of the oldest literary forms of the postclassical world, a meeting place of image and voice, passion and reason, elegy and ode, the sonnet has engaged almost every notable poet writing in a Western language. Seeing how each writer meets the challenge of transforming an inherited pattern heightens our understanding of the living conversation between past and present. When a sonnet is true to its nature, it encompasses contradiction and arrives at resolution or revelation.

In English literature, the story of the sonnet begins with translations of Petrarch, which gave the form and its rich cargo of images another life in another language. This anthology represents the full tradition of the sonnet in English, tracing its separation from its Italian origins, its multifaceted development from the Elizabethan era to the Romantic and the Victorian, and its popularity as a vehicle of protest among poets of the Harlem Renaissance and the poets who served in the First World War. It also includes an extensive selection of poems from the twentieth century, which saw a sonnet revival. In contemporary poetry, the form keeps living the double life it has always led—as private confession and public memorial. The reader will follow the sonnet's evolution over time, experiencing firsthand how historical, political, and structural pressures engender innovation, subversion, and renewal.

One of the remarkable things about sonnets is how the act of writing them became a competitive sport (sonneteering); and the joy of playing the game, of pushing oneself to the limit in a bounded space with a set of rather arbitrary rules that soon become second nature, is part of the attraction for both writer and reader, player and spectator. The reader of a sonnet participates in the game. One will discover on reading sonnets in the context of this anthology how form configures meaning just as meaning shapes form, how sonnets speak to each other across the ages, and how different authors embrace different struggles at different times: from romantic love to religious crisis to social justice. Looking closely at the architecture of a poem and the recurrent motifs inherent in a particular mode, one enters the protean world of a literary form.

The sonnet was born in a royal court, but more than half its body is of folk origin. The first sonnets on record were written in Sicilian dialect in the early thirteenth century, probably between 1225 and 1230, by an attorney named Giacomo da Lentino, *il Notaio* (1188–1240), one of fourteen notaries employed in the court of Frederick II (1194–1250), king of Sicily (1197–1250), German king (1212–1250), and emperor of the Holy Roman empire (1220–1250)—known throughout Europe for having assembled a "republic of scholars." Giacomo da Lentino, the senior poet in the Sicilian School of court poetry, was celebrated in his own lifetime and memorialized by Dante in the *Purgatorio*. His legal education, along with his training in logic, rhetoric, theology, mathematics, and philosophy, prepared him for a position of power in the court's inner circle; undoubtedly it shaped his imagination. Poetry was part of the culture of the court, composing and exchanging poems a form of intellectual entertainment. We cannot enter da Lentino's creative process, but we do know he invented the form. He created it out of something familiar to anyone in his culture, the *strambotto,* an eight-line stanza (an octave rhyming abab abab) commonly found in songs that were sung by Sicilian peasants. To this he added six more lines (a sestet rhyming cde cde), making a very new thing, a restless pattern refusing symmetry—a poem that turned and spoke to itself. Though nothing is extraordinary about either of these two parts, the alchemy of that particular combination created a novel form that was soon being imitated by other members of the court, including the emperor. The circulation of sonnets created a subculture that, as is often the case, entered the culture at large. The form took on a life of its own; soon it was traveling far.

A notary (*notaio,* in Italian) practices a branch of law that specializes in the preparation and execution of legal documents rather than litigation. In the time of da Lentino, notaries belonged to an exclusive guild whose members were responsible for writing and preparing birth, marriage, and death certificates, wills, deeds, and contracts. To this day in Italy, the sale or transfer of property—from a used car to a grand estate—requires a *notaio.* One cannot get much further from a legal document than a poem: in law, every attempt is made to avoid ambiguity so that interpretation can be controlled, limited to a particular, intended meaning. A poem thrives on ambiguity. But it is this radical difference between the objective and the subjective that a notary would face in creating a document for a client. The words on paper say nothing of the subjective reality of a life, of the individual soul. The sonnet is as extreme in its subjectivity as a legal document is in its objectivity. Within its severely restricted boundaries, it opens itself to matters that know no bound.

The word "sonnet" (*sonetto* in Italian, *sonetti* being the plural), meaning "little song" or "little sound," may have its origins in *suonare* (or *sonare*), an infinitive verb meaning "to sound," "to ring," "to play"; or *suono,* a masculine noun meaning "sound." Paul Oppenheimer finds in Dante's *La Vita Nuova* (1294) the first occurrence in print of the word *sonetto,* which Dante mentions without discussing its meaning. "The first critical discussion of the sonnet," Oppenheimer tells us, appears in *De vulgari eloquentia,* Dante's treatise on the development of literature in the vernacular, written in Latin around 1304. There we come across the word *sonitus,* which Dante uses as an equivalent term for *sonetto*—a special term, according to Oppenheimer, for the kind of poem we recognize as a sonnet: a lyric meant to be read (to oneself or to others) instead of sung. Dante uses this term in his treatise to refer to poems (including his own sonnets) that make a "soft noise," their words arranged harmonically but not necessarily set to music. In *The Birth of the Modern Mind: Self, Consciousness, and the Invention of the Sonnet,* Oppenheimer examines "the logic of a form that turned expression inward." He identifies the sonnet as "the first lyric form since the fall of the Roman Empire intended not for music or performance but for silent reading"—a form that embodies a self-consciousness present in classical literature and philosophy but absent in medieval European literature, which tends to lead away from the self (and the vanity of self-involvement) to a knowledge of God. As "an instrument of self-reflection," the sonnet became a self-generating system, and meditation became a fashion.

Though no one has solved the enigma of the sestet, Oppenheimer disagrees with those who posit the six lines as a sleight-of-hand decision or out-of-the-blue creative addition. For him, the number six in relation to eight, and the tendency of the last two lines of an Italian sonnet to form a separate, though unrhymed, rhetorical unit—thereby placing the octave in relation to the twelve lines containing it—confirm his suspicion that da Lentino was influenced by the Pythagorean-Platonic theory of numbers, elucidated in Plato's *Timaeus.* According to Oppenheimer, Plato's *Timaeus* was a text studied carefully by the members of the elite group surrounding the emperor, a man who believed in the evidence of his senses more than in the teachings of the Church. To prove his theory, Oppenheimer refers to a discussion of harmonic proportion in Rudolph Wittkower's groundbreaking study, *Architectural Principles in the Age of Humanism*: "Three terms are in 'harmonic' proportion when the distance of the two extremes from the mean is the same fraction of their own quantity. . . . In Palladio's example 6:8:12 the mean 8 exceeds 6 by ⅓ of 6 and is exceeded by 12 by ⅓ of 12. . . ." Wittkower shows how a definition of harmonic proportion in the *Timaeus* (36) directly informed the theory of the Renaissance architect Palladio. Looking at those three numbers, Oppenheimer sees the numerical relations of the sonnet, its ancient architecture.

By concentrating on the "harmonic" relation of six, eight, and twelve, Oppenheimer avoids the number fourteen in his discussion of the ratios present in the structure of the sonnet. He makes a crucial leap in locating the origin and underpinnings of the sonnet form in the *Timaeus*. But there is a second theory of proportionality in the *Timaeus*, and that is the ideal ratio proposed by Pythagoras—the Golden Mean or Golden Section, later called the Divine Proportion—a ratio that characterizes the motion of the world soul in its entirety:

A   B   C

$$BC : AB = AB : AC$$

Plato, in the *Timaeus* (35b to 36c), divides the vibrations in the world soul animating the cosmos into two sets of intervals which, though dissonant, can be brought into dynamic harmony through the skill of creative and rational agency. The demiurge, with the help of intelligent persuasion (48), can achieve the precarious balance between necessity and chance, a balance of which the harmonies between the two sets of sonic intervals are but a similitude. The sonnet's ratios can be seen as the formal rules by which the poet can imitate the demiurge's artistic achievement and, by composing the poem, harmonize his, and perhaps the reader's, soul. Contemporary architects and designers still use the calculation for the Golden Mean, but in isolation from the larger and dynamic philosophic context. And composers often remark on how the structure of a musical composition will break into this same ratio: the smaller is to the larger what the larger is to the whole. Even the intermission of a performance tends to occur a bit later than the midpoint.

Since a ratio of eight to five is actually a true approximation to the Golden Mean, it may be more likely that da Lentino, familiar with the significance of these ratios, instinctively gravitated toward an asymmetrical form—and that when he came to the number of lines for completing the form, he chose the even number six rather than the odd number five so that he could balance out the pattern of rhyme. A poet has more latitude than an architect or a mathematician, and can stretch a theory at will. It is also possible that da Lentino wanted to use the number six specifically: it is the first perfect number in Pythagorean number theory, the sum of all its divisors ($6 = 1 + 2 + 3$). It is fascinating to consider that those two numbers, 5 and 8, as well as their sum of 13, are consecutive integers in the infinite sequence 1, 1, 2, 3, 5, 8, 13, 21 . . . of the

Fibonacci series, of which the first two terms are 1 and 1 and each succeeding term is the sum of the two preceding terms. The algorithm that generates this sequence, named after the Italian mathematician Leonardo Pisano Fibonacci (1170–1250), who proposed it, has been of longstanding interest, especially since Jacques Binet demonstrated in 1843 that the ratios of successive pairs of Fibonacci numbers converge upon the Golden Section.

If these speculations sound far-fetched, consider the following: Frederick II began corresponding with Fibonacci when scholars at his court informed him of the importance of Fibonacci's theories proposed in *Liber Abbaci* (1202), "book of the abacus," the book that introduced the Hindu-Arabic place-valued decimal system and Arabic numerals into Europe; the Fibonacci series appears in this work, as well. In 1225, when the emperor's itinerant court convened in Pisa (Fibonacci's home town), the great mathematician was invited to meet Frederick II. Members of the court presented especially challenging problems to Fibonacci, who sent his solutions back to the emperor. What seems like esoteric information was probably an ongoing subject of dinner conversation. That is the atmosphere in which da Lentino composed the first sonnets ever written.

But perhaps the number fourteen also alludes to the number of notaries in the court, da Lentino's body of readers, including himself, or maybe the thirteen other notaries, plus the emperor. Biblical numerology theory suggests other possibilities: a baptismal font has eight sides, the number eight signifying the first day of the new life, following the seventh day, the Sabbath; the number six recalled the six days of creation (and after the sixth line of the sestet, the poet rests). In music, an octave is the only interval to appear as a constant in the scales of nearly every culture. Eight, for the pagans, is the number of the sun, symbolizing perfection, because it repeats the first term in a series of seven and therefore makes a circle. Eight is the symbol of the circle, of immortality; it is also associated with Caesar Augustus, the first emperor of the Roman empire. The power of eight is still with us in the sign for infinity: the number eight resting on its side.

Perhaps to align himself with Augustus and also with the Church, Emperor Frederick II built Castel del Monte, a huge eight-sided Gothic castle, on one of the Murge hills in Apulia, which became his favorite retreat. Built around 1240, Castel del Monte is one of a series of two hundred fortresses Frederick II built after he returned from the Crusades, but it is the only one constructed on an octagonal plan; each of its angles is strengthened by a tall octagonal tower. More than two centuries later, Raphael would fabricate not an eight- but a fourteen-sided polygon (the mystical number seven, doubled), an anomalous composite he based on his studies of classical architecture for the *tempietto* (little temple) that leads to the vanishing point in his painting *The Marriage of the Virgin*, where human and cosmic time unite and where pagan, Hebrew, and Christian perspectives converge.

Independence from musical performance freed the sonnet to exist as a self-sufficient microcosm, inviting a reader to follow its maze of meaning and sound at whatever pace one preferred. The social context encouraged the element of gamesmanship, and the structure of the form promoted intimacy, acknowledging a deep privacy of individual experience while affirming the possibility of shaping subjective experience in objectively recognizable patterns.

The sonnet is a simulacrum of the Renaissance, a reawakening of ancient values, the revival of classical learning, a movement effecting change in the very depiction of reality, from literature and the visual arts to descriptions of human nature and the cosmos. Evolving from the humanism of Petrarch (1304–1374), it began in the city-states of northern Italy, flowering steadily throughout the fifteenth century, the *quattrocento* (Masaccio, Brunelleschi, Uccello, Alberti, Fra Angelico, Piero della Francesca, Botticelli, da Vinci, Machiavelli, Michelangelo). Not until the reign of Elizabeth did the Renaissance flourish in England. Conte Giovanni Pico della Mirandola (1463–1494), in his *Oration on the Dignity of Man*, epitomized its sensibility when he stated that man is the center of the universe, the measure of all things. In the measured room of its stanza, the sonnet embodied a new way of thinking and being. It made space for the self to hold audience with the "inmost" self we may take for granted but often have trouble naming—a psychological or metaphysical entity called soul, mind, the *cogito*, consciousness. We refer to the process of engaging this inmost self (a silent, interior dialogue) as self-consciousness.

The sonnet, a mode of introspection, a crystallization of the process of thought, of a self arriving at self-consciousness, in many ways is born from the same confluence of pagan and Christian sources to which scholars attribute the rise of the Renaissance: the meeting of medieval theology with newly translated works of Greek and Latin literature, history, and philosophy (the "classics"), and an acute awareness of the classical past—its ubiquitous splendor and utter decline—resulting from the excavation of Roman ruins and the archaeological studies that followed. In terms of the development of the sonnet, we should also consider the discovery—in Petrarch's lifetime—of a manuscript containing the work of Catullus (87 B.C.–54? B.C.), the Roman poet whose poems dissecting the torment of his passionate love for Claudia had been lost since antiquity, and which Petrarch closely imitated in his early sonnets. Catullus began his life as a poet by translating Sappho's poems to Lesbia; he also imitated Sappho by giving the same fictional name—"Lesbia"—to his beloved, thereby creating an atmosphere that seems intimate and artful at once.

In European history, Petrarch represents a turning point, an intellectual and aesthetic revolution inaugurating a sensibility that is modern in its focus on the individual—on human aspiration and the importance of introspection in the development of identity, on the signature of a unique personality. A diplomat and classical scholar, as well as an ordained priest, Petrarch is considered the first secular poet, the first humanist, his work a bridge between medieval and Renaissance thought. The sonnets of Dante Alighieri (1265–1321) already represent a break with the tradition of courtly love poetry and its conventional vocabulary for describing the perfect teeth, hair, lips, and eyes of the chaste, beautiful, elusive, untouchable Lady. In the context of medieval literature, Dante sounds like a man writing from personal experience, though his experience leads him to a beatific vision, not fulfillment on earth. In *La Vita Nuova*, a sonnet sequence (the first ever written), dream notebook, and treatise on verse rolled into one, Dante frankly discusses the terrifying love he feels for Beatrice: his confusion over the way her grace, goodness, and ethereal beauty dominate his mind, and his struggle to decide whether he should give himself over to the force of such an absolute love or reject its power, which threatens to destroy his mental and physical health. Many of his meditations exploring the nature of love take the form of sonnets, whose structure he explains in great detail in the prose commentary surrounding the poems. Some of these he sends to older, established poets in the hope they will be able to interpret his dreams or advise him, as well as determine the merit of his writing. Reading *La Vita Nuova* is like watching someone perform a combination of psychoanalysis and literary criticism upon the text he has become: Dante shows empathy for his subject, while maintaining professional detachment.

Both Dante and Petrarch project a self that suffers the contrary passions of a never-ending, unrequited love for an unattainable, unresponsive she-lord, whose regal being takes on a value formerly reserved for a divinity. Though such a concept of love has its roots in the troubadour tradition of Provençal love poetry, in Dante the object of one's attention becomes a means to Christian salvation for an individual soul, and a reflection of divine love. Comparing Dante with Petrarch, we could say that for the former, the scales balancing reason and desire finally reach a state of equilibrium, whereas for the latter the scales never cease quivering, unmistakably imbalanced in favor of desire. Beatrice leads Dante to God, and praise alone is the adequate response, becoming the joyous purpose of his life once he turns away from his own suffering. Petrarch is more involved with discovering his own psyche through the existential crisis that Laura precipitates whenever he sees or imagines her.

In Petrarch, we see a man as much of the flesh as the spirit, who finds no end to his desire and no end to his suffering. Still, we make a mistake if we confuse Petrarch's conception of romantic longing with our own, which tends to include the hope of sexual union in the formula: Petrarch's poet/lover, at war with the carnal element of his desire, loves against his will, hating in himself what drives him on to love. His attraction to Laura's alluring aura, charged with what we read as boundless erotic energy, attaches him to a virtuous, flesh-and-blood woman unwavering in her chastity (and married to another man). The difference, according to the scholar Aldo Scaglione, lies in the fact that Petrarch "sets himself against Dante by making Laura not a way to God, as Beatrice had been, but the objective correlative of God, divinity on earth, the love of God descended into the creature." Laura is essential to the construction of his identity—and to its fragmentation, from which he makes himself anew. Though she will always remain beyond his grasp, Laura is his chance for immortality; like Apollo pursuing Daphne, he will not go empty-handed if he wins the laurel.

The history of the sonnet is partly a history of increasing realism in the attitude to the beloved, a move from sacred to secular, general to particular, allegory to metaphor, symbol to image, and a parallel increasing realism in the poet's attitude to the sources of literary creation as being the substance of daily life—the singularity of lived experience—instead of a system of ideal, abstract concepts. Translations of Aristotle's *Poetics*, with its mimetic theory of representation, accelerated this transition, from the moment his newly recovered work became more widely available in the sixteenth century. As S. K. Heninger, Jr., points out in his outstanding essay, "Sequences, Systems, Models: Sidney and the Secularization of Sonnets," Sir Philip Sidney (1554–1586) immediately acknowledges Aristotle's influence when he claims, in his treatise *The Defence of Poesie*, that "Poesy . . . is an imitation," that "it is not rhyming and versing that maketh a poet . . . but it is that feigning notable images of virtues, vices, or what else."

In other words, as Heninger says, under the influence of Aristotle "poetry was sloughing off its identity as a formal art dependent on metrification and was instead developing its potential as a narrative and depictive art." Paramount for Sidney was the ability to conjure an image that, by example, could teach and delight the reader, creating a fictional world to convey a system of values. Sidney, in 1582, writing the first Petrarchan sonnet sequence in English, played a pivotal role in bringing about the transition from a concept of poetic creation based on abstract, neoplatonic models to a concrete, empirical one based on the observation of human behavior. This dramatic realism, reflecting the increasing secularization of culture, leads from the sublime hallucinations of Petrarch's sonnets to Laura to the rampant ambiguity of Shakespeare's sonnets to the Dark Lady, who is no celestial supermodel, and whose erotic attraction cannot be explained by any blazon—any catalogue of visual splendor. Her hold on the speaker is therefore more mysterious and powerful.

The prototypical Renaissance sonneteer uses Reason to comprehend emotion, and knows or seems to know the absurdity of the position he is arguing. Trained in logic and rhetoric from early youth, and often in the law, poets of both the Italian and English Renaissance internalized patterns of thought that shaped whatever they wrote. The sense of wit and of desperation match each other: argument arrives at the limits of logic and praise arrives at the limits of language. In the hands of Elizabethan poets who experimented with the sonnet, adapting its structure to suit their own habits of speech and thought, the form consolidated into a standard pattern, the one we call Shakespearean. As with most traditions, once the pattern became stable and recognizable, writers began experimenting with it anew, usually respecting its overall shape but continually pushing its boundaries. Change has its own rhythm, dependent on both will and chance.

The building blocks of any sonnet are the quatrain, the tercet, and the couplet, which contribute to larger units of sound and thought—octave and sestet—and the quatorzain as a whole. Though it has been argued that only the Italian sonnet comprises an octave and sestet, in most sonnets a change in strategy begins after the eighth line, evidence perhaps that a trace of the sonnet's original binary structure refuses to go away. The poem needs to have something happen near its center, but a bit off center. It disorients the reader by refusing perfect symmetry. This asymmetry is so essential to the nature of the sonnet that we are even more disoriented when a poem starts out behaving like a sonnet but then divides neatly in two. A sonnet with stanzas of seven and seven feels like an anomaly, and in fact it is. Sometimes a poet will write a sonnet in a totally traditional rhyme scheme, but introduce a break, designated by white space, that divides the sonnet in an unconventional way—for example, just before the last line, or immediately after the first line. Still, this deviation usually becomes part of the meaning of the poem, just as any small change carries great weight in a system of strict observance. Sonnets are sometimes very narrow, with lines less than half the metrical length we expect (Bogan, Bishop, Merrill). In other cases, a line is missing (Yeats, Voigt, Hollander) or added on (Frost, Robert Lowell), or one line is significantly shorter than the others (Keats, Peacock), as if severed. Sometimes there is no rhyme pattern at all (Blake, Beddoes, Rich). What makes such a poem a sonnet, then? Usually, that it feels like one, someone familiar with the tradition will say—either because of the way the poet has handled the subject or arranged the ratio of parts, or because he or she has made a series of sonnetlike maneuvers.

In this anthology, I have included a number of poems that defy or redefine the sonnet tradition, invoking the form they have broken. Some of these variations, such as George Meredith's *Modern Love*, a lyric sequence that consists of sixteen-line stanzas telling the story of the breakdown of a marriage, have already entered the tradition. Long before that, Milton composed what is called a caudated sonnet (two three-line "tails" added to fourteen lines), borrowing a form that had been popular among Italian poets in the fifteenth century, and later on Gerard Manley Hopkins imitated Milton's invention and then invented his own, a form he called the curtal sonnet because it is curtailed (its ten and a half lines simulate the proportions of a Petrarchan sonnet). The title of Yeats's thirteen-line sonnet, "The Fascination of What's Difficult," wryly encapsulates his brawny ambivalence. Though none of the sections in Adrienne Rich's sequence "Contradictions: Tracking Poems" are traditional sonnets, they participate in the sonnet tradition—building a lyric argument from vision and reason, enacting the drama of reconciling opposing forces, urgently speaking of the most private and public matters in one breath.

Changes in the profile of the sonnet are a dramatic gesture on the part of the poet. As we become acclimated to the sonnet environment, we experience a literary gesture as if it were a physical act. The poet seems to be saying, "Look what I have done," pointing to the past and the future at once. This self-consciousness has its roots in the first stages of the form's history, when individual poets exchanged sonnets they had written, often addressing them to each other or to poets they admired. In such an exacting form, whose pattern constantly repeated itself, the sonnet called attention to its own behavior and to the requirements those strictures placed on the writer. Lady Mary Wroth's (1587?–1652?) "A Crowne of Sonetts Dedicated to Love" (p. 66), beginning "In this strang labourinth how shall I turne," is about the elaborate and unpredictable pathways of romantic love, and of restoring equilibrium. This "crown" of fourteen sonnets falls at the end of an intricately structured sequence of eighty-three sonnets and twenty songs entitled *Pamphilia to Amphilanthus* ("All-Loving" to "Lover of Two"), concerning true (constant) versus unfaithful love. In addition to reflecting back on the larger sequence, it is a commentary on the problem of writing a crown, which requires that the last line of each sonnet become the thread leading the poet to the next sonnet in the series— which will have to begin with that preceding line, until the cycle concludes by repeating the very first line of the crown (which can range from seven to fourteen sonnets). And it is no coincidence that the first line in this remarkable crown, and therefore the last, ends with the word "turne," or that Mary Wroth's conceit turns a myth upside down and its speaker plays the roles of both Ariadne and Theseus: she is the one lost in the maze, and the one who must give herself the thread to lead herself out of it. A crown itself is a strange labyrinth, and composing one is a strange labor, too, as the Elizabethan spelling (labourinth) reveals to us.

To appreciate the richness and complexity of any particular sonnet, as well as the legacy of its tradition, it is important to understand not only the two basic ways in which the form can be structured, but also the significant differences between those characteristic structures. According to Paul Fussell,

> If the shape of the Petrarchan sonnet, with its two slightly unbalanced sections devoted to pressure and release, seems to accord with the dynamics of much emotional experience, the shape of the Shakespearean, with its smaller units and its "commentary couplet," seems to accord with the modes of the intellectual, analytic, and even satiric operations of the human sensibility.

The two types of sonnets, the Italian or Petrarchan and the English or Shakespearean, have each spurred variations, which renew the form from within (see Appendix for examples). But each type has an essential structure that functions as an armature or template.

In the Italian sonnet, lines are arranged in a rhyme pattern that makes the poem fall into two unequal sections, the octave (the first eight lines) and the sestet (the six lines that follow). The *volta,* initiating a "turn" or change in tone, mood, voice, tempo, or perspective—a shift in focus, a swerve in logic, a change of heart—occurs after the eighth line, or in the space between the eighth and ninth lines, which in many cases is indicated by a blank space on the page. Binary forces are still at work in the clear-cut divisions of the English sonnet, whose symmetrical quatrains precede a keen terminal couplet calling so much attention to itself that we forget the tide began to turn somewhat earlier. For though the *volta* occurs much later on in the space of an English sonnet, a significant rhetorical shift often appears after the eighth line, anticipating the more unmistakable change that will ensue, setting up in advance a very different method of closure while looking back to its predecessor. In Italian, *volta* (a feminine noun) can refer to a change that is temporal, as in *prossima volta,* "next time," or spatial, as in "a bend." In architecture, it is the term for a vault, which forms the supporting structure of a roof or ceiling—an apt metaphor, as the *volta* supports and defines the structure of the sonnet. Turning marks time and its passage: in an Italian sonnet, the poet has less time before the turn arrives, but more space in which to make the turn, more time to amplify the aftermath.

The rhyme scheme for the octave of an Italian sonnet is abbaabba (*rima baciata:* "kissing rhyme"), called "envelope rhyme" in English. The first sonnets ever written, however, used the Sicilian octave: abababab (*rima alternata*). The scheme for the Italian sestet is cdecde (*rima incatenata*), a pattern of interlacing rhyme. The most common sestet variation is a pattern of alternating rhymes, cdcdcd, called the Sicilian sestet, which is rather confusing, since many of the early Sicilian sonnets use the Italian sestet. The octave actually contains two parts, since the abba pattern repeats itself, and the same can be said for the cde pattern of the first three lines of an Italian sestet, which also repeats itself. Even though the lines of a Sicilian sestet can be read as a set of three (cd cd cd) or as a pair of enclosed rhymes (cdc dcd), they tend to behave as two, not three, units, and commonly appear as two tercets on the page. The early Sicilian sonnets signified the division between octave and sestet by capitalizing the letter beginning the first and the ninth lines, and setting those two lines farther to the left side of the page than the other lines. In time, poets played with the blank space of an empty line to emphasize units of rhyme and give other visual cues.

With or without a blank line denoting a break between stanzas, we experience the units of four-plus-four and three-plus-three as discrete, because of the way rhyme—and meter—establish the limit of a line, overriding demarcations of sense noted by punctuation, syntax, and logic. The repetition of the rhyme scheme of the first quatrain makes us intuit a pattern of sound, and this leads us to expect further repetition, causing us to experience the cde rhyme scheme of the first tercet as a sharp deviation, rather than a simple change. Furthermore, since the Italian octave, like its Sicilian predecessor, turns on only two rhymes, but the quatrains that compose it are in envelope rhyme (that is, two lines that rhyme are enveloped by two lines that rhyme), the end of the first quatrain shares its rhyme with the beginning of the second. This rhyming couplet in the middle of the Italian octave has a curious effect: it makes the two quatrains stand out as separate subunits, and at the same time it joins them together, blurring the border between them, doubling the sense of closure. As a result, the octave presents itself to us as a dense sonic unit.

The poet can play inside this space, carrying sense from one quatrain to the next or allowing ideas, images, and rhetorical gestures to fall neatly into place within those particular subunits. But usually something happens after the eighth line, just before the ninth begins or somewhere within it (as in the case of Milton and certain poets following his lead). In the sestet, whether the poet deploys the Italian (cdecde) or the Sicilian (cdcdcd) version, no two succeeding lines rhyme with each other. It is the sestet's more open sense of rhyme that most clearly distinguishes the Italian sonnet from the English. Other variations for the sestet do exist, however (see Appendix), including that of the French sonnet, in which a rhyming couplet occurs in lines nine and ten, immediately after the *volta*. We so strongly identify a terminal rhyming couplet (any rhyming pair of lines in iambic pentameter is called a heroic couplet) as the signature of the Shakespearean sonnet that we may experience as English a sonnet that, except for its last two lines, has an Italian rhyme scheme and is actually a hybrid (see Donne's *Holy Sonnets*).

Guitone d'Arezzo (1230–1294), the central figure in the Tuscan School of court poetry, introduced *rima baciata* into the sonnet's octave (abbaabba rather than abababab), and thereby established the Italian pattern, the one that was used by Cavalcanti (to whom Dante sent his first sonnets), and by Dante and Petrarch. D'Arezzo's modification added a new dimension of closure to the octave, one that sharpened the contrast between octave and sestet, allowing the change from envelope to open rhyme (alternating, or linking) to signal the turn. Thereafter, Italian poets worked with that one basic model, variations of the rhyme pattern taking place only in the sestet. In the rare instances that the last two lines of an Italian sonnet rhyme with each other, they are not set off from the rest of the poem as an independent couplet, since they still refer back to a pattern of rhyme and a train of thought that precede them. They do not exist as a separate unit of thought, as in the English sonnet, whose closing couplet is almost always aphoristic, an impression strongly reinforced by an independent pair of rhymes.

Though the rhyming couplet is the most obvious innovation marking the difference between Petrarchan and English sonnets, this couplet is even more surprising in light of the rhyme scheme that precedes it. The English sonnet is made of a succession of three Sicilian quatrains (abab) arranged in a pattern called alternating, or open, rhyme, followed by a closing couplet: abab cdcd efef gg. The rhymes in each quatrain do not carry over into the quatrain that follows, though often there is an echoing of consonants or vowels. As we well know from Shakespeare's sonnets, these four-line units have the potential to build to a momentum that will fulfill itself in the rhyming couplet of the final two lines, whose force and wit must close the poem convincingly, maintaining a separate identity by virtue of their radical (within the system of the sonnet) departure from the pattern of the preceding lines. Because the rhyme scheme of each quatrain in the English sonnet is distinctly different from the one before it, there is space in each to introduce a new set of sounds, images, and thoughts. These the reader will perceive as more clearly demarcated than in the Italian sonnet, because no rhymes overlap. But because none of the rhymes overlap, the rhyming couplet, so strikingly different in both sound and tone, can feel tacked on, added as an afterthought that had to be there not so much to answer the need of the poem as to fit the requirements of the formula. A poem built on such a structure risks being too static from start to finish, or too neatly fitted together; it demands enormous rhetorical skill and a metamorphic imagination to unify these distinctly different parts into a cohesive whole.

The advantages of this form for a poet writing in English are great, however, because English offers a broader spectrum of rhymes from which to choose. The Italian sonnet poses a serious challenge for poets writing in English because of major differences in the phonetic properties of the two languages. The prescribed Petrarchan rhyme pattern, turning on four or five rhymes, evolved from a language in which rhymes occur in a narrower spectrum, though with a greater frequency: so many Italian words end in the same cluster of syllables, the same pattern of consonants and vowels, a function of grammatical formations as well as the fact that every noun possesses a gender with which every related article and adjective, and in many cases the verb, must agree (*mamma mia* is a far cry from "my mother"). In Italian, it is difficult not to rhyme, whereas in English a poem can easily sound strained if the same rhyme repeats more than twice. Perhaps it was inevitable that a poet writing in English would have to come up with a different scheme to allow a wider variation of rhymes to govern the poem. And as soon as more rhymes are introduced into the same space of fourteen lines, the distribution of lines into rhyming units—and therefore the proportions of the units—had to change: either the number of lines forming a pattern of rhyme or the number of rhyming units had to increase. Since an Italian sonnet has four or five rhymes, whereas the English variety has seven, that alone was sufficient cause for many poets to abandon the Italian model, apart from the need to establish distance from the form's origins and create a new identity in the period of turbulent linguistic change that characterizes the English Renaissance.

The need for poets to separate themselves from the Italian model becomes understandable if we recall that the first sonnets written in English were actually translations by poets searching for new material at a time when the language and literary culture were going through a great transition. Petrarch was the most eminent intellectual in Europe by the time Geoffrey Chaucer (1343?–1400) made his first journey to Italy, from December 1372 to May 1373, to begin negotiations with the Genoese concerning an English port for their commerce and with the Florentines concerning loans for King Edward III. Reading Dante, Petrarch, and Boccaccio gave Chaucer another literary horizon and another perspective on ways of personifying love. His translation of a sonnet written by Petrarch (*Canzoniere*, 132), embedded in his long poem *Troilus and Criseyde,* is "Canticus Troili," the song that Troilus sings when he first sees—and falls in love with—Criseyde. Like the rest of the epic, Troilus's song is written in rhyme royal (a pattern of Scottish origin that rhymes ababbcc), not in sonnet form, though he certainly could have simulated the shape of a sonnet, since he was working with a stanza pattern that adds up to fourteen when doubled. Chaucer translates from one poetic form to another, deploying a pattern integral to his own sensibility; he recognizes in rhyme royal an apt formal vehicle, rather than imitating the Petrarchan rhyme scheme and attempting to write a sonnet in English. Thus he possesses Petrarch's poem, registering a shift in the consciousness of his hero without interrupting the structure of his epic.

If we look at those twenty-one lines by Chaucer (p. lxxvii), though, we see that he begins his third stanza where Petrarch begins the first tercet; i.e., that he locates the most significant break after a pattern has completely repeated itself, in an analogous place. In Petrarch's poem the long "o" dominates the last two lines: so even though no rhyming couplet closes this or any of his sonnets, those lines are joined together by a repetition of the same vowel. The rhyming couplet of Chaucer's second stanza repeats the long "e" of the second, fourth, and fifth lines of the first stanza, thereby introducing a sense of closure at the fourteenth line, although the song continues for another stanza. By weaving the same sound into the end of his second stanza, Chaucer invites us to return to the first, to the original source of that sound, and thus to experience these two stanzas as one sonic entity, echoing the cohesion Petrarch maintains in an octave. Elaborating on key phrases in *Canzoniere*, 132, Chaucer devotes a full stanza of rhyme royal to each of Petrarch's two quatrains, taking fourteen lines to do what Petrarch accomplishes in eight. Yet he seems to acknowledge the imbalance inherent in a sonnet, since he translates Petrarch's sestet in the space of seven lines, which form the final rhyme royal stanza of "Canticus Troili." Chaucer's lyric behaves more like a song than a sonnet, and that is what it is—more a spoken performance than a passage of compressed introspection. In this way, Chaucer frames his translation of Petrarch's sonnet, a cameo set in his epic.

During his travels on diplomatic missions to Italy and Spain in the 1530s, Sir Thomas Wyatt (1503?–1542), a courtier-poet who served King Henry VIII, encountered the sonnet and carried it back to the early Tudor court, which was already becoming a center of humanist learning, as well as a place where love and death had a literal as well as figurative relation. Wyatt imitated Petrarch's mosaic of ideas and startling metaphors, reshaping them to his sensibility while altering certain aspects of the form. Wyatt preserved the pattern of the Italian octave (abbaabba), but treated the sestet differently by dividing it into a quatrain (cddc) and a couplet (ee); and he slightly modified the Italian hendecasyllabic line, reducing the number of syllables from eleven to ten. Henry Howard, Earl of Surrey (1517?–1547), a friend of Wyatt's who was active in the same Tudor court until his execution on trumped-up charges, further adapted the form, splitting the octave in two by using a different set of rhymes in the second quatrain: now three separate quatrains led up to a closing couplet. It was Surrey's innovation (a quatrain sometimes in envelope rhyme, sometimes in alternating rhyme) that enabled the sonnet to house seven rhymes, creating the impression of three even steps leading to an abrupt closure. Eventually, the pattern of alternating rhyme that Surrey introduced became the norm for the quatrain, and the sonnet in English stabilized into the type we recognize as Shakespearean. If we compare "The longe love, that in my thought doeth harbar" (p. 3), Wyatt's translation of Petrarch's *Canzoniere*, 140, with "Love that liveth and reigneth in my thought," Surrey's adaptation of the same sonnet (p. 7), we confront a rather astounding degree of difference. Not only do we face two utterly different literary personalities, each with his own cadences, diction, and phrasing, but we also discern a contrast in emotional coloring that results from the mandate of each poet's choice of rhyme scheme. Wyatt's imitation feels more passionate, moving in waves toward its melancholy conclusion, whereas the persona in Surrey's version sounds more objective, more distant from the sorrow he reports. Nevertheless, Wyatt and Surrey share an "anti-Petrarchan" ambivalence toward the source of desire.

Made from old metal, the sonnet had become the newly minted coin of a realm, circulating widely on the Continent, spreading to many European countries, Portugal, Spain, France, and present-day Croatia (the Dalmatian coast was then under Venetian rule) among the earliest. It was a mature form in many vernacular languages by the time Wyatt and Surrey brought it into English. But the process of assimilation was relatively slow, and the sonnet lived an underground existence for several decades, entering the public domain in 1557 with the publication of *Tottel's Miscellany*, one of the most influential anthologies of the early English Renaissance.

When the term "sonnet" was initially used in English, it referred to any short poem about love; the words "song" and "sonnet" were interchangeable. George Gascoigne (1539–1578), a poet and critic, was the first English writer to define the form in print in a way we might recognize, with a limit of fourteen lines, a line length of ten syllables, and a rhyme scheme that would become the norm. In "Certayne Notes of Instruction Concerning the Making of Verse or Ryme in English" (1575), Gascoigne provides a clear-cut, if overly rigid, working definition for Elizabethan poets writing in their native tongue:

> Then have you Sonnets, some thinke that all Poemes (being short) may be called Sonets, as in deede it is a diminutive worde derived of *Sonare*, but yet I can beste allowe to call those Sonets which are of fouretene lynes, every line conteyning tenne syllables. The firste twelve do ryme in staves of four lines by crosse meetre, and the last twoo ryming togither do conclude the whole.

Luckily for English poetry, poets liberated themselves from the strict criterion of ten syllables, which had derived from an attempt to model a line of verse on the principles of classical prosody, rules that work for Latin and Greek but ultimately fail when applied to English. In a highly accented language such as English, the stress pattern of the line determines its metrical identity more than the precise number of syllables in that line. The quality matters as much as the quantity. A line of iambic pentameter (an accentual-syllabic meter with five rising stresses in a row) is elastic enough to accommodate deviations and substitutions without losing its identity. Contracting and expanding, the limits of the pentameter line contribute to the paradox of the sonnet, where formal structures elicit spontaneous gestures, artifice produces colloquial rhythm, and inherited patterns summon idiomatic speech.

The English sonnet came into its own as a vital form in the 1590s, during the reign of Queen Elizabeth (b. 1533, r. 1558–1603), a time of strong interest in things foreign, an aggressively Protestant foreign policy, and a growing pride in developing a national literature written in the vernacular rather than Latin. Shortly after Elizabeth's accession to the throne in 1558, a young reform Protestant named Anne Locke (1533?–1595) returned to England from Geneva and published the first sonnet sequence in English, *A Meditation of a Penitent Sinner: Written in maner of a Paraphrase upon the 51 Psalme of David* (1560), a series of linked prayers in the Calvinist mode of meditation on a biblical text (p. 8). Locke's work doesn't seem to have made a ripple in literary circles, and it had no imitators. Of course, we do not know the effect her beautifully crafted devotional sequence had on those who read it in private.

Thirty years later, Sir Philip Sidney's extraordinary sonnet sequence, *Astrophel and Stella*, first appeared in print in 1591 (five years after his death), "taking the English sonnet form at a bound virtually from birth to maturity," as Maurice Evans notes. Thus was inaugurated a vogue, a virtual sonneteering craze. Countless imitations followed, until the sonnet was soon an object of parody or satire. When Shakespeare says "My mistress' eyes are nothing like the sun" (p. 50), he writes as both a poet/lover and a reader who has come across far too many such descriptions, recalling for himself and his audience the gaudy shopping list of ideal feminine features. These were the very sort of hyperbolic comparisons associated with Petrarchism, the name given to the widespread sonneteering trend on the Continent, which followed in the wake of Petrarch's monumental sequence, the *Canzoniere*, or *Rime sparse* (Petrarch himself reacted against artificiality, though he was blamed for the abuses of his imitators). But Shakespeare is doing something else, as well: he is clearing the stage for a new way of thinking and speaking about love and time, death and the power of rhyme. He begins with the assumption that love is like nothing else but itself: it is beyond compare, beyond comparison. Yet this reflection beyond reflection mirrors the self-reflexive nature of the sonnet, its tendency to implode in its solitary cell. The unrepeatable instant is suspended and refracted in verbal and acoustical repetition; the unreproducible being produces an echo of everlasting absence.

In the extended sonnet sequence, from the very beginning of its tradition, we see how poets respond to the pressure of repetition, and how the problem of redundancy may find its solution in the variation of rhyme patterns. In *Astrophel and Stella*, which comprises 108 sonnets and eleven songs interspersed among them, Sidney (1554–1586) varies the rhyme pattern from sonnet to sonnet, and the variations are easy to recognize, but we cannot predict what will happen from one to another. One sonnet will have an octave rhyming abbaabba, another the ababbcbc pattern that Edmund Spenser (1552?–1599) later uses in composing his *Amoretti*. Sometimes Sidney returns to the pattern governing the first sonnet in his sequence, the ababababab rhyme scheme typical of the earliest Sicilian sonnets; then he throws us off the track with yet another permutation. Surely Sidney is having a good time exhausting the possibilities of rhyme by making a virtual encyclopedia of sound effects.

The variation of rhyme schemes from one sonnet to another is striking in the context of any sequence: by changing the pattern, the poet introduces a rift in the overall flow, conducting us through the experience that the entire sequence unfolds, and shaping the experience between the sonnets as well as within them. Clusters will form and dissolve, falling into place like fragments in a kaleidoscope. The white space of a stanza break (a slight pause, like a musical rest), or the often unmarked interval in the shift from one set of rhymes to the next, resides also in the space between sonnets. And the shift in pattern often allows the poet to shift focus. This method of registering change is an essential technique for the lyric poet, for whom narrative devices denoting transition are not only extraneous to the poem but also destructive to its movement. In the delicately calibrated world of the sonnet, language that serves a solely expository function is usually fatal; instead, the lyric poet must convey information rhythmically and metaphorically. An entire world of emotion and meaning is articulated through sound and image.

Perhaps in response to Spenser's attraction to the Italian form, in conjunction with his understanding the problems inherent in writing a Petrarchan sonnet in English, Spenser adapted the English sonnet into a pattern preserving much of the Italian sonnet's musicality and capacity for tracing an emotional arc, while allowing him greater freedom of movement within the sounds of his own language. The Spenserian sonnet begins the way other English sonnets usually do, with a quatrain rhyming abab. But though each quatrain is Sicilian, the first line of each succeeding quatrain picks up the rhyme closing the last line of the preceding quatrain, creating a strong link between the first and second quatrains, and then between the second and third (abab bcbc cdcd). The last two lines (ee) are a distinct rhyming couplet. There are five instead of seven rhyme sounds, and the overall effect, as has been noted by many readers, is much more organic than the typical English sonnet, since the contours of the quatrains overlap, their edges blending into each other: the linking rhymes make the quatrains coalesce, and rhetoric is absorbed into music. The pattern feels gentle, and even in its logic is never aggressive. We can read the Spenserian sonnet as a hinge linking two traditions, the Continental and the British. Those two traditions coexisted so strongly in his imagination that the form Spenser developed for his *Amoretti* (1595) seems the manifestation of a harmonic union of intellectual and emotional affinities. And the sequence, dedicated to his future wife, was a marriage gift.

Looking at Spenser's innovation, we see how the overlapping rhymes between his quatrains occur in exactly the same place they do in the Petrarchan octave, only Spenser has recourse to the wider range of rhymes, and uses the Sicilian quatrain (abab alternating rhyme) rather than the Italian (abba envelope rhyme). Whereas the Petrarchan sonnet introduces a new set of sounds after the eighth line, foregrounding the position of the *volta,* Spenser's pattern dampens the effect of a break after the octave. Even though after line eight he may shift direction rhetorically or syntactically, he continues with a quatrain (cdcd) that is linked by rhyme to the quatrain preceding it. Only after line twelve does he change course, closing with the rhyming couplet that suddenly reorients the reader to the unmistakable terrain of the English sonnet. And because of the nature of the rhyme scheme he has established, we have encountered two other rhyming couplets already, owing to the overlapping rhymes joining the first three quatrains to each other. In the octave of a traditional Petrarchan sonnet (abbaabba), there are three places in which a line rhymes with the line immediately following it. A Spenserian sonnet also contains three rhyming couplets, but the third appears in the last two lines of the sestet. As a result, the closing couplet of the Spenserian sonnet invokes the Italian and the English model simultaneously, and likewise deviates from each of those two established types. We are disoriented and reoriented at every turn.

This distinct unit of sound in a Spenserian sonnet, a rhyming couplet whose sense flows from the preceding quatrain, parallels the final two lines of a Petrarchan sonnet, which often are set off rhetorically—existing as a unit of meaning, though not as a unit of rhyme. There is even speculation that the rhyming couplet closing an Elizabethan sonnet, which first appears in Wyatt's and Surrey's translations of Petrarch, originated in response to a perceived change of course in the last two lines of the sestet.

In any given sonnet, patterns of rhyme, syntax, and meaning may generate and reinforce one another, or they may exist in dynamic tension or in counterpoint—or even alternate among these possibilities. In the sonnet sequence, the options expand exponentially, as does the pressure on the poet to introduce variation into the series. The fear of redundancy results in originality—which is tempered by the formal/technical dilemma, as well as the daunting achievement of the past. Pushed to the brink of his or her abilities, the poet must draw upon the full resources of the language, tapping unknown reserves of feeling and thought.

How does one break from monotony and free oneself successfully from conformity in the typical Shakespearean sonnet, which commits the poet to a set pattern and allows no option at any point to vary the rhyme scheme? Let us look at how William Shakespeare (1564–1616) himself handles the problem, which is quite considerable in a collection of 154 sonnets, almost all of which adhere strictly to the pattern associated with his name. Sonnet 27, "Weary with toil, I haste me to my bed" (p. 42), presents in miniature a solution to the problem of poetic composition, when writer and reader are already on intimate terms with both pattern and substance. Conflating, as sonneteers have from the start, the language of religious devotion and of courtly romance, Shakespeare invokes two of the most conventional conceits of the tradition: the weary lover's unceasing pursuit of the beloved, a journey he likens to a "zealous pilgrimage," and the image ("thy shadow") of the beloved, whose face and form recurrently appear to "my soul's imaginary sight," illuminating the darkness and leaving the mind as restless by night as the body had been by day. Putting aside Shakespeare's genius for generating exquisite metaphors, delicious paradoxes, and efficacious images in lines whose rhythm, texture, and syntax seem inexhaustible in their possible permutations, let us pay attention to how he calls forth the vision of this ideal figure solely through his modulation of sound among the words that form the rhyme scheme. As he exposes the working of the mind, so the working of his sonnet works its spell upon us.

The two sets of rhymes forming the pattern of the first quatrain are closer to each other than we expect with an abab pattern, because all four lines end with the same consonant ("bed," "tired," "head," "expired"). The word ending the first line of the following quatrain ("abide"), though introducing the new rhyme that begins the cdcd pattern, also ends with a "d," and in addition contains the long "i" of "expired," which ended the last line of the first quatrain. Every step forward leads the reader back. In fact, not until the sixth line does Shakespeare deviate from this repetition, when he introduces "thee," making that word shine in all its difference. Since the end of the next line must rhyme with "abide," only "thee" creates the possibility for opening the pattern to a new set of sounds. By pairing "thee" with "see," he finishes his second quatrain with an apparently simple rhyme, whose sonic relief and freshness are nonetheless ironic and ingenious, since "thee" and "see" join the sleepless pilgrim to what will keep him awake.

The new set of sounds serves to introduce the image that causes the speaker exhaustion and delight—before that image actually enters the poem. The sound prefigures the image: the word "thee" enters the sonnet before the image of "thee" appears, since in the eighth line the speaker is still "Looking on darkness which the blind do see." A shift occurs at this point in the poem, at the end of the eighth line, just at the word "see," giving special weight to the octave, making us experience it as a structural unit, especially since the first two quatrains have had so much in common. The sense of this octave as a significant unit containing two interrelated quatrains is underscored by the beginning of the ninth line, "Save," a monosyllable that refuses to stay put in its range of meaning—and a basic rhetorical strategy in arguments moving in one direction and then changing course. What saves the speaker—and proves to be the exception to the rule of unremitting darkness—serves as a pivot for the rest of the poem, a moment of promise that leads to the oasis of the third quatrain, a mirage that feeds "the soul's imaginary sight." We can locate a turning point between "see" and "save," within the framework of a pattern that will ultimately end, as all English sonnets do, in a heroic couplet, whose summarizing quality deflates the expansive tone, undermining the visionary moment.

But before we reach that closing couplet, Sonnet 27 begins to open up sonically: new sounds ("sight" / "view," rhyming with "night" / "new") are admitted into the system, leaving the "d" behind, or so it seems. Yet there is still a subtle yoking together of vowels in the continuation of the long "i" returning us to the "i" of "tired," "expired," "abide," and "wide," then issuing from "sight," "night," into the closing couplet ("mind" / "find"). In fact, the bright difference of sound exists solely in "thee" and "see," until we reach "view" and "new," words whose sound affirms their sense, insinuating possibility through the quality of their open vowel (ū), which leads us to beginnings, openings, and sets up the heroic couplet more starkly. The places in the poem of maximum hope and renewal, of relief from redundancy, occur in the four lines ending in vowels rather than in consonants. Despite the obvious shift initiated by "Lo" at the beginning of line thirteen, the poet's summary of the situation returns us acoustically to "d," the poem's dominant consonant. The sonnet circles back to where it began, save that the pilgrim, who cannot reach his destination, has located the ideal object in his mind's eye. Seeing saves—save that seeing the shadow that renews the face of night keeps the speaker in the same unquiet state.

After a hefty dose of earthly sentiment, by the early seventeenth century the sacred returns to the sonnet with a vengeance. The transfiguration from a poem of love to a poem of religious devotion carries the form back to its origins, to an attitude of chaste worship; but now the sublime object is nothing less than God, without the Madonna, without the Lady, without any female, dead or alive, as intermediary. Sometimes this renouncing of the world comes from an author who shows considerable appetite for the flesh in other poems, as is the case with John Donne (1572–1631), whose secular verse represents some of the greatest erotic poetry in English. In his *Holy Sonnets*, using the rhetoric of an ardent suitor, Donne depicts desire for union with God in metaphors of carnal passion. He often reverses stereotypes and employs paradoxes to challenge conventions that still persist, as when he pleads with God to ravish him in order to save him from damnation. Sidney and Shakespeare also wrote sonnets on shame and sin, on the futility of "lower" things, renouncing the fading pleasures of life on earth.

Sonnets renouncing "the world" seem to be written primarily by men. For much of history, women have not been free to acknowledge eros, so presumably they would have no need to renounce it. Male sexuality may have something to do with this disgust for desire—an attitude shaped by physiological differences shaping psychological differences shaped by religious upbringing. The need to create distance from a powerful female figure manifests itself in the love triangles that recur in the early history of the sonnet, in which the woman is bound to another man, or to God, keeping her unavailable to the poet/lover until an early death takes her from the world, at which point the speaker is free to obsess about her, since she no longer represents a carnal temptation. In Shakespeare's sonnets, the speaker is drawn to a fair Young Man who represents the Platonic ideal of manhood, but this fair friend is somehow entangled with the same Dark Lady to whom the speaker is bound. Rita Dove's sonnets in *Mother Love* examine a different sort of love triangle, the longing of Demeter, goddess of fertility, for her maiden daughter Persephone, who is bound to Hades, god of death. Myth and history meet in the figure of Elizabeth I, the Virgin Queen, a supremely unattainable Other, an object of amorous, religious, and political devotion. As Jane Hedley spells it out in *Power in Verse:* "the cult of Elizabeth" became "an ideological project; the Petrarchan paradigm could be used interchangeably for private courtship and for the depiction of ruler-to-subject relations." In the new Anglican Church, the veneration of the Virgin Mary could be transferred to the Queen.

It is impossible to overestimate the importance of Catholicism in the evolution of the sonnet. The worship of the Virgin Mary, a girl who is a mother and yet a child, who suckles a baby boy and holds in her arms a mortally wounded man who is also a god (making him, in theological terms, her father, her brother, her husband, and her son), produced a culture of icons in the visual arts and a cult of ideal images in the verbal arts. The sonnet is one of its artifacts. Christian iconography endlessly retells a story of blissful attachment, unbearable loss, and miraculous reunion; adoration, humiliation, and glorification. Paradox suffuses the sonnet, and one primary antecedent of this pervasiveness is probably the concept of the Trinity, of a three-in-one godhead wholly human and wholly divine. But paradox was also one of the principal figures in classical rhetoric, which itself shaped the language of Christian theology. The religious sonnet fulfills the possibility that Augustine opens in his spiritual autobiography, his *Confessions*: memory and imagination liberate the soul from bondage to the past, serving the function of redemption.

With the Protestant Reformation, changes that had long been occurring underground surfaced as a revolution, and the privacy of devotion dependent on the act of reading—direct contact with the Word, without intervention from authority, making literacy a requisite for salvation—fostered the ongoing development of the sonnet. The Protestant faith does not require even its clergy to relinquish the world or reject the possibility of fulfillment on earth. In fact, sexual love within the bond of holy matrimony is considered, as in Spenser, a means of celebrating God—an attitude that has its roots in Judaism. The consummation of love in marriage is encouraged for both clergy and lay members of a congregation. That is what Spenser's poet-persona has in mind as he arrives at his beguiling conclusion in Sonnet 68 of the *Amoretti,* wooing even on Easter Sunday in the year-long courtship of his bride-to-be: "So let us love, deare love, lyke as we ought: / love is the lesson which the Lord us taught." George Herbert (1593–1633), an Anglican priest, dedicated all of his poems to praise, celebrating a love-feast with his Lord: their ingenuity of structure is the result of a labor of love for God, not a bid for worldly glory and fame, as in the case of Petrarch. Herbert's sonnets are not as extreme or passionate as Donne's, but he is not violently clashing against himself the way Donne seems to be—nor did he suffer so many hardships in his life on earth.

Whereas Donne's artistic/theological struggle is with the very materiality of the Word, Herbert's is more with the formal and semantic dimensions of language—a struggle to give free rein to his intellect and art while keeping in check the poet's pride at mastery, at making spectacular artifice. Artifice must serve the Maker, reflecting divinity. In keeping with his faith, Herbert does not let his talent go to waste: he uses his verbal gift and skill to praise the Creation through his poetic creations, which together construct a work called *The Temple.* He beautifully demonstrates his understanding of the limits of language with the wit and humility that combine in "Prayer," a Shakespearean sonnet defining its own title through a catalogue of phrases that float free of any syntactical hierarchy and never arrive at any predicate; instead, the poem concludes without an assertion and ends without a definite conclusion, only "something understood." The gorgeous plainness of "something" is its ability to mean anything to anyone, to generalize without losing distinction, to conclude without placing one thing above or below another. Prayer is a turning within the self that originates in a self turning toward an Other in supplication, vulnerable as a lover. In "Prayer," we see how the pressure of closure, especially present the moment one begins writing a Shakespearean sonnet, leads to Herbert's subtle rebellion against the rules of English syntax, which tell us that the subject of a sentence always has a predicate. Refusing predication, "Prayer" is predicated on itself, on the sanctity of the unspoken, and on the mutually "understood" intransitive verb whose infinitive is "to be": it comes into being without asserting transitive action.

John Milton (1608–1674), who wrote a number of his sonnets in Italian, invariably prefers the Petrarchan model, adhering to its rhyme scheme while experimenting with tempo and volume, with the movement of rhythm and syntax within and across the framework of the pattern. The more pragmatic, compartmentalizing quality of the English sonnet does not seem congenial to his character, to the gravity of his voluptuous sentences, his waves of speech that will not pause to take a breath. Perhaps he distrusted the English sonnet, especially its witty closure, which so easily infiltrates a poem from the opening line. His verse flows uncurbed, not even pausing to acknowledge the place of the *volta*. Meaning is woven on a giant loom of sound, and sound prevails, orchestrating meaning, as in the recurrence of the long "o" that echoes throughout "On the Late Massacre in Piedmont" ("Avenge, O Lord, thy slaughtered saints, whose bones"). But though Milton moves within the form without making a sharp turn or tonal shift in any one place, there is tension the moment he crosses the octave's threshold.

In a poem exploring inner conflict, it makes sense that the poem's structure would guide us through the process of arriving at a moment of change, from an impasse to a clearing. But in a poem that begins and ends in resolution, with an unambivalent speaker, we might expect a very different movement. When division occurs for Milton, it is not within a self fragmented by the dazzling splendor of an Other, but a division between himself and a social or political Other; he is not a house divided against himself, to paraphrase Augustine. The house is divided, and he knows where he stands. Religious and political conviction may contribute to how Milton handles the *volta*, but his artistic independence and iconoclastic spirit inform his technique just as profoundly. Especially in his later sonnets, Milton dissolves the division of octave and sestet while obeying the strictures of the Petrarchan rhyme scheme. Milton's organic approach to the forces at work in a sonnet corresponds with Michelangelo's sculptural approach to architecture more than a hundred years earlier, which was based on his knowledge of human anatomy, "a radical departure from Renaissance tradition," as James S. Ackerman tells us: "By thinking of buildings as organisms, he changed the concept of architectural design from the static one produced by a system of predetermined proportions to a dynamic one in which members would be integrated by the suggestion of muscular power."

In one of his greatest poems, "Methought I saw my late espousèd Saint" (p. 82), surely indebted to Dante in its visionary timbre, and also a precursor of the Romantics, Milton treats the *volta* as if it were a physical barrier between this world and the next. Many readers have remarked on the astonishing power of this sonnet to embody in its structure the inexplicable reality of a dream. His deceased wife, beloved by him and irrevocably lost, visits him at night, veiled yet shining until the moment she inclines to embrace him, and he awakens to the night, and to his state of perpetual blindness. In the eighth line of the octave, he speaks of hoping once more "to have / Full sight of her in Heaven without restraint," and after the comma following "restraint" she materializes as a brilliant moving image. No visual description of her appears in the octave, and she slips into the poem "without restraint," occupying four lines. (In lines nine through twelve of Shakespeare's Sonnet 27, the beloved image also emits the most light.) The turn is more shocking, coming as it does just after we would expect it, just after we are prepared for it by the rhyme scheme. The last two lines of the poem are a single sentence, and therefore are set off syntactically, as in an English sonnet. Still, they complete the pattern (cdcdcd) of an Italian sonnet; and Milton manages to keep this separate unit from sounding like an epigram by filling it with dramatic monosyllables, nouns and verbs whose staccato rhythm is counterpointed by a succession of long vowels that make those unremitting lines sound heavy and light at once.

The sonnet is a poem of process, a movement that leads from image to insight, from inquiry to understanding. As readers and writers, we must be willing to enter a situation or mood that will carry us somewhere we cannot predict, however well equipped we may be. The emotional or technical confidence of the poet enables a greater degree of risk. But one does not start out knowing how or where one will end, only that one will have to stop after the fourteenth line. This type of progression is antithetical to the modus operandi of the eighteenth-century tradition, where one begins with one's conclusion, thinking deductively, not inductively. Maybe that is why so few notable sonnets were written during this time period, and why those that were written tended to be satirical, or on minor, more occasional subjects. An exception to the rule is Charlotte Smith (1749–1806), whose *Elegiac Sonnets* (1784) rekindled an interest in the form and influenced Samuel Taylor Coleridge, Leigh Hunt, and John Keats. Smith's sonnets reflect on the experience of being lost, without a goal, in a receptive state that Keats would call "negative capability," and thus seem to shed some light on the dilemma facing the eighteenth-century poet. The writer of a sonnet must take the chance of not arriving anywhere significant at all. The prototypical poem of the eighteenth century is not only long, because of the prevailing interest in the epic genre, but also opens with a confident position or hypothesis. On the other hand, the eighteenth-century poem's primary means of organizing thought was the heroic couplet, so perhaps the epigrammatic quality of the English sonnet remained.

The sea change we intuit when reading poems of the Romantic period after reading eighteenth-century verse is a shift in ways of organizing patterns of perception and cognition, a shift in how one arrives at psychological and metaphysical knowledge. The preoccupation with the lost paradise of childhood and the world of dreams lends itself to the sonnet form and partakes of that form's tradition of recording moments of upheaval or illumination in mind and heart. Milton as poet and revolutionary, as influence and example, along with their own desire to recapture the richness of Shakespearean diction, informed the strong revival of the sonnet tradition among the Romantics, whose elation and dejection were a consequence of public as well as private matters. The crisis of the French Revolution, the resurrection and destruction of utopian ideals, and the longing for Liberty, a powerful, nurturing goddess, were all shaping forces in their work and their lives. The need to follow and fulfill epic impulses in a time when epic was no longer possible might have contributed to the resurging interest in sonnets in both the Romantic and the Victorian eras, since the sonnet sequence is monumental in impulse yet suited to bursts of creative energy and insight that are freed from linear time (as in film, where flashbacks, freeze-frames, fast-forwarding, panning, and zooming are by now traditional techniques and the splicing together of disjointed frames to create montage resembles the splitting/binding effect of the *volta*). A sonnet needs an object around which to turn, just as a person needs an ideal in order to construct ontological meaning. To become the object it is (to constitute itself), the sonnet needs an object.

Wordsworth discovered, in the sonnets of Milton, the possibility for expressing unity of spirit and unity of form—of making an "orbicular body" that resembled "a dewdrop." The way in which Wordsworth "took fire" from Milton's sonnets is central to Jennifer Ann Wagner's study of the nineteenth-century English sonnet, *A Moment's Monument*. Exploring how "Wordsworth's admiration of Milton's sonnets is won because of that poet's projection of voice far beyond the confines of conventional lyric," and how "the scope of address changes . . . from an audience of one to an audience of a nation," Wagner brilliantly demonstrates how sonnets of the Romantic period are grounded in a visionary poetics and therefore feel and move differently, internally unified in a way that sonnets of the English Renaissance are not. For Milton was already writing sonnets that, if not ignoring the *volta* entirely, rushed through that point to the end of the poem. But in Dante, as well, there is a change in his sonnets when he comes to the turning point of his life in relation to Beatrice and decides not to write any longer about her effect on him, turning instead to writing poems that praise her. The integration of spirit that resulted from this decision, the release from inner turmoil and conflict, the letting go into an attitude of praise, certainly resonate with the unity of being that the Romantic poets sought, though for the Romantics it was nature that became the Muse, the ideal object, the ultimate subject of praise, the only believable image of immortality.

It is interesting to consider that the turning point in Petrarch's life was when, on resting a moment while climbing Mount Ventoux, he opened his copy of Saint Augustine's *Confessions* and alighted by chance on a passage in which Augustine discusses how people look at the mountains and the fields and the stars but not at or into themselves. We could say that by the time of the Romantic Movement, after a long journey inward, the sonnet returns to the outer world. Of course, the Romantic poets were just as concerned with psychology as any poets before them; yet the means of escaping or discovering the self is usually not in finding an image of the human beloved within the heart, or in meditating on the image of Christ or a kingdom of God—but in engaging the world of nature and the secular images of everyday life. Wordsworth, Coleridge, Clare, and Keats frequently muse on emotions or changes in mood, on how those changes are reflected in the natural world and provoked by natural processes. Nature is the divine sanctuary, the object of worship, the ideal Other the poet would like to join in blissful union—free of the weight of self-consciousness and of history.

Prometheus, the Titan of Greek legend who created the first human out of clay, who brought fire to humanity (and therefore knowledge, and the burden of knowledge) by stealing a spark from heaven and carrying it to earth in a stalk of fennel, was considered with suspicion in the ancient world, but embraced as a hero during the Romantic era—as a champion of freedom from tyranny and a symbol of democratic ideals. The early Christian Church found a way to embrace him by making him into a symbol of the Passion. Mary Shelley's novel *Frankenstein,* subtitled *The Modern Prometheus,* is a critique of such titanic ambitions (and it is of course the ambitious, godlike scientist and intellectual, not the sensitive monster, who is named Frankenstein); it is a critique, as well, of those unrestrained Promethean impulses which her husband, Percy Bysshe Shelley (1792–1822), celebrated in his verse drama, *Prometheus Unbound.* Shelley's ambivalent relationship to power and to the empires of the past—veering between attraction and repulsion—appears on a much smaller scale in his well-known sonnet "Ozymandias" (p. 103). Shelley wrote this poem in a competition with his friend Horace Smith (p. 99) after they viewed ancient Egyptian artifacts on display at the British Museum. (Ozymandias is the Greek name for the monarch Ramses II, who reigned in Egypt in the thirteenth century B.C.).

The originality of Shelley's poem is due in part to his recognition that a sonnet can incorporate several voices, a possibility that the sonnet tradition richly offers and the *volta* licenses—whether the dialogue is between a self at odds

with itself or engaged in an I/Thou relation with a lover or a Lord. The open-
ing line, journalistic in strategy, gives the "traveller from an antique land" the
stage. The traveller's discourse occupies most of the lines, framed by the opening
statement and the final three lines, which contain an observation whose objec-
tivity removes us from the speaking subject. The sonnet is dramatic in character,
leaving it up to the reader to make the inferences and judgments. Information
is reported without reflection, but the organization of information elicits cer-
tain conclusions: we cannot avoid reflecting back on the image of colossal
power after hearing the words engraved on the pedestal, which in a matter of a
few lines gives life to the "lifeless things" and impresses us with the totality of
loss, the ruler's arrogance and ruin, and the power of time. As in Shakespeare,
who opened the sonnet's thematic possibilities to the full gamut of life on earth
and treated the form as a lyric independent of all other lyrics, even if part of a
sequence, "Ozymandias" stands on its own, self-contained, telling us that only
words, not images, survive, or only images made from words. "Ozymandias" is
like a shard from which we read a civilization, or a snapshot whose caption
alone has survived the annihilation of a culture. Natural forces destroy the mon-
ument, and the level sand, which is a product of time, and which human beings
use to measure time, stretches into a distance that seems serene.

   The structure is telling: as in many Italian sonnets, an image dominates the
octave; the sestet, which introduces the pedestal on which the words of Ozy-
mandias appear, is the poem's pedestal. The only line in the octave without a
matching rhyme ends with "lifeless things"; and the only line without a match-
ing rhyme in the sestet ends with "king of kings." The extra lines we have to
travel to connect "kings" and "things" make us more aware of those two words,
and emphasize their ironic relation. Within a year, Shelley would write his son-
net entitled "England in 1819," an invective against the mad king George III
(1738–1820), in which he derides "Rulers who neither see, nor feel, nor
know, / But leech-like to their fainting country cling." Moving from rage to
apocalyptic hope, Shelley leaves us with the image of a "glorious Phantom,"
who is none other than Prometheus, the Spirit of Liberty.

Many schoolchildren are familiar with part of the inscription engraved on the
pedestal of the Statue of Liberty, yet most people do not realize that those
words are the last five lines of a sonnet written by Emma Lazarus (1849–1887),
a New Yorker of Portuguese Jewish descent who fought for the rights of
refugees. "The New Colossus" (p. 153), from which those lines are taken, alludes
to Shelley's "Ozymandias," contrasting two radically opposite conceptions of
leadership and statehood—one based on conquest and domination, the other
on compassion and inclusion. Like her Romantic predecessor, Lazarus is at-
tracted to the Promethean struggle for independence from brute tyrannical
force, human or divine: she describes "A mighty woman with a torch, whose

flame / Is the imprisoned lightning, and her name / Mother of Exiles." These two colossal figures represent utterly different values; and that is what her sonnet says to us about empire, and emblems of power. Her portrait of *ideal* authority, of strength equal to empathy, is distinctively female.

In "The New Colossus," Lazarus takes from Shelley the strategy of direct discourse, for both poets have created monuments that speak as we enter the sonnet's sestet. What the Statue of Liberty tells us, the power of that eloquent image whose words now belong to the world, owes a debt to how Lazarus read Shelley and to how Shelley reread the French Revolution when Napoleon's crew of artists returned from Egypt with a drawing of the massive head of Ramses II, "that colossal wreck" found lying in the sand. In still more recent popular culture, "Ozymandias" and "The New Colossus" ironically converge in the uncanny closing scene of the film *Planet of the Apes,* when Liberty's head and raised arm are all that remain in the rubble. But looming behind Shelley and Lazarus was yet another creation built to conquer time, Shakespeare's Sonnet 55: "Not marble nor the gilded monuments / Of princes shall outlive this pow'rful rime." Whether courtly lover or social reformer, the sonnet-maker is embroiled in the dialectic of power—of mastery or surrender.

The sonnets of Gerard Manley Hopkins (1844–1889) are some of the most intellectually and emotionally demanding and rewarding lyric poems in English literature. A poet of the Victorian era who finally gained an audience in the twentieth century, after his friend and fellow-poet Robert Bridges published an edition of his work in 1918, Hopkins charted the course that led him "to passion's end" in a sequence of three sonnets, "The Beginning of the End," written in 1865. The sequence is subtitled "a neglected lover's address to his mistress." A year later, however, Hopkins joined the Catholic Church; in 1868, he decided to become a priest, burned copies of his poems, believing that writing conflicted with his vocation, and became a novitiate of the Jesuit order. It was after entering the priesthood that he wrote the poems representing his greatest achievement: sonnets radically experimental in their rhythm, syntax, and diction, in which he explores his complex relationship to himself and to God—the distance or closeness to his Lord that determines his state of mind. Collectively they form a journal of the struggle between hope and despair, anguish and ecstasy, which vie in him as fiercely as the contrary passions of a Petrarchan lover. Hopkins's intense awareness of the smallest iota of rhythm and meaning is equaled by his sensitivity to the most microscopic detail in the natural world, and by his vast range of reference, from the notebooks of Charles Darwin to the pre-Socratic philosophy of Heraclitus. Hopkins's life and work embody the paradox of containing passion (for Creator and Creation) in strict boundaries—the sonnet form an emblem of the mortal frame that binds us to death and awakens us through the senses to the intimation of an eternal present.

Ironic reversals, intrinsic to the sonnet tradition, appear frequently in the poets who fought and wrote during the First World War, often with little time between the fighting and the writing. Wilfred Owen (1893–1918), who in early youth wrote sonnets on pastoral subjects, did not abandon the sonnet when war became his subject—that is, when he turned from poetry as a refuge from reality to poetry as a vehicle for expressing outrage and conjuring the hell of trench warfare. Instead, he overhauled the sonnet's character, with Milton as a major antecedent in a long line of poets writing sonnets about intolerance, inequality, and injustice. Owen's famous poem "Dulce et Decorum Est" (p. 192) is rarely recognized for what it is, a double sonnet, the first part appearing to be Italian in its structure (octave and sestet), the other an upside-down English sonnet—as if the two traditions mirrored each other in a muddy pool. The total reversal of ideals (young men portrayed as "old beggars," glorious war depicted as useless slaughter) is echoed in Owen's wrenching and twisting of the sonnet form, in his grotesque repetition of "drowning" (rather than finding a neat rhyme); and the ugliness of the images attests to the traditional qualities of horror and to Owen's horror at that tradition. This poem's form cannot be separated from its meaning; it informs the meaning throughout. A double sonnet among court poets served the purpose of double praise, the suitor's redoubled labor an index of his desire to persuade, to prove himself worthy of an ideal. Owen's more modern suit was a double plea to end a brutally senseless war.

In the same decades, many poets of the Harlem Renaissance wrote sonnets, revising the tradition while employing it to gain a place in American culture. It was a way to claim their humanity through a form that, from its inception, fostered the expression of individual consciousness while reflecting in its metaphors and paradoxes the contradictory aspects of being in the world—the tensions between self and Other, the unending desire for an unattainable ideal. When Winston Churchill addressed the House of Commons during the Second World War, he read aloud one of the most impassioned testaments to courage and dignity in the English language, "If We Must Die" (p. 181), a sonnet written by Claude McKay (1890–1948) in response to the Harlem race riots of 1919: "If we must die, let it not be like hogs / Hunted and penned in an inglorious spot, / While round us bark the mad and hungry dogs, / Making their mock at our accursed lot." The power of this poem to embody the struggle for racial equality while reviving the sonnet as a means of persuasion and moral validation, and likewise its capacity to transcend the occasion that evoked it—reaching people of another culture in the midst of an entirely different historical crisis—are themselves living proof of the sonnet's plasticity, volatility, and resiliency. McKay deftly uses each quatrain to advance each step in his argument, but his dramatic signaling of a turn at the beginning of his sestet ("O kinsmen! we must meet the common foe!") aligns the sonnet with the Petrarchan model, despite its Shakespearean rhyme scheme and rhetorical structure; McKay then turns the sonnet again, deploying a Shakespearean closing couplet, whose decisive resolution is an avowal of fortitude, solidarity, resistance, and honor.

Reading another of McKay's sonnets, entitled "America" (p. 182), one becomes aware of how thoroughly McKay, who was born in Jamaica and moved to Harlem in 1914, absorbed the sonnet tradition. He mastered its pattern and power, gravitating to its heritage to articulate both his own artistic aims and his ethical passions. In "America" he ingeniously reverses the conventional trope of dark and light, black and white. That is, he reverses Shakespeare's reversal, with an added twist: a dark-skinned man addresses white ("fair"?) America, personified here as a tormenting, alluring woman unfairly depriving him of what he desires. The speaker cannot extricate himself from the culture whose vigor gives him strength "against her hate"; he cannot stop loving the disdainful mistress who feeds him the "bread of bitterness." McKay closes with a direct allusion to the ending of Shelley's "Ozymandias," thereby converting his own poem into a prophecy of the self-destructive force of racism for the future of his nation. His "America" ends: "Beneath the touch of time's unerring hand, / Like priceless treasures sinking in the sand."

Robert Lowell (1917–1977) collected a large group of sonnets into a book he entitled *Notebook,* and printed a telling afterword in that volume. His commentary demonstrates how the sonnet attracts ambition, an impulse toward emulation, and a desire to subvert both the form itself and perhaps his own ambition: "My meter, fourteen-line unrhymed blank verse sections, is fairly strict at first and elsewhere, but often corrupts in single lines to the freedom of prose. Even with this license, I fear I have failed to avoid the themes and gigantism of the sonnet." The gravitational pull of the sonnet and its tradition was too strong for Lowell to resist, and he wanted to enter its force field. On some level, he knew what he was doing, that he was getting into something big, though he tried to diminish his expectations of himself and poetry. Writing a sonnet in blank verse is not a symptom of humility for Lowell, for it aligns him with Shakespearean drama and Miltonic epic; it suggests a stripping away of rhyme's sensual artifice in the service of a graphic, antilyrical puritan realism, as if rhyme were a temptation to be resisted. Tellingly, at the moments of rapture in *Notebook,* Lowell often "reverts" to rhyme and to the measure of the Muses.

"Dolphin" (p. 232) is a self-portrait of a "man of craft" guided by surprise: in other words, a portrait of the kind of person who would write a sonnet and need to write one. After Lowell's speaker admits he has "plotted perhaps too freely with my life," confessing that he has caused too much injury to himself and others to ask for compassion, he reaches the poem's fourteenth line, which is followed by a dash and the white space of a stanza break. Then there is one additional, fifteenth, isolated line—"my eyes have seen what my hand did"—as if that extra line were itself a description of what he has done, not only in that poem but in his life, and in his whole life in art. The extra line is a chilling, heart-breaking admission of excess, of shame, of unabashed self-awareness, of conscience. Reading this poem, we attend upon the act of consciousness becoming conscience, which in the sonnet occurs at the *volta*. In this case, however, the *volta* shifts location and occurs after the poem should be over. And so the position of recognition is tragic, coming as it does here after the ending—coming too late and yet, being part of the poem, not too late, at least for the poem. "Dolphin" is a sad speculation on a belated realization that makes the reader participate in the process of a self facing himself: an audience watches a man in audience with himself. We are back to the position we have found ourselves in when reading sonnets of the Renaissance. The saving grace here is not God, or a beloved human, but the Dolphin, another mammal, an emblem of the Muse who guides him in his craft. Not a human being, but not a god either. And if art is a consolation here, it is still not enough. The shape and movement of this sonnet tell us so.

In "American Sonnet" (p. 276) Billy Collins (B. 1941), who writes in a comic, surrealistic vein, plays on the preconceived notion of both the sonnet and the Americanization of things. Though his poem certainly doesn't look like a sonnet (it really isn't one, in either a classical or a far-fetched sense), and we would not think of sonnets at all in relation to this poem if not for its droll, flat title announcing itself as one of them (a contradiction in terms to anyone who can see its shape or feel its contours in Braille), on close inspection we realize that Collins has something up his sleeve other than false advertising. The basic image of this poem—its principal conceit, the picture postcard—is a paradigm of the sonnet. The strategy of calling forth a compelling image in the octave and commenting on it in the sestet is mirrored in Collins's portrayal of the very way a picture postcard functions: we look at the picture, then *turn* it over and read the message. The popularity of sending postcards to impress a few readers and compress information is not unlike the popularity of sonneteering. And how ingenious of Collins to transmogrify the most crucial moment in any sonnet, the *volta,* into the reader's actual turning of the card. We are back to the power of brevity; to the genius of that Sicilian notary, clearly someone with sufficient practice at writing a "brief" and putting a case together in a concise, convincing manner. And the sonnet itself, however far it has gone in its history, has never completely left its roots—whether religious, erotic, or political motives drive the logic of its imagery, rhetoric, and music.

Seamus Heaney's exquisitely painful closing couplet in the third part of "Clearances" (p. 275), a sequence of eight sonnets written as an elegy for his mother, exemplifies the inextricable bond between meaning and rhyme. The sonnet begins with an image of the bond between mother and son: "When all the others were away at Mass / I was all hers as we peeled potatoes." The scene could have been painted by Vermeer, a picture of domestic bliss, of "things to share / Gleaming in a bucket of clean water." The poem looks like a traditional Petrarchan sonnet, an octave and a sestet with one blank space separating the poem into two parts. But Heaney (B. 1939) is very free with the rhyme pattern, not following any particular scheme and relying more on off-rhyme. He avoids perfect rhyme until the last two lines of the poem, the closing couplet of a Shakespearean sonnet, importing Shakespeare's meditations on Time along with it.

In the space between octave and sestet, between immediacy and memory, the mother dies. We are prepared for this event by the off-rhyme in the last two lines of the octave ("splashes" / "senses"), which works with the white space that follows (the break before the sestet) to "bring us to our senses"; still, we are jolted from the dreamy childhood memory of this shared moment—as the author is—when the "parish priest at her bedside" appears with hammer and tongs at the beginning of the sestet. Once we enter the sestet, the speed of the poem quickens, moving inexorably to its concluding image of a mother and son peeling potatoes, this time a more compressed description. With less space for the poet to work in, the poet must face the end of the poem. Out of nowhere, the memory appears to him of "her head bent towards my head, / Her breath in mine, our fluent dipping knives— / Never closer the whole rest of our lives." The first and only perfect rhyming couplet in the poem brings together "knives" and "lives." And though the knives are there to peel potatoes, not to do damage to human flesh ("lives"), the environment these two words live in leads us to consider them over and over. The sameness of sound ironically juxtaposes life with an instrument of death; moreover, the idea of a safe yet dangerous closeness persists in haunting us, for the intimacy between mother and son is separated only by the fine line of those "fluent dipping knives," which brings the mother and son together in a drama devoid of speech.

Part of the emotional power of this sonnet results from how Heaney faces the technical problem of the heroic couplet, which encourages wit and more cerebral insights. He closes with a rhyming of image and thought, an image that cannot be contained and a thought that encapsulates its meaning yet ramifies its mystery. "Lives" finish the poem, not "knives." And the couplet also invokes the knife cutting the umbilical cord at the birth of the child. The thing that separated mother and son now brings them together as close as they will ever again be in life. The terminal couplet, so problematic in an elegiac mode, because of its nature and its history, led Heaney to the problem he so brilliantly solves, and movingly resolves. Knowing the burden of the formal problem, and the burden of fulfilling the promise of the sonnet tradition, increases our involvement in the struggle the poet faces in grappling with the form and with the subject.

In Eavan Boland's sonnet "Heroic" (p. 291), we come full circle in the history of the form, which itself is partially a chronicle of subjects re-creating themselves (constructing identity) in relation to objects. Boland (B. 1944) has made giving voice to the speechless ideal object, to the female behind the archetypal female of Irish myth and lore, a central motif of her work. The speaking monument that is her sonnet bears witness to its own history, and to the memory of a young woman confronting the statue of a hero. The poem is dialectical on every level, announcing its complexity in the first line, with two sets of terms that seem to be joined and opposed simultaneously: "Sex and history. And skin and bone." The unsettling finality of the cold phrase "Sex and history" reverberates throughout the poem, until it becomes an unsettling ambiguity: the idea of sex as an act engendering a history (in human or mythic time) and that of sex as a gender with a history—and the false, conventional distinction between women as beings of nature (biology) and men as beings of culture. It is "history" that is remembered, that lasts: the record of deeds inscribed on paper, engraved in stone, or imitated in monuments built to celebrate a "heroic" ideal. Boland's title teeters on the edge of a precipice without a noun to support it, asking us to conjure an image.

The speaker portrays the girl she used to be, on a Sunday, the day of worship. It is a day of rest, oppressive in its stillness, and it isolates her from the faithful, who are called to devotion by the bells. She is seeking something outside herself that is not in the church but in the world, something that will confirm who she is and call her to a faith in her own powers—for which no image exists. Boland recalls the young woman—still in school, still single—walking in the rain in her restlessness until she meets a patriot "made of drenched stone. / His lips were still speaking. The gun / he held had just killed someone." Eloquence of speech and economy of action unite in the figure of this man drawing the attention of the girl. The speaker remembers how she looked at him, and how "He stared past me without recognition."

"Heroic" is mesmerizing acoustically, because the entire sonnet turns on only a few vowels, primarily a long "o" (as if Boland were alluding to the pattern of assonance in Milton's sonnet "On the Late Massacre in Piedmont"), and on one consonant, the "n" in "bone" (the word ending the first line), which echoes at the end of every line of the poem: in "rain" and "stone," in "no one" and "heroine." The flickering rhymes and off-rhymes form a set of shifting subunits that stretch across a scaffold of stanzas delineating the basic structural possibilities of the sonnet: quatrain, tercet, and couplet. The poem coalesces into one composite body of sound, but the eye sees five individual stanzas; the formal pattern fluctuates like water, but the phrasing is as adamant as stone. The consistency of off-rhyme and rhyme sets up an unrelenting mercurial pattern that does not stop until we reach that last word, "heroine," which is the sonic template of the poem—containing the "o" of "bone," "own," and "stone," and embedded in "devotion" and "recognition."

The poet has made the portrait of a woman who realizes she is not recognized, who arrives at a blank space of time (marked by a stanza break) in which she undergoes a transformation from mute devotion to meditative silence to a prayer, "whispered so that no one / could hear it but him: *make me a heroine.*" Moving her lips, she breaks the spell the monument has held over her. The speaker relives that solitary moment of recognition in which she made the emotional and intellectual turn that repeats the turn intrinsic to a sonnet: an arresting image outside the self leads the self inward, where insight translates the silent self into intimate speech. The final stanza's finely calibrated irony refuses neat resolution. The speaker, addressing a stone figure who seems to come to life in the rain, comes into her own—recognizes herself—in relation to an ideal object whose solidity she would like to emulate, but on her own terms. She wishes her own tongue were made of stone so that she might be immortalized—but for her words, not for her beauty. Poetry is an art of making one's tongue into stone, but a stone that speaks. The words ending the four lines of the last stanza tell their own story: "rain," "stone," "no one," "heroine." And in terms of pure sound, and the logic of rhyme, adding a single breath (the aspirated "h") to "no one" makes "heroine." With a breath, Boland creates her.

"Heroic" refuses to fit or fill any one mold: it will not stop moving, yet it will not cease forming itself into patterns. This is not due to Boland's unwillingness to make a commitment to one type of sonnet or another, but to her reenvisioning the form, creating a fluid pattern committed to flux, while never ceasing to register the history of previous commitments. In terms of structure and sound, as well as meaning, the poem transcends polarities of soft and hard, female and male, water and stone, ultimately transcending dialectic. The five stanzas make it impossible to identify the poem as belonging to one type: it is not bipartite, nor does it break into the four parts of an Italian sonnet (8, 6 or 4, 4, 3, 3) or the four parts of an English sonnet (4, 4, 4, 2). Adding an extra step to the sonnet, Boland reforms it from within. The *volta* seems to occur after the eighth line, where the most dramatic action is reported and a corresponding inner action—one that is intellectual and emotional—begins to transform the speaker. The interlinear space between line eight and line nine is the moment between action and contemplation. The innovative five-part structure disguises this turn, but it is clearly there; the five stanzas give the sonnet a center, whose tercet also has a dead center: "His lips were still speaking. The gun." That line constitutes the central occasion of the poem, portraying a particular sex with a particular history facing a particular sex with a particular history, contemplating a "heroic" action. Bearing witness leads to an act of speech and the deed of the written poem: reflection emanates outward from this center.

Once again, the sonnet leaves us with the mystery of public and private utterance, the struggle of the self to transcend the self in relation to an ideal within one's sight and beyond one's grasp, the image of a voice born in the space between disintegration of one world and the emergence of another.

Boland pares the sonnet down to its essentials, as stark as the opening phrase, erecting a monument that exists only in words and depends on the tongue for survival. Looking results in knowledge, which turns into speech. Here the man is the object, yet that is nothing new: he is the archetype, the hero, caught eternally in the moment of deadly action. But the girl is the one who is moving, wandering, searching, not eternally the same but in the process of mortal change. She reforms herself in relation to him, but as a subject, not a love object (in the Platonic scheme, he would fit perfectly). His image brings her closer to her ideal, but that does not mean she wants to imitate his action. The final turn of the poem, set up on every level, affirmed and supported by a building made of sound, posited by its own rhyming opposite, the anonymity of "no one," occurs in a syllable that changes "hero" into "heroine."

This anthology is really an autobiography—not of any one person, but of the life of a literary form that from its conception has given birth, or rebirth, to many poetic identities, and to countless poems. The sonnets collected here in these pages belong to a community whose borders keep shifting, and whose uniquely defined constitution makes "contraries meet in one" (Donne). As if speaking for the sonnet as much as for herself, Gwendolyn Brooks says, "Still do I keep my look, my identity"; "little painted poem of god" ends a sonnet by E. E. Cummings, who draws a line that shuttles between idolatry and iconoclasm. "Now, you great stanza, you heroic mould," begins Louise Bogan, addressing "Single Sonnet" to a form whose self-defining pattern and lineage invite us to take liberties—to address the lines of that lineage, to readdress them elsewhere in other lines, invoking another self and another poem. The sonnet provided the impetus for Keats's odes, whose stanza structure emerged from a marriage of the Italian and the English forms (the first four lines being the quatrain of a Shakespearean sonnet, which he joined to the sestet of a typical Petrarchan sonnet). And Shelley's sonnet cycle "Ode to the West Wind," praising the fleeting spirit that renewed him, was composed on a bank of the Arno in the *terza rima* pattern invented by Dante, who six hundred years before had started composing a sonnet in praise of Beatrice as he heard the wind moving the water while he walked along the same riverbank.

"We love the things we love for what they are," says Robert Frost, adding an extra line to one of his sonnets, defying the form he loved throughout his life. "Love is not all: it is not meat nor drink," says Edna St. Vincent Millay; "love is not love," says William Shakespeare; "it is funny; you will be dead some day," says E. E. Cummings; "Life's cache / is flesh, flesh, and flesh," says Molly Peacock; "Thou hast made me, and shall thy work decay?" asks John Donne; "What did I know, what did I know / of love's austere and lonely offices," asks Robert Hayden; "Lackyng my love I go from place to place," says Edmund Spenser; "from bar to bar in terror I shall move," says Denis Johnson; "Did you love well what very soon you left?" asks Marilyn Hacker; "Nay I have done, you get no more of me," says Michael Drayton; "You may have all things from me, save my breath," begins Louise Bogan; "it will be short, it will take all your breath," says Adrienne Rich; "I recall everything, but more than all, / Words being nothing now," begins a double sonnet of Anthony Hecht; "love is not love / Which alters when it alteration finds," says Shakespeare again, again altering everything.

" 'If no love is, O God, what fele I so?' " asks Chaucer, translating himself in the act of translating Petrarch, whose "scattered rhymes" sparked a revolution of the imagination that lives on in many other languages, as we know from the enduring lyric monuments that commemorate loss, love, and spiritual freedom, surviving the ruins of time. Sonnets represent some of the major achievements of the twentieth century, from Rilke's *Sonnets to Orpheus* in German to Neruda's *100 Love Sonnets* in Spanish, from the classical purity of Anna Akhmatova in Russian and Paul Valéry in French to the anarchic announcements of Tomaž Šalamun writing in Slovenian, the old language of a newly independent state that built its identity on the spirit of poetry—a nation that features a sonnet by France Prešeren (1800–1849) on the back of one of its banknotes, his face on the front, honoring the Romantic poet whose crown connected Slovenian poetry to the lyric line of Dante and Petrarch, brought the vernacular language to its peak, and helped insure the survival of a culture.

Passion and reason, sense and intellect, faith and doubt continue to animate our everyday existence. The intensity of reason confronting the intensity of emotion, the clash and chemistry of that meeting in the space of the sonnet, speak to us because we are still astounded by the power of feeling to overcome us, and we still marvel at how reason allows us to detach, to stand outside ourselves for a moment. The need to survive and transcend consuming emotion, the need to succumb to the sway of feeling, the need to order life meaningfully with the awareness that pattern can mean sanity and freedom or stasis and stagnation, the need to pursue an ideal—all these urges occupy us still. The sonnet changes whoever stands upon "its scanty plot of ground." It thrives because it offers a haven for complex emotions and memories, an innate holding pattern and stopping point, a guarantee that however dangerous or overwhelming the subject, the duration of the encounter will be brief. Because the temporal frame is set in advance, the material, however difficult, is free to surface—an image whose meaning begins to unfold as time draws to a close.

The sonnet is a room for sounding these irreconcilable oppositions and making sense of them, and for registering the edge of understanding, in which passion and reason somehow lead to an inward transformation, experienced silently yet surfacing in language that points to a border beyond which language cannot go. It brings us—perhaps—to a place where both the poet and the reader must lose themselves to find themselves, where lovers in the labyrinth begin, in the words of Mary Wroth, "to leave all, and take the thread of love."

Proem

from *Canzoniere*

132

S' amor non è, che dunque è quel ch' io sento?
ma s' egli è amor, per Dio, che cosa et quale?
se bona, ond' è l'effetto aspro mortale?
se ria, ond' è sì dolce ogni tormento?

S' a mia voglia ardo, ond' è 'l pianto e lamento?
s' a mal mio grado, il lamentar che vale?
O viva morte, o dilettoso male,
come puoi tanto in me s' io nol consento?

Et s' io 'l consento, a gran torto mi doglio.
Fra sì contrari venti in frale barca
mi trovo in alto mar senza governo,

sì lieve di saver, d' error sì carca
ch' i' medesmo non so quel ch' io mi voglio,
e tremo a mezza state, ardendo il verno.

❖ GEOFFREY CHAUCER ❖

from *Troilus and Criseyde*

CANTICUS TROILI

"If no love is, O God, what fele I so?
And if love is, what thing and which is he?
If love be good, from whennes cometh my woo?
If it be wikke, a wonder thynketh me,
When every torment and adversite
That cometh of hym, may to me savory thinke,
For ay thurst I, the more that ich it drynke.

"And if that at myn owen lust I brenne,
From whennes cometh my waillynge and my pleynte?
If harm agree me, wherto pleyne I thenne?
I noot, ne whi unwery that I feynte.
O quike deth, O swete harm so queynte,
How may of the in me swich quantite,
But if that I consente that it be?

"And if that I consente, I wrongfully
Compleyne, iwis. Thus possed to and fro,
Al stereless withinne a boot am I
Amydde the see, bitwixen wyndes two,
That in contrarie stonden evere mo.
Allas! what is this wondre maladie?
For hete of cold, for cold of hete, I dye."

[*after the Italian of Petrarch's* Canzoniere, 132]

The Penguin Book of the Sonnet

❖

❖ SIR THOMAS WYATT ❖

"The longe love, that in my thought doeth harbar"

The longe love, that in my thought doeth harbar
   And in myn hert doeth kepe his residence
   Into my face preseth with bold pretence,
   And therin campeth, spreding his baner.
She that me lerneth to love and suffre
   And will that my trust, and lustes negligence
   Be reinèd by reason, shame, and reverence
   With his hardines taketh displeasure.
Wherewithall, unto the hertes forrest he fleith,
   Leving his entreprise with payne and cry
   And there him hideth and not appereth.
What may I do when my maister fereth,
   But, in the felde, with him to lyve and dye?
   For goode is the liff, ending faithfully.

[*after the Italian of Petrarch*]

"Who so list to hounte I know where is an hynde"

Who so list to hounte I know where is an hynde;
   But as for me, helas, I may no more:
   The vayne travaill hath weried me so sore,
   I ame of theim that farthest cometh behinde;
Yet may I by no meanes my weried mynde
   Drawe from the Diere: but as she fleeth afore
   Faynting I folowe; I leve off therefore,
   Sithens in a nett I seke to hold the wynde.
Who list her hount I put him owte of dowbte,
   As well as I may spend his tyme in vain:
   And graven with Diamondes in letters plain
There is written her faier neck rounde abowte:
   'Noli me tangere for Cesars I ame,
   And wylde for to hold though I seme tame.'

[*after the Italian of Petrarch*]

Farewell, Love, and all thy lawes for ever;
    Thy bayted hookes shall tangill me no more;
    Senec and Plato call me from thy lore,
    To perfaict welth my wit for to endever.
In blynde errour when I did perséver,
    Thy sherpe repulce that pricketh ay so sore
    Hath taught me to sett in tryfels no store
    And scape forth syns libertie is liefer.
Therefore, farewell; goo trouble yonger hertes
    And in me clayme no more authoritie;
    With idill yeuth goo use thy propertie
And theron spend thy many britill dertes:
    For hetherto though I have lost all my tyme,
    Me lusteth no lenger rotten boughes to clyme.

"My galy chargèd with forgetfulnes"

My galy chargèd with forgetfulnes
    Thorrough sharpe sees in wynter nyghtes doeth pas
    Twene Rock and Rock; and eke myn ennemy, Alas,
    That is my lorde, sterith with cruelnes;
And every houre a thought in readines,
    As tho that deth were light in suche a case;
    An endles wynd doeth tere the sayll a pace
    Of forcèd sightes and trusty ferefulnes.
A rayn of tearis, a clowde of derk disdain
    Hath done the wearied cordes great hinderaunce,
    Wrethèd with errour and eke with ignoraunce.
The starres be hid that led me to this pain;
    Drownèd is reason that should me confórt,
    And I remain dispering of the port.

                    [*after the Italian of Petrarch*]

"I find no peace, and all my war is done"

I find no peace, and all my war is done,
I fear, and hope. I burn, and freeze like ice.
I fly above the wind, yet can I not arise.
And naught I have, and all the world I season.
That loseth nor locketh holdeth me in prison,
And holdeth me not, yet can I 'scape nowise:
Nor letteth me live nor die at my devise,
And yet of death it giveth me occasion.
Without eyen I see, and without tongue I 'plain;
I desire to perish, and yet I ask health;
I love another, and thus I hate myself;
I feed me in sorrow, and laugh at all my pain.
    Likewise displeaseth me both death and life,
    And my delight is causer of this strife.

[after the Italian of Petrarch]

❖ HENRY HOWARD, EARL OF SURREY ❖

"The soote season, that bud and blome furth bringes"

The soote season, that bud and blome furth bringes,
With grene hath clad the hill and eke the vale;
The nightingale with fethers new she singes;
The turtle to her make hath tolde her tale.
Somer is come, for every spray nowe springes;
The hart hath hong his olde hed on the pale;
The buck in brake his winter cote he flinges;
The fishes flote with newe repairèd scale;
The adder all her sloughe awaye she slinges;
The swift swalow pursueth the flyes smale;
The busy bee her honye now she minges;
Winter is worne that was the flowers bale.
    And thus I see among these pleasant thinges
    Eche care decayes, and yet my sorow springes.

[after the Italian of Petrarch]

"Alas, so all thinges nowe doe holde their peace"

Alas, so all thinges nowe doe holde their peace,
Heaven and earth disturbèd in nothing;
The beastes, the ayer, the birdes their song doe cease;
The nightes chare the starres aboute dothe bring.
Calme is the sea, the waves worke lesse and lesse;
So am not I, whom love alas doth wring,
Bringing before my face the great encrease
Of my desires, whereat I wepe and syng
In joye and wo as in a doutfull ease.
For my swete thoughtes sometyme doe pleasure bring,
But by and by the cause of my disease
Geves me a pang that inwardly dothe sting,
    When that I thinke what griefe it is againe
    To live and lacke the thing should ridde my paine.

[after the Italian of Petrarch]

"I never saw you, madam, lay apart"

I never saw you, madam, lay apart
    Your cornet black, in cold nor yet in heat,
    Sith first ye knew of my desire so great,
Which other fancies chased clean from my heart.
Whiles to my self I did the thought reserve,
    That so unware did wound my woeful breast,
    Pity I saw within your heart did rest.
But since ye knew I did you love and serve,
Your golden tress was clad alway in black,
    Your smiling looks were hid thus evermore,
    All that withdrawn that I did crave so sore.
So doth this cornet govern me, alack!
    In summer's sun, in winter breath of frost,
    Of your fair eyes whereby the light is lost.

"Love that liveth and reigneth in my thought"

Love that liveth and reigneth in my thought,
That built his seat within my captive breast,
Clad in the arms wherein with me he fought,
Oft in my face he doth his banner rest.
She that me taught to love and suffer pain,
My doubtful hope and eke my hot desire
With shamefast cloak to shadow and refrain,
Her smiling grace converteth straight to ire;
And coward love then to the heart apace
Taketh his flight, whereas he lurks and plains
His purpose lost, and dare not show his face.
For my lord's guilt thus faultless bide I pains;
Yet from my lord shall not my foot remove,—
Sweet is his death that takes his end by love.

[after the Italian of Petrarch]

❖ ANNE LOCKE ❖

*from A Meditation of a Penitent Sinner: Written in maner of a Paraphrase
upon the 51 Psalme of David*

Loe prostrate, Lorde, before thy face I lye   *Cast me not*
With sighes depe drawne depe sorrow to expresse,   *away from thy*
O Lord of mercie, mercie do I crye: *face and take not*
Dryve me not from thy face in my distresse,   *thy holy spirit*
Thy face of mercie and of swete relefe   *from me.*
The face that fedes angels with onely sight,
The face of comfort in extremest grefe
Take not away the succour of thy sprite,
Thy holy sprite, which is myn onely stay,
The stay that when despeir assaileth me,
In faintest hope yet moveth me to pray,
To pray for mercy, and to pray to thee.
Lord, cast me not from presence of thy face,
Nor take from me the spirite of thy grace.

But render me my wonted joyes againe,   *Restore to me the*
Which sinne hath reft, and planted in theyr place   *comforte of thy*
Doubt of thy mercie ground of all my paine.   *saving helpe, &*
The tast that thy love whylome did embrace   *stablishe me with*
My cheerfull soule, the signes that dyd assure   *thy free spirit.*
My felyng ghost of favour in thy sight,
Are fled from me, and wretched I endure
Senselesse of grace the absence of thy sprite.
Restore my joyes, and make me fele againe
The swete retorne of grace that I have lost,
That I may hope I pray not all in vayne.
With thy free sprite confirme my feble ghost,
To hold my faith from ruine and decay
With fast affiance and assured stay.

"That self-same tongue which first did thee entreat"

That self-same tongue which first did thee entreat
To link thy liking with my lucky love,
That trusty tongue must now these words repeat,
I love thee still, my fancy cannot move.
That dreadless heart which durst attempt the thought
To win thy will with mine for to consent,
Maintains that vow which love in me first wrought,
I love thee still, and never shall repent.
That happy hand which hardly did touch
Thy tender body to my deep delight,
Shall serve with sword to prove my passion such
As loves thee still, much more than it can write.
    Thus love I still with tongue, hand, heart and all,
    And when I change, let vengeance on me fall.

A SONET WRITTEN IN PRAYSE OF THE BROWNE BEAUTIE, COMPILED FOR THE LOVE OF MISTRESSE *E.P.* AS FOLOWETH

The thriftles thred which pampred beauty spinnes,
In thraldom binds the foolish gazing eyes:
As cruell Spyders with their crafty ginnes,
In worthlesse webbes doe snare the simple Flies.
The garments gay, the glittring golden gite,
The tysing talk which floweth from *Pallas* pooles:
The painted pale, the (too much) red made white,
Are smyling baytes to fishe for loving fooles.
But lo, when eld in toothlesse mouth appeares,
And whoary heares in steed of beauties blaze:
Than Had I wist, doth teach repenting yeares,
The tickle track of craftie *Cupides* maze.
Twixt faire and foule therfore, twixt great and small,
A lovely nutbrowne face is best of all.

               Si fortunatus infælix.

from *Licia or Poems of Love*

20

First did I fear, when first my love began,
Possessed in fits by watchful jealousy;
I sought to keep what I by favor wan,
And brooked no partner in my love to be.
But tyrant sickness fed upon my love,
And spread his ensigns, dyed with color white;
Then was suspicion glad for to remove,
And, loving much, did fear to lose her quite.
Erect, fair sweet, the colors thou didst wear;
Dislodge thy griefs, the short'ners of content;
For now of life, not love, is all my fear,
Lest life and love be both together spent.
    Live but, fair love, and banish thy disease,
    And love, kind heart, both when and whom thou please.

❖ EDMUND SPENSER ❖

from *Amoretti*

I

Happy ye leaves when as those lilly hands,
    which hold my life in their dead-doing might
    shall handle you and hold in love's soft bands,
    lyke captives trembling at the victor's sight.
And happy lines, on which with starry light
    those lamping eyes will deigne sometimes to look
    and reade the sorrowes of my dying spright,
    written with teares in hart's close bleeding book.
And happy rymes, bath'd in the sacred brooke
    of *Helicon* whence she derived is,
    when ye behold that Angel's blessed looke,
    my soule's long-lacked foode, my heaven's blis.
Leaves, lines, and rymes, seeke her to please alone,
    whom if ye please, I care for other none.

8

More then most faire, full of the living fire,
    kindled above unto the maker neere:
    no eies but joyes, in which al powers conspire
    that to the world naught else be counted deare:
Thrugh your bright beams doth not the blinded guest
    shoot out his darts to base affections' wound?
    but Angels come to lead fraile mindes to rest
    in chast desires on heavenly beauty bound.
You frame my thoughts and fashion me within;
    you stop my toung, and teach my hart to speake;
    you calme the storme that passion did begin,
    strong thrugh your cause, but by your vertue weak.
Dark is the world, where your light shined never;
    well is he borne, that may behold you ever.

18

The rolling wheele that runneth often round,
    the hardest steele in tract of time doth teare;
    and drizling drops that often doe redound,
    the firmest flint doth in continuance weare.
Yet cannot I with many a dropping teare
    and long intreaty soften her hard hart,
    that she will once vouchsafe my plaint to heare,
    or looke with pitty on my payneful smart.
But when I pleade, she bids me play my part,
    and when I weep, she sayes teares are but water:
    and when I sigh, she sayes I know the art,
    and when I waile, she turnes hir selfe to laughter.
So doe I weepe, and wayle, and pleade in vaine,
    whiles she as steele and flint doth still remayne.

22

This holy season fit to fast and pray,
    men to devotion ought to be inclynd:
    therefore, I lykewise on so holy day,
    for my sweet Saynt some service fit will find.
Her temple fayre is built within my mind,
    in which her glorious ymage placed is,
    on which my thoughts doo day and night attend
    lyke sacred priests that never thinke amisse.
There I to her, as th'author of my blisse,
    will builde an altar to appease her yre;
    and on the same my hart will sacrifise,
    burning in flames of pure and chast desyre:
The which vouchsafe, O goddesse, to accept,
    amongst thy deerest relicks to be kept.

23

Penelope for her *Ulisses'* sake,
    deviz'd a Web her wooers to deceave;
    in which the worke that she all day did make
    the same at night she did againe unreave.
Such subtile craft my Damzell doth conceave,
    th'importune suit of my desire to shonne:
    for all that I in many dayes doo weave,
    in one short houre I find by her undonne.
So when I thinke to end that I begonne,
    I must begin and never bring to end;
    for with one looke she spils that long I sponne,
    and with one word my whole year's work doth rend.
Such labour like the Spyder's web I fynd,
    whose fruitlesse worke is broken with least wynd.

30

My love is lyke to yse, and I to fyre:
    how comes it then that this her cold so great
    is not dissolv'd through my so hot desyre,
    but harder growes the more I her intreat?
Or how comes it that my exceeding heat
    is not delayed by her hart frosen cold,
    but that I burne much more in boyling sweat,
    and feele my flames augmented manifold?
What more miraculous thing may be told
    that fire, which all thing melts, should harden yse:
    and yse which is congeald with sencelesse cold,
    should kindle fyre by wonderfull devyse?
Such is the powre of love in gentle mind
    that it can alter all the course of kynd.

37

What guyle is this, that those her golden tresses,
    she doth attyre under a net of gold,
    and with sly skill so cunningly them dresses,
    that which is gold or heare may scarse be told?
Is it that men's frayle eyes, which gaze too bold,
    she may entangle in that golden snare;
    and being caught, may craftily enfold
    theyr weaker harts, which are not wel aware?
Take heed therefore, myne eyes, how ye doe stare
    henceforth too rashly on that guilefull net,
    in which if ever ye entrapped are,
    out of her bands ye by no meanes shall get.
Fondnesse it were for any being free
    to covet fetters, though they golden bee.

45

Leave, lady, in your glasse of christall clene
    your goodly selfe for evermore to vew,
    and in my selfe, my inward selfe I meane,
    most lively-lyke behold your semblant trew.
Within my hart, though hardly it can shew
    thing so divine to vew of earthly eye,
    the fayre Idea of your celestiall hew
    and every part remaines immortally:
And were it not that through your cruelty
    with sorrow dimmed and deformd it were,
    the goodly ymage of your visnomy
    clearer then christall would therein appere.
But if your selfe in me ye playne will see,
    remove the cause by which your fayre beames darkned be.

67

Lyke as a huntsman after weary chace,
    seeing the game from him escapt away,
    sits downe to rest him in some shady place,
    with panting hounds beguiled of their pray:
So after long pursuit and vaine assay,
    when I all weary had the chace forsooke,
    the gentle deare returnd the selfe-same way,
    thinking to quench her thirst at the next brooke.
There she beholding me with mylder looke,
    sought not to fly, but fearelesse still did bide;
    till I in hand her yet halfe trembling tooke,
    and with her owne goodwill hir fyrmely tyde.
Strange thing me seemd to see a beast so wyld,
    so goodly wonne with her owne will beguyld.

68

Most glorious Lord of lyfe that on this day
　　didst make thy triumph over death and sin,
　　and having harrowd hell didst bring away
　　captivity thence captive us to win:
This joyous day, deare Lord, with joy begin,
　　and grant that we for whom thou diddest dye,
　　being with thy deare blood clene washt from sin,
　　may live for ever in felicity:
And that thy love we weighing worthily,
　　may likewise love thee for the same againe;
　　and for thy sake that all lyke deare didst buy,
　　with love may one another entertayne.
So let us love, deare love, lyke as we ought:
　　love is the lesson which the Lord us taught.

71

I joy to see how in your drawen work,
　　your selfe unto the Bee ye doe compare;
　　and me unto the Spyder that doth lurke
　　in close awayt to catch her unaware.
Right so your selfe were caught in cunning snare
　　of a deare foe, and thralled to his love;
　　in whose streight bands ye now captived are
　　so firmely, that ye never may remove.
But as your worke is woven all above
　　with woodbynd flowers and fragrant Eglantine,
　　so sweet your prison you in time shall prove,
　　with many deare delights bedecked fyne.
And all thensforth eternall peace shall see,
　　betweene the Spyder and the gentle Bee.

75

One day I wrote her name upon the strand,
    but came the waves and washed it away:
    agayne I wrote it with a second hand,
    but came the tyde, and made my paynes his pray.
Vayne man, sayd she, that doest in vaine assay
    a mortall thing so to immortalize,
    for I my selve shall lyke to this decay,
    and eek my name bee wyped out lykewize.
Not so, (quod I) let baser things devize
    to dy in dust, but you shall live by fame:
    my verse your vertues rare shall eternize,
    and in the hevens wryte your glorious name:
Where, whenas death shall all the world subdew,
    our love shall live, and later life renew.

78

Lackyng my love I go from place to place,
    lyke a young fawne that late hath lost the hynd;
    and seeke each where, where last I sawe her face,
    whose ymage yet I carry fresh in mynd.
I seeke the fields with her late footing synd,
    I seeke her bowre with her late presence deckt,
    yet nor in field nor bowre I her can fynd;
    yet field and bowre are full of her aspect.
But when myne eyes I thereunto direct,
    they ydly back returne to me agayne,
    and when I hope to see theyr trew object,
    I fynd my selfe but fed with fancies vayne.
Ceasse then, myne eyes, to seeke her selfe to see,
    and let my thoughts behold her selfe in mee.

79

Men call you fayre, and you doe credit it,
 for that your selfe ye dayly such doe see:
 but the trew fayre, that is the gentle wit
 and vertuous mind, is much more praysd of me.
For all the rest, how ever fayre it be,
 shall turne to nought and loose that glorious hew:
 but onely that is permanent and free
 from frayle corruption, that doth flesh ensew.
That is true beautie: that doth argue you
 to be divine and borne of heavenly seed,
 deriv'd from that fayre Spirit, from whom al true
 and perfect beauty did at first proceed.
He onely fayre, and what he fayre hath made:
 all other fayre lyke flowres untymely fade.

81

Fayre is my love, when her fayre golden heares
 with the loose wynd ye waving chance to marke:
 fayre when the rose in her red cheekes appeares,
 or in her eyes the fyre of love does sparke.
Fayre when her brest lyke a rich laden barke,
 with pretious merchandize she forth doth lay:
 fayre when that cloud of pryde, which oft doth dark
 her goodly light, with smiles she drives away.
But fayrest she, when so she doth display
 the gate with pearles and rubyes richly dight,
 throgh which her words so wise do make their way
 to beare the message of her gentle spright.
The rest be works of nature's wonderment,
 but this the worke of hart's astonishment.

from *Cælica*

38

Cælica, I overnight was finely used,
Lodged in the midst of paradise, your heart;
Kind thoughts had charge I might not be refused,
Of every fruit and flower I had part.

But curious knowledge, blown with busy flame,
The sweetest fruits had in down shadows hidden,
And for it found mine eyes had seen the same,
I from my paradise was straight forbidden.

Where that 'cur, rumor, runs in every place,
Barking with care, begotten out of fear;
And glassy honor, tender of disgrace,
Stand seraphim to see I come not there;
    While that fine soil which all these joys did yield,
    By broken fence is proved a common field.

39

The *nurse-life* wheat, within his green husk growing,
Flatters our hope, and tickles our desire,
Nature's true riches in sweet beauties showing,
Which set all hearts, with labour's love, on fire.

No less fair is the wheat when golden ear
Shows unto hope the joys of near enjoying:
Fair and sweet is the bud, more sweet and fair
The rose, which proves that time is not destroying.

Cælica, your youth, the morning of delight,
Enamelled o'er with beauties white and red,
All sense and thoughts did to belief invite,
That love and glory there are brought to bed;
And your ripe years love none; he goes no higher,
    Turns all the spirits of man into desire.

In night when colours all to black are cast,
Distinction lost, or gone down with the light;
The eye a watch to inward senses plac'd,
Not seeing, yet still having power of sight,
Gives vain alarums to the inward sense,
Where fear stirr'd up with witty tyranny,
Confounds all powers, and thorough self-offence,
Doth forge and raise impossibility:
Such is in thick depriving darknesses,
Proper reflections of the error be,
And images of self-confusednesses,
Which hurt imaginations only see;
And from this nothing seen, tells news of devils,
Which but expressions be of inward evils.

❖ SIR PHILIP SIDNEY ❖

from *The Countess of Pembroke's Arcadia*

"My true love hath my hart, and I have his"

My true love hath my hart, and I have his,
By just exchange, one for the other giv'ne.
I holde his deare, and myne he cannot misse:
There never was a better bargaine driv'ne.

His hart in me, keepes me and him in one,
My hart in him, his thoughtes and senses guides:
He loves my hart, for once it was his owne:
I cherish his, because in me it bides.

His hart his wound receavèd from my sight:
My hart was wounded, with his wounded hart,
For as from me, on him his hurt did light,
So still me thought in me his hurt did smart:
   Both equall hurt, in this change sought our blisse:
   My true love hath my hart and I have his.

from *Astrophel and Stella*

1

Loving in truth, and faine in verse my love to show,
That she (deare she) might take some pleasure of my paine;
Pleasure might cause her reade, reading might make her know,
Knowledge might pitie winne, and pitie grace obtaine,
I sought fit words to paint the blackest face of woe,
Studying inventions fine her wits to entertaine;
Oft turning others' leaves, to see if thence would flow
Some fresh and fruitfull showers upon my sunne-burn'd braine.
But words came halting forth, wanting Invention's stay;
Invention, Nature's child, fled step-dame Studie's blowes,
And others' feete still seem'd but strangers in my way.
Thus great with child to speake, and helplesse in my throwes,
Biting my trewand pen, beating my selfe for spite,
"Foole," said my Muse to me, "looke in thy heart and write."

3

Let daintie wits crie on the Sisters nine,
That bravely maskt, their fancies may be told:
Or *Pindare's* Apes, flaunt they in phrases fine,
Enam'ling with pied flowers their thoughts of gold:
Or else let them in statelier glorie shine,
Ennobling new found Tropes with problemes old:
Or with strange similies enrich each line,
Of herbes or beastes, which *Inde* or *Afrike* hold.
For me in sooth, no Muse but one I know:
Phrases and Problemes from my reach do grow,
And strange things cost too deare for my poore sprites.
How then? Even thus: in *Stella's* face I reed
What Love and Beautie be; then all my deed
But Copying is what in her Nature writes.

5

It is most true that eyes are form'd to serve
The inward light, and that the heavenly part
Ought to be king, from whose rules who do swerve,
　　Rebels to Nature, strive for their owne smart.
　　It is most true, what we call *Cupid's* dart,
An image is, which for our selves we carve,
And, fooles, adore in temple of our hart,
Till that good God make Church and Churchman starve.
　　True, that true Beautie Vertue is indeed,
Whereof this Beautie can be but a shade
Which elements with mortall mixture breed:
True, that on earth we are but pilgrims made,
　　And should in soule up to our countrey move:
　　True, and yet true that I must *Stella* love.

31

With how sad steps, O Moone, thou climb'st the skies,
　　How silently, and with how wanne a face;
　　What, may it be that even in heav'nly place
That busie archer his sharpe arrowes tries?
Sure, if that long-with-*Love*-acquainted eyes
　　Can judge of *Love,* thou feel'st a Lover's case;
　　I reade it in thy lookes; thy languisht grace
To me that feele the like, thy state descries.
　　Then ev'n of fellowship, O Moone, tell me
Is constant *Love* deem'd there but want of wit?
Are Beauties there as proud as here they be?
Do they above love to be lov'd, and yet
　　Those Lovers scorne whom that *Love* doth possesse?
　　Do they call *Vertue* there ungratefulnesse?

37

My mouth doth water, and my breast doth swell,
    My tongue doth itch, my thoughts in labour be:
    Listen then, Lordings, with good eare to me,
For of my life I must a riddle tell.
Towardes *Aurora's* Court a Nymph doth dwell,
    Rich in all beauties which man's eye can see;
    Beauties so farre from reach of words, that we
Abase her praise, saying she doth excell:
    Rich in the treasure of deserv'd renowne,
Rich in the riches of a royall hart,
Rich in those gifts which give th'eternall crowne;
Who, though most rich in these and everie part
    Which make the patents of true wordly blisse,
    Hath no misfortune, but that Rich she is.

39

Come sleepe, O sleepe, the certaine knot of peace,
The baiting place of wit, the balme of woe,
The poore man's wealth, the prisoner's release,
Th'indifferent Judge betweene the high and low;
With shield of proofe shield me from out the prease
Of those fierce darts dispaire at me doth throw:
O make in me those civill warres to cease;
I will good tribute pay if thou do so.
    Take thou of me smooth pillowes, sweetest bed,
A chamber deafe to noise, and blind to light;
A rosie garland, and a wearie hed;
And if these things, as being thine by right,
    Move not thy heavy grace, thou shalt in me,
    Livelier then else-where, *Stella's* image see.

41

Having this day my horse, my hand, my launce
   Guided so well that I obtain'd the prize,
   Both by the judgement of the English eyes,
And of some sent from that sweet enemie *Fraunce*;
Horsemen my skill in horsmanship advaunce,
   Towne-folkes my strength; a daintier judge applies
   His praise to sleight, which from good use doth rise:
Some luckie wits impute it but to chaunce:
   Others, because of both sides I do take
My bloud from them, who did excell in this,
Thinke Nature me a man of armes did make.
How farre they shoote awrie! The true cause is
   Stella lookt on, and from her heav'nly face
   Sent forth the beames which made so faire my race.

47

What, have I thus betrayed my libertie?
   Can those blacke beames such burning markes engrave
   In my free side? or am I borne a slave,
Whose necke becomes such yoke of tyranny?
Or want I sense to feele my miserie?
   Or sprite, disdaine of such disdaine to have,
   Who for long faith, tho dayly helpe I crave,
May get no almes but scorne of beggerie?
   Vertue awake; Beautie but beautie is:
I may, I must, I can, I will, I do
Leave following that, which it is gaine to misse.
Let her go. Soft, but here she comes. Go to,
   Unkind, I love you not: O me, that eye
   Doth make my heart give to my tongue the lie.

49

I on my horse, and *Love* on me doth trie
   Our horsmanships, while by strange worke I prove
   A horsman to my horse, a horse to *Love*;
And now man's wrongs in me, poore beast, descrie.
The raines wherewith my Rider doth me tie
   Are humbled thoughts, which bit of Reverence move,
   Curb'd in with feare, but with guilt bosse above
Of Hope, which makes it seeme faire to the eye.
   The Wand is Will; thou Fancie, Saddle art,
Girt fast by memorie, and while I spurre
My horse, he spurres with sharpe desire my hart:
He sits me fast, how ever I do sturre;
   And now hath made me to his hand so right,
   That in the Manage myselfe takes delight.

54

Because I breathe not love to everie one,
   Nor do not use set colours for to weare,
   Nor nourish speciall lockes of vowed haire,
Nor give each speech a full point of a grone,
The courtly Nymphs, acquainted with the mone
   Of them, who in their lips *Love's* standerd beare,
   "What he?" say they of me, "now I dare sweare,
He cannot love: no, no, let him alone."
   And thinke so still, so *Stella* know my mind.
Professe in deed I do not *Cupid's* art;
But you, faire maides, at length this true shall find,
That his right badge is but worne in the hart:
   Dumbe Swannes, not chatring Pies, do Lovers prove;
   They love indeed who quake to say they love.

63

O Grammer rules, O now your vertues show;
    So children still reade you with awfull eyes,
    As my young Dove may, in your precepts wise,
Her graunt to me by her owne vertue know.
For late with heart most high, with eyes most low,
    I crav'd the thing which ever she denies:
    She, lightning *Love,* displaying *Venus'* skies,
Least once should not be heard, twise said, "No, No."
    Sing then, my Muse, now *Io Pean* sing;
    Heav'ns, envy not at my high triumphing,
But Grammer's force with sweet successe confirme;
    For Grammer sayes (O this, deare *Stella,* weighe,)
    For Grammer sayes (to Grammer who sayes nay?)
That in one speech two Negatives affirme.

71

Who will in fairest booke of Nature know
    How Vertue may best lodg'd in beautie be,
    Let him but learne of *Love* to reade in thee,
Stella, those faire lines which true goodnesse show.
There shall he find all vices' overthrow,
    Not by rude force, but sweetest soveraigntie
    Of reason, from whose light those night-birds flie,
That inward sunne in thine eyes shineth so:
    And not content to be Perfection's heire
Thy selfe, doest strive all minds that way to move,
Who marke in thee what is in thee most faire.
So while thy beautie drawes the heart to love,
    As fast thy Vertue bends that love to good:
    "But ah," Desire still cries, "give me some food."

73

Love still a boy, and oft a wanton is,
School'd onely by his mother's tender eye:
What wonder then if he his lesson misse,
When for so soft a rod deare play he trie?
And yet, my Starre, because a sugred kisse
In sport I suckt, while she asleepe did lie,
Doth lowre, nay, chide; nay, threat for only this:
Sweet, it was saucie *Love,* not humble I.
  But no scuse serves, she makes her wrath appeare
  In Beautie's throne; see now who dares come neare
Those scarlet judges, threatning bloudy paine?
  O heav'nly foole, thy most kisse-worthie face
  Anger invests with such a lovely grace,
That Anger' selfe I needs must kisse againe.

90

Stella, thinke not that I by verse seeke fame,
  Who seeke, who hope, who love, who live but thee;
  Thine eyes my pride, thy lips my history:
If thou praise not, all other praise is shame.
Nor so ambitious am I, as to frame
  A nest for my yong praise in Lawrell tree:
  In truth I sweare, I wish not there should be
Graved in mine Epitaph a Poet's name:
  Ne if I would, could I just title make,
That any laud to me thereof should grow,
Without my plumes from others' wings I take.
For nothing from my wit or will doth flow,
  Since all my words thy beauty doth endite,
  And love doth hold my hand, and makes me write.

from *Certaine Sonnets*

"Leave me, O Love, which reachest but to dust"

Leave me, O Love, which reachest but to dust,
And thou, my mind, aspire to higher things:
Grow rich in that which never taketh rust:
What ever fades but fading pleasure brings.
  Draw in thy beames, and humble all thy might
To that sweet yoke, where lasting freedomes be,
Which breakes the clowdes and opens forth the light,
That doth both shine and give us sight to see.
  O take fast hold, let that light be thy guide,
In this small course which birth drawes out to death,
And thinke how evill becommeth him to slide,
Who seeketh heav'n, and comes of heav'nly breath.
  Then farewell world, thy uttermost I see:
  Eternall Love maintaine thy life in me.

❖ SIR WALTER RALEGH ❖

A VISION UPON THIS CONCEIPT OF THE FAERY QUEENE

Methought I saw the grave where Laura lay,
Within that temple where the vestal flame
Was wont to burn; and passing by that way
To see that buried dust of living fame,
Whose tomb fair Love and fairer Virtue kept,
All suddenly I saw the Faery Queen:
At whose approach the soul of Petrarch wept;
And from thenceforth those Graces were not seen,
For they this Queen attended; in whose stead
Oblivion laid him down on Laura's hearse.
Hereat the hardest stones were seen to bleed,
And groans of buried ghosts the heavens did pierce,
  Where Homer's spright did tremble all for grief,
  And cursed the access of that celestial thief.

A secret murder hath been done of late—
Unkindness found to be the bloody knife;
And she that did the deed a dame of state,
Fair, gracious, wise, as any beareth life.

To quit herself, this answer did she make:
Mistrust (quoth she) hath brought him to his end,
Which makes the man so much himself mistake,
To lay the guilt unto his guiltless friend.

Lady, not so. Not feared I found my death,
For no desert thus murdered is my mind.
And yet before I yield my fainting breath,
I quit the killer, though I blame the kind.

You kill unkind; I die, and yet am true—
For at your sight my wound doth bleed anew.

TO HIS SON

Three things there be that prosper up apace
And flourish, whilst they grow asunder far;
But on a day, they meet all in one place,
And when they meet they one another mar:
And they be these—the wood, the weed, the wag.
The wood is that which makes the gallows tree;
The weed is that which strings the hangman's bag;
The wag, my pretty knave, betokeneth thee.
Mark well, dear boy, whilst these assemble not,
Green springs the tree, hemp grows, the wag is wild;
But when they meet, it makes the timber rot,
It frets the halter, and it chokes the child.
    Then bless thee, and beware, and let us pray
    We part not with thee at this meeting day.

❖ THOMAS LODGE ❖

from *Phillis: Honoured with Pastorall Sonnets, Elegies and amorous delights*

I hope and feare, I pray and hould my peace,
Now freeze my thoughtes and straight they frie againe;
I now admire and straight my wounders cease,
I loose my bondes and yet my self restraine:
    This likes me most that leaves me discontent,
My courage serves and yet my heart doth fail;
My will doth clime whereas my hopes are spent,
I laugh at love, yet when he comes I quaile.
    The more I strive, the duller bide I still,
I would be thrald, and yet I freedome love;
I would redresse, yet hourly feede myne ill,
I would repine, and dare not once reprove;
    And for my love I am bereft of power,
    And strengthlesse strive my weaknes to devoure.

❖ GEORGE CHAPMAN ❖

from *A Coronet for his Mistress Philosophy*

Muses that sing Love's sensual empery,
And lovers kindling your enraged fires
At Cupid's bonfires burning in the eye,
Blown with the empty breath of vain desires,—
You that prefer the painted cabinet
Before the wealthy jewels it doth store ye,
That all your joys in dying figures set,
And stain the living substance of your glory;
Abjure those joys, abhor their memory,
And let my Love the honoured subject be
Of love, and honour's complete history;
Your eyes were never yet let in to see
The majesty and riches of the mind,
But dwell in darkness; for your god is blind.

❖ HENRY CONSTABLE ❖

from *Diana*

Needs must I leave and yet needs must I love
In vayne my witt doth paynt in verse my woe
Disdaine in thee dispaire in me doth showe
How by my witte I doe my follie prove

All this my heart from love can never move
Love is not in my hearte, no Lady no,
My hearte is love it selfe; till I forgoe
My hearte, I never can my love remove.

How shall I then leave love? I do entend
Not to crave grace but yet to wish it still
Not to prayse thee, but beautie to commend
And so by beauties prayse, prayse thee I will
    For as my hearte is love, love not in me
    So beautie thou beautie is not in thee.

❖ MARK ALEXANDER BOYD ❖

SONET

Fra banc to banc, fra wod to wod, I rin
    Owrhailit with my feble fantasie,
    Lyc til a leif that fallis from a trie
    Or til a reid owrblawin with the win'.
Twa gods gyds me: the ane of tham is blin',
    Ye, and a bairn brocht up in vanitie;
    The nixt a wyf ingenrit of the se,
    And lichter nor a dauphin with hir fin.
Unhappie is the man for evirmaire
    That teils the sand and sawis in the aire,
    Bot twyse unhappier is he, I lairn,
That feidis in his hairt a mad desyre,
    And follows on a woman throu the fyre,
    Led be a blind and teichit be a bairn.

from *To Delia*

34

Looke, *Delia,* how wee steeme the half-blowne Rose,
   The image of thy blush, and Sommer's honour,
   Whilst in her tender greene shee doth inclose
   The pure sweet beauty Time bestowes upon her:
No sooner spreades her glory in the ayre,
   But straight her ful-blowne pride is in declining;
   Shee then is scorn'd, that late adorn'd the fayre:
   So clowdes thy beautie, after fairest shining.
No Aprill can revive thy withred flowers,
   Whose blooming grace adornes thy glory now:
   Swift speedy Time, feathred with flying howers,
   Dissolves the beautie of the fairest brow.
O let not then such riches waste in vaine;
But love whist thou maist be lov'd againe.

49

Care-charmer Sleepe, sonne of the sable Night,
   Brother to death, in silent darknes borne;
   Relieve my languish, and restore the light,
   With darke forgetting of my care's returne:
And let the day be time enough to mourne
   The shipwrack of my ill-adventred youth:
   Let waking eyes suffice to waile their scorne,
   Without the torment of the night's untruth.
Cease dreames, th'imag'ry of our day desires,
   To modell forth the passions of the morrow:
   Never let rysing Sunne approve you lyers,
   To adde more griefe to agravate my sorrow.
Still let me sleepe, imbracing clowdes in vaine,
And never wake to feele the daye's disdayne.

50

Let others sing of Knights and Palladines
    In aged accents and untimely words,
    Paint shadowes in imaginarie lines,
    Which wel the reach of their high wits records:
But I must sing of thee and those faire eyes;
    Autentique shall my verse in time to come,
    When yet th'unborne shall say, "Loe, where she lyes,
    Whose beauty made him speak that else was dombe."
These are the Arkes, the Trophies I erect,
    That fortifie thy name against old age;
    And these thy sacred vertues must protect
    Against the darke, and Time's consuming rage.
Though th'error of my youth they shall discover,
Suffice, they shew I liv'd and was thy lover.

❖   MICHAEL DRAYTON   ❖

from *Idea in Sixtie Three Sonnets*

5

Nothing but No and I, and I and No:
How fals it out so strangely you reply?
I tell yee (Faire) I'le not be answered so.
With this affirming No, denying I.
I say, "I Love"; you sleightly answere "I":
I say, "You Love"; you peule me out a No:
I say, "I Die"; you Eccho me with "I":
"Save mee", I Crie; you sigh me out a No.
Must Woe and I have naught but No and I?
No I am I, if I no more can have:
Answere no more; with Silence make reply,
And let me take my selfe what I doe crave;
    Let No and I with I and you be so:
    Then answere No and I, and I and No.

6

How many paltry, foolish, painted things,
That now in Coaches trouble ev'ry Street,
Shall be forgotten, whom no Poet sings,
Ere they be well wrap'd in their winding Sheet!
Where I to thee Eternitie shall give,
When nothing else remayneth of these dayes,
And Queenes hereafter shall be glad to live
Upon the Almes of thy superfluous prayse:
Virgins and Matrons reading these my Rimes,
Shall be so much delighted with thy story,
That they shall grieve they liv'd not in these Times,
To have seene thee, their Sexe's onely glory:
    So shalt thou flye above the vulgar Throng,
    Still to survive in my immortal Song.

7

Love, in a Humor, play'd the Prodigall,
And bad my Senses to a solemn Feast:
Yet more to Grace the company withall,
Invites my Heart to be the chiefest Ghest:
No other Drinke would serve this Glutton's turne
But precious Teares distilling from mine Eyne,
Which with my Sighes this Epicure doth burne,
Quaffing Carowses in this costly Wine;
Where, in his Cups o'rcome with foule Excesse,
Straightwayes he plays a swagg'ring Ruffin's part,
And at the Banquet, in his Drunkennesse,
Slew his deare Friend, my kind and truest Heart:
    A gentle warning (Friends) thus may you see,
    What 'tis to keepe a Drunkard companie.

Since to obtaine thee nothing me will sted,
I have a Med'cine that shall cure my Love:
The powder of her Heart dry'd, when she is dead,
That Gold nor Honour ne'r had pow'r to move;
Mix'd with her Teares, that ne'r her true-Love crost,
Nor at Fifteene ne'r long'd to be a Bride;
Boyl'd with her Sighes, in giving up the Ghost,
That for her late deceased Husband dy'd:
Into the same then let a Woman breathe,
That being chid, did never word replie,
With one thrice-marry'd's Pray'rs, that did bequeath
A Legacie to stale Virginitie.
    If this Receit have not the pow'r to winne me,
    Little I'le say, but thinke the Devill's in me.

38

Sitting alone, Love bids me goe and write;
Reason plucks back, commanding me to stay,
Boasting that she doth still direct the way,
Or else Love were unable to indite:
Love growing angry, vexed at the Spleene,
And scorning Reason's maymed Argument,
Straight taxeth Reason wanting to invent
Where she with Love conversing hath not beene:
Reason, reproched with this coy Disdaine,
Despiteth Love, and laugheth at her Folly;
And Love, contemning Reason's reason wholly,
Thought it in weight too light by many a Graine:
    Reason, put back, doth out of sight remove,
    And Love alone picks reason out of love.

Since ther's no helpe, Come let us kisse and part,
Nay, I have done: You get no more of Me,
And I am glad, yea glad with all my heart,
That thus so cleanly I my Selfe can free;
Shake hands for ever, Cancell all our Vowes,
And when We meet at any time againe,
Be it not seene in either of our Browes,
That we one jot of former Love reteyne:
Now at the last gaspe of Love's latest Breath,
When his Pulse fayling, Passion speechlesse lies,
When Faith is kneeling by his bed of Death,
And Innocence is closing up his eyes,
  Now if thou would'st, when all have given him over,
  From Death to Life thou might'st him yet recover.

❖ JOHN DAVIES OF HEREFORD ❖

"Some blaze the precious beauties of their loves"

Some blaze the precious beauties of their loves
By precious stones, and other some by flowers,
Some by the planets and celestial powers,
Or by what else their fancy best approves;
Yet I by none of these will blazon mine,
But only say her self herself is like,
For those similitudes I much mislike
That are much used, though they be divine.
In saying she is like herself, I say
She hath no like, for she is past compare.
Then who aright commends this creature rare
Must say, "She is"; and there of force must stay,
  Because by words she cannot be expressed;
  So say, "She is," and wond'ring owe the rest.

Although we do not all the good we love,
But still, in love, desire to do the same;
Nor leave the sins we hate, but hating move
Our soul and body's powers their powers to tame;
The good we do God takes as done aright,
That we desire to do he takes as done;
The sin we shun he will with grace requite,
And not impute the sin we seek to shun.
But good desires produce no worser deeds,
For God doth both together lightly give,
Because he knows a righteous man must needs
By faith, that works by love, forever live.
    Then to do nought but only in desire
    Is love that burns, but burns like painted fire.

THE AUTHOR LOVING THESE HOMELY MEATS SPECIALLY, VIZ.: CREAM, PANCAKES, BUTTERED PIPPIN–PIES (LAUGH, GOOD PEOPLE) AND TOBACCO; WRIT TO THAT WORTHY AND VIRTUOUS GENTLEWOMAN, WHOM HE CALLETH MISTRESS, AS FOLLOWETH

If there were, oh! an Hellespont of cream
Between us, milk-white mistress, I would swim
To you, to show to both my love's extreme,
Leander-like,—yea! dive from brim to brim.
But met I with a buttered pippin-pie
Floating upon 't, that would I make my boat
To waft me to you without jeopardy,
Though sea-sick I might be while it did float.
Yet if a storm should rise, by night or day,
Of sugar-snows and hail of caraways,
Then, if I found a pancake in my way,
It like a plank should bring me to your kays;
    Which having found, if they tobacco kept,
    The smoke should dry me well before I slept.

❖ CHARLES BEST ❖

OF THE MOON

Look how the pale queen of the silent night
    Doth cause the Ocean to attend upon her,
And he, as long as she is in his sight,
    With his full tide is ready her to honour;
But when the silver waggon of the Moon
    Is mounted up so high he cannot follow,
The sea calls home his crystal waves to moan,
    And with low ebb doth manifest his sorrow.
So you, that are the sovereign of my heart,
    Have all my joys attending on your will,
My joys low-ebbing when you do depart—
    When you return, their tide my heart doth fill:
      So as you come, and as you do depart,
      Joys ebb and flow within my tender heart.

❖ WILLIAM SHAKESPEARE ❖

from *Love's Labour's Lost* [ACT IV, SCENE III]

Did not the heavenly rhetoric of thine eye,
'Gainst whom the world cannot hold argument,
Persuade my heart to this false perjury?
Vows for thee broke deserve not punishment.
A woman I forswore, but I will prove,
Thou being a goddess, I forswore not thee.
My vow was earthly, thou a heavenly love;
Thy grace being gained cures all disgrace in me.
Vows are but breath, and breath a vapor is.
Then thou, fair sun, which on my earth doth shine,
Exhalest this vapor-vow; in thee it is.
If broken then, it is no fault of mine.
If by me broke, what fool is not so wise
To lose an oath to win a paradise?

from *Romeo and Juliet* [ACT I, SCENE V]

ROMEO. If I profane with my unworthiest hand
This holy shrine, the gentle fine is this,
My lips, two blushing pilgrims, ready stand
To smooth that rough touch with a tender kiss.

JULIET. Good pilgrim, you do wrong your hand too much,
Which mannerly devotion shows in this;
For saints have hands that pilgrims' hands do touch,
And palm to palm is holy palmers' kiss.

ROMEO. Have not saints lips, and holy palmers too?
JULIET. Aye, pilgrim, lips that they must use in prayer.
ROMEO. Oh then, dear saint, let lips do what hands do.
Then pray. Grant thou, lest faith turn to despair.

JULIET. Saints do not move, though grant for prayers' sake.
ROMEO. Then move not while my prayer's effect I take.

from *Sonnets*

I

From fairest creatures we desire increase,
That thereby beauty's rose might never die,
But as the riper should by time decease,
His tender heir might bear his memory:
But thou, contracted to thine own bright eyes,
Feed'st thy light's flame with self-substantial fuel,
Making a famine where abundance lies,
Thyself thy foe, to thy sweet self too cruel.
Thou that art now the world's fresh ornament,
And only herald to the gaudy spring,
Within thine own bud buriest thy content,
And, tender churl, mak'st waste in niggarding:
　　Pity the world, or else this glutton be,
　　To eat the world's due, by the grave and thee.

3

Look in thy glass, and tell the face thou viewest
Now is the time that face should form another,
Whose fresh repair if now thou not renewest,
Thou dost beguile the world, unbless some mother.
For where is she so fair whose uneared womb
Disdains the tillage of thy husbandry?
Or who is he so fond will be the tomb
Of his self-love, to stop posterity?
Thou art thy mother's glass, and she in thee
Calls back the lovely April of her prime;
So thou through windows of thine age shalt see,
Despite of wrinkles, this thy golden time.
    But if thou live rememb'red not to be,
    Die single, and thine image dies with thee.

13

O, that you were yourself, but, love, you are
No longer yours than you yourself here live:
Against this coming end you should prepare,
And your sweet semblance to some other give.
So should that beauty which you hold in lease
Find no determination; then you were
Yourself again after yourself's decease
When your sweet issue your sweet form should bear.
Who lets so fair a house fall to decay,
Which husbandry in honor might uphold
Against the stormy gusts of winter's day
And barren rage of death's eternal cold?
    O, none but unthrifts! Dear my love, you know
    You had a father—let your son say so.

18

Shall I compare thee to a summer's day?
Thou art more lovely and more temperate.
Rough winds do shake the darling buds of May,
And summer's lease hath all too short a date.
Sometime too hot the eye of heaven shines,
And often is his gold complexion dimmed;
And every fair from fair sometime declines,
By chance, or nature's changing course, untrimmed:
But thy eternal summer shall not fade
Nor lose possession of that fair thou ow'st,
Nor shall Death brag thou wand'rest in his shade
When in eternal lines to time thou grow'st.
    So long as men can breathe or eyes can see,
    So long lives this, and this gives life to thee.

19

Devouring Time, blunt thou the lion's paws,
And make the earth devour her own sweet brood;
Pluck the keen teeth from the fierce tiger's jaws,
And burn the long-lived phoenix in her blood;
Make glad and sorry seasons as thou fleet'st,
And do whate'er thou wilt, swift-footed Time,
To the wide world and all her fading sweets,
But I forbid thee one most heinous crime:
O, carve not with thy hours my love's fair brow,
Nor draw no lines there with thine antique pen;
Him in thy course untainted do allow
For beauty's pattern to succeeding men.
    Yet do thy worst, old Time: despite thy wrong,
    My love shall in my verse ever live young.

20

A woman's face, with Nature's own hand painted,
Hast thou, the master-mistress of my passion;
A woman's gentle heart, but not acquainted
With shifting change, as is false women's fashion;
An eye more bright than theirs, less false in rolling,
Gilding the object whereupon it gazeth;
A man in hue all hues in his controlling,
Which steals men's eyes and women's souls amazeth.
And for a woman wert thou first created,
Till Nature as she wrought thee fell a-doting,
And by addition me of thee defeated
By adding one thing to my purpose nothing.
    But since she pricked thee out for women's pleasure,
    Mine be thy love, and thy love's use their treasure.

24

Mine eye hath played the painter and hath stelled
Thy beauty's form in table of my heart;
My body is the frame wherein 'tis held,
And perspective it is best painter's art.
For through the painter must you see his skill
To find where your true image pictured lies,
Which in my bosom's shop is hanging still,
That hath his windows glazèd with thine eyes.
Now see what good turns eyes for eyes have done:
Mine eyes have drawn thy shape, and thine for me
Are windows to my breast, wherethrough the sun
Delights to peep, to gaze therein on thee.
    Yet eyes this cunning want to grace their art;
    They draw but what they see, know not the heart.

27

Weary with toil, I haste me to my bed,
The dear repose for limbs with travel tired,
But then begins a journey in my head
To work my mind when body's work's expired;
For then my thoughts, from far where I abide,
Intend a zealous pilgrimage to thee,
And keep my drooping eyelids open wide,
Looking on darkness which the blind do see;
Save that my soul's imaginary sight
Presents thy shadow to my sightless view,
Which, like a jewel hung in ghastly night,
Makes black night beauteous and her old face new.
    Lo, thus, by day my limbs, by night my mind,
    For thee and for myself no quiet find.

29

When, in disgrace with Fortune and men's eyes,
I all alone beweep my outcast state,
And trouble deaf heaven with my bootless cries,
And look upon myself and curse my fate,
Wishing me like to one more rich in hope,
Featured like him, like him with friends possessed,
Desiring this man's art, and that man's scope,
With what I most enjoy contented least;
Yet in these thoughts myself almost despising,
Haply I think on thee, and then my state,
Like to the lark at break of day arising
From sullen earth, sings hymns at heaven's gate;
    For thy sweet love rememb'red such wealth brings
    That then I scorn to change my state with kings.

53

What is your substance, whereof are you made,
That millions of strange shadows on you tend?
Since every one hath, every one, one shade,
And you, but one, can every shadow lend.
Describe Adonis, and the counterfeit
Is poorly imitated after you.
On Helen's cheek all art of beauty set,
And you in Grecian tires are painted new.
Speak of the spring and foison of the year:
The one doth shadow of your beauty show,
The other as your bounty doth appear,
And you in every blessèd shape we know.
   In all external grace you have some part,
   But you like none, none you, for constant heart.

55

Not marble nor the gilded monuments
Of princes shall outlive this pow'rful rime,
But you shall shine more bright in these contents
Than unswept stone, besmeared with sluttish time.
When wasteful war shall statues overturn,
And broils root out the work of masonry,
Nor Mars his sword nor war's quick fire shall burn
The living record of your memory.
'Gainst death and all oblivious enmity
Shall you pace forth; your praise shall still find room
Even in the eyes of all posterity
That wear this world out to the ending doom.
   So, till the judgment that yourself arise,
   You live in this, and dwell in lovers' eyes.

57

Being your slave, what should I do but tend
Upon the hours and times of your desire?
I have no precious time at all to spend,
Nor services to do till you require.
Nor dare I chide the world-without-end hour
Whilst I, my sovereign, watch the clock for you,
Nor think the bitterness of absence sour
When you have bid your servant once adieu.
Nor dare I question with my jealious thought
Where you may be, or your affairs suppose,
But, like a sad slave, stay and think of nought
Save where you are how happy you make those.
  So true a fool is love that in your will,
  Though you do anything, he thinks no ill.

60

Like as the waves make towards the pebbled shore,
So do our minutes hasten to their end;
Each changing place with that which goes before,
In sequent toil all forwards do contend.
Nativity, once in the main of light,
Crawls to maturity, wherewith being crowned,
Crooked eclipses 'gainst his glory fight,
And Time that gave doth now his gift confound.
Time doth transfix the flourish set on youth
And delves the parallels in beauty's brow,
Feeds on the rarities of nature's truth,
And nothing stands but for his scythe to mow:
  And yet to times in hope my verse shall stand,
  Praising thy worth, despite his cruel hand.

65

Since brass, nor stone, nor earth, nor boundless sea,
But sad mortality o'ersways their power,
How with this rage shall beauty hold a plea,
Whose action is no stronger than a flower?
O, how shall summer's honey breath hold out
Against the wrackful siege of batt'ring days,
When rocks impregnable are not so stout,
Nor gates of steel so strong but Time decays?
O fearful meditation: where, alack,
Shall Time's best jewel from Time's chest lie hid?
Or what strong hand can hold his swift foot back,
Or who his spoil of beauty can forbid?
    O, none, unless this miracle have might,
    That in black ink my love may still shine bright.

71

No longer mourn for me when I am dead
Than you shall hear the surly sullen bell
Give warning to the world that I am fled
From this vile world, with vilest worms to dwell.
Nay, if you read this line, remember not
The hand that writ it, for I love you so
That I in your sweet thoughts would be forgot
If thinking on me then should make you woe.
O, if, I say, you look upon this verse
When I, perhaps, compounded am with clay,
Do not so much as my poor name rehearse,
But let your love even with my life decay,
    Lest the wise world should look into your moan
    And mock you with me after I am gone.

73

That time of year thou mayst in me behold
When yellow leaves, or none, or few, do hang
Upon those boughs which shake against the cold,
Bare ruined choirs where late the sweet birds sang.
In me thou seest the twilight of such day
As after sunset fadeth in the west,
Which by and by black night doth take away,
Death's second self that seals up all in rest.
In me thou seest the glowing of such fire
That on the ashes of his youth doth lie,
As the deathbed whereon it must expire,
Consumed with that which it was nourished by.
    This thou perceiv'st, which makes thy love more strong,
    To love that well which thou must leave ere long.

94

They that have pow'r to hurt and will do none,
That do not do the thing they most do show,
Who, moving others, are themselves as stone,
Unmovèd, cold, and to temptation slow;
They rightly do inherit heaven's graces
And husband nature's riches from expense;
They are the lords and owners of their faces,
Others but stewards of their excellence.
The summer's flow'r is to the summer sweet,
Though to itself it only live and die;
But if that flow'r with base infection meet,
The basest weed outbraves his dignity:
    For sweetest things turn sourest by their deeds;
    Lilies that fester smell far worse than weeds.

105

Let not my love be called idolatry,
Nor my belovèd as an idol show,
Since all alike my songs and praises be
To one, of one, still such, and ever so.
Kind is my love to-day, to-morrow kind,
Still constant in a wondrous excellence;
Therefore my verse, to constancy confined,
One thing expressing, leaves out difference.
"Fair, kind, and true" is all my argument,
"Fair, kind, and true" varying to other words;
And in this change is my invention spent,
Three themes in one, which wondrous scope affords.
    Fair, kind, and true have often lived alone,
    Which three till now never kept seat in one.

106

When in the chronicle of wasted time
I see descriptions of the fairest wights,
And beauty making beautiful old rime
In praise of ladies dead and lovely knights;
Then, in the blazon of sweet beauty's best,
Of hand, of foot, of lip, of eye, of brow,
I see their antique pen would have expressed
Even such a beauty as you master now.
So all their praises are but prophecies
Of this our time, all you prefiguring;
And, for they looked but with divining eyes,
They had not skill enough your worth to sing:
    For we, which now behold these present days,
    Have eyes to wonder, but lack tongues to praise.

116

Let me not to the marriage of true minds
Admit impediments; love is not love
Which alters when it alteration finds
Or bends with the remover to remove.
O, no, it is an ever-fixèd mark
That looks on tempests and is never shaken;
It is the star to every wand'ring bark,
Whose worth's unknown, although his height be taken.
Love's not Time's fool, though rosy lips and cheeks
Within his bending sickle's compass come;
Love alters not with his brief hours and weeks,
But bears it out even to the edge of doom.
    If this be error, and upon me proved,
    I never writ, nor no man ever loved.

127

In the old age black was not counted fair,
Or, if it were, it bore not beauty's name;
But now is black beauty's successive heir,
And beauty slandered with a bastard shame;
For since each hand hath put on nature's power,
Fairing the foul with art's false borrowed face,
Sweet beauty hath no name, no holy bower,
But is profaned, if not lives in disgrace.
Therefore my mistress' brows are raven black,
Her eyes so suited, and they mourners seem
At such who, not born fair, no beauty lack,
Sland'ring creation with a false esteem:
    Yet so they mourn, becoming of their woe,
    That every tongue says beauty should look so.

128

How oft, when thou, my music, music play'st
Upon that blessèd wood whose motion sounds
With thy sweet fingers when thou gently sway'st
The wiry concord that mine ear confounds,
Do I envy those jacks that nimble leap
To kiss the tender inward of thy hand,
Whilst my poor lips, which should that harvest reap,
At the wood's boldness by thee blushing stand.
To be so tickled they would change their state
And situation with those dancing chips
O'er whom thy fingers walk with gentle gait,
Making dead wood more blest than living lips.
    Since saucy jacks so happy are in this,
    Give them thy fingers, me thy lips to kiss.

129

Th' expense of spirit in a waste of shame
Is lust in action; and, till action, lust
Is perjured, murd'rous, bloody, full of blame,
Savage, extreme, rude, cruel, not to trust;
Enjoyed no sooner but despisèd straight;
Past reason hunted, and no sooner had,
Past reason hated as a swallowed bait
On purpose laid to make the taker mad:
Mad in pursuit, and in possession so;
Had, having, and in quest to have, extreme;
A bliss in proof, and proved, a very woe;
Before, a joy proposed; behind, a dream.
    All this the world well knows; yet none knows well
    To shun the heaven that leads men to this hell.

130

My mistress' eyes are nothing like the sun;
Coral is far more red than her lips' red;
If snow be white, why then her breasts are dun;
If hairs be wires, black wires grow on her head.
I have seen roses damasked, red and white,
But no such roses see I in her cheeks;
And in some perfumes is there more delight
Than in the breath that from my mistress reeks.
I love to hear her speak; yet well I know
That music hath a far more pleasing sound:
I grant I never saw a goddess go;
My mistress, when she walks, treads on the ground.
    And yet, by heaven, I think my love as rare
    As any she belied with false compare.

134

So, now I have confessed that he is thine
And I myself am mortgaged to thy will,
Myself I'll forfeit, so that other mine
Thou wilt restore to be my comfort still:
But thou wilt not, nor he will not be free,
For thou art covetous, and he is kind;
He learned but surety-like to write for me
Under that bond that him as fast doth bind.
The statute of thy beauty thou wilt take,
Thou usurer that put'st forth all to use,
And sue a friend came debtor for my sake;
So him I lose through my unkind abuse.
    Him have I lost, thou hast both him and me;
    He pays the whole, and yet am I not free.

138

When my love swears that she is made of truth
I do believe her, though I know she lies,
That she might think me some untutored youth,
Unlearnèd in the world's false subtilties.
Thus vainly thinking that she thinks me young,
Although she knows my days are past the best,
Simply I credit her false-speaking tongue;
On both sides thus is simple truth suppressed.
But wherefore says she not she is unjust?
And wherefore say not I that I am old?
O, love's best habit is in seeming trust,
And age in love loves not to have years told.
    Therefore I lie with her and she with me,
    And in our faults by lies we flattered be.

141

In faith, I do not love thee with mine eyes,
For they in thee a thousand errors note;
But 'tis my heart that loves what they despise,
Who in despite of view is pleased to dote.
Nor are mine ears with thy tongue's tune delighted,
Nor tender feeling to base touches prone,
Nor taste, nor smell, desire to be invited
To any sensual feast with thee alone;
But my five wits nor my five senses can
Dissuade one foolish heart from serving thee,
Who leaves unswayed the likeness of a man,
Thy proud heart's slave and vassal wretch to be:
    Only my plague thus far I count my gain,
    That she that makes me sin awards me pain.

144

Two loves I have, of comfort and despair,
Which like two spirits do suggest me still:
The better angel is a man right fair,
The worser spirit a woman colored ill.
To win me soon to hell, my female evil
Tempteth my better angel from my side,
And would corrupt my saint to be a devil,
Wooing his purity with her foul pride.
And whether that my angel be turned fiend
Suspect I may, yet not directly tell;
But being both from me, both to each friend,
I guess one angel in another's hell.
    Yet this shall I ne'er know, but live in doubt,
    Till my bad angel fire my good one out.

146

Poor soul, the center of my sinful earth,
[Pressed by] these rebel pow'rs that thee array,
Why dost thou pine within and suffer dearth,
Painting thy outward walls so costly gay?
Why so large cost, having so short a lease,
Dost thou upon thy fading mansion spend?
Shall worms, inheritors of this excess,
Eat up thy charge? Is this thy body's end?
Then, soul, live thou upon thy servant's loss,
And let that pine to aggravate thy store;
Buy terms divine in selling hours of dross;
Within be fed, without be rich no more:
    So shalt thou feed on Death, that feeds on men,
    And Death once dead, there's no more dying then.

147

My love is as a fever, longing still
For that which longer nurseth the disease,
Feeding on that which doth preserve the ill,
Th' uncertain sickly appetite to please.
My reason, the physician to my love,
Angry that his prescriptions are not kept,
Hath left me, and I desperate now approve
Desire is death, which physic did except.
Past cure I am, now reason is past care,
And frantic-mad with evermore unrest;
My thoughts and my discourse as madmen's are,
At random from the truth vainly expressed:
　　For I have sworn thee fair, and thought thee bright,
　　Who art as black as hell, as dark as night.

151

Love is too young to know what conscience is;
Yet who knows not conscience is born of love?
Then, gentle cheater, urge not my amiss,
Lest guilty of my faults thy sweet self prove.
For, thou betraying me, I do betray
My nobler part to my gross body's treason;
My soul doth tell my body that he may
Triumph in love; flesh stays no farther reason,
But, rising at thy name, doth point out thee
As his triumphant prize. Proud of this pride,
He is contented thy poor drudge to be,
To stand in thy affairs, fall by thy side.
　　No want of conscience hold it that I call
　　Her "love" for whose dear love I rise and fall.

❖ JAMES I ❖

AN EPITAPH ON SIR PHILIP SIDNEY

Thou mighty Mars, the god of soldiers brave,
And thou, Minerva, that does in wit excel,
And thou, Apollo, that does knowledge have
Of every art that from Parnassus fell,
With all the sisters that thereon do dwell,
Lament for him who duly served you all,
Whom-in you wisely all your arts did mell,—
Bewail, I say, his unexpected fall.
I need not in remembrance for to call
His youth, his race, the hope had of him aye,
Since that in him doth cruel death appall
Both manhood, wit, and learning every way.
    Now in the bed of honor doth he rest,
    And evermore of him shall live the best.

❖ SIR JOHN DAVIES ❖

from *Gullinge Sonnets*

Mine Eye, myne eare, my will, my witt, my harte,
Did see, did heare, did like, discerne, did love,
Her face, her speche, her fashion, judgement, arte,
Which did charme, please, delighte, confounde and move.
Then fancie, humor, love, conceipte, and thoughte
Did soe drawe, force, intyse, perswade, devise,
That she was wonne, mov'd, caryed, compast, wrought,
To thinck me kinde, true, comelie, valyant, wise.
That heaven, earth, hell, my folly and her pride
Did worke, contrive, labor, conspire and sweare
To make me scorn'd, vile, cast of, bace, defyed
With her my love, my lighte, my life, my deare;
So that my harte, my witt, will, eare, and eye
Doth greive, lament, sorrowe, dispaire and dye.

❖ ❖ ❖

If you would know the love which I you bear,
Compare it to the Ring which your fair hand
Shall make more precious when you shall it wear:
So my love's nature you shall understand.
Is it of metal pure? so you shall prove
My love, which ne'er disloyal thought did stain.
Hath it no end? so endless is my love,
Unless you it destroy with your disdain.
Doth it the purer wax the more 'tis tried?
So doth my love: yet herein they dissent,
That whereas gold, the more 'tis purified,
By waxing less doth show some part is spent,
My love doth wax more pure by your more trying,
And yet increaseth in the purifying.

❖ JOHN DONNE ❖

LA CORONA

I

Deign at my hands this crown of prayer and praise,
Weaved in my low devout melancholy,
Thou which of good, hast, yea art treasury,
All changing unchanged Ancient of days,
But do not, with a vile crown of frail bays,
Reward my muse's white sincerity,
But what thy thorny crown gained, that give me,
A crown of glory, which doth flower always;
The ends crown our works, but thou crown'st our ends,
For, at our end begins our endless rest,
This first last end, now zealously possessed,
With a strong sober thirst, my soul attends.
'Tis time that heart and voice be lifted high,
Salvation to all that will is nigh.

2   ANNUNCIATION

Salvation to all that will is nigh,
That all, which always is all everywhere,
Which cannot sin, and yet all sins must bear,
Which cannot die, yet cannot choose but die,
Lo, faithful Virgin, yields himself to lie
In prison, in thy womb; and though he there
Can take no sin, nor thou give, yet he 'will wear
Taken from thence, flesh, which death's force may try.
Ere by the spheres time was created, thou
Wast in his mind, who is thy son, and brother,
Whom thou conceiv'st, conceived; yea thou art now
Thy maker's maker, and thy father's mother,
Thou' hast light in dark; and shutt'st in little room,
Immensity cloistered in thy dear womb.

3   NATIVITY

Immensity cloistered in thy dear womb,
Now leaves his well-beloved imprisonment,
There he hath made himself to his intent
Weak enough, now into our world to come;
But oh, for thee, for him, hath th' inn no room?
Yet lay him in this stall, and from the orient,
Stars, and wisemen will travel to prevent
Th' effect of Herod's jealous general doom.
See'st thou, my soul, with thy faith's eyes, how he
Which fills all place, yet none holds him, doth lie?
Was not his pity towards thee wondrous high,
That would have need to be pitied by thee?
Kiss him, and with him into Egypt go,
With his kind mother, who partakes thy woe.

4   TEMPLE

With his kind mother who partakes thy woe,
Joseph turn back; see where your child doth sit,
Blowing, yea blowing out those sparks of wit,
Which himself on the Doctors did bestow;
The Word but lately could not speak, and lo
It suddenly speaks wonders, whence comes it,
That all which was, and all which should be writ,
A shallow seeming child, should deeply know?
His godhead was not soul to his manhood,
Nor had time mellowed him to this ripeness,
But as for one which hath a long task, 'tis good,
With the sun to begin his business,
He in his age's morning thus began
By miracles exceeding power of man.

5   CRUCIFYING

By miracles exceeding power of man,
He faith in some, envy in some begat,
For, what weak spirits admire, ambitious hate;
In both affections many to him ran,
But oh! the worst are most, they will and can,
Alas, and do, unto the immaculate,
Whose creature Fate is, now prescribe a fate,
Measuring self-life's infinity to a span,
Nay to an inch. Lo, where condemned he
Bears his own cross, with pain, yet by and by
When it bears him, he must bear more and die.
Now thou are lifted up, draw me to thee,
And at thy death giving such liberal dole,
Moist, with one drop of thy blood, my dry soul.

6   RESURRECTION

Moist with one drop of thy blood, my dry soul
Shall (though she now be in extreme degree
Too stony hard, and yet too fleshly,) be
Freed by that drop, from being starved, hard, or foul,
And life, by this death abled, shall control
Death, whom thy death slew; nor shall to me
Fear of first or last death, bring misery,
If in thy little book my name thou enrol,
Flesh in that long sleep is not putrefied,
But made that there, of which, and for which 'twas;
Nor can by other means be glorified.
May then sin's sleep, and death's soon from me pass,
That waked from both, I again risen may
Salute the last, and everlasting day.

7   ASCENSION

Salute the last and everlasting day,
Joy at the uprising of this sun, and son,
Ye whose just tears, or tribulation
Have purely washed, or burnt your drossy clay;
Behold the highest, parting hence away,
Lightens the dark clouds, which he treads upon,
Nor doth he by ascending, show alone,
But first he, and he first enters the way.
O strong ram, which hast battered heaven for me,
Mild lamb, which with thy blood, hast marked the path;
Bright torch, which shin'st, that I the way may see,
Oh, with thine own blood quench thine own just wrath,
And if thy holy Spirit, my Muse did raise,
Deign at my hands this crown of prayer and praise.

from *Holy Sonnets*

I

Thou hast made me, and shall thy work decay?
Repair me now, for now mine end doth haste,
I run to death, and death meets me as fast,
And all my pleasures are like yesterday,
I dare not move my dim eyes any way,
Despair behind, and death before doth cast
Such terror, and my feeble flesh doth waste
By sin in it, which it towards hell doth weigh;
Only thou art above, and when towards thee
By thy leave I can look, I rise again;
But our old subtle foe so tempteth me,
That not one hour I can myself sustain;
Thy Grace may wing me to prevent his art,
And thou like adamant draw mine iron heart.

5

I am a little world made cunningly
Of elements, and an angelic sprite,
But black sin hath betrayed to endless night
My world's both parts, and, oh, both parts must die.
You which beyond that heaven which was most high
Have found new spheres, and of new lands can write,
Pour new seas in mine eyes, that so I might
Drown my world with my weeping earnestly,
Or wash it if it must be drowned no more:
But oh it must be burnt; alas the fire
Of lust and envy have burnt it heretofore,
And made it fouler; let their flames retire,
And burn me O Lord, with a fiery zeal
Of thee and thy house, which doth in eating heal.

6

This is my play's last scene, here heavens appoint
My pilgrimage's last mile; and my race
Idly, yet quickly run, hath this last pace,
My span's last inch, my minute's latest point,
And gluttonous death, will instantly unjoint
My body, and soul, and I shall sleep a space,
But my'ever-waking part shall see that face,
Whose fear already shakes my every joint:
Then, as my soul, to heaven her first seat, takes flight,
And earth-born body, in the earth shall dwell,
So, fall my sins, that all may have their right,
To where they are bred, and would press me, to hell.
Impute me righteous, thus purged of evil,
For thus I leave the world, the flesh, and devil.

7

At the round earth's imagined corners, blow
Your trumpets, angels, and arise, arise
From death, you numberless infinities
Of souls, and to your scattered bodies go,
All whom the flood did, and fire shall o'erthrow,
All whom war, dearth, age, agues, tyrannies,
Despair, law, chance, hath slain, and you whose eyes,
Shall behold God, and never taste death's woe.
But let them sleep, Lord, and me mourn a space,
For, if above all these, my sins abound,
'Tis late to ask abundance of thy grace,
When we are there; here on this lowly ground,
Teach me how to repent; for that's as good
As if thou hadst sealed my pardon, with thy blood.

10

Death be not proud, though some have callèd thee
Mighty and dreadful, for, thou art not so,
For, those, whom thou think'st, thou dost overthrow,
Die not, poor death, nor yet canst thou kill me;
From rest and sleep, which but thy pictures be,
Much pleasure, then from thee, much more must flow,
And soonest our best men with thee do go,
Rest of their bones, and soul's delivery.
Thou art slave to fate, chance, kings, and desperate men,
And dost with poison, war, and sickness dwell,
And poppy, or charms can make us sleep as well,
And better than thy stroke; why swell'st thou then?
One short sleep past, we wake eternally,
And death shall be no more, Death thou shalt die.

13

What if this present were the world's last night?
Mark in my heart, O soul, where thou dost dwell,
The picture of Christ crucified, and tell
Whether that countenance can thee affright,
Tears in his eyes quench the amazing light,
Blood fills his frowns, which from his pierced head fell,
And can that tongue adjudge thee unto hell,
Which prayed forgiveness for his foes' fierce spite?
No, no; but as in my idolatry
I said to all my profane mistresses,
Beauty, of pity, foulness only is
A sign of rigour: so I say to thee,
To wicked spirits are horrid shapes assigned,
This beauteous form assures a piteous mind.

14

Batter my heart, three-personed God; for, you
As yet but knock, breathe, shine, and seek to mend;
That I may rise, and stand, o'erthrow me, and bend
Your force, to break, blow, burn, and make me new.
I, like an usurped town, to another due,
Labour to admit you, but oh, to no end,
Reason your viceroy in me, me should defend,
But is captived, and proves weak or untrue,
Yet dearly I love you, and would be loved fain,
But am betrothed unto your enemy,
Divorce me, untie, or break that knot again,
Take me to you, imprison me, for I
Except you enthral me, never shall be free,
Nor ever chaste, except you ravish me.

18

Show me dear Christ, thy spouse, so bright and clear.
What, is it she, which on the other shore
Goes richly painted? or which robbed and tore
Laments and mourns in Germany and here?
Sleeps she a thousand, then peeps up one year?
Is she self truth and errs? now new, now outwore?
Doth she, and did she, and shall she evermore
On one, on seven, or on no hill appear?
Dwells she with us, or like adventuring knights
First travail we to seek and then make love?
Betray kind husband thy spouse to our sights,
And let mine amorous soul court thy mild dove,
Who is most true, and pleasing to thee, then
When she'is embraced and open to most men.

19

Oh, to vex me, contraries meet in one:
Inconstancy unnaturally hath begot
A constant habit; that when I would not
I change in vows, and in devotion.
As humorous is my contrition
As my profane love, and as soon forgot:
As riddlingly distempered, cold and hot,
As praying, as mute; as infinite, as none.
I durst not view heaven yesterday; and today
In prayers, and flattering speeches I court God:
Tomorrow I quake with true fear of his rod.
So my devout fits come and go away
Like a fantastic ague: save that here
Those are my best days, when I shake with fear.

❖ ❖ ❖

SONNET. THE TOKEN

Send me some token, that my hope may live,
    Or that my easeless thoughts may sleep and rest;
Send me some honey to make sweet my hive,
    That in my passions I may hope the best.
I beg no riband wrought with thine own hands,
    To knit our loves in the fantastic strain
Of new-touched youth; nor ring to show the stands
    Of our affection, that as that's round and plain,
So should our loves meet in simplicity;
    No, nor the corals which thy wrist enfold,
Laced up together in congruity,
    To show our thoughts should rest in the same hold;
No, nor thy picture, though most gracious,
    And most desired, because best like the best;
Nor witty lines, which are most copious,
    Within the writings which thou hast addressed.

Send me nor this, nor that, to increase my store,
But swear thou think'st I love thee, and no more.

❖ BEN JONSON ❖

A SONNET TO THE NOBLE LADY, THE LADY MARY WROTH

I that have been a lover, and could shew it,
   Though not in these, in rithmes not wholly dumb,
   Since I exscribe your sonnets, am become
   A better lover, and much better poet.
Nor is my Muse or I ashamed to owe it
   To those true numerous graces; whereof some
   But charm the senses, others overcome
   Both brains and hearts; and mine now best do know it:
For in your verse all Cupid's armoury,
   His flames, his shafts, his quiver, and his bow,
   His very eyes are yours to overthrow.
But then his mother's sweets you so apply,
   Her joys, her smiles, her loves, as readers take
   For Venus' ceston every line you make.

❖ LORD HERBERT OF CHERBURY ❖

SONNET TO BLACK IT SELF

Thou Black, wherein all colours are compos'd,
And unto which they all at last return,
Thou colour of the Sun where it doth burn,
And shadow, where it cools, in thee is clos'd
Whatever nature can or hath dispos'd
In any other hue: from thee do rise
Those tempers and complexions, which, disclos'd
As parts of thee, do work as mysteries
Of that thy hidden power: when thou dost reign,
The characters of fate shine in the Skies,
And tell us what the Heavens do ordain,
But when Earth's common light shines to our eyes,
Thou so retirest thyself, that thy disdain
All revelation unto Man denies.

❖ WILLIAM DRUMMOND ❖
OF HAWTHORNDEN

"I know that all beneath the moon decays"

I know that all beneath the moon decays,
And what by mortals in this world is brought,
In Time's great periods shall return to nought;
That fairest states have fatal nights and days;
I know how all the Muse's heavenly lays,
With toil of spright which are so dearly bought,
As idle sounds of few or none are sought,
And that nought lighter is than airy praise.
I know frail beauty like the purple flower,
To which one morn oft birth and death affords;
That love a jarring is of minds' accords,
Where sense and will invassal reason's power:
Know what I list, this all can not me move,
But that, O me! I both must write and love.

"Sleep, Silence' child, sweet father of soft rest"

Sleep, Silence' child, sweet father of soft rest,
Prince whose approach peace to all mortals brings,
Indifferent host to shepherds and to kings,
Sole comforter of minds with grief opprest;
Lo, by thy charming-rod all breathing things
Lie slumbering, with forgetfulness possest,
And yet o'er me to spread thy drowsy wings
Thou spares, alas! who cannot be thy guest.
Since I am thine, O come, but with that face
To inward light which thou art wont to show;
With feigned solace each a true-felt woe;
Or if, deaf god, thou do deny that grace,
Come as thou wilt, and what thou wilt bequeath,—
I long to kiss the image of my death.

❖ LADY MARY WROTH ❖

from *Pamphilia to Amphilanthus*

A CROWNE OF SONETTS DEDICATED TO LOVE

In this strang labourinth how shall I turne?
    wayes are on all sids while the way I miss:
    if to the right hand, ther, in love I burne;
    lett mee goe forward, therin danger is;

If to the left, suspition hinders bliss,
    lett mee turne back, shame cries I ought returne
    nor fainte though crosses with my fortunes kiss;
    stand still is harder, allthough sure to mourne;

Thus lett mee take the right, or left hand way;
    goe forward, or stand still, or back retire;
    I must thes doubts indure with out allay
    or help, butt traveile find for my best hire;

yett that which most my troubled sence doth move
is to leave all, and take the thread of love,

2

Is to leave all, and take the thread of love
    which line straite leads unto the soules content
    wher choyce delights with pleasures wings doe move,
    and idle phant'sie never roome had lent,

When chaste thoughts guide us then owr minds ar bent
    to take that good which ills from us remove,
    light of true love, brings fruite which none repent
    butt constant lovers seeke, and wish to prove;

Love is the shining starr of blessings light;
    the fervent fire of zeale, the roote of peace,
    that lasting lampe fed with the oyle of right;
    Image of fayth, and wombe for joyes increase.

Love is true vertu, and his ends delight,
his flames ar joyes, his bands true lovers might.

3

His flames ar joyes, his bands true lovers might,
    noe staine is ther butt pure, as purest white,
    wher noe clowde can apeere to dimm his light,
    nor spott defile, butt shame will soone requite,

Heere are affections, tri'de by loves just might
    as gold by fire, and black desernd by white,
    Error by truthe, and darknes knowne by light,
    wher faith is vallwed for love to requite,

Please him, and serve him, glory in his might,
    and firme hee'll bee, as innosencye white,
    cleere as th'ayre, warme as sunn beames, as day light,
    just as truthe, constant as fate, joy'd to requite,

Then love obay, strive to observe his might,
and bee in his brave court a glorious light;

4

And bee in his brave court a gloriouse light,
    shine in the eyes of faith, and constancie,
    maintaine the fires of love still burning bright
    nott slightly sparkling butt light flaming bee

Never to slack till earth noe stars can see,
    till sunn, and Moone doe leave to us dark night,
    and secound Chaose once againe doe free
    us, and the world from all devisions spite,

Till then, affections which his followers are
    governe our harts, and prove his powers gaine
    to taste this pleasing sting seek with all care
    for hapy smarting is itt with smale paine,

such as although, itt pierce your tender hart
and burne, yett burning you will love the smart;

5

And burne, yett burning you will love the smart,
    when you shall feele the weight of true desire,
    soe pleasing, as you would nott wish your part
    of burden showld bee missing from that fire;

Butt faithfull and unfained heate aspire
    which sinne abolisheth, and doth impart
    saulves to all feares, with vertues which inspire
    soules with devine love, which showes his chaste art,

And guide hee is to joyings; open eyes
    hee hath to hapines, and best can learne
    us means how to deserve, this hee descries,
    who blind yett doth our hidenest thought deserne.

Thus may wee gaine since living in blest love
hee may our profitt, and owr Tuter prove,

6

Hee may owr profitt, and our Tuter prove
    in whom alone wee doe this power finde,
    to joine tow harts as in one frame to move;
    tow bodies, butt one soule to rule the minde;

Eyes with much care to one deere object bind
    eares to each others speech as if above
    all els they sweet, and learned were; this kind
    content of lovers wittniseth true love,

Itt doth inrich the witts, and makes you see
    that in your self, which you knew nott before,
    forcing you to admire such guifts showld bee
    hid from your knowledg, yett in you the store;

Millions of thes adorne the throne of Love
how blest bee they then, who his favours prove

7

How blest bee they then, who his favors prove
    a lyfe wherof the birth is just desire,
    breeding sweet flames which hearts invite to move
    in those lov'd eyes which kindles Cupids fire,

And nurse his longings with his thoughts intire,
    fixt on the heat of wishes formd by love,
    yett as wher fire distroys this doth respire,
    increase, and foster all delights above;

Love will a painter make you, such, as you
    shall able bee to drawe your only deere
    more lively, parfett, lasting, and more true
    then rarest woorkmen, and to you more neere,

Thes be the least, then needs must all confess
Hee that shunns love doth love him self the less

8

Hee that shunns love doth love him self the less
    and cursed hee whos spiritt nott admires
    the worth of love, wher endles blessednes
    raines, and commands, maintaind by heavnly fires

made of Vertu, join'de by truth, blowne by desires
    strengthned by worth, renued by carefullnes
    flaming in never changing thoughts, briers
    of jelousie shall heere miss wellcomnes;

nor coldly pass in the pursuites of love
    like one longe frozen in a sea of ise,
    and yett butt chastly lett your passions move
    noe thought from vertuouse love your minds intise.

Never to other ends your phant'sies place
butt wher they may returne with honors grace,

9

Butt wher they may returne with honors grace
   wher Venus follyes can noe harbour winn
   butt chased ar as worthles of the face
   or stile of love who hath lasiviouse binn.

Oure harts ar subjects to her sunn; wher sinn
   never did dwell, nor rest one minutes space;
   what faults hee hath, in her, did still begin,
   and from her brest hee suckd his fleeting pace,

If lust bee counted love t'is faulcely nam'd
   by wikednes a fayrer gloss to sett
   upon that Vice, which els makes men asham'd
   in the owne frase to warrant butt begett

This childe for love, who ought like monster borne
bee from the court of Love, and reason torne.

10

Bee from the court of Love, and reason torne
   for Love in reason now doth putt his trust,
   desert, and liking are together borne
   children of love, and reason parents just,

Reason adviser is, love ruler must
   bee of the state which crowne hee long hath worne
   yett soe as neither will in least mistrust
   the government wher noe feare is of scorne,

Then reverence both theyr mights thus made butt one,
   butt wantones, and all those errors shun,
   which wrongers bee, impostures, and alone
   maintainers of all follyes ill begunn;

Fruit of a sowre, and unwholsome ground
unprofitably pleasing, and unsound

11

Unprofitably pleasing, and unsound
    when heaven gave liberty to frayle dull earth
    to bringe forth plenty that in ills abound
    which ripest yett doe bring a sertaine dearth.

A timeles, and unseasonable birth
    planted in ill, in wurse time springing found,
    which hemlock like might feed a sick-witts mirthe
    wher unruld vapors swimm in endles rounde,

Then joy wee nott in what wee ought to shun
    wher shady pleasures showe, butt true borne fires
    ar quite quench'd out, or by poore ashes wunn
    awhile to keepe those coole, and wann desires.

O noe lett love his glory have and might
bee given to him who triumphs in his right

12

Bee given to him who triumphs in his right
    nor vading bee, butt like those blossooms fayre
    which fall for good, and lose theyr coulers bright
    yett dy nott, butt with fruite theyr loss repaire

soe may love make you pale with loving care
    when sweet injoying shall restore that light
    more cleare in beauty then wee can compare
    if nott to Venus in her chosen night.

And who soe give them selves in this deere kind
    thes hapinesses shall attend them still
    to bee suplyd with joys, inrichd in mind
    with treasures of contents, and pleasures fill,

Thus love to bee devine doth heere apeere
free from all fogs butt shining faire, and cleere;

13

Free from all fogs butt shining faire, and cleere
  wise in all good, and innosent in ill
  wher holly friendship is esteemed deere
  with truth in love, and justice in our will,

In love thes titles only have theyr fill
  of hapy lyfe maintainer, and the meere
  defence of right, the punnisher of skill,
  and fraude; from whence directnes doth apeere,

To thee then lord commander of all harts,
  ruller of owr affections kinde, and just
  great king of Love, my soule from fained smarts
  or thought of change I offer to your trust

This crowne, my self, and all that I have more
except my hart which you beestow'd beefore;

14

Except my hart which you beestow'd before,
  and for a signe of conquest gave away
  as worthles to bee kept in your choyse store
  yett one more spotles with you doth nott stay.

The tribute which my hart doth truly pay
  faith untouch'd is, pure thoughts discharge the score
  of depts for mee, wher constancy bears sway,
  and rules as Lord, unharm'd by envyes sore,

Yett other mischiefs faile nott to attend,
  as enimies to you, my foes must bee;
  curst jealousie doth all her forces bend
  to my undoing; thus my harmes I see.

Soe though in Love I fervently doe burne,
In this strange labourinth how shall I turne?

TO HIS MISTRESS OBJECTING TO HIM NEITHER TOYING NOR TALKING

You say I love not, 'cause I do not play
   Still with your curls, and kiss the time away.
   You blame me, too, because I can't devise
   Some sport to please those babies in your eyes;—
By Love's religion, I must here confess it,
   The most I love, when I the least express it.
   Small griefs find tongues; full casks are ever found
   To give, if any, yet but little sound.
Deep waters noiseless are; and this we know,
   That chiding streams betray small depth below.
   So when love speechless is, she doth express
   A depth in love, and that depth bottomless.
Now, since my love is tongueless, know me such,
   Who speak but little, 'cause I love so much.

TO HIS EVER-LOVING GOD

Can I not come to Thee, my God, for these
So very-many-meeting hindrances,
That slack my pace; but yet not make me stay?
Who slowly goes, rids (in the end) his way.
Cleere Thou my paths, or shorten Thou my miles,
Remove the barrs, or lift me o're the stiles:
Since rough the way is, help me when I call,
And take me up; or els prevent the fall.
I kenn my home; and it affords some ease,
To see far off the smoaking Villages.
Fain would I rest; yet covet not to die,
For feare of future-biting penurie:
No, no, (my God) Thou know'st my wishes be
To leave this life, not loving it, but Thee.

❖ GEORGE HERBERT ❖

TWO SONNETS SENT TO HIS MOTHER, NEW–YEAR 1609/10

My God, where is that ancient heat towards thee,
　　Wherewith whole showls of *Martyrs* once did burn,
　　Besides their other flames? Doth Poetry
Wear *Venus* Livery? only serve her turn?
Why are not *Sonnets* made of thee? and layes
　　Upon thine Altar burnt? Cannot thy love
　　Heighten a spirit to sound out thy praise
As well as any she? Cannot thy *Dove*
Out-strip their *Cupid* easily in flight?
　　Or, since thy wayes are deep, and still the same,
　　Will not a verse run smooth that bears thy name?
Why doth that fire, which by thy power and might
　　Each breast does feel, no braver fuel choose
　　Than that, which one day Worms may chance refuse?

Sure, Lord, there is enough in thee to dry
　　Oceans of *Ink*; for, as the Deluge did
　　Cover the Earth, so doth thy Majesty:
Each Cloud distills thy praise, and doth forbid
Poets to turn it to another use.
　　Roses and *Lillies* speak thee; and to make
　　A pair of Cheeks of them, is thy abuse.
Why should I *Womens eyes* for Chrystal take?
Such poor invention burns in their low mind
　　Whose fire is wild, and doth not upward go
　　To praise, and on thee, Lord, some *Ink* bestow.
Open the bones, and you shall nothing find
　　In the best *face* but *filth,* when, Lord, in thee
　　The *beauty* lies in the *discovery.*

REDEMPTION

Having been tenant long to a rich Lord,
   Not thriving, I resolved to be bold,
   And make a suit unto him, to afford
A new small-rented lease, and cancel th' old.

In Heaven at his manor I him sought:
   They told me there, that he was lately gone
   About some land, which he had dearly bought
Long since on earth, to take possession.

I straight return'd, and knowing his great birth,
   Sought him accordingly in great resorts;
   In cities, theatres, gardens, parks, and courts:
At length I heard a ragged noise and mirth

   Of thieves and murderers: there I him espied,
   Who straight, *Your suit is granted,* said, and died.

PRAYER

Prayer, the Church's banquet, Angel's age,
   God's breath in man returning to his birth,
   The soul in paraphrase, heart in pilgrimage,
The Christian plummet sounding heaven and earth;

Engine against th' Almighty, sinner's tower,
   Reversed thunder, Christ-side-piercing spear,
   The six days' world-transposing in an hour,
A kind of tune, which all things hear and fear;

Softness, and peace, and joy, and love, and bliss,
   Exalted Manna, gladness of the best,
   Heaven in ordinary, men well drest,
The Milky Way, the bird of Paradise,

   Church-bells beyond the stars heard, the soul's blood,
   The land of spices, something understood.

LOVE (I)

Immortall Love, authour of this great frame,
    Sprung from that beautie which can never fade;
    How hath man parcel'd out thy glorious name,
And thrown it on that dust which thou hast made,
While mortall love doth all the title gain!
    Which siding with invention, they together
    Bear all the sway, possessing heart and brain,
(Thy workmanship) and give thee share in neither.
Wit fancies beautie, beautie raiseth wit:
    The world is theirs; they two play out the game,
    Thou standing by: and though thy glorious name
Wrought our deliverance from th' infernall pit,
    Who sings thy praise? onely a skarf or glove
    Doth warm our hands, and make them write of love.

THE SONNE

Let forrain nations of their language boast,
What fine varietie each tongue affords:
I like our language, as our men and coast:
Who cannot dress it well, want wit, not words.
How neatly doe we give one onely name
To parents issue and the sunnes bright starre!
A sonne is light and fruit; a fruitfull flame
Chasing the fathers dimnesse, carri'd farre
From the first man in th' East, to fresh and new
Western discov'ries of posteritie.
So in one word our Lords humilitie
We turn upon him in a sense most true:
    For what Christ once in humblenesse began,
    We him in glorie call, *The Sonne of Man.*

THE H. SCRIPTURES (I)

Oh Book! infinite sweetnesse! let my heart
   Suck ev'ry letter, and a hony gain,
   Precious for any grief in any part;
To cleare the breast, to mollifie all pain.
Thou art all health, health thriving till it make
   A full eternitie: thou art a masse
   Of strange delights, where we may wish & take.
Ladies, look here; this is the thankfull glasse,
That mends the lookers eyes: this is the well
   That washes what it shows. Who can indeare
   Thy praise too much? thou art heav'ns Lidger here,
Working against the states of death and hell.
   Thou art joyes handsell: heav'n lies flat in thee,
   Subject to ev'ry mounters bended knee.

THE H. SCRIPTURES (II)

Oh that I knew how all thy lights combine,
   And the configurations of their glorie!
   Seeing not onely how each verse doth shine,
But all the constellations of the storie.
This verse marks that, and both do make a motion
   Unto a third, that ten leaves off doth lie:
   Then as dispersed herbs do watch a potion,
These three make up some Christians destinie:
Such are thy secrets, which my life makes good,
   And comments on thee: for in ev'ry thing
   Thy words do finde me out, & parallels bring,
And in another make me understood.
   Starres are poore books, & oftentimes do misse:
   This book of starres lights to eternall blisse.

❖ JOHN MILTON ❖

O NIGHTINGALE!

O Nightingale! that on yon bloomy spray
    Warblest at eve, when all the woods are still,
    Thou with fresh hope the lover's heart dost fill,
    While the jolly hours lead on propitious May.
Thy liquid notes that close the eye of day,
    First heard before the shallow cuckoo's bill,
    Portend success in love. O, if Jove's will
    Have linked that amorous power to thy soft lay,
Now timely sing, ere the rude bird of hate
    Foretell my hopeless doom, in some grove nigh;
    As thou from year to year hast sung too late
For my relief, yet hadst no reason why.
    Whether the Muse or Love call thee his mate,
    Both them I serve, and of their train am I.

HOW SOON HATH TIME

How soon hath Time, the subtle thief of youth,
    Stoln on his wing my three and twentieth year!
    My hasting days fly on with full career,
    But my late spring no bud or blossom shew'th.
Perhaps my semblance might deceive the truth,
    That I to manhood am arrived so near,
    And inward ripeness doth much less appear,
    That some more timely-happy spirits endu'th.
Yet be it less or more, or soon or slow,
    It shall be still in strictest measure even
    To that same lot, however mean or high,
Toward which Time leads me, and the will of Heaven;
    All is, if I have grace to use it so,
    As ever in my great Taskmaster's eye.

TO MR. H. LAWES, ON HIS AIRS

Harry, whose tuneful and well-measured song
   First taught our English music how to span
   Words with just note and accent, not to scan
   With Midas' ears, committing short and long,
Thy worth and skill exempts thee from the throng,
   With praise enough for Envy to look wan;
   To after-age thou shalt be writ the man
   That with smooth air couldst humor best our tongue.
Thou honor'st Verse, and Verse must lend her wing
   To honor thee, the priest of Phœbus' choir,
   That tun'st their happiest lines in hymn or story.
Dante shall give Fame leave to set thee higher
   Than his Casella, whom he wooed to sing,
   Met in the milder shades of Purgatory.

ON THE DETRACTION WHICH FOLLOWED UPON
MY WRITING CERTAIN TREATISES

A book was writ of late called *Tetrachordon,*
And woven close, both matter, form and style;
The subject new, it walked the town a while,
Numbering good intellects: now seldom pored on.
Cries the stall-reader, "Bless us! what a word on
A title-page is this!"; and some in file
Stand spelling false, while one might walk to Mile-
End Green. Why is it harder, sirs, than *Gordon,*
Colkitto, or *Macdonnel,* or *Galasp*?
Those rugged names to our like mouths grow sleek,
That would have made Quintalian stare and gasp.
Thy age, like ours, O soul of Sir John Cheek,
Hated not learning worse than toad or asp,
When thou taught'st Cambridge and King Edward Greek.

ON THE NEW FORCERS OF CONSCIENCE UNDER
THE LONG PARLIAMENT

Because you have thrown off your prelate lord,
    And with stiff vows renounced his liturgy,
    To seize the widowed whore Plurality
    From them whose sin ye envied, not abhorred,
Dare ye for this adjure the civil sword
    To force our consciences that Christ set free,
    And ride us with a classic hierarchy
    Taught ye by mere A. S. and Rutherford?
Men whose life, learning, faith and pure intent
    Would have been held in high esteem with Paul
    Must now be named and printed heretics
By shallow Edwards and Scotch what d'ye call:
    But we do hope to find out all your tricks,
    Your plots and packings worse than those of Trent,
               That so the Parliament
May with their wholesome and preventive shears
Clip your phylacteries, though balk your ears,
               And succor our just fears
When they shall read this clearly in your charge
New *presbyter* is but old *priest* writ large.

TO THE LORD GENERAL CROMWELL

Cromwell, our chief of men, who through a cloud,
    Not of war only, but detractions rude,
    Guided by faith and matchless fortitude,
    To peace and truth thy glorious way hast ploughed,
And on the neck of crownèd Fortune proud
    Hast reared God's trophies, and His work pursued,
    While Darwen stream, with blood of Scots imbrued,
    And Dunbar field, resounds thy praises loud,
And Worcester's laureate wreath: yet much remains
    To conquer still; peace hath her victories
    No less renowned than war: new foes arise,
Threatening to bind our souls with secular chains.
    Help us to save free conscience from the paw
    Of hireling wolves, whose gospel is their maw.

ON THE LATE MASSACRE IN PIEDMONT

Avenge, O Lord, thy slaughtered saints, whose bones
   Lie scattered on the Alpine mountains cold,
   Even them who kept thy truth so pure of old
   When all our fathers worshiped stocks and stones,
Forget not: in thy book record their groans
   Who were thy sheep and in their ancient fold
   Slain by the bloody Piedmontese that rolled
   Mother with infant down the rocks. Their moans
The vales redoubled to the hills, and they
   To Heaven. Their martyred blood and ashes sow
   O'er all th' Italian fields where still doth sway
The triple tyrant: that from these may grow
   A hundredfold, who having learnt thy way
   Early may fly the Babylonian woe.

"When I consider how my light is spent"

When I consider how my light is spent
   Ere half my days, in this dark world and wide,
   And that one talent which is death to hide
   Lodged with me useless, though my soul more bent
To serve therewith my Maker, and present
   My true account, lest he returning chide;
   "Doth God exact day-labour, light denied?"
   I fondly ask; but Patience to prevent
That murmur, soon replies, "God doth not need
   Either man's work or his own gifts; who best
   Bear his mild yoke, they serve him best. His state
Is kingly. Thousands at his bidding speed
   And post o'er land and ocean without rest:
   They also serve who only stand and wait."

Methought I saw my late espousèd Saint
    Brought to me like Alcestis from the grave,
      Whom Jove's great son to her glad husband gave,
      Rescued from death by force, though pale and faint.
Mine, as whom washt from spot of child-bed taint
    Purification in the Old Law did save,
      And such, as yet once more I trust to have
      Full sight of her in Heaven without restraint,
Came vested all in white, pure as her mind.
    Her face was veiled; yet to my fancied sight
      Love, sweetness, goodness, in her person shined
So clear as in no face with more delight.
    But O, as to embrace me she inclined,
      I waked, she fled, and day brought back my night.

❖ CHARLES COTTON ❖

RESOLUTION IN FOUR SONNETS, OF A POETICAL QUESTION PUT TO ME BY A FRIEND, CONCERNING FOUR RURAL SISTERS

I

Alice is tall and upright as a pine,
White as blanched almonds, or the falling snow,
Sweet as are damask roses when they blow,
And doubtless fruitful as the swelling vine.

Ripe to be cut, and ready to be pressed,
Her full cheeked beauties very well appear,
And a year's fruit she loses every year,
Wanting a man t' improve her to the best.

Full fain she would be husbanded, and yet,
Alas! she cannot a fit laborer get
To cultivate her to her own content:

Fain would she be (God wot) about her task,
And yet (forsooth) she is too proud to ask,
And (which is worse) too modest to consent.

2

Marg'ret of humbler stature by the head
Is (as it oft falls out with yellow hair)
Than her fair sister, yet so much more fair,
As her pure white is better mixed with red.

This, hotter than the other ten to one,
Longs to be put unto her mother's trade,
And loud proclaims she lives too long a maid,
Wishing for one t' untie her virgin zone.

She finds virginity a kind of ware,
That's very very troublesome to bear,
And being gone, she thinks will ne'er be mist:

And yet withal, the girl has so much grace,
To call for help I know she wants the face,
Though asked, I know not how she would resist.

3

Mary is black, and taller than the last,
Yet equal in perfection and desire,
To the one's melting snow, and t' other's fire,
As with whose black their fairness is defaced.

She pants as much for love as th' other two,
But she so virtuous is, or else so wise,
That she will win or will not love a prize,
And upon but good terms will never do:

Therefore, who her will conquer ought to be
At least as full of love and wit as she,
Or he shall ne'er gain favor at her hands:

Nay, though he have a pretty store of brains,
Shall only have his labor for his pains,
Unless he offer more than she demands.

4

Martha is not so tall, nor yet so fair
As any of the other lovely three,
Her chiefest grace is poor simplicity,
Yet were the rest away, she were a star.

She's fair enough, only she wants the art
To set her beauties off as they can do,
And that's the cause she ne'er heard any woo,
Nor ever yet made conquest of a heart:

And yet her blood's as boiling as the best,
Which, pretty soul, does so disturb her rest,
And makes her languish so, she's fit to die.

Poor thing, I doubt she still must lie alone,
For being like to be attacked by none,
She's no more wit to ask than to deny.

❖ THOMAS GRAY ❖

ON THE DEATH OF MR. RICHARD WEST

In vain to me the smiling mornings shine,
And redd'ning Phoebus lifts his golden fire:
The birds in vain their amorous descant join;
Or cheerful fields resume their green attire:
These ears, alas! for other notes repine,
A different object do these eyes require.
My lonely anguish melts no heart but mine;
And in my breast the imperfect joys expire.
Yet morning smiles the busy race to cheer,
And new-born pleasure brings to happier men:
The fields to all their wonted tribute bear:
To warm their little loves the birds complain:
I fruitless mourn to him, that cannot hear,
And weep the more, because I weep in vain.

❖ THOMAS WARTON, THE YOUNGER ❖

TO THE RIVER LODON

Ah! what a weary race my feet have run
Since first I trod thy banks with alders crowned,
And thought my way was all through fairy ground,
Beneath thy azure sky and golden sun,
Where first my Muse to lisp her notes begun.
While pensive Memory traces back the round
Which fills the varied interval between,
Much pleasure, more of sorrow, marks the scene.
Sweet native stream, those skies and suns so pure
No more return to cheer my evening road,
Yet still one joy remains, that not obscure
Nor useless all my vacant days have flowed
From Youth's grey dawn to manhood's prime mature,
Nor with the Muse's laurel unbestowed.

❖ ANNA SEWARD ❖

TO MR. HENRY CARY, ON THE PUBLICATION OF HIS SONNETS

Prais'd be the Poet, who the Sonnet's claim,
    Severest of the orders that belong
    Distinct and separate to the Delphic song,
    Shall venerate, nor its appropriate name
Lawless assume. Peculiar is its frame,
    From him derived, who shunn'd the city throng,
    And warbled sweet thy rocks and streams among,
    Lonely Valclusa!—and that heir of fame,
Our greater MILTON, hath, by many a lay
    Form'd on that arduous model, fully shown
    That English verse may happily display
Those strict energic measures, which alone
    Deserve the name of Sonnet, and convey
    A grandeur, grace and spirit, all their own.

TO THE MOON

Queen of the silver bow!—by thy pale beam,
Alone and pensive, I delight to stray,
And watch thy shadow trembling in the stream,
Or mark the floating clouds that cross thy way.
And while I gaze, thy mild and placid light
Sheds a soft calm upon my troubled breast;
And oft I think—fair planet of the night—
That in thy orb, the wretched may have rest:
The sufferers of the earth perhaps may go,
Released by Death—to thy benignant sphere,
And the sad children of Despair and Woe
Forget, in thee, their cup of sorrow here.
Oh! that I soon may reach thy world serene,
Poor wearied pilgrim—in this toiling scene!

TO SLEEP

Come balmy Sleep! tired Nature's soft resort!
On these sad temples all thy poppies shed;
And bid gay dreams from Morpheus' airy court,
Float in light vision round my aching head!
Secure of all thy blessings, partial Power!
On his hard bed the peasant throws him down;
And the poor sea boy, in the rudest hour,
Enjoys thee more than he who wears a crown.
Clasped in her faithful shepherd's guardian arms,
Well may the village girl sweet slumbers prove,
And they, O gentle Sleep! still taste thy charms,
Who wake to labor, liberty and love.
But still thy opiate aid dost thou deny
To calm the anxious breast; to close the streaming eye.

Huge vapors brood above the clifted shore,
   Night on the ocean settles, dark and mute,
Save where is heard the repercussive roar
   Of drowsy billows, on the rugged foot
Of rocks remote; or still more distant tone
   Of seamen in the anchored bark that tell
The watch relieved; or one deep voice alone
   Singing the hour, and bidding "Strike the bell."
All is black shadow, but the lucid line
   Marked by the light surf on the level sand,
Or where afar the ship-lights faintly shine
   Like wandering fairy fires, that oft on land
Mislead the pilgrim—such the dubious ray
That wavering reason lends, in life's long darkling way.

❖ WILLIAM BLAKE ❖

TO THE EVENING STAR

Thou fair-hair'd angel of the evening,
Now, while the sun rests on the mountains, light
Thy bright torch of love; thy radiant crown
Put on, and smile upon our evening bed!
Smile on our loves; and, while thou drawest the
Blue curtains of the sky, scatter thy silver dew
On every flower that shuts its sweet eyes
In timely sleep. Let thy west wind sleep on
The lake; speak silence with thy glimmering eyes,
And wash the dusk with silver. Soon, full soon,
Dost thou withdraw; then the wolf rages wide,
And the lion glares thro' the dun forest:
The fleeces of our flocks are cover'd with
Thy sacred dew: protect them with thine influence.

❖ ROBERT BURNS ❖

A SONNET UPON SONNETS

Fourteen, a sonneteer thy praises sings;
What magic myst'ries in that number lie!
Your hen hath fourteen eggs beneath her wings
That fourteen chickens to the roost may fly.
Fourteen full pounds the jockey's stone must be;
His age fourteen—a horse's prime is past.
Fourteen long hours too oft the Bard must fast;
Fourteen bright bumpers—bliss he ne'er must see!
Before fourteen, a dozen yields the strife;
Before fourteen—e'en thirteen's strength is vain.
Fourteen good years—a woman gives us life;
Fourteen good men—we lose that life again.
What lucubrations can be more upon it?
Fourteen good measur'd verses make a sonnet.

❖ THOMAS RUSSELL ❖

TO THE SPIDER

Ingenious insect, but of ruthless mould,
   Whose savage craft, as Nature taught, designs
   A mazy web of death, the filmy lines,
   That form thy circling labyrinth, enfold
Each thoughtless fly, that wanders near thy hold,
   Sad victim of thy guile; nor aught avail
   His silken wings, nor coat of glossy mail,
   Nor varying hues of azure, jet, or gold:
Yet, though thus ill the fluttering captive fares,
   Whom heedless of the fraud thy toils trepan,
   Thy tyrant-fang, that slays the stranger, spares
The bloody brothers of thy cruel clan;
   While man against his fellows spreads his snares,
   Then most delighted, when his prey is man.

❖ ELIZABETH COBBOLD ❖

from *Sonnets of Laura*

I.   REPROACH

Ah! little cause has Petrarch to complain,
    Since thus he boasts his wound, thus vaunts the smart,
While Laura struggles to conceal the pain
    Derived from silence and a bursting heart:
For dear she holds the Poet and his lay:
    But this avowal meets no human ear,
Nor shall the conscious eye of tell-tale day
    Behold her shed the unavailing tear.
For this, with watchful and incessant care
    She tries each varied art, each strange disguise
While cold indifference marks her studied air,
    Smiles on her cheek, and lords it o'er her sighs.
The world shall sympathize with Petrarch's woe,
While night and silence only Laura's know.

❖ WILLIAM WORDSWORTH ❖

"Nuns fret not at their convent's narrow room"

Nuns fret not at their convent's narrow room;
And hermits are contented with their cells;
And students with their pensive citadels;
Maids at the wheel, the weaver at his loom,
Sit blithe and happy; bees that soar for bloom,
High as the highest Peak of Furness-fells,
Will murmur by the hour in foxglove bells:
In truth the prison, unto which we doom
Ourselves, no prison is: and hence for me,
In sundry moods, 'twas pastime to be bound
Within the Sonnet's scanty plot of ground;
Pleased if some Souls (for such there needs must be)
Who have felt the weight of too much liberty,
Should find brief solace there, as I have found.

Earth has not anything to show more fair:
Dull would he be of soul who could pass by
A sight so touching in its majesty:
This City now doth, like a garment, wear
The beauty of the morning; silent, bare,
Ships, towers, domes, theatres, and temples lie
Open unto the fields, and to the sky;
All bright and glittering in the smokeless air.
Never did sun more beautifully steep
In his first splendour, valley, rock, or hill;
Ne'er saw I, never felt, a calm so deep!
The river glideth at his own sweet will:
Dear God! the very houses seem asleep;
And all that mighty heart is lying still!

"The world is too much with us; late and soon"

The world is too much with us; late and soon,
Getting and spending, we lay waste our powers:
Little we see in Nature that is ours;
We have given our hearts away, a sordid boon!
This sea that bares her bosom to the moon;
The winds that will be howling at all hours
And are up-gathered now like sleeping flowers;
For this, for every thing, we are out of tune;
It moves us not—Great God! I'd rather be
A Pagan suckled in a creed outworn;
So might I, standing on this pleasant lea,
Have glimpses that would make me less forlorn;
Have sight of Proteus coming from the sea;
Or hear old Triton blow his wreathed horn.

"It is a beauteous evening, calm and free"

It is a beauteous evening, calm and free;
The holy time is quiet as a nun
Breathless with adoration; the broad sun
Is sinking down in its tranquillity;
The gentleness of heaven is on the Sea:
Listen! the mighty Being is awake,
And doth with his eternal motion make
A sound like thunder—everlastingly.
Dear Child! dear Girl! that walkest with me here,
If thou appear'st untouched by solemn thought,
Thy nature is not therefore less divine:
Thou liest in Abraham's bosom all the year;
And worshipp'st at the Temple's inner shrine,
God being with thee when we know it not.

from *Sonnets Dedicated to Liberty*

TO TOUSSAINT L'OUVERTURE

Toussaint, the most unhappy Man of Men!
Whether the rural milk-maid by her cow
Sing in thy hearing, or thou liest now
Alone in some deep dungeon's earless den,
O miserable chieftain! where and when
Wilt thou find patience? Yet die not; do thou
Wear rather in thy bonds a cheerful brow:
Though fallen thyself, never to rise again,
Live, and take comfort. Thou hast left behind
Powers that will work for thee; air, earth, and skies;
There's not a breathing of the common wind
That will forget thee; thou has great allies;
Thy friends are exultations, agonies,
And love, and Man's unconquerable mind.

Milton! thou should'st be living at this hour:
England hath need of thee: she is a fen
Of stagnant waters: altar, sword and pen,
Fireside, the heroic wealth of hall and bower,
Have forfeited their ancient English dower
Of inward happiness. We are selfish men;
Oh! raise us up, return to us again;
And give us manners, virtue, freedom, power.
Thy soul was like a star and dwelt apart:
Thou hadst a voice whose sound was like the sea:
Pure as the naked heavens, majestic, free,
So didst thou travel on life's common way,
In cheerful godliness; and yet thy heart
The lowliest duties on itself did lay.

❖   ❖   ❖

"It is no Spirit who from heaven hath flown"

It is no Spirit who from heaven hath flown,
And is descending on his embassy;
Nor Traveller gone from earth the heavens to espy!
'Tis Hesperus—there he stands with glittering crown,
First admonition that the sun is down!
For yet it is broad day-light: clouds pass by;
A few are near him still—and now the sky,
He hath it to himself—'tis all his own.
O most ambitious Star! an inquest wrought
Within me when I recognized thy light;
A moment I was startled at the sight:
And, while I gazed, there came to me a thought
That I might step beyond my natural race
As thou seem'st now to do; might one day trace
Some ground not mine; and, strong her strength above,
My Soul, an Apparition in the place,
Tread there with steps that no one shall reprove!

Surprised by joy—impatient as the wind
I turned to share the transport—Oh! with whom
But thee, long buried in the silent tomb,
That spot which no vicissitude can find?
Love, faithful love, recalled thee to my mind—
But how could I forget thee?—Through what power,
Even for the least division of an hour,
Have I been so beguiled as to be blind
To my most grievous loss?—That thought's return
Was the worst pang that sorrow ever bore,
Save one, one only, when I stood forlorn,
Knowing my heart's best treasure was no more;
That neither present time, nor years unborn
Could to my sight that heavenly face restore.

from *The River Duddon, A Series of Sonnets*

III

How shall I paint thee?—Be this naked stone
My seat while I give way to such intent;
Pleased could my verse, a speaking monument,
Make to the eyes of men thy features known.
But as of all those tripping lambs not one
Outruns his fellows, so hath nature lent
To thy beginning nought that doth present
Peculiar grounds for hope to build upon.
To dignify the spot that gives thee birth,
No sign of hoar Antiquity's esteem
Appears, and none of modern fortune's care;
Yet thou thyself hast round thee shed a gleam
Of brilliant moss, instinct with freshness rare;
Prompt offering to thy foster-mother, Earth!

47

Why sleeps the future, as a snake enrolled,
Coil within coil, at noon-tide? For the WORD
Yields, if with unpresumptuous faith explored,
Power at whose touch the sluggard shall unfold
His drowsy rings. Look forth!—that Stream behold,
THAT STREAM upon whose bosom we have passed
Floating at ease while nations have effaced
Nations, and Death has gathered to his fold
Long lines of mighty Kings—look forth, my Soul!
(Nor in this vision be thou slow to trust)
The living Waters, less and less by guilt
Stained and polluted, brighten as they roll,
Till they have reached the eternal City—built
For the perfected Spirits of the just!

❖ ❖ ❖

"Scorn not the Sonnet; critic, you have frowned"

Scorn not the Sonnet; critic, you have frowned,
Mindless of its just honors;—with this key
Shakespeare unlocked his heart; the melody
Of this small lute gave ease to Petrarch's wound;
A thousand times this pipe did Tasso sound;
Camöens soothed with it an exile's grief;
The Sonnet glittered a gay myrtle leaf
Amid the cypress with which Dante crowned
His visionary brow: a glow-worm lamp,
It cheered mild Spenser, called from Faery-land
To struggle through dark ways; and when a damp
Fell round the path of Milton, in his hand
The thing became a trumpet, whence he blew
Soul-animating strains—alas, too few!

TO THE RIVER OTTER

Dear native brook! wild streamlet of the West!
How many various-fated years have passed,
What happy, and what mournful hours, since last
I skimmed the smooth thin stone along thy breast,
Numbering its light leaps! Yet so deep imprest
Sink the sweet scenes of childhood, that mine eyes
I never shut amid the sunny ray,
But straight with all their tints thy waters rise,
Thy crossing plank, thy marge with willows gray,
And bedded sand that, veined with various dyes,
Gleamed through thy bright transparence. On my way,
Visions of childhood! oft have ye beguiled
Lone manhood's cares, yet waking fondest sighs:
Ah! that once more I were a careless child.

TO NATURE

It may indeed be phantasy when I
Essay to draw from all created things
Deep, heartfelt, inward joy that closely clings;
And trace in leaves and flowers that round me lie
Lessons of love and earnest piety.
So let it be; and if the wide world rings
In mock of this belief, to me it brings
Nor fear, nor grief, nor vain perplexity.
So will I build my altar in the fields,
And the blue sky my fretted dome shall be,
And the sweet fragrance that the wild flower yields
Shall be the incense I will yield to Thee,
Thee only God! and Thou shalt not despise
Even me, the priest of this poor sacrifice.

TO A FRIEND, WHO ASKED HOW I FELT, WHEN THE
NURSE FIRST PRESENTED MY INFANT TO ME

Charles! my slow heart was only sad, when first
I scanned that face of feeble infancy:
For dimly on my thoughtful spirit burst
All I had been, and all my babe might be!
But when I saw it on its mother's arm,
And hanging at her bosom (she the while
Bent o'er its features with a tearful smile)
Then I was thrilled and melted, and most warm
Impressed a father's kiss: and all beguiled
Of dark remembrance, and presageful fear,
I seemed to see an angel's form appear.—
'Twas even thine, beloved woman mild!
So for the mother's sake the child was dear,
And dearer was the mother for the child.

WORK WITHOUT HOPE

All Nature seems at work. Slugs leave their lair—
The bees are stirring—birds are on the wing—
And Winter, slumbering in the open air,
Wears on his smiling face a dream of Spring!
And I, the while, the sole unbusy thing,
Nor honey make, nor pair, nor build, nor sing.

Yet well I ken the banks where amaranths blow,
Have traced the fount where streams of nectar flow.
Bloom, O ye amaranths! bloom for whom ye may,
For me ye bloom not! Glide, rich streams, away!
With lips unbrighten'd, wreathless brow, I stroll:
And would you learn the spells that drowse my soul?
Work without Hope draws nectar in a sieve,
And Hope without an object cannot live.

from *Poems on the Slave Trade*

VI

High in the air exposed the slave is hung
   To all the birds of Heaven, their living food!
He groans not, though awaked by that fierce sun
   New torturers live to drink their parent blood!
He groans not, though the gorging vulture tear
   The quivering fiber! Hither gaze O ye
   Who tore this man from peace and liberty!
Gaze hither ye who weigh with scrupulous care
The right and prudent; for beyond the grave
   There is another world! and call to mind,
   Ere your decrees proclaim to all mankind
Murder is legalized, that there the slave
Before the Eternal, "thunder-tongued shall plead
Against the deep damnation of your deed."

❖ ❖ ❖

TO A GOOSE

If thou didst feed on western plains of yore;
Or waddle wide with flat and flabby feet
Over some Cambrian mountain's plashy moor;
Or find in farmer's yard a safe retreat
From gypsy thieves, and foxes sly and fleet;
If thy gray quills, by lawyer guided, trace
Deeds big with ruin to some wretched race,
Or love-sick poet's sonnet, sad and sweet,
Wailing the rigor of his lady fair;
Or if, the drudge of housemaid's daily toil,
Cobwebs and dust thy pinions white besoil,
Departed Goose! I neither know nor care.
But this I know, that we pronounced thee fine,
Seasoned with sage and onions, and port wine.

❖ CHARLES LAMB ❖

THE FAMILY NAME

What reason first imposed thee, gentle name,
Name that my father bore, and his sire's sire,
Without reproach? we trace our stream no higher;
And I, a childless man, may end the same.
Perchance some shepherd on Lincolnian plains,
In manners guileless as his own sweet flocks,
Received thee first amid the merry mocks
And arch allusions of his fellow swains.
Perchance from Salem's holier fields returned,
With glory gotten on the heads abhorred
Of faithless Saracens, some martial lord
Took His meek title, in whose zeal he burned.
Whate'er the fount whence thy beginnings came,
No deed of mine shall shame thee, gentle name.

❖ JOSEPH BLANCO WHITE ❖

TO NIGHT

Mysterious Night! when our first parent knew
    Thee from report divine, and heard thy name,
    Did he not tremble for this lovely frame,
This glorious canopy of light and blue.
Yet 'neath a curtain of translucent dew,
    Bathed in the rays of the great setting flame,
    Hesperus with the host of heaven came,
And lo! creation widened in man's view.
Who could have thought such darkness lay concealed
    Within thy beams, O Sun! or who could find,
Whilst fly and leaf and insect stood revealed,
    That to such countless orbs thou mad'st us blind!
        Why do we then shun Death with anxious strife?
        If Light can thus deceive, wherefore not Life?

❖ HORACE SMITH ❖

OZYMANDIAS

In Egypt's sandy silence, all alone,
   Stands a gigantic leg, which far off throws
   The only shadow that the desert knows:—
"I am great Ozymandias," saith the stone,
   "The King of Kings; this mighty City shows
The wonders of my hand."—The city's gone,—
   Nought but the leg remaining to disclose
The site of this forgotten Babylon.

We wonder,—and some hunter may express
Wonder like ours, when through the wilderness
   Where London stood, holding the wolf in chase,
He meets some fragment huge, and stops to guess
   What powerful but unrecorded race
   Once dwelt in that annihilated place.

❖ EBENEZER ELLIOTT ❖

"In these days, every mother's son or daughter"

In these days, every mother's son or daughter
Writes verse, which no one reads except the writer,
Although, uninked, the paper would be whiter,
And worth, per ream, a hare, when you have caught her.
Hundreds of unstaunched Shelleys daily water
Unanswering dust; a thousand Wordsworths scribble;
And twice a thousand Corn Law Rhymers dribble
Rhymed prose, unread. Hymners of fraud and slaughter,
By cant called other names, alone find buyers—
Who buy, but read not. "What a loss in paper,"
Groans each immortal of the host of sighers!
"What profanation of the midnight taper
In expirations vile! But I write well,
And wisely print. Why don't my poems sell?"

❖ MARTHA HANSON ❖

"How proudly Man usurps the power to reign"

How proudly Man usurps the power to reign,
   In every climate of the world is known,
   From the cold regions of the Northern Zone,
To where the South extends his boundless main.
Yet in this wide expanse, no realm we find,
   To boast a Woman, who the yoke disdained;
   And with intrepid soul, that freedom claimed,
Which Heaven impartial, gave all human kind.
With soul too proud, to bear the servile chain,
   Or to usurping Man, submissive bow,
   Though poorest of the names, record can show,
Ages unborn, with wonder, shall proclaim
The pride of one unyielding Female thine,
Dear native England! and the name be mine.

❖ MARY F. JOHNSON ❖

THE IDIOT GIRL

Start not at her, who, in fantastic guise,
   Comes wildly chanting in a dirge-like tone,
With big tears trembling in her vacant eyes,
   And uncoifed tresses by the breezes blown.
Recoil not from the harmless idiot maid,
   Who often from a rugged beldame creeps
To yon deserted cottage in the shade,
   And its fallen stones, to guard the entrance, heaps.
There was the home where passed her early years
   With parents now withdrawn to final rest,
Who proved how infant helplessness endears;
   And of a numerous offspring loved her best.
Now wails she, as she rudely blocks the door,
"They both are in, and will come out no more."

❖ LEIGH HUNT ❖

TO THE GRASSHOPPER AND THE CRICKET

Green little vaulter in the sunny grass,
    Catching your heart up at the feel of June,
    Sole voice that's heard amidst the lazy noon,
When even the bees lag at the summoning brass;
And you, warm little housekeeper, who class
    With those who think the candles come too soon,
    Loving the fire, and with your tricksome tune
Nick the glad silent moments as they pass;
O, sweet and tiny cousin! that belong,
    One to the fields, the other to the hearth,
Both have your sunshine; both though small are strong
    At your clear hearts; and both were sent on earth
To sing in thoughtful ears this natural song:
    In doors and out, summer and winter, Mirth.

❖ GEORGE GORDON, LORD BYRON ❖

ON CHILLON

Eternal spirit of the chainless mind!
    Brightest in dungeons, Liberty! thou art,
    For there thy habitation is the heart—
The heart which love of thee alone can bind;
And when thy sons to fetters are consigned—
    To fetters, and the damp vault's dayless gloom,
    Their country conquers with their martyrdom,
And Freedom's fame finds wings on every wind.
Chillon! thy prison is a holy place,
    And thy sad floor an altar—for 'twas trod,
Until his very steps have left a trace
    Worn, as if thy cold pavement were a sod,
By Bonnivard!—May none those marks efface!
    For they appeal from tyranny to God.

Rousseau—Voltaire—our Gibbon—and de Staël—
   Leman! these names are worthy of thy shore,
   Thy shore of names like these! wert thou no more,
Their memory thy remembrance would recall:
To them thy banks were lovely as to all,
   But they have made them lovelier, for the lore
   Of mighty minds doth hallow in the core
Of human hearts the ruin of a wall
   Where dwelt the wise and wondrous; but by *thee*
How much more, Lake of Beauty! do we feel,
   In sweetly gliding o'er thy crystal sea,
The wild glow of that not ungentle zeal,
   Which of the heirs of immortality
Is proud, and makes the breath of glory real!

❖ PERCY BYSSHE SHELLEY ❖

TO WORDSWORTH

Poet of Nature, thou hast wept to know
That things depart which never may return:
Childhood and youth, friendship and love's first glow,
Have fled like sweet dreams, leaving thee to mourn.
These common woes I feel. One loss is mine
Which thou too feel'st, yet I alone deplore.
Thou wert as a lone star, whose light did shine
On some frail bark in winter's midnight roar:
Thou hast like to a rock-built refuge stood
Above the blind and battling multitude:
In honored poverty thy voice did weave
Songs consecrate to truth and liberty,—
Deserting these, thou leavest me to grieve,
Thus having been, that thou shouldst cease to be.

I hated thee, fallen tyrant! I did groan
To think that a most unambitious slave,
Like thou, shouldst dance and revel on the grave
Of Liberty. Thou mightst have built thy throne
Where it had stood even now: thou didst prefer
A frail and bloody pomp which Time has swept
In fragments towards Oblivion. Massacre,
For this I prayed, would on thy sleep have crept,
Treason and Slavery, Rapine, Fear, and Lust,
And stifled thee, their minister. I know
Too late, since thou and France are in the dust,
That Virtue owns a more eternal foe
Than Force or Fraud: old Custom, legal Crime,
And bloody Faith the foulest birth of Time.

OZYMANDIAS

I met a traveller from an antique land
Who said: Two vast and trunkless legs of stone
Stand in the desert. Near them, on the sand,
Half sunk, a shattered visage lies, whose frown,
And wrinkled lip, and sneer of cold command,
Tell that its sculptor well those passions read
Which yet survive, stamped on these lifeless things,
The hand that mocked them and the heart that fed;
And on the pedestal these words appear:
"My name is Ozymandias, king of kings:
Look on my works, ye Mighty, and despair!"
Nothing beside remains. Round the decay
Of that colossal wreck, boundless and bare
The lone and level sands stretch far away.

ENGLAND IN 1819

An old, mad, blind, despised, and dying king,—
Princes, the dregs of their dull race, who flow
Through public scorn,—mud from a muddy spring,—
Rulers who neither see, nor feel, nor know,
But leech-like to their fainting country cling,
Till they drop, blind in blood, without a blow,—
A people starved and stabbed in the untilled field,—
An army, which liberticide and prey
Makes as a two-edged sword to all who wield,—
Golden and sanguine laws which tempt and slay;
Religion Christless, Godless—a book sealed;
A Senate,—Time's worst statute unrepealed,—
Are graves, from which a glorious Phantom may
Burst, to illumine our tempestuous day.

ODE TO THE WEST WIND

I

O wild West Wind, thou breath of Autumn's being,
Thou, from whose unseen presence the leaves dead
Are driven, like ghosts from an enchanter fleeing,

Yellow, and black, and pale, and hectic red,
Pestilence-stricken multitudes: O, thou,
Who chariotest to their dark wintry bed

The winged seeds, where they lie cold and low,
Each like a corpse within its grave, until
Thine azure sister of the spring shall blow

Her clarion o'er the dreaming earth, and fill
(Driving sweet buds like flocks to feed in air)
With living hues and odors plain and hill:

Wild Spirit, which art moving everywhere;
Destroyer and preserver; hear, O hear!

II

Thou on whose stream, 'mid the steep sky's commotion,
Loose clouds like earth's decaying leaves are shed,
Shook from the tangled boughs of Heaven and Ocean,

Angels of rain and lightning: there are spread
One the blue surface of thine aery surge,
Like the bright hair uplifted from the head

Of some fierce Mænad, even from the dim verge
Of the horizon to the zenith's height
The locks of the approaching storm. Thou Dirge

Of the dying year, to which this closing night
Will be the dome of a vast sepulchre,
Vaulted with all thy congregated might

Of vapours, from whose solid atmosphere
Black rain and fire and hail will burst: O, hear!

III

Thou who didst waken from his summer dreams
The blue Mediterranean, where he lay,
Lulled by the coil of his crystalline streams,

Beside a pumice isle in Baiæ's bay,
And saw in sleep old palaces and towers
Quivering within the wave's intenser day,

All overgrown with azure moss and flowers
So sweet, the sense faints picturing them! Thou
For whose path the Atlantic's level powers

Cleave themselves into chasms, while far below
The sea-blooms and the oozy woods which wear
The sapless foliage of the ocean, know

Thy voice, and suddenly grow grey with fear,
And tremble and despoil themselves: O, hear!

IV

If I were a dead leaf thou mightest bear;
If I were a swift cloud to fly with thee;
A wave to pant beneath thy power, and share

The impulse of thy strength, only less free
Than thou, O Uncontrollable! If even
I were as in my boyhood, and could be

The comrade of thy wanderings over Heaven,
As then, when to outstrip thy skiey speed
Scarce seemed a vision; I would ne'er have striven

As thus with thee in prayer in my sore need.
Oh! lift me as wave, a leaf, a cloud!
I fall upon the thorns of life! I bleed!

A heavy weight of hours has chained and bowed
One too like thee: tameless, and swift, and proud.

V

Make me thy lyre, even as the forest is:
What if my leaves are falling like its own!
The tumult of thy mighty harmonies

Will take from both a deep, autumnal tone,
Sweet though in sadness. Be thou, Spirit fierce,
My spirit! Be thou me, impetuous one!

Drive my dead thoughts over the universe
Like withered leaves to quicken a new birth!
And, by the incantation of this verse,

Scatter, as from an unextinguished hearth
Ashes and sparks, my words among mankind!
Be through my lips to unawakened Earth

The trumpet of a prophecy! O Wind,
If Winter comes, can Spring be far behind?

❖ JOHN CLARE ❖

TO WORDSWORTH

Wordsworth I love, his books are like the fields,
   Not filled with flowers, but works of human kind;
The pleasant weed a fragrant pleasure yields,
   The briar and broomwood shaken by the wind,
The thorn and bramble o'er the water shoot
   A finer flower than gardens e'er gave birth,
The aged huntsman grubbing up the root—
   I love them all as tenants of the earth:
Where genius is, there often die the seeds;
   What critics throw away I love the more;
I love to stoop and look among the weeds,
   To find a flower I never knew before;
Wordsworth, go on—a greater poet be;
Merit will live, though parties disagree!

HEN'S NEST

Among the orchard weeds, from every search,
Snugly and sure, the old hen's nest is made,
Who cackles every morning from her perch
To tell the servant girl new eggs are laid;
Who lays her washing by; and far and near
Goes seeking all about from day to day,
And stung with nettles tramples everywhere;
But still the cackling pullet lays away.
The boy on Sundays goes the stack to pull
In hopes to find her there, but naught is seen,
And takes his hat and thinks to find it full,
She's laid so long so many might have been.
But naught is found and all is given o'er
Till the young brood come chirping to the door.

TO JOHN CLARE

Well, honest John, how fare you now at home?
The spring is come, and birds are building nests;
The old cock-robin to the sty is come,
With olive feathers and its ruddy breast;
And the old cock, with wattles and red comb,
Struts with the hens, and seems to like some best,
Then crows, and looks about for little crumbs,
Swept out by little folks an hour ago;
The pigs sleep in the sty; the bookman comes—
The little boy lets home-close nesting go,
And pockets tops and taws, where daisies blow,
To look at the new number just laid down,
With lots of pictures, and good stories too,
And Jack the Giant Killer's high renown.

THE HAPPY BIRD

The happy white-throat on the swaying bough,
Rocked by the impulse of the gadding wind
That ushers in the showers of April, now
Carols right joyously; and now reclined,
Crouching, she clings close to her moving seat,
To keep her hold;—and till the wind for rest
Pauses, she mutters inward melodies,
That seem her heart's rich thinkings to repeat.
But when the branch is still, her little breast
Swells out in rapture's gushing symphonies;
And then, against her brown wing softly prest,
The wind comes playing, an enraptured guest;
This way and that she swings—till gusts arise
More boisterous in their play, then off she flies.

THE THRUSH'S NEST

Within a thick and spreading hawthorn bush,
That overhung a molehill large and round,
I heard from morn to morn a merry thrush
Sing hymns to sunrise, and I drank the sound
With joy, and, often an intruding guest,
I watched her secret toils from day to day—
How true she warped the moss, to form a nest,
And modelled it within with wood and clay;
And by and by, like heath-bells gilt with dew,
There lay her shining eggs, as bright as flowers,
Ink-spotted-over shells of greeny blue:
And there I witnessed in the sunny hours
A brood of nature's minstrels chirp and fly,
Glad as that sunshine and the laughing sky.

❖ JOHN KEATS ❖

ON FIRST LOOKING INTO CHAPMAN'S HOMER

Much have I travell'd in the realms of gold,
    And many goodly states and kingdoms seen;
    Round many western islands have I been
Which bards in fealty to Apollo hold.
Oft of one wide expanse had I been told
    That deep-brow'd Homer ruled as his demesne;
    Yet did I never breathe its pure serene
Till I heard Chapman speak out loud and bold:
Then felt I like some watcher of the skies
    When a new planet swims into his ken;
Or like stout Cortez when with eagle eyes
    He star'd at the Pacific—and all his men
Look'd at each other with a wild surmise—
    Silent, upon a peak in Darien.

Small, busy flames play through the fresh laid coals,
   And their faint cracklings o'er our silence creep
   Like whispers of the household gods that keep
A gentle empire o'er fraternal souls.
And while, for rhymes, I search around the poles,
   Your eyes are fixed, as in poetic sleep,
   Upon the lore so voluble and deep,
That aye at fall of night our care condoles.
This is your birthday, Tom, and I rejoice
   That thus it passes smoothly, quietly.
Many such eves of gently whisp'ring noise
   May we together pass, and calmly try
What are this world's true joys,—ere the great voice
   From its fair face, shall bid our spirits fly.

"Great spirits now on earth are sojourning"

Great spirits now on earth are sojourning;
   He of the cloud, the cataract, the lake,
   Who on Helvellyn's summit, wide awake,
Catches his freshness from archangel's wing:
He of the rose, the violet, the spring,
   The social smile, the chain for freedom's sake:
   And lo!—whose stedfastness would never take
A meaner sound than Raphael's whispering.
And other spirits there are standing apart
   Upon the forehead of the age to come;
These, these will give the world another heart,
   And other pulses. Hear ye not the hum
Of mighty workings?—
   Listen awhile ye nations, and be dumb.

The poetry of earth is never dead:
   When all the birds are faint with the hot sun,
   And hide in cooling trees, a voice will run
From hedge to hedge about the new-mown mead;
That is the Grasshopper's—he takes the lead
   In summer luxury,—he has never done
   With his delights; for when tired out with fun
He rests at ease beneath some pleasant weed.
The poetry of earth is ceasing never:
   On a lone winter evening, when the frost
     Has wrought a silence, from the stove there shrills
The Cricket's song, in warmth increasing ever,
   And seems to one in drowsiness half lost,
     The Grasshopper's among some grassy hills.

"When I have fears that I may cease to be"

When I have fears that I may cease to be
   Before my pen has glean'd my teeming brain,
Before high piled books, in charactry,
   Hold like rich garners the full ripen'd grain;
When I behold, upon the night's starr'd face,
   Huge cloudy symbols of a high romance,
And think that I may never live to trace
   Their shadows, with the magic hand of chance;
And when I feel, fair creature of an hour,
   That I shall never look upon thee more,
Never have relish in the fairy power
   Of unreflecting love;—then on the shore
Of the wide world I stand alone, and think
Till love and fame to nothingness do sink.

Standing aloof in giant ignorance,
 Of thee I hear and of the Cyclades,
As one who sits ashore and longs perchance
 To visit dolphin-coral in deep seas.
So wast thou blind,—but then the veil was rent,
 For Jove uncurtain'd heaven to let thee live,
And Neptune made for thee a spumy tent,
 And Pan made sing for thee his forest-hive,
Aye on the shores of darkness there is light,
 And precipices show untrodden green,
There is a budding morrow in midnight,
 There is a triple sight in blindness keen;
Such seeing hadst thou, as it once befel
To Dian, Queen of Earth, and Heaven, and Hell.

"Bright star, would I were stedfast as thou art"

Bright star, would I were stedfast as thou art—
 Not in lone splendor hung aloft the night,
And watching, with eternal lids apart,
 Like nature's patient, sleepless eremite,
The moving waters at their priestlike task
 Of pure ablution round earth's human shores,
Or gazing on the new soft-fallen mask
 Of snow upon the mountains and the moors;
No—yet still stedfast, still unchangeable,
 Pillow'd upon my fair love's ripening breast,
To feel for ever its soft swell and fall,
 Awake for ever in a sweet unrest,
Still, still to hear her tender-taken breath,
And so live ever—or else swoon to death.

O soft embalmer of the still midnight,
  Shutting with careful fingers and benign
Our gloom-pleas'd eyes, embower'd from the light,
  Enshaded in forgetfulness divine:
O soothest Sleep! if so it please thee, close,
  In midst of this thine hymn, my willing eyes,
Or wait the Amen ere thy poppy throws
  Around my bed its lulling charities.
Then save me or the passed day will shine
  Upon my pillow, breeding many woes:
Save me from curious conscience, that still hoards
  Its strength for darkness, burrowing like the mole;
Turn the key deftly in the oiled wards,
  And seal the hushed casket of my soul.

"If by dull rhymes our English must be chain'd"

If by dull rhymes our English must be chain'd,
  And, like Andromeda, the sonnet sweet
Fetter'd, in spite of pained loveliness;
Let us find out, if we must be constrain'd,
  Sandals more interwoven and complete
To fit the naked foot of Poesy;
Let us inspect the lyre, and weigh the stress
Of every chord, and see what may be gain'd
  By ear industrious, and attention meet;
Misers of sound and syllable, no less
Than Midas of his coinage, let us be
  Jealous of dead leaves in the bay wreath crown;
So, if we may not let the muse be free,
  She will be bound with garlands of her own.

I cry your mercy—pity—love!—aye, love,
    Merciful love that tantalises not,
One-thoughted, never wand'ring, guileless love,
    Unmask'd, and being seen—without a blot!
O, let me have thee whole,—all,—all—be mine!
    That shape, that fairness, that sweet minor zest
Of love, your kiss, those hands, those eyes divine,
    That warm, white, lucent, million-pleasured breast,—
Yourself—your soul—in pity give me all,
    Withhold no atom's atom or I die,
Or living on perhaps, your wretched thrall,
    Forget, in the mist of idle misery,
Life's purposes,—the palate of my mind
Losing its gust, and my ambition blind.

❖ HARTLEY COLERIDGE ❖

TO A FRIEND

When we were idlers with the loitering rills,
The need of human love we little noted:
Our love was nature; and the peace that floated
On the white mist, and dwelt upon the hills,
To sweet accord subdued our wayward wills:
One soul was ours, one mind, one heart devoted,
That, wisely doating, asked not why it doated,
And ours the unknown joy, which knowing kills.
But now I find how dear thou wert to me;
That man is more than half of nature's treasure,
Of that fair beauty which no eye can see,
Of that sweet music which no ear can measure;
And now the streams may sing for others' pleasure,
The hills sleep on in their eternity.

"Let me not deem that I was made in vain"

Let me not deem that I was made in vain,
Or that my being was an accident
Which Fate, in working its sublime intent,
Not wished to be, to hinder would not deign.
Each drop uncounted in a storm of rain
Hath its own mission, and is duly sent
To its own leaf or blade, not idly spent
'Mid myriad dimples on the shipless main.
The very shadow of an insect's wing,
For which the violet cared not while it stayed,
Yet felt the lighter for its vanishing,
Proved that the sun was shining by its shade.
Then can a drop of the eternal spring,
Shadow of living lights, in vain be made?

"Think upon Death, 'tis good to think of Death"

Think upon Death, 'tis good to think of Death,
But better far to think upon the Dead.
Death is a spectre with a bony head,
Or the mere mortal body without breath,
The state foredoomed of every son of Seth,
Decomposition—dust, or dreamless sleep.
But the dear Dead are they for whom we weep,
For whom I credit all the Bible saith.
Dead is my father, dead is my good mother,
And what on earth have I to do but die?
But if by grace I reach the blessed sky,
I fain would see the same, and not another;
The very father that I used to see,
The mother that has nursed me on her knee.

TO NIGHT

So thou art come again, old black-winged night,
　　Like a huge bird, between us and the sun,
Hiding, with out-stretched form, the genial light;
　　And still, beneath thine icy bosom's dun
And cloudy plumage, hatching fog-breathed blight,
　　And embryo storms, and crabbed frosts, that shun
Day's warm caress. The owls from ivied loop
　　Are shrieking homage, as thou cowerest high,
Like sable crow pausing in eager stoop
　　On the dim world thou gluttest thy clouded eye,
Silently waiting latest time's fell whoop,
　　When thou shalt quit thine eyrie in the sky,
To pounce upon the world with eager claw,
And tomb time, death, and substance in thy maw.

A CROCODILE

Hard by the lilied Nile I saw
A duskish river-dragon stretched along,
The brown habergeon of his limbs enamelled
With sanguine almandines and rainy pearl:
And on his back there lay a young one sleeping,
No bigger than a mouse; with eyes like beads,
And a small fragment of its speckled egg
Remaining on its harmless, pulpy snout;
A thing to laugh at, as it gaped to catch
The baulking merry flies. In the iron jaws
Of the great devil-beast, like a pale soul
Fluttering in rocky hell, lightsomely flew
A snowy trochilus, with roseate beak
Tearing the hairy leeches from his throat.

FINITE AND INFINITE

The wind sounds only in opposing straits,
The sea, beside the shore; man's spirit rends
Its quiet only up against the ends
Of wants and oppositions, loves and hates,
Where, worked and worn by passionate debates,
And losing by the loss it apprehends,
The flesh rocks round, and every breath it sends
Is ravelled to a sigh. All tortured states
Suppose a straitened place. Jehovah Lord,
Make room for rest, around me! out of sight
Now float me, of the vexing land abhorred,
Till in deep calms of space my soul may right
Her nature,—shoot large sail on lengthening cord,
And rush exultant on the Infinite.

from *Sonnets from the Portuguese*

I

I thought once how Theocritus had sung
Of the sweet years, the dear and wished-for years,
Who each one in a gracious hand appears
To bear a gift for mortals, old or young:
And, as I mused it in his antique tongue,
I saw, in gradual vision through my tears,
The sweet, sad years, the melancholy years,
Those of my own life, who by turns had flung
A shadow across me. Straightway I was 'ware,
So weeping, how a mystic Shape did move
Behind me, and drew me backward by the hair;
And a voice said in mastery, while I strove,—
"Guess now who holds thee?"—"Death!" I said. But, there,
The silver answer rang—"Not Death, but Love."

VII

The face of all the world is changed, I think,
Since first I heard the footsteps of thy soul
Move still, oh, still, beside me; as they stole
Betwixt me and the dreadful outer brink
Of obvious death, where I who thought to sink
Was caught up into love, and taught the whole
Of life in a new rhythm. The cup of dole
God gave for baptism, I am fain to drink,
And praise its sweetness, sweet, with thee anear.
The names of country, heaven, are changed away
For where thou art or shalt be, there or here;
And this—this lute and song—loved yesterday,
(The singing angels know) are only dear,
Because thy name moves right in what they say.

XIII

And wilt thou have me fashion into speech
The love I bear thee, finding words enough,
And hold the torch out, while the winds are rough,
Between our faces, to cast light on each?—
I drop it at thy feet. I cannot teach
My hand to hold my spirit so far off
From myself—me—that I should bring thee proof
In words, of love hid in me out of reach.
Nay, let the silence of my womanhood
Commend my woman-love to thy belief,—
Seeing that I stand unwon, however wooed,
And rend the garment of my life, in brief,
By a most dauntless, voiceless fortitude,
Lest one touch of this heart convey its grief.

XVIII

I never gave a lock of hair away
To a man, Dearest, except this to thee,
Which now upon my fingers thoughtfully,
I ring out to the full brown length and say
"Take it." My day of youth went yesterday;
My hair no longer bounds to my foot's glee,
Nor plant I it from rose or myrtle-tree,
As girls do, any more. It only may
Now shade on two pale cheeks, the mark of tears,
Taught drooping from the head that hangs aside
Through sorrow's trick. I thought the funeral-shears
Would take this first; but Love is justified:
Take it thou,—finding pure, from all those years,
The kiss my mother left here when she died.

XLII

How do I love thee? Let me count the ways.
I love thee to the depth and breadth and height
My soul can reach, when feeling out of sight
For the ends of Being and Ideal Grace.
I love thee to the level of everyday's
Most quiet need, by sun and candlelight.
I love thee freely, as men strive for Right;
I love thee purely, as they turn from Praise;
I love thee with the passion put to use
In my old griefs, and with my childhood's faith;
I love thee with a love I seemed to lose
With my lost saints,—I love thee with the breath,
Smiles, tears, of all my life!—and, if God choose,
I shall but love thee better after death.

CHAUCER

An old man in a lodge within a park;
   The chamber walls depicted all around
   With portraitures of huntsman, hawk, and hound,
   And the hurt deer. He listeneth to the lark,
Whose song comes with the sunshine through the dark
   Of painted glass in leaden lattice bound;
   He listeneth and he laugheth at the sound,
   Then writeth in a book like any clerk.
He is the poet of the dawn, who wrote
   The Canterbury Tales, and his old age
   Made beautiful with song; and as I read
I hear the crowing cock, I hear the note
   Of lark and linnet, and from every page
   Rise odors of ploughed field or flowery mead.

THE CROSS OF SNOW

In the long, sleepless watches of the night,
   A gentle face—the face of one long dead—
   Looks at me from the wall, where round its head
   The night-lamp casts a halo of pale light.
Here in this room she died; and soul more white
   Never through martyrdom of fire was led
   To its repose; nor can in books be read
   The legend of a life more benedight.
There is a mountain in the distant West
   That, sun-defying, in its deep ravines
   Displays a cross of snow upon its side.
Such is the cross I wear upon my breast
   These eighteen years, through all the changing scenes
   And seasons, changeless since the day she died.

❖ CHARLES TENNYSON TURNER ❖

LETTY'S GLOBE

When Letty had scarce passed her third glad year,
And her young artless words began to flow,
One day we gave the child a coloured sphere
Of the wide earth, that she might mark and know,
By tint and outline, all its sea and land.
She patted all the world; old empires peeped
Between her baby fingers. Her soft hand
Was welcome at all frontiers. How she leaped,
And laughed, and prattled, in her world-wide bliss.
But when we turned her sweet unlearned eye
On our own isle, she raised a joyous cry,
"Oh! yes, I see it. Letty's home is there!"
And while she hid all England with a kiss,
Bright over Europe fell her golden hair.

ON THE ECLIPSE OF THE MOON OF OCTOBER 1865

One little noise of life remained—I heard
The train pause in the distance, then rush by,
Brawling and hushing, like some busy fly
That murmurs and then settles; nothing stirred
Beside. The shadow of our travelling earth
Hung on the silver moon, which mutely went
Through that grand process, without token sent,
Or any sign to call a gazer forth,
Had I not chanced to see; dumb was the vault
Of heaven, and dumb the fields—no zephyr swept
The forest walks, or through the coppice crept;
Nor other sound the stillness did assault,
Save that faint-brawling railway's move and halt;
So perfect was the silence Nature kept.

❖ EDGAR ALLAN POE ❖

TO SCIENCE

Science, true daughter of Old Time thou art!
    Who alterest all things with thy peering eyes.
Why preyest thou thus upon the poet's heart,
    Vulture, whose wings are dull realities?
How should he love thee, or how deem thee wise,
    Who wouldst not leave him in his wandering
To seek for treasure in the jeweled skies,
    Albeit he soared with an undaunted wing?
Hast thou not dragged Diana from her car,
    And driven the Hamadryad from the wood
To seek a shelter in some happier star?
    Hast thou not torn the Naiad from her flood,
The Elfin from the green grass, and from me
The summer dream beneath the tamarind tree?

❖ ALFRED, LORD TENNYSON ❖

"If I were loved, as I desire to be"

If I were loved, as I desire to be,
What is there in the great sphere of the earth,
And range of evil between death and birth,
That I should fear,—if I were loved by thee?
All the inner, all the outer world of pain
Clear love would pierce and cleave, if thou wert mine,
As I have heard that, somewhere in the main,
Fresh-water springs come up through bitter brine.
'Twere joy, not fear, clasped hand in hand with thee,
To wait for death—mute—careless of all ills,
Apart upon a mountain, though the surge
Of some new deluge from a thousand hills
Flung leagues of roaring foam into the gorge
Below us, as far on as eye could see.

Mine be the strength of spirit fierce and free,
Like some broad river rushing down alone,
With the selfsame impulse wherewith he was thrown
From his loud fount upon the echoing lea:—
Which with increasing might doth forward flee
By town, and tower, and hill, and cape, and isle,
And in the middle of the green salt sea
Keeps his blue waters fresh for many a mile.
Mine be the power which ever to its sway
Will win the wise at once, and by degrees
May into uncongenial spirits flow;
Even as the great gulfstream of Florida
Floats far away into the Northern seas
The lavish growths of southern Mexico.

❖ ROBERT BROWNING ❖

WHY I AM A LIBERAL

"Why?" Because all I haply can and do,
  And that I am now, all I hope to be,—
  Whence comes it save from fortune setting free
Body and soul the purpose to pursue,
God traced for both? If letters not a few,
  Of prejudice, convention, fall from me,
  These shall I bid men—each in his degree
Also God-guided—bear, and gaily, too?
But little do or can the best of us:
  That little is achieved through Liberty.
Who, then, dares hold, emancipated thus,
  His fellow shall continue bound? Not I,
Who live, love, labor freely, nor discuss
  A brother's right to freedom. That is "Why."

❖ JONES VERY ❖

YOURSELF

'Tis to yourself I speak; you cannot know
Him whom I call in speaking such a one,
For you beneath the ground lie buried low,
Which he alone as living walks upon:
You may at times have heard him speak to you,
And often wished perchance that you were he;
And I must ever wish that it were true,
For then you could hold fellowship with me:
But now you hear us talk as strangers, met
Above the room wherein you lie abed;
A word perhaps loud spoken you may get,
Or hear our feet when heavily they tread;
But he who speaks, or him who's spoken to,
Must both remain as strangers still to you.

❖ AUBREY THOMAS DE VERE ❖

THE SUN GOD

I saw the Master of the Sun. He stood
    High in his luminous car, himself more bright;
    An Archer of immeasurable might:
On his left shoulder hung his quiver'd load;
Spurn'd by his steeds the eastern mountains glowed;
    Forward his eagle eye and bow of Light
He bent, and while both hands that arch embowed,
    Shaft after shaft pursued the flying night.
No wings profaned that godlike form: around
    His neck high held an ever-moving crowd
Of locks hung glistening: while such perfect sound
    Fell from his bowstring that th' ethereal dome
Thrilled as a dew-drop; and each passing cloud
    Expanded, whitening like the ocean foam.

from *Brother and Sister*

I

I cannot choose but think upon the time
When our two lives grew like two buds that kiss
At lightest thrill from the bee's swinging chime,
Because the one so near the other is.

He was the elder and a little man
Of forty inches, bound to show no dread,
And I the girl that puppy-like now ran,
Now lagged behind my brother's larger tread.

I held him wise, and when he talked to me
Of snakes and birds, and which God loved the best,
I thought his knowledge marked the boundary
Where men grew blind, though angels knew the rest.

  If he said "Hush!" I tried to hold my breath;
  Wherever he said "Come!" I stepped in faith.

XI

School parted us; we never found again
That childish world where our two spirits mingled
Like scents from varying roses that remain
One sweetness, nor can evermore be singled.

Yet the twin habit of that early time
Lingered for long about the heart and tongue:
We had been natives of one happy clime,
And its dear accent to our utterance clung,

Till the dire years whose awful name is Change
Had grasped our souls still yearning in divorce,
And pitiless shaped them in two forms that range
Two elements which sever their life's course.

  But were another childhood-world my share,
  I would be born a little sister there.

❖ JAMES RUSSELL LOWELL ❖

THE STREET

They pass me by like shadows, crowds on crowds,
Dim ghosts of men, that hover to and fro,
Hugging their bodies round them like thin shrouds
Wherein their souls were buried long ago:
They trampled on their youth, and faith, and love,
They cast their hope of human-kind away,
With Heaven's clear messages they madly strove,
And conquered,—and their spirits turned to clay:
Lo! how they wander round the world, their grave,
Whose ever-gaping maw by such is fed,
Gibbering at living men, and idly rave,
"We only truly live, but ye are dead."
Alas! poor fools, the anointed eye may trace
A dead soul's epitaph in every face!

❖ FREDERICK GODDARD TUCKERMAN ❖

from *Sonnets, First Series*

10

An upper chamber in a darkened house,
Where, ere his footsteps reached ripe manhood's brink,
Terror and anguish were his lot to drink;
I cannot rid the thought nor hold it close
But dimly dream upon that man alone:
Now though the autumn clouds most softly pass,
The cricket chides beneath the doorstep stone
And greener than the season grows the grass.
Nor can I drop my lids nor shade my brows,
But there he stands beside the lifted sash;
And with a swooning of the heart, I think
Where the black shingles slope to meet the boughs
And, shattered on the roof like smallest snows,
The tiny petals of the mountain ash.

28

Not the round natural world, not the deep mind,
The reconcilement holds: the blue abyss
Collects it not; our arrows sink amiss
And but in Him may we our import find.
The agony to know, the grief, the bliss
Of toil, is vain and vain: clots of the sod
Gathered in heat and haste and flung behind
To blind ourselves and others, what but this
Still grasping dust and sowing toward the wind?
No more thy meaning seek, thine anguish plead,
But leaving straining thought and stammering word,
Across the barren azure pass to God;
Shooting the void in silence like a bird,
A bird that shuts his wings for better speed.

from *Sonnets, Second Series*

7

His heart was in his garden; but his brain
Wandered at will among the fiery stars:
Bards, heroes, prophets, Homers, Hamilcars,
With many angels, stood, his eye to gain;
The devils, too, were his familiars.
And yet the cunning florist held his eyes
Close to the ground,—a tulip-bulb his prize,—
And talked of tan and bone-dust, cutworms, grubs,
As though all Nature held no higher strain;
Or, if he spoke of Art, he made the theme
Flow through box-borders, turf, and flower-tubs;
Or, like a garden-engine's, steered the stream,—
Now spouted rainbows to the silent skies;
Now kept it flat, and raked the walks and shrubs.

29

How oft in schoolboy-days, from the school's sway
Have I run forth to Nature as to a friend,—
With some pretext of o'erwrought sight, to spend
My school-time in green meadows far away!
Careless of summoning bell, or clocks that strike,
I marked with flowers the minutes of my day:
For still the eye that shrank from hated hours,
Dazzled with decimal and dividend,
Knew each bleached alder-root that plashed across
The bubbling brook, and every mass of moss;
Could tell the month, too, by the vervain-spike,—
How far the ring of purple tiny flowers
Had climbed; just starting, may-be, with the May,
Half-high, or tapering off at Summer's end.

❖ MATTHEW ARNOLD ❖

SHAKESPEARE

Others abide our question. Thou art free.
We ask and ask. Thou smilest and art still,
Out-topping knowledge. For the loftiest hill
Who to the stars uncrowns his majesty,
Planting his steadfast footsteps in the sea,
Making the heaven of heavens his dwelling-place,
Spears but the cloudy border of his base
To the foiled searching of mortality.
And thou, who didst the stars and sunbeams know,
Self-schooled, self-scanned, self-honoured, self-secure,
Didst tread on earth unguessed at. Better so!
All pains the immortal spirit must endure,
All weakness which impairs, all griefs which bow,
Find their sole speech in that victorious brow.

WEST LONDON

Crouched on the pavement, close by Belgrave Square,
A tramp I saw, ill, moody, and tongue-tied.
A babe was in her arms, and at her side
A girl; their clothes were rags, their feet were bare.

Some laboring men, whose work lay somewhere there,
Passed opposite; she touched her girl, who hied
Across, and begged, and came back satisfied.
The rich she had let pass with frozen stare.

Thought I: "Above her state this spirit towers;
She will not ask of aliens, but of friends,
Of sharers in a common human fate.

"She turns from that cold succor, which attends
The unknown little from the unknowing great,
And points us to a better time than ours."

❖ SYDNEY DOBELL ❖

THE ARMY SURGEON

Over that breathing waste of friends and foes,
The wounded and the dying, hour by hour,—
In will a thousand, yet but one in power,—
He labours thro' the red and groaning day.
The fearful moorland where the myriads lay
Moved as a moving field of mangled worms.
And as a raw brood, orphaned in the storms,
Thrust up their heads if the wind bend a spray
Above them, but when the bare branch performs
No sweet parental office, sink away
With hopeless chirp of woe, so as he goes
Around his feet in clamorous agony
They rise and fall; and all the seething plain
Bubbles a cauldron vast of many-coloured pain.

from *Modern Love*

I

By this he knew she wept with waking eyes:
That, at his hand's light quiver by her head,
The strange low sobs that shook their common bed
Were called into her with a sharp surprise,
And strangled mute, like little gaping snakes,
Dreadfully venomous to him. She lay
Stone-still, and the long darkness flowed away
With muffled pulses. Then, as midnight makes
Her giant heart of Memory and Tears
Drink the pale drug of silence, and so beat
Sleep's heavy measure, they from head to feet
Were moveless, looking through their dead black years,
By vain regret scrawled over the blank wall.
Like sculptured effigies they might be seen
Upon their marriage-tomb, the sword between;
Each wishing for the sword that severs all.

XVII

At dinner, she is hostess, I am host.
Went the feast ever cheerfuller? She keeps
The Topic over intellectual deeps
In buoyancy afloat. They see no ghost.
With sparkling surface-eyes we ply the ball:
It is in truth a most contagious game:
HIDING THE SKELETON, shall be its name.
Such play as this the devils might appall!
But here's the greater wonder; in that we,
Enamored of an acting naught can tire,
Each other, like true hypocrites, admire;
Warm-lighted looks, Love's ephemeræ,
Shoot gaily o'er the dishes and the wine.
We waken envy of our happy lot.
Fast, sweet, and golden, shows the marriage-knot.
Dear guests, you now have seen Love's corpse-light shine.

XXX

What are we first? First, animals; and next
Intelligences at a leap; on whom
Pale lies the distant shadow of the tomb,
And all that draweth on the tomb for text.
Into which state comes Love, the crowning sun:
Beneath whose light the shadow loses form.
We are the lords of life, and life is warm.
Intelligence and instinct now are one.
But nature says: "My children most they seem
When they least know me: therefore I decree
That they shall suffer." Swift doth young Love flee,
And we stand wakened, shivering from our dream.
Then if we study Nature we are wise.
Thus do the few who live but with the day:
The scientific animals are they—
Lady, this is my sonnet to your eyes.

XXXIV

Madam would speak with me. So, now it comes:
The Deluge or else Fire! She's well; she thanks
My husbandship. Our chain on silence clanks.
Time leers between, above his twiddling thumbs.
Am I quite well? Most excellent in health!
The journals, too, I diligently peruse.
Vesuvius is expected to give news:
Niagara is no noisier. By stealth
Our eyes dart scrutinizing snakes. She's glad
I'm happy, says her quivering under-lip.
"And are not you?" "How can I be?" "Take ship!
For happiness is somewhere to be had."
"Nowhere for me!" Her voice is barely heard.
I am not melted, and make no pretence.
With commonplace I freeze her, tongue and sense.
Niagara or Vesuvius is deferred.

XLVII

We saw the swallows gathering in the sky,
And in the osier-isle we heard them noise.
We had not to look back on summer joys,
Or forward to a summer of bright dye:
But in the largeness of the evening earth
Our spirits grew as we went side by side.
The hour became her husband and my bride.
Love that had robbed us so, thus blessed our dearth!
The pilgrims of the year waxed very loud
In multitudinous chatterings, as the flood
Full brown came from the West, and like pale blood
Expanded to the upper crimson cloud.
Love that had robbed us of immortal things,
This little moment mercifully gave,
Where I have seen across the twilight wave
The swan sail with her young beneath her wings.

XLIX

He found her by the ocean's moaning verge,
Nor any wicked change in her discerned;
And she believed his old love had returned,
Which was her exultation, and her scourge.
She took his hand, and walked with him, and seemed
The wife he sought, though shadow-like and dry.
She had one terror, lest her heart should sigh,
And tell her loudly she no longer dreamed.
She dared not say, "This is my breast: look in."
But there's a strength to help the desperate weak.
That night he learned how silence best can speak
The awful things when Pity pleads for Sin.
About the middle of the night her call
Was heard, and he came wondering to the bed.
"Now kiss me, dear! it may be, now!" she said.
Lethe had passed those lips, and he knew all.

L

Thus piteously Love closed what he begat:
The union of this ever-diverse pair!
These two were rapid falcons in a snare,
Condemned to do the flitting of the bat.
Lovers beneath the singing sky of May,
They wandered once; clear as the dew on flowers:
But they fed not on the advancing hours:
Their hearts held cravings for the buried day.
Then each applied to each that fatal knife,
Deep questioning, which probes to endless dole.
Ah, what a dusty answer gets the soul
When hot for certainties in this our life!—
In tragic hints here see what evermore
Moves dark as yonder midnight ocean's force,
Thundering like ramping hosts of warrior horse,
To throw that faint thin line upon the shore!

❖ ❖ ❖

LUCIFER IN STARLIGHT

On a starred night Prince Lucifer uprose.
Tired of his dark dominion swung the fiend
Above the rolling ball in cloud part screened,
Where sinners hugged their spectre of repose.
Poor prey to his hot fit of pride were those.
And now upon his western wing he leaned,
Now his huge bulk o'er Africa careened,
Now the black planet shadowed Arctic snows.
Soaring through wider zones that pricked his scars
With memory of the old revolt from Awe,
He reached a middle height, and at the stars,
Which are the brain of heaven, he looked, and sank.
Around the ancient track marched, rank on rank,
The army of unalterable law.

❖ DANTE GABRIEL ROSSETTI ❖

from *The House of Life*

INTRODUCTORY SONNET

A Sonnet is a moment's monument,—
   Memorial from the Soul's eternity
   To one dead deathless hour. Look that it be,
Whether for lustral rite or dire portent,
Or its own arduous fullness reverent:
   Carve it in ivory or in ebony
   As Day or Night shall rule; and let Time see
Its flowering crest impearled and orient.

A Sonnet is a coin: its face reveals
   The soul,—its converse, to what Power 'tis due:—
Whether for tribute to the august appeals
   Of Life, or dower in Love's high retinue
It serve, or, mid the dark wharf's cavernous breath,
In Charon's palm it pay the toll to Death.

XV   THE BIRTH-BOND

Have you not noted, in some family
   Where two were born of a first marriage-bed,
   How still they own their gracious bond, though fed
And nursed on the forgotten breast and knee?—
How to their father's children they shall be
   In act and thought of one goodwill; but each
   Shall for the other have, in silence speech,
And in a word complete community?

Even so, when first I saw you, seemed it, love,
   That among souls allied to mine was yet
   One nearer kindred than life hinted of.
O born with me somewhere that men forget,
And though in years of sight and sound unmet,
   Known for my soul's birth-partner well enough!

XIX SILENT NOON

Your hands lie open in the long fresh grass,—
   The finger-points look through like rosy blooms:
   Your eyes smile peace. The pasture gleams and glooms
'Neath billowing skies that scatter and amass.
All round our nest, far as the eye can pass,
   Are golden kingcup-fields with silver edge
   Where the cow-parsley skirts the hawthorn-hedge.
'Tis visible silence, still as the hour-glass.

Deep in the sun-searched growths the dragon-fly
Hangs like a blue thread loosened from the sky:—
   So this wing'd hour is dropt to us from above.
Oh! clasp we to our hearts, for deathless dower,
This close-companioned inarticulate hour
   When twofold silence was the song of love.

LIII WITHOUT HER

What of her glass without her? the blank grey
   There where the pool is blind of the moon's face.
   Her dress without her? the tossed empty space
Of cloud-rack whence the moon has passed away.
Her paths without her? Day's appointed sway
   Usurped by desolate night. Her pillowed place
   Without her! Tears, Ah me! for love's good grace
And cold forgetfulness of night or day.

What of the heart without her? Nay, poor heart,
   Of thee what word remains ere speech be still?
   A wayfarer by barren ways and chill,
Steep ways and weary, without her thou art,
Where the long cloud, the long wood's counterpart,
   Sheds doubled darkness up the labouring hill.

LXXXIII   BARREN SPRING

Once more the changed year's turning wheel returns:
　　And as a girl sails balanced in the wind,
　　And now before and now again behind
Stoops as it swoops, with cheek that laughs and burns,
So Spring comes merry towards me here, but earns
　　No answering smile from me, whose life is twin'd
　　With the dead boughs that winter still must bind,
And whom today the Spring no more concerns.

Behold, this crocus is a withering flame;
　　This snowdrop, snow; this apple-blossom's part
　　To breed the fruit that breeds the serpent's art.
Nay, for these Spring-flowers, turn thy face from them
Nor stay till on the year's last lily-stem
　　The white cup shrivels round the golden heart.

XCVII   A SUPERSCRIPTION

Look in my face; my name is Might-have-been;
　　I am also called No-more, Too-late, Farewell;
　　Unto thine ear I hold the dead-sea shell
Cast up thy Life's foam-fretted feet between,
Unto thine eyes the glass where that is seen
　　Which had Life's form and Love's, but by my spell
　　Is now a shaken shadow intolerable,
Of ultimate things unuttered the frail screen.

Mark me, how still I am! But should there dart
　　One moment through thy soul the soft surprise
　　Of that winged Peace which lulls the breath of sighs,—
Then shalt thou see me smile, and turn apart
Thy visage of mine ambush at thy heart,
　　Sleepless, with cold commemorative eyes.

REST

O Earth, lie heavily upon her eyes;
   Seal her sweet eyes weary of watching, Earth;
   Lie close around her; leave no room for mirth
With its harsh laughter, nor for sound of sighs.
She hath no questions, she hath no replies,
   Hushed in and curtained with a blessèd dearth
   Of all that irked her from the hour of birth;
With stillness that is almost Paradise.
Darkness more clear than noon-day holdeth her,
   Silence more musical than any song;
Even her very heart has ceased to stir:
Until the morning of Eternity
Her rest shall not begin nor end, but be;
   And when she wakes she will not think it long.

IN AN ARTIST'S STUDIO

One face looks out from all his canvases,
   One selfsame figure sits or walks or leans:
   We found her hidden just behind those screens,
That mirror gave back all her loveliness.
A queen in opal or in ruby dress,
   A nameless girl in freshest summer-greens,
   A saint, an angel—every canvas means
The same one meaning, neither more nor less.
He feeds upon her face by day and night,
   And she with true kind eyes looks back on him,
Fair as the moon and joyful as the light:
   Not wan with waiting, not with sorrow dim;
Not as she is, but was when hope shone bright;
   Not as she is, but as she fills his dream.

from *The Thread of Life*

"Thus am I mine own prison. Everything"

Thus am I mine own prison. Everything
   Around me free and sunny and at ease:
   Or if in shadow, in a shade of trees
Which the sun kisses, where the gay birds sing
And where all winds make virtuous murmuring;
   Where bees are found, with honey for the bees;
   Where sounds are music, and where silences
Are music of an unlike fashioning.
Then gaze I at the merry-making crew,
   And smile a moment and a moment sigh
Thinking: Why cannot I rejoice with you?
   But soon I put the foolish fancy by:
I am not what I have nor what I do;
   But what I was I am, I am even I.

❖ ALGERNON CHARLES SWINBURNE ❖

COR CORDIUM

O heart of hearts, the chalice of love's fire,
Hid round with flowers and all the bounty of bloom;
O wonderful and perfect heart, for whom
The lyrist liberty made life a lyre;
O heavenly heart, at whose most dear desire
Dead love, living and singing, cleft his tomb,
And with him risen and regent in death's room
All day thy choral pulses rang full choir;
O heart whose beating blood was running song,
O sole thing sweeter than thine own songs were,
Help us for thy free love's sake to be free,
True for thy truth's sake, for thy strength's sake strong,
Till very liberty make clean and fair
The nursing earth as the sepulchral sea.

O son of man, by lying tongues adored,
   By slaughterous hands of slaves with feet red-shod
   In carnage deep as ever Christian trod
Profaned with prayer and sacrifice abhorred
And incense from the trembling tyrant's horde,
   Brute worshipers or wielders of the rod,
   Most murderous even of all that call thee God,
Most treacherous even that ever called thee Lord;
Face loved of little children long ago,
   Head hated of the priests and rulers then,
     If thou see this, or hear these hounds of thine
     Run ravening as the Gadarean swine,
Say, was not this thy Passion, to foreknow
   In death's worst hour the works of Christian men?

❖ THOMAS HARDY ❖

HAP

If but some vengeful god would call to me
From up the sky, and laugh: "Thou suffering thing,
Know that thy sorrow is my ecstasy,
That thy love's loss is my hate's profiting!"

Then would I bear it, clench myself, and die,
Steeled by the sense of ire unmerited;
Half-eased in that a Powerfuller than I
Had willed and meted me the tears I shed.

But not so. How arrives it joy lies slain,
And why unblooms the best hope ever sown?
—Crass Casualty obstructs the sun and rain,
And dicing Time for gladness casts a moan. . . .
These purblind Doomsters had as readily strown
Blisses about my pilgrimage as pain.

SHE, TO HIM (I)

When you shall see me in the toils of Time,
My lauded beauties carried off from me,
My eyes no longer stars as in their prime,
My name forgot of Maiden Fair and Free;

When in your being heart concedes to mind,
And judgement, though you scarce its process know,
Recalls the excellences I once enshrined,
And you are irk'd that they have wither'd so;

Remembering mine the loss is, not the blame,
That Sportsman Time but rears his brood to kill,
Knowing me in my soul the very same—
One who would die to spare you touch of ill!—
Will you not grant to old affection's claim
The hand of friendship down Life's sunless hill?

SHE, TO HIM (II)

Perhaps, long hence, when I have passed away,
Some other's feature, accent, thought like mine,
Will carry you back to what I used to say,
And bring some memory of your love's decline.

Then you may pause awhile and think, "Poor jade!"
And yield a sigh to me—as ample due,
Not as the tittle of a debt unpaid
To one who could resign her all to you—

And thus reflecting, you will never see
That your thin thought, in two small words conveyed,
Was no such fleeting phantom-thought to me,
But the Whole Life wherein my part was played;
And you amid its fitful masquerade
A Thought—as I in your life seem to be!

IN THE OLD THEATRE, FIESOLE (APRIL 1887)

I traced the Circus whose gray stones incline
Where Rome and dim Etruria interjoin,
Till came a child who showed an ancient coin
That bore the image of a Constantine.

She lightly passed; nor did she once opine
How, better than all books, she had raised for me
In swift perspective Europe's history
Through the vast years of Cæsar's sceptred line.

For in my distant plot of English loam
'Twas but to delve, and straightway there to find
Coins of like impress. As with one half blind
Whom common simples cure, her act flashed home
In that mute moment to my opened mind
The power, the pride, the reach of perished Rome.

AT A LUNAR ECLIPSE

Thy shadow, Earth, from Pole to Central Sea,
Now steals along upon the Moon's meek shine
In even monochrome and curving line
Of imperturbable serenity.

How shall I link such sun-cast symmetry
With the torn troubled form I know as thine,
That profile, placid as a brow divine,
With continents of moil and misery?

And can immense Mortality but throw
So small a shade, and Heaven's high human scheme
Be hemmed within the coasts yon arc implies?

Is such the stellar gauge of earthly show,
Nation at war with nation, brains that teem,
Heroes, and women fairer than the skies?

A CHURCH ROMANCE

She turned in the high pew, until her sight
Swept the west gallery, and caught its row
Of music-men with viol, book, and bow
Against the sinking sad tower-window light.

She turned again; and in her pride's despite
One strenuous viol's inspirer seemed to throw
A message from his string to her below,
Which said: "I claim thee as my own forthright!"

Thus their hearts' bond began, in due time signed.
And long years thence, when Age had scared Romance,
At some old attitude of his or glance
That gallery-scene would break upon her mind,
With him as minstrel, ardent, young, and trim,
Bowing "New Sabbath" or "Mount Ephraim."

OVER THE COFFIN

They stand confronting, the coffin between,
His wife of old, and his wife of late,
And the dead man whose they both had been
Seems listening aloof, as to things past date.
—"I have called," says the first. "Do you marvel or not?"
"In truth," says the second, "I do—somewhat."

"Well, there was a word to be said by me! . . .
I divorced that man because of you—
It seemed I must do it, boundenly;
But now I am older, and tell you true,
For life is little, and dead lies he;
I would I had let alone you two!
And both of us, scorning parochial ways,
Had lived like the wives in the patriarchs' days."

We are getting to the end of visioning
The impossible within this universe,
Such as that better whiles may follow worse,
And that our race may mend by reasoning.

We know that even as larks in cages sing
Unthoughtful of deliverance from the curse
That holds them lifelong in a latticed hearse,
We ply spasmodically our pleasuring.

And that when nations set them to lay waste
Their neighbours' heritage by foot and horse,
And hack their pleasant plains in festering seams,
They may again,—not warely, or from taste,
But tickled mad by some demonic force.—
Yes. We are getting to the end of dreams!

❖ ROBERT BRIDGES ❖

"While yet we wait for spring, and from the dry"

While yet we wait for spring, and from the dry
And blackening east that so embitters March,
Well-housed must watch grey fields and meadows parch,
And driven dust and withering snowflake fly;
Already in glimpses of the tarnish'd sky
The sun is warm and beckons to the larch,
And where the covert hazels interarch
Their tassell'd twigs, fair beds of primrose lie.

Beneath the crisp and wintry carpet hid
A million buds but stay their blossoming;
And trustful birds have built their nests amid
The shuddering boughs, and only wait to sing
Till one soft shower from the south shall bid,
And hither tempt the pilgrim steps of spring.

GOD'S GRANDEUR

The world is charged with the grandeur of God.
 It will flame out, like shining from shook foil;
 It gathers to a greatness, like the ooze of oil
Crushed. Why do men then now not reck his rod?
Generations have trod, have trod, have trod;
 And all is seared with trade; bleared, smeared with toil;
 And wears man's smudge and shares man's smell: the soil
Is bare now, nor can foot feel, being shod.

And for all this, nature is never spent;
 There lives the dearest freshness deep down things;
And though the last lights off the black West went
 Oh, morning, at the brown brink eastward, springs—
Because the Holy Ghost over the bent
 World broods with warm breast and with ah! bright wings.

"As kingfishers catch fire, dragonflies draw flame"

As kingfishers catch fire, dragonflies draw flame;
 As tumbled over rim in roundy wells
 Stones ring; like each tucked string tells, each hung bell's
Bow swung finds tongue to fling out broad its name;
Each mortal thing does one thing and the same:
 Deals out that being indoors each one dwells;
 Selves—goes its self; *myself* it speaks and spells,
Crying *What I do is me; for that I came.*

I say more: the just man justices;
 Keeps grace: that keeps all his goings graces;
Acts in God's eye what in God's eye he is—
 Christ. For Christ plays in ten thousand places,
Lovely in limbs, and lovely in eyes not his
 To the Father through the features of men's faces.

SPRING

Nothing is so beautiful as Spring—
　　When weeds, in wheels, shoot long and lovely and lush;
　　Thrush's eggs look little low heavens, and thrush
Through the echoing timber does so rinse and wring
The ear, it strikes like lightnings to hear him sing;
　　The glassy peartree leaves and blooms, they brush
　　The descending blue; that blue is all in a rush
With richness; the racing lambs too have fair their fling.

What is all this juice and all this joy?
　　A strain of the earth's sweet being in the beginning
In Eden's garden.—Have, get before it cloy,
　　Before it cloud, Christ, lord, and sour with sinning,
Innocent mind and Mayday in girl and boy,
　　Most, O maid's child, thy choice and worthy the winning.

THE WINDHOVER

To Christ Our Lord

I caught this morning morning's minion, king-
　　dom of daylight's dauphin, dapple-dáwn-drawn Falcon, in his riding
　　Of the rólling level úndernéath him steady áir, and stríding
High there, how he rung upon the rein of a wimpling wing
In his ecstasy! then off, off forth on swing,
　　As a skate's heel sweeps smooth on a bow-bend: the hurl and gliding
　　Rebuffed the big wind. My heart in hiding
Stirred for a bird,—the achieve of, the mastery of the thing!

Brute beauty and valour and act, oh, air, pride, plume, here
　　Buckle! AND the fire that breaks from thee then, a billion
Times told lovelier, more dangerous, O my chevalier!

　　No wónder of it: shéer plód makes plóugh down síllion
Shine, and blue-bleak embers, ah my dear,
　　Fall, gáll themsélves, and gásh góld-vermílion.

PIED BEAUTY

Glory be to God for dappled things—
    For skies of couple-colour as a brinded cow;
      For rose-moles all in stipple upon trout that swim;
Fresh-firecoal chestnut-falls; finches' wings;
    Landscape plotted and pieced—fold, fallow, and plough;
      And áll trades, their gear and tackle and trim.

All things counter, original, spáre, strange;
    Whatever is fickle, frecklèd (who knows how?)
      With swíft, slów; sweet, sóur; adázzle, dím;
He fathers-forth whose beauty is pást change:
                    Práise hím.

THE CAGED SKYLARK

As a dare-gale skylark scanted in a dull cage,
    Man's mounting spirit in his bone-house, mean house, dwells—
    That bird beyond the remembering hís free fells;
This in drudgery, day-labouring-out life's age.

Though aloft on turf or perch or poor low stage
    Both sing sometímes the sweetest, sweetest spells,
    Yet both droop deadly sómetimes in their cells
Or wring their barriers in bursts of fear or rage.

Not that the sweet-fowl, song-fowl, needs no rest—
Why, hear him, hear him babble and drop down to his nest,
    But his own nest, wild nest, no prison.

Man's spirit will be flesh-bound, when found at best,
But úncúmberèd: meadow-dówn is nót distréssed
    For a ráinbow fóoting it nor hé for his bónes rísen.

PEACE

When will you ever, Peace, wild wooddove, shy wings shut,
Your round me roaming end, and under be my boughs?
When, when, Peace, will you, Peace?—I'll not play hypocrite

To own my heart: I yield you do come sometimes; but
That piecemeal peace is poor piece. What pure peace allows
Alarms of wars, the daunting, wars, the death of it?   \

O surely, reaving Peace, my Lord should leave in lieu
Some good! And so he does leave Patience exquisite,
That plumes to Peace thereafter. And when Peace here does house
He comes with work to do, he does not come to coo,
                    He comes to brood and sit.

FELIX RANDAL

Félix Rándal the fárrier, O is he déad then? my dúty all énded,
Who have watched his mould of man, big-boned and hardy-handsome
Pining, pining, till time when reason rambled in it and some
Fatal four disorders, fleshed there, all contended?

Sickness broke him. Impatient, he cursed at first, but mended
Being anointed and all; though a heavenlier heart began some
Mónths éarlier, since I had our swéet repriéve and ránsom
Téndered to him. Áh well, God rést him áll road éver he offénded!

This séeing the síck endéars them tó us, us tóo it endéars.
My tongue had taught thee comfort, touch had quenched thy tears,
Thy tears that touched my heart, child, Felix, poor Felix Randal;

How far from then forethought of, all thy more boisterous years,
When thou at the random grim forge, powerful amidst peers,
Didst fettle for the great grey drayhorse his bright and battering sandal!

"I wake and feel the fell of dark, not day"

I wake and feel the fell of dark, not day.
What hours, O what black hours we have spent
This night! what sights you, heart, saw; ways you went!
And more must, in yet longer light's delay.

With witness I speak this. But where I say
Hours I mean years, mean life. And my lament
Is cries countless, cries like dead letters sent
To dearest him that lives alas! away.

I am gall, I am heartburn. God's most deep decree
Bitter would have me taste: my taste was me;
Bones built in me, flesh filled, blood brimmed the curse.

Selfyeast of spirit a dull dough sours. I see
The lost are like this, and their scourge to be
As I am mine, their sweating selves; but worse.

"No worst, there is none. Pitched past pitch of grief"

No worst, there is none. Pitched past pitch of grief,
More pangs will, schooled at forepangs, wilder wring.
Comforter, where, where is your comforting?
Mary, mother of us, where is your relief?
My cries heave, herds-long; huddle in a main, a chief-
Woe, wórld-sorrow; on an áge-old ánvil wínce and síng—
Then lull, then leave off. Fury had shrieked "No ling-
Ering! Let me be fell: force I must be brief."
O the mind, mind has mountains; cliffs of fall
Frightful, sheer, no-man-fathomed. Hold them cheap
May who ne'er hung there. Nor does long our small
Durance deal with that steep or deep. Here! creep,
Wretch, under a comfort serves in a whirlwind: all
Life death does end and each day dies with sleep.

"Not, I'll not, carrion comfort, Despair, not feast on thee"

Not, I'll not, carrion comfort, Despair, not feast on thee;
Not untwist—slack they may be—these last strands of man
In me ór, most weary, cry *I can no more*. I can;
Can something, hope, wish day come, not choose not to be.

But ah, but O thou terrible, why wouldst thou rude on me
Thy wring-earth right foot rock? lay a lionlimb against me? scan
With darksome devouring eyes my bruisèd bones? and fan,
O in turns of tempest, me heaped there; me frantic to avoid thee and
       flee?

Why? That my chaff might fly; my grain lie, sheer and clear.
Nay in all that toil, that coil, since (seems) I kissed the rod,
Hand rather, my heart lo! lapped strength, stole joy, would laugh, cheer.

Cheer whóm though? The héro whose héaven-handling flúng me, fóot
       tród
Me? or mé that fóught him? O whích one? is it eách one? That níght,
       that year
Of now done darkness I wretch lay wrestling with (my God!) my God.

THAT NATURE IS A HERACLITEAN FIRE AND
OF THE COMFORT OF THE RESURRECTION

Cloud-puffball, torn tufts, tossed pillows | flaunt forth, then chevy on an air-
Built thoroughfare: heaven-roysterers, in gay-gangs | they throng; they
       glitter in marches.
Down roughcast, down dazzling whitewash, | wherever an elm arches,
Shivelights and shadowtackle in long | lashes lace, lance, and pair.
Delightfully the bright wind boisterous | ropes, wrestles, beats earth bare
Of yestertempest's creases; in pool and rutpeel parches
Squandering ooze to squeezed | dough, crust, dust; stanches, starches
Squadroned masks and manmarks | treadmire toil there
Footfretted in it. Million-fuèled, | nature's bonfire burns on.
But quench her bonniest, dearest | to her, her clearest-selvèd spark
Man, how fast his firedint, | his mark on mind, is gone!
Both are in an únfathomable, all is in an enormous dark
Drowned. O pity an indig | nation! Manshape, that shone
Sheer off, disseveral, a star, | death blots black out; nor mark
       Is any of him at all so stark
But vastness blurs and time | beats level. Enough! The Resurrection,
A heart's-clarion! Away grief's gasping, | joyless days, dejection.
       Across my foundering deck shone
A beacon, an eternal beam. | Flesh fade, and mortal trash
Fall to the residuary worm; | world's wildfire, leave but ash:
       In a flash, at a trumpet crash,
I am all at once what Christ is, | since he was what I am, and
This Jack, joke, poor potsherd, | patch, matchwood, immortal diamond,
       Is immortal diamond.

"Thou art indeed just, Lord, if I contend"

Justus quidem tu es, Domine,
si disputem tecum; verumtamen justa loquar ad te:
quare via impiorum prosperatur? &c. (JEREM. *xii* I.)

Thou art indeed just, Lord, if I contend
With thee; but, sir, so what I plead is just.
Why do sinners' ways prosper? and why must
Disappointment all I endeavour end?

Wert thou my enemy, O thou my friend,
How wouldst thou worse, I wonder, than thou dost
Defeat, thwart me? Oh, the sots and thralls of lust
Do in spare hours more thrive than I that spend,

Sir, life upon thy cause. See, banks and brakes
Now, leavèd how thick! lacèd they are again
With fretty chervil, look, and fresh wind shakes

Them; birds build—but not I build; no, but strain,
Time's eunuch, and not breed one work that wakes.
Mine, O thou lord of life, send my roots rain.

TO R. B.

The fine delight that fathers thought; the strong
Spur, live and lancing like the blowpipe flame,
Breathes once and, quenchèd faster than it came,
Leaves yet the mind a mother of immortal song.

Nine months she then, nay years, nine years she long
Within her wears, bears, cares and combs the same:
The widow of an insight lost she lives, with aim
Now known and hand at work now never wrong.

Sweet fire the sire of muse, my soul needs this;
I want the one rapture of an inspiration.
O then if in my lagging lines you miss

The roll, the rise, the carol, the creation,
My winter world, that scarcely breathes that bliss
Now, yields you, with some sighs, our explanation.

❖ EUGENE LEE–HAMILTON ❖

LUTHER TO A BLUEBOTTLE FLY (1540)

Ay, buzz and buzz away. Dost thou suppose
  I know not who thou art, who all today
  Hast vexed and plagued me, as I write and pray,
And dared to settle on my very nose?

Thou thinkest thou canst trip me while I doze?
  Each time I snatch at thee thou slipp'st away;
  But wait till my next sermon: I will lay
Thee in the dust, thou Father of all Foes.

Ay, buzz about my Bible. But I wot,
  Unless thou wish to shrivel, thou'lt not dare
To settle on the page, thou live blue blot!

Out, Beelzebub, or thou wilt make me swear.
  Buzz back to Hell: old Martin fears thee not,
Thou god of Flies, though thou shouldst fill the air!

❖ ALICE CHRISTINA MEYNELL ❖

TO A DAISY

Slight as thou art, thou art enough to hide,
  Like all created things, secrets from me,
  And stand a barrier to eternity.
And I, how can I praise thee well and wide
From where I dwell—upon the hither side?
  Thou little veil for so great mystery,
  When shall I penetrate all things and thee,
And then look back? For this I must abide,
Till thou shalt grow and fold and be unfurled
Literally between me and the world.
  Then I shall drink from in beneath a spring,
And from a poet's side shall read his book.
O daisy mine, what will it be to look
  From God's side even on such a simple thing?

❖ EMMA LAZARUS ❖

THE NEW COLOSSUS

Not like the brazen giant of Greek fame,
With conquering limbs astride from land to land,
Here at our sea-washed, sunset-gates shall stand
A mighty woman with a torch, whose flame
Is the imprisoned lightning, and her name
Mother of Exiles. From her beacon-hand
Glows world-wide welcome, her mild eyes command
The air-bridged harbor that twin-cities frame.
"Keep, ancient lands, your storied pomp!" cries she,
With silent lips. "Give me your tired, your poor,
Your huddled masses yearning to breathe free,
The wretched refuse of your teeming shore,
Send these, the homeless, tempest-tost to me,
I lift my lamp beside the golden door!"

❖ OSCAR WILDE ❖

ON THE SALE BY AUCTION OF KEATS' LOVE LETTERS

These are the letters which Endymion wrote
To one he loved in secret, and apart.
And now the brawlers of the auction mart
Bargain and bid for each poor blotted note,
Ay! for each separate pulse of passion quote
The merchant's price. I think they love not art
Who break the crystal of a poet's heart
That small and sickly eyes may glare and gloat.
Is it not said that many years ago,
In a far Eastern town, some soldiers ran
With torches through the midnight, and began
To wrangle for mean raiment, and to throw
Dice for the garments of a wretched man,
Not knowing the God's wonder, or His woe?

HÉLAS

To drift with every passion till my soul
Is a stringed lute on which all winds can play,
Is it for this that I have given away
Mine ancient wisdom, and austere control?
Methinks my life is a twice-written scroll
Scrawled over on some boyish holiday
With idle songs for pipe and virelay,
Which do but mar the secret of the whole.
Surely there was a time I might have trod
The sunlit heights, and from life's dissonance
Struck one clear chord to reach the ears of God.
Is that time dead? lo! with a little rod
I did but touch the honey of romance—
And must I lose a soul's inheritance?

❖ FRANCIS THOMPSON ❖

ALL'S VAST

O nothing, in this corporal earth of man,
    That to the imminent heaven of his high soul
Responds with color and with shadow, can
    Lack correlated greatness. If the scroll
Where thoughts lie fast in spell of hieroglyph
    Be mighty through its mighty inhabitants;
If God be in His Name; grave potence if
    The sounds unbind of hieratic chants;
All's vast that vastness means. Nay, I affirm
    Nature is whole in her least things exprest,
Nor know we with what scope God builds the worm.
        Our towns are copied fragments from our breast;
            And all man's Babylons strive but to impart
            The grandeurs of his Babylonian heart.

THE FOLLY OF BEING COMFORTED

One that is ever kind said yesterday:
"Your well-belovèd's hair has threads of grey,
And little shadows come about her eyes;
Time can but make it easier to be wise
Though now it seem impossible, and so
All that you need is patience."

　　　　　　　　　　Heart cries, "No,
I have not a crumb of comfort, not a grain.
Time can but make her beauty over again:
Because of that great nobleness of hers
The fire that stirs about her, when she stirs,
Burns but more clearly. O she had not these ways
When all the wild summer was in her gaze."

O heart! O heart! if she'd but turn her head,
You'd know the folly of being comforted.

THE FASCINATION OF WHAT'S DIFFICULT

The fascination of what's difficult
Has dried the sap out of my veins, and rent
Spontaneous joy and natural content
Out of my heart. There's something ails our colt
That must, as if it had not holy blood
Nor on Olympus leaped from cloud to cloud,
Shiver under the lash, strain, sweat and jolt
As though it dragged road-metal. My curse on plays
That have to be set up in fifty ways,
On the day's war with every knave and dolt,
Theatre business, management of men.
I swear before the dawn comes round again
I'll find the stable and pull out the bolt.

Dear Craoibhin Aoibhin, look into our case.
When we are high and airy hundreds say
That if we hold that flight they'll leave the place,
While those same hundreds mock another day
Because we have made our art of common things,
So bitterly, you'd dream they longed to look
All their lives through into some drift of wings.
You've dandled them and fed them from the book
And know them to the bone; impart to us—
We'll keep the secret—a new trick to please.
Is there a bridle for this Proteus
That turns and changes like his draughty seas?
Or is there none, most popular of men,
But when they mock us, that we mock again?

(*Imitated from Ronsard*)

"While I, from that reed-throated whisperer"

While I, from that reed-throated whisperer
Who comes at need, although not now as once
A clear articulation in the air,
But inwardly, surmise companions
Beyond the fling of the dull ass's hoof
—Ben Jonson's phrase—and find when June is come
At Kyle-na-no under that ancient roof
A sterner conscience and a friendlier home,
I can forgive even that wrong of wrongs,
Those undreamt accidents that have made me
—Seeing that Fame has perished this long while,
Being but a part of ancient ceremony—
Notorious, till all my priceless things
Are but a post the passing dogs defile.

A sudden blow; the great wings beating still
Above the staggering girl, her thighs caressed
By the dark webs, her nape caught in his bill,
He holds her helpless breast upon his breast.

How can those terrified vague fingers push
The feathered glory from her loosening thighs?
And how can body, laid in that white rush,
But feel the strange heart beating where it lies?

A shudder in the loins engenders there
The broken wall, the burning roof and tower
And Agamemnon dead.
                              Being so caught up,
So mastered by the brute blood of the air,
Did she put on his knowledge with his power
Before the indifferent beak could let her drop?

MERU

Civilisation is hooped together, brought
Under a rule, under the semblance of peace
By manifold illusion; but man's life is thought,
And he, despite his terror, cannot cease
Ravening through century after century,
Ravening, raging, and uprooting that he may come
Into the desolation of reality:
Egypt and Greece, good-bye, and good-bye, Rome!
Hermits upon Mount Meru or Everest,
Caverned in night under the drifted snow,
Or where that snow and winter's dreadful blast
Beat down upon their naked bodies, know
That day brings round the night, that before dawn
His glory and his monuments are gone.

A CRAZED GIRL

That crazed girl improvising her music,
Her poetry, dancing upon the shore,
Her soul in division from itself
Climbing, falling she knew not where,
Hiding amid the cargo of a steamship,
Her knee-cap broken, that girl I declare
A beautiful lofty thing, or a thing
Heroically lost, heroically found.

No matter what disaster occurred
She stood in desperate music wound,
Wound, wound, and she made in her triumph
Where the bales and the baskets lay
No common intelligible sound
But sang, "O sea-starved, hungry sea."

HIGH TALK

Processions that lack high stilts have nothing that catches the eye.
What if my great-granddad had a pair that were twenty foot high,
And mine were but fifteen foot, no modern stalks upon higher,
Some rogue of the world stole them to patch up a fence or a fire.
Because piebald ponies, led bears, caged lions, make but poor shows,
Because children demand Daddy-long-legs upon his timber toes,
Because women in the upper storeys demand a face at the pane,
That patching old heels they may shriek, I take to chisel and plane.

Malachi Stilt-Jack am I, whatever I learned has run wild,
From collar to collar, from stilt to stilt, from father to child.
All metaphor, Malachi, stilts and all. A barnacle goose
Far up in the stretches of night; night splits and the dawn breaks loose;
I, through the terrible novelty of light, stalk on, stalk on;
Those great sea-horses bare their teeth and laugh at the dawn.

❖ ERNEST DOWSON ❖

A LAST WORD

Let us go hence: the night is now at hand;
The day is overworn, the birds all flown;
And we have reaped the crops the gods have sown;
Despair and death; deep darkness o'er the land,
Broods like an owl; we cannot understand
Laughter or tears, for we have only known
Surpassing vanity: vain things alone
Have driven our perverse and aimless band.
Let us go hence, somewhither strange and cold,
To Hollow Lands where just men and unjust
Find end of labour, where's rest for the old,
Freedom to all from love and fear and lust.
Twine our torn hands! O pray the earth enfold
Our life-sick hearts and turn them into dust.

❖ EDWARD ARLINGTON ROBINSON ❖

FIRELIGHT

Ten years together without yet a cloud,
They seek each other's eyes at intervals
Of gratefulness to firelight and four walls
For love's obliteration of the crowd.
Serenely and perennially endowed
And bowered as few may be, their joy recalls
No snake, no sword, and over them there falls
The blessing of what neither says aloud.

Wiser for silence, they were not so glad
Were she to read the graven tale of lines
On the wan face of one somewhere alone;
Nor were they more content could he have had
Her thoughts a moment since of one who shines
Apart, and would be hers if he had known.

CALVARY

Friendless and faint, with martyred steps and slow,
Faint for the flesh, but for the spirit free,
Stung by the mob that came to see the show,
The Master toiled along to Calvary;
We gibed him, as he went, with houndish glee,
Till his dimmed eyes for us did overflow;
We cursed his vengeless hands thrice wretchedly,—
And this was nineteen hundred years ago.

But after nineteen hundred years the shame
Still clings, and we have not made good the loss
That outraged faith has entered in his name.
Ah, when shall come love's courage to be strong!
Tell me, O Lord—tell me, O Lord, how long
Are we to keep Christ writhing on the cross!

CLIFF KLINGENHAGEN

Cliff Klingenhagen had me in to dine
With him one day; and after soup and meat,
And all the other things there were to eat,
Cliff took two glasses and filled one with wine
And one with wormwood. Then, without a sign
For me to choose at all, he took the draught
Of bitterness himself, and lightly quaffed
It off, and said the other one was mine.

And when I asked him what the deuce he meant
By doing that, he only looked at me
And smiled, and said it was a way of his.
And though I know the fellow, I have spent
Long time a-wondering when I shall be
As happy as Cliff Klingenhagen is.

REUBEN BRIGHT

Because he was a butcher and thereby
Did earn an honest living (and did right),
I would not have you think that Reuben Bright
Was any more a brute than you or I;
For when they told him that his wife must die,
He stared at them, and shook with grief and fright,
And cried like a great baby half that night,
And made the women cry to see him cry.

And after she was dead, and he had paid
The singers and the sexton and the rest,
He packed a lot of things that she had made
Most mournfully away in an old chest
Of hers, and put some chopped-up cedar boughs
In with them, and tore down the slaughter house.

CREDO

I cannot find my way: there is no star
In all the shrouded heavens anywhere;
And there is not a whisper in the air
Of any living voice but one so far
That I can hear it only as a bar
Of lost, imperial music, played when fair
And angel fingers wove, and unaware,
Dead leaves to garlands where no roses are.

No, there is not a glimmer, nor a call,
For one that welcomes, welcomes when he fears,
The black and awful chaos of the night;
For through it all—above, beyond it all—
I know the far-sent message of the years,
I feel the coming glory of the Light.

SONNET

The master and the slave go hand in hand,
Though touch be lost. The poet is a slave,
And there be kings do sorrowfully crave
The joyance that a scullion may command.
But, ah, the sonnet-slave must understand
The mission of his bondage, or the grave
May clasp his bones, or ever he shall save
The perfect word that is the poet's wand.

The sonnet is a crown, whereof the rhymes
Are for Thought's purest gold the jewel-stones;
But shapes and echoes that are never done
Will haunt the workshop, as regret sometimes
Will bring with human yearning to sad thrones
The crash of battles that are never won.

THE SHEAVES

Where long the shadows of the wind had rolled,
Green wheat was yielding to the change assigned;
And as by some vast magic undivined
The world was turning slowly into gold.
Like nothing that was ever bought or sold
It waited there, the body and the mind;
And with a mighty meaning of a kind
That tells the more the more it is not told.

So in a land where all days are not fair,
Fair days went on till on another day
A thousand golden sheaves were lying there,
Shining and still, but not for long to stay—
As if a thousand girls with golden hair
Might rise from where they slept and go away.

❖ JAMES WELDON JOHNSON ❖

MOTHER NIGHT

Eternities before the first-born day,
  Or ere the first sun fledged his wings of flame,
  Calm Night, the everlasting and the same,
  A brooding mother over chaos lay.
And whirling suns shall blaze and then decay,
  Shall run their fiery courses and then claim
  The haven of the darkness whence they came;
  Back to Nirvanic peace shall grope their way.

So when my feeble sun of life burns out,
  And sounded is the hour for my long sleep,
  I shall, full weary of the feverish light,
Welcome the darkness without fear or doubt,
  And heavy-lidded, I shall softly creep
  Into the quiet bosom of the Night.

❖ PAUL LAURENCE DUNBAR ❖

ROBERT GOULD SHAW

Why was it that the thunder voice of Fate
  Should call thee, studious, from the classic groves,
  Where calm-eyed Pallas with still footsteps roves,
And charge thee seek the turmoil of the State?
What bade thee hear the voice and rise elate,
  Leave home and kindred and thy spicy loaves,
  To lead th' unlettered and despised droves
To manhood's home and thunder at the gate?

Far better the slow blaze of Learning's light,
  The cool and quiet of her dearer fane,
Than this hot terror of a hopeless fight,
  This cold endurance of the final pain,—
Since thou and those who with thee died for right
  Have died, the Present teaches, but in vain!

Ah, Douglass, we have fall'n on evil days,
　　Such days as thou, not even thou didst know,
　　When thee, the eyes of that harsh long ago
Saw, salient, at the cross of devious ways,
And all the country heard thee with amaze.
　　Not ended then, the passionate ebb and flow,
　　The awful tide that battled to and fro;
We ride amid a tempest of dispraise.

Now, when the waves of swift dissension swarm,
　　And Honor, the strong pilot, lieth stark,
Oh, for thy voice high-sounding o'er the storm,
　　For thy strong arm to guide the shivering bark,
The blast-defying power of thy form,
　　To give us comfort through the lonely dark.

❖　AMY LOWELL　❖

TO JOHN KEATS

Great master! Boyish, sympathetic man!
　　Whose orbed and ripened genius lightly hung
　　From life's slim, twisted tendril and there swung
In crimson-sphered completeness; guardian
Of crystal portals through whose openings fan
　　The spicèd winds which blew when earth was young,
　　Scattering wreaths of stars, as Jove once flung
A golden shower from heights cerulean.
　　Crumbled before thy majesty we bow.
　　Forget thy empurpled state, thy panoply
Of greatness, and be merciful and near;
　　A youth who trudged the highroad we tread now
　　Singing the miles behind him; so may we
Faint throbbings of thy music overhear.

"Be still. The Hanging Gardens were a dream"

Be still. The Hanging Gardens were a dream
That over Persian roses flew to kiss
The curled lashes of Semiramis.
Troy never was, nor green Skamander stream.
Provence and Troubadour are merest lies,
The glorious hair of Venice was a beam
Made with Titian's eye. The sunsets seem,
The world is very old and nothing is.
Be still. Thou foolish thing, thou canst not wake,
Nor thy tears wedge thy soldered lids apart,
But patter in the darkness of thy heart.
Thy brain is plagued. Thou art a frightened owl
Blind with the light of life thou'ldst not forsake,
And error loves and nourishes thy soul.

SIX O'CLOCK

Now burst above the city's cold twilight
The piercing whistles and the tower-clocks:
For day is done. Along the frozen docks
The workmen set their ragged shirts aright.
Thro' factory doors a stream of dingy light
Follows the scrimmage as it quickly flocks
To hut and home among the snow's gray blocks.—
I love you, human labourers. Good-night!
Good-night to all the blackened arms that ache!
Good-night to every sick and sweated brow,
To the poor girl that strength and love forsake,
To the poor boy who can no more! I vow
The victim soon shall shudder at the stake
And fall in blood: we bring him even now.

THE HILL

Breathless, we flung us on the windy hill,
  Laughed in the sun, and kissed the lovely grass.
  You said, "Through glory and ecstasy we pass;
Wind, sun, and earth remain, the birds sing still,
When we are old, are old. . . ." "And when we die
  All's over that is ours; and life burns on
Through other lovers, other lips," said I,
  "Heart of my heart, our heaven is now, is won!"

"We are Earth's best, that learnt her lesson here.
  Life is our cry. We have kept the faith!" we said;
  "We shall go down with unreluctant tread
Rose-crowned into the darkness!" . . . Proud we were,
And laughed, that had such brave true things to say.
—And then you suddenly cried, and turned away.

CLOUDS

Down the blue night the unending columns press
  In noiseless tumult, break and wave and flow,
  Now tread the far South, or lift rounds of snow
Up to the white moon's hidden loveliness.
Some pause in their grave wandering comradeless,
  And turn with profound gesture vague and slow,
  As who would pray good for the world, but know
Their benediction empty as they bless.

They say that the Dead die not, but remain
  Near to the rich heirs of their grief and mirth.
    I think they ride the calm mid-heaven, as these,
In wise majestic melancholy train,
    And watch the moon, and the still-raging seas,
    And men, coming and going on the earth.

A MEMORY

Somewhile before the dawn I rose, and stept
   Softly along the dim way to your room,
   And found you sleeping in the quiet gloom,
And holiness about you as you slept.
I knelt there; till your waking fingers crept
   About my head, and held it. I had rest
   Unhoped this side of Heaven, beneath your breast.
I knelt a long time, still; nor even wept.

It was great wrong you did me; and for gain
Of that poor moment's kindliness, and ease,
And sleepy mother-comfort!
                 Child, you know
How easily love leaps out to dreams like these,
Who has seen them true. And love that's wakened so
Takes all too long to lay asleep again.

from *1914*

THE SOLDIER

If I should die, think only this of me;
   That there's some corner of a foreign field
That is for ever England. There shall be
   In that rich earth a richer dust concealed;
A dust whom England bore, shaped, made aware,
   Gave, once, her flowers to love, her ways to roam,
A body of England's breathing English air,
   Washed by the rivers, blessed by suns of home.

And think, this heart, all evil shed away,
   A pulse in the eternal mind, no less
     Gives somewhere back the thoughts by England given;
Her sights and sounds; dreams happy as her day;
   And laughter, learned of friends; and gentleness,
     In hearts at peace, under an English heaven.

❖ ALICE DUNBAR–NELSON ❖

SONNET

I had no thought of violets of late,
The wild, shy kind that spring beneath your feet
In wistful April days, when lovers mate
And wander through the fields in raptures sweet.
The thought of violets meant florists' shops,
And bows and pins, and perfumed papers fine;
And garish lights, and mincing little fops
And cabarets and songs, and deadening wine.
So far from sweet real things my thoughts had strayed,
I had forgot wide fields, and clear brown streams;
The perfect loveliness that God has made,—
Wild violets shy and Heaven-mounting dreams.
And now—unwittingly, you've made me dream
Of violets, and my soul's forgotten gleam.

❖ ROBERT FROST ❖

A DREAM PANG

I had withdrawn in forest, and my song
Was swallowed up in leaves that blew alway;
And to the forest edge you came one day
(This was my dream) and looked and pondered long,
But did not enter, though the wish was strong:
You shook your pensive head as who should say,
"I dare not—too far in his footsteps stray—
He must seek me would he undo the wrong."

Not far, but near, I stood and saw it all,
Behind low boughs the trees let down outside;
And the sweet pang it cost me not to call
And tell you that I saw does still abide.
But 'tis not true that thus I dwelt aloof,
For the wood wakes, and you are here for proof.

MOWING

There was never a sound beside the wood but one,
And that was my long scythe whispering to the ground.
What was it it whispered? I knew not well myself;
Perhaps it was something about the heat of the sun,
Something, perhaps, about the lack of sound—
And that was why it whispered and did not speak.
It was no dream of the gift of idle hours,
Or easy gold at the hand of fay or elf:
Anything more than the truth would have seemed too weak
To the earnest love that laid the swale in rows,
Not without feeble-pointed spikes of flowers
(Pale orchises), and scared a bright green snake.
The fact is the sweetest dream that labor knows.
My long scythe whispered and left the hay to make.

MEETING AND PASSING

As I went down the hill along the wall
There was a gate I had leaned at for the view
And had just turned from when I first saw you
As you came up the hill. We met. But all
We did that day was mingle great and small
Footprints in summer dust as if we drew
The figure of our being less than two
But more than one as yet. Your parasol
Pointed the decimal off with one deep thrust.
And all the time we talked you seemed to see
Something down there to smile at in the dust.
(Oh, it was without prejudice to me!)
Afterward I went past what you had passed
Before we met, and you what I had passed.

HYLA BROOK

By June our brook's run out of song and speed.
Sought for much after that, it will be found
Either to have gone groping underground
(And taken with it all the Hyla breed
That shouted in the mist a month ago,
Like ghost of sleigh bells in a ghost of snow)—
Or flourished and come up in jewelweed,
Weak foliage that is blown upon and bent,
Even against the way its waters went.
Its bed is left a faded paper sheet
Of dead leaves stuck together by the heat—
A brook to none but who remember long.
This as it will be seen is other far
Than with brooks taken otherwhere in song.
We love the things we love for what they are.

THE OVEN BIRD

There is a singer everyone has heard,
Loud, a mid-summer and a mid-wood bird,
Who makes the solid tree trunks sound again.
He says that leaves are old and that for flowers
Mid-summer is to spring as one to ten.
He says the early petal-fall is past,
When pear and cherry bloom went down in showers
On sunny days a moment overcast;
And comes that other fall we name the fall.
He says the highway dust is over all.
The bird would cease and be as other birds
But that he knows in singing not to sing.
The question that he frames in all but words
Is what to make of a diminished thing.

RANGE–FINDING

The battle rent a cobweb diamond-strung
And cut a flower beside a groundbird's nest
Before it stained a single human breast.
The stricken flower bent double and so hung.
And still the bird revisited her young.
A butterfly its fall had dispossessed,
A moment sought in air his flower of rest,
Then lightly stooped to it and fluttering clung.
On the bare upland pasture there had spread
O'ernight 'twixt mullein stalks a wheel of thread
And straining cables wet with silver dew.
A sudden passing bullet shook it dry.
The indwelling spider ran to greet the fly,
But finding nothing, sullenly withdrew.

ACQUAINTED WITH THE NIGHT

I have been one acquainted with the night.
I have walked out in rain—and back in rain.
I have outwalked the furthest city light.

I have looked down the saddest city lane.
I have passed by the watchman on his beat
And dropped my eyes, unwilling to explain.

I have stood still and stopped the sound of feet
When far away an interrupted cry
Came over houses from another street,

But not to call me back or say good-by;
And further still at an unearthly height
One luminary clock against the sky

Proclaimed the time was neither wrong nor right.
I have been one acquainted with the night.

DESIGN

I found a dimpled spider, fat and white,
On a white heal-all, holding up a moth
Like a white piece of rigid satin cloth—
Assorted characters of death and blight
Mixed ready to begin the morning right,
Like the ingredients of a witches' broth—
A snow-drop spider, a flower like a froth,
And dead wings carried like a paper kite.

What had that flower to do with being white,
The wayside blue and innocent heal-all?
What brought the kindred spider to that height,
Then steered the white moth thither in the night?
What but design of darkness to appall?—
If design govern in a thing so small.

THE SILKEN TENT

She is as in a field a silken tent
At midday when a sunny summer breeze
Has dried the dew and all its ropes relent,
So that in guys it gently sways at ease,
And its supporting central cedar pole,
That is its pinnacle to heavenward
And signifies the sureness of the soul,
Seems to owe naught to any single cord,
But strictly held by none, is loosely bound
By countless silken ties of love and thought
To everything on earth the compass round,
And only by one's going slightly taut
In the capriciousness of summer air
Is of the slightest bondage made aware.

He would declare and could himself believe
That the birds there in all the garden round
From having heard the daylong voice of Eve
Had added to their own an oversound,
Her tone of meaning but without the words.
Admittedly an eloquence so soft
Could only have had an influence on birds
When call or laughter carried it aloft.
Be that as may be, she was in their song.
Moreover her voice upon their voices crossed
Had now persisted in the woods so long
That probably it never would be lost.
Never again would birds' song be the same.
And to do that to birds was why she came.

❖ EDWARD THOMAS ❖

SOME EYES CONDEMN

Some eyes condemn the earth they gaze upon:
Some wait patiently till they know far more
Than earth can tell them: some laugh at the whole
As folly of another's making: one
I knew that laughed because he saw, from core
To rind, not one thing worth the laugh his soul
Had ready at waking: some eyes have begun
With laughing; some stand startled at the door.

Others, too, I have seen rest, question, roll,
Dance, shoot. And many I have loved watching. Some
I could not take my eyes from till they turned
And loving died. I had not found my goal.
But thinking of your eyes, dear, I become
Dumb: for they flamed and it was me they burned.

Men heard this roar of parleying starlings, saw,
 A thousand years ago even as now,
 Black rooks with white gulls following the plough
So that the first are last until a caw
Commands that last are first again,—a law
 Which was of old when one, like me, dreamed how
 A thousand years might dust lie on his brow
Yet thus would birds do between hedge and shaw.

Time swims before me, making as a day
 A thousand years, while the broad ploughland oak
 Roars mill-like and men strike and bear the stroke
 Of war as ever, audacious or resigned,
And God still sits aloft in the array
 That we have wrought him, stone-deaf and stone-blind.

❖   EZRA POUND   ❖

A VIRGINAL

No, no! Go from me. I have left her lately.
I will not spoil my sheath with lesser brightness,
For my surrounding air hath a new lightness;
Slight are her arms, yet they have bound me straitly
And left me cloaked as with a gauze of ether;
As with sweet leaves; as with subtle clearness.
Oh, I have picked up magic in her nearness
To sheathe me half in half the things that sheathe her.
No, no! Go from me. I have still the flavor,
Soft as spring wind that's come from birchen bowers.
Green come the shoots, aye April in the branches,
As winter's wound with her sleight hand she staunches,
Hath of the trees a likeness of the savor:
As white their bark, so white this lady's hours.

❖ ELINOR WYLIE ❖

from *Wild Peaches*

I

When the world turns completely upside down
You say we'll emigrate to the Eastern Shore
Aboard a river-boat from Baltimore;
We'll live among wild peach trees, miles from town,
You'll wear a coonskin cap, and I a gown
Homespun, dyed butternut's dark gold colour.
Lost, like your lotus-eating ancestor,
We'll swim in milk and honey till we drown.

The winter will be short, the summer long,
The autumn amber-hued, sunny and hot,
Tasting of cider and of scuppernong;
All seasons sweet, but autumn best of all.
The squirrels in their silver fur will fall
Like falling leaves, like fruit, before your shot.

2

The autumn frosts will lie upon the grass
Like bloom on grapes of purple-brown and gold.
The misted early mornings will be cold;
The little puddles will be roofed with glass.
The sun, which burns from copper into brass,
Melts these at noon, and makes the boys unfold
Their knitted mufflers; full as they can hold,
Fat pockets dribble chestnuts as they pass.

Peaches grow wild, and pigs can live in clover;
A barrel of salted herrings lasts a year;
The spring begins before the winter's over.
By February you may find the skins
Of garter snakes and water moccasins
Dwindled and harsh, dead-white and cloudy-clear.

❖ ❖ ❖

SONNET

When, in the dear beginning of the fever
Whose one remedial physic must be death,
I drew the light and unembittered breath
Of ecstasy, then was I brave and clever;
No pinch of dust presumed to whisper "never";
The soul had exorcised the body's wraith,
In sacred madness and severer faith,
And this delirium should endure forever.

Then was my throat obedient as a reed
Wherein a demigod is audible;
But now its stops are practised to foretell
Only the mortal doom, the murderous deed:
Yet, if my love is pleased to whistle once,
The silver still cries out above the bronze.

A LODGING FOR THE NIGHT

If I had lightly given at the first
The lightest favours that you first demanded;
Had I been prodigal and open-handed
Of this dead body in its dream immersed;
My flesh and not my spirit had been pierced:
Your appetite was casual and candid;
Thus, for an hour, had endured and ended
My love, in violation and reversed.

Alas, because I would not draw the bolt
And take you to my bed, you now assume
The likeness of an angel in revolt
Turned from a low inhospitable room,
Until your fiery image has enchanted
And ravished the poor soul you never wanted.

❖ SIEGFRIED SASSOON ❖

DREAMERS

Soldiers are citizens of death's grey land,
   Drawing no dividend from time's tomorrows.
In the great hour of destiny they stand,
   Each with his feuds, and jealousies, and sorrows.

Soldiers are sworn to action; they must win
   Some flaming, fatal climax with their lives.
Soldiers are dreamers, when the guns begin
   They think of firelit homes, clean beds, and wives.

I see them in foul dug-outs, gnawed by rats,
   And in the ruined trenches, lashed with rain,
Dreaming of things they did with balls and bats,
   And mocked by hopeless longing to regain
Bank-holidays, and picture shows, and spats,
   And going to the office in the train.

GLORY OF WOMEN

You love us when we're heroes, home on leave,
Or wounded in a mentionable place.
You worship decorations; you believe
That chivalry redeems the war's disgrace.
You make us shells. You listen with delight,
By tales of dirt and danger fondly thrilled.
You crown our distant ardours while we fight,
And mourn our laurelled memories when we're killed.
You can't believe that British troops "retire"
When hell's last horror breaks them, and they run,
Trampling the terrible corpses—blind with blood.
   O German mother dreaming by the fire,
While you are knitting socks to send your son
His face is trodden deeper in the mud.

Who will remember, passing through this Gate,
The unheroic Dead who fed the guns?
Who shall absolve the foulness of their fate,—
Those doomed, conscripted, unvictorious ones?
    Crudely renewed, the Salient holds its own.
    Paid are its dim defenders by this pomp;
    Paid, with a pile of peace-complacent stone,
    The armies who endured that sullen swamp.

Here was the world's worst wound. And here with pride
"Their name liveth for ever," the Gateway claims.
Was ever an immolation so belied
As these intolerably nameless names?
Well might the Dead who struggled in the slime
Rise and deride this sepulchre of crime.

❖ ROBINSON JEFFERS ❖

LOVE THE WILD SWAN

"I hate my verses, every line, every word.
Oh pale and brittle pencils ever to try
One grass-blade's curve, or the throat of one bird
That clings to twig, ruffled against white sky.
Oh cracked and twilight mirrors ever to catch
One color, one glinting flash, of the splendor of things.
Unlucky hunter, Oh bullets of wax,
The lion beauty, the wild-swan wings, the storm of the wings."
—This wild swan of a world is no hunter's game.
Better bullets than yours would miss the white breast,
Better mirrors than yours would crack in the flame.
Does it matter whether you hate your . . . self? At least
Love your eyes that can see, your mind that can
Hear the music, the thunder of the wings. Love the wild swan.

❖ MARIANNE MOORE ❖

NO SWAN SO FINE

"No water so still as the
    dead fountains of Versailles." No swan,
with swart blind look askance
and gondoliering legs, so fine
    as the chintz china one with fawn-
brown eyes and toothed gold
collar on to show whose bird it was.

Lodged in the Louis Fifteenth
    candelabrum-tree of cockscomb-
tinted buttons, dahlias,
sea-urchins, and everlastings,
    it perches on the branching foam
of polished sculptured
flowers—at ease and tall. The king is dead.

❖ EDWIN MUIR ❖

MILTON

Milton, his face set fair for Paradise,
And knowing that he and Paradise were lost
In separate desolation, bravely crossed
Into his second night and paid his price.
There towards the end he to the dark tower came
Set square in the gate, a mass of blackened stone
Crowned with vermilion fiends like streamers blown
From a great funnel filled with roaring flame.

Shut in his darkness, these he could not see,
But heard the steely clamour known too well
On Saturday nights in every street in Hell.
Where, past the devilish din, could Paradise be?
A footstep more, and his unblinded eyes
Saw far and near the fields of Paradise.

from *The Dry Salvages* [OPENING STANZA]

I do not know much about gods; but I think that the river
Is a strong brown god—sullen, untamed and intractable,
Patient to some degree, at first recognised as a frontier;
Useful, untrustworthy, as a conveyor of commerce;
Then only a problem confronting the builder of bridges.
The problem once solved, the brown god is almost forgotten
By the dwellers in cities—ever, however, implacable,
Keeping his seasons and rages, destroyer, reminder
Of what men choose to forget. Unhonoured, unpropitiated
By worshippers of the machine, but waiting, watching and waiting.
His rhythm was present in the nursery bedroom,
In the rank ailanthus of the April dooryard,
In the smell of grapes on the autumn table,
And the evening circle in the winter gaslight.

❖ JOHN CROWE RANSOM ❖

PIAZZA PIECE

—I am a gentleman in a dustcoat trying
To make you hear. Your ears are soft and small
And listen to an old man not at all,
They want the young men's whispering and sighing.
But see the roses on your trellis dying
And hear the spectral singing of the moon;
For I must have my lovely lady soon,
I am a gentleman in a dustcoat trying.

—I am a lady young in beauty waiting
Until my truelove comes, and then we kiss.
But what grey man among the vines is this
Whose words are dry and faint as in a dream?
Back from my trellis, Sir, before I scream!
I am a lady young in beauty waiting.

❖ CLAUDE McKAY ❖

IF WE MUST DIE

If we must die, let it not be like hogs
Hunted and penned in an inglorious spot,
While round us bark the mad and hungry dogs,
Making their mock at our accursed lot.
If we must die, O let us nobly die,
So that our precious blood may not be shed
In vain; then even the monsters we defy
Shall be constrained to honor us though dead!
O kinsmen! we must meet the common foe!
Though far outnumbered let us show us brave,
And for their thousand blows deal one deathblow!
What though before us lies the open grave?
Like men we'll face the murderous, cowardly pack,
Pressed to the wall, dying, but fighting back!

THE HARLEM DANCER

Applauding youths laughed with young prostitutes
And watched her perfect, half-clothed body sway;
Her voice was like the sound of blended flutes
Blown by black players upon a picnic day.
She sang and danced on gracefully and calm,
The light gauze hanging loose about her form;
To me she seemed a proudly-swaying palm
Grown lovelier for passing through a storm.
Upon her swarthy neck black shiny curls
Luxuriant fell; and tossing coins in praise,
The wine-flushed, bold-eyed boys, and even the girls,
Devoured her shape with eager, passionate gaze;
But looking at her falsely-smiling face,
I knew her self was not in that strange place.

Although she feeds me bread of bitterness,
And sinks into my throat her tiger's tooth,
Stealing my breath of life, I will confess
I love this cultured hell that tests my youth!
Her vigor flows like tides into my blood,
Giving me strength erect against her hate.
Her bigness sweeps my being like a flood.
Yet as a rebel fronts a king in state,
I stand within her walls with not a shred
Of terror, malice, not a word of jeer.
Darkly I gaze into the days ahead,
And see her might and granite wonders there,
Beneath the touch of time's unerring hand,
Like priceless treasures sinking in the sand.

❖ ARCHIBALD MacLEISH ❖

THE END OF THE WORLD

Quite unexpectedly as Vasserot
The armless ambidextrian was lighting
A match between his great and second toe
And Ralph the lion was engaged in biting
The neck of Madame Sossman while the drum
Pointed, and Teeny was about to cough
In waltz time swinging Jocko by the thumb—
Quite unexpectedly the top blew off:

And there, there overhead, there, there, hung over
Those thousands of white faces, those dazed eyes,
There in the starless dark the poise, the hover,
There with vast wings across the canceled skies,
There in the sudden blackness the black pall
Of nothing, nothing, nothing—nothing at all.

The concierge at the front gate where relatives
Half after two till four Mondays and Fridays
Do not turn always to look at the hospital,
Brown now and rusty with sunlight and bare
As the day you died in it, stump of the knee gangrenous,

"Le ciel dans les yeux" and the flea-bitten priest with the wafer
Forgiving you everything—You!—the concierge hadn't
Heard of you: *"Rimbaud? Comment s'écrit ça, Rimbaud?"*

But Sidis the, well, American dealer in manuscripts—
Sidis has sold the original ink decree:
Verlaine versus Verlaine (Divorce) with your name as
How do we say between gentlemen—anyway all
OK, the facts, the actual story . . .

Men remember you, dead boy—the lover of verses!

❖ EDNA ST. VINCENT MILLAY ❖

"Thou art not lovelier than lilacs,—no"

Thou art not lovelier than lilacs,—no,
Nor honeysuckle; thou art not more fair
Than small white single poppies,—I can bear
Thy beauty; though I bend before thee, though
From left to right, now knowing where to go,
I turn my troubled eyes, nor here nor there
Find any refuge from thee, yet I swear
So has it been with mist,—with moonlight so.
Like him who day by day unto his draught
Of delicate poison adds him one drop more
Till he may drink unharmed the death of ten,
Even so, inured to beauty, who have quaffed
Each hour more deeply than the hour before,
I drink—and live—what has destroyed some men.

"Time does not bring relief; you all have lied"

Time does not bring relief; you all have lied
Who told me time would ease me of my pain!
I miss him in the weeping of the rain;
I want him at the shrinking of the tide;
The old snows melt from every mountain-side,
And last year's leaves are smoke in every lane;
But last year's bitter loving must remain
Heaped on my heart, and my old thoughts abide.
There are a hundred places where I fear
To go,—so with his memory they brim.
And entering with relief some quiet place
Where never fell his foot or shone his face
I say, "There is no memory of him here!"
And so stand stricken, so remembering him.

"If I should learn, in some quite casual way"

If I should learn, in some quite casual way,
That you were gone, not to return again—
Read from the back-page of a paper, say,
Held by a neighbor in a subway train,
How at the corner of this avenue
And such a street (so are the papers filled)
A hurrying man, who happened to be you,
At noon today had happened to be killed,
I should not cry aloud—I could not cry
Aloud, or wring my hands in such a place—
I should but watch the station lights rush by
With a more careful interest on my face;
Or raise my eyes and read with greater care
Where to store furs and how to treat the hair.

"Oh, think not I am faithful to a vow!"

Oh, think not I am faithful to a vow!
Faithless am I save to love's self alone.
Were you not lovely I would leave you now:
After the feet of beauty fly my own.
Were you not still my hunger's rarest food,
And water ever to my wildest thirst,
I would desert you—think not but I would!—
And seek another as I sought you first.
But you are mobile as the veering air,
And all your charms more changeful than the tide,
Wherefore to be inconstant is no care:
I have but to continue at your side.
So wanton, light and false, my love, are you,
I am most faithless when I most am true.

"Pity me not because the light of day"

Pity me not because the light of day
At close of day no longer walks the sky;
Pity me not for beauties passed away
From field and thicket as the year goes by;
Pity me not the waning of the moon,
Nor that the ebbing tide goes out to sea,
Nor that a man's desire is hushed so soon,
And you no longer look with love on me.
This have I known always: Love is no more
Than the wide blossom which the wind assails,
Than the great tide that treads the shifting shore,
Strewing fresh wreckage gathered in the gales:
Pity me that the heart is slow to learn
What the swift mind beholds at every turn.

"I shall go back again to the bleak shore"

I shall go back again to the bleak shore
And build a little shanty on the sand,
In such a way that the extremest band
Of brittle seaweed will escape my door
But by a yard or two; and nevermore
Shall I return to take you by the hand;
I shall be gone to what I understand,
And happier than I ever was before.
The love that stood a moment in your eyes,
The words that lay a moment on your tongue,
Are one with all that in a moment dies,
A little under-said and over-sung.
But I shall find the sullen rocks and skies
Unchanged from what they were when I was young.

"I, being born a woman and distressed"

I, being born a woman and distressed
By all the needs and notions of my kind,
Am urged by your propinquity to find
Your person fair, and feel a certain zest
To bear your body's weight upon my breast:
So subtly is the fume of life designed,
To clarify the pulse and cloud the mind,
And leave me once again undone, possessed.
Think not for this, however, the poor treason
Of my stout blood against my staggering brain,
I shall remember you with love, or season
My scorn with pity,—let me make it plain:
I find this frenzy insufficient reason
For conversation when we meet again.

"What lips my lips have kissed, and where, and why"

What lips my lips have kissed, and where, and why,
I have forgotten, and what arms have lain
Under my head till morning; but the rain
Is full of ghosts tonight, that tap and sigh
Upon the glass and listen for reply,
And in my heart there stirs a quiet pain
For unremembered lads that not again
Will turn to me at midnight with a cry.
Thus in the winter stands the lonely tree,
Nor knows what birds have vanished one by one,
Yet knows its boughs more silent than before:
I cannot say what loves have come and gone,
I only know that summer sang in me
A little while, that in me sings no more.

"Still will I harvest beauty where it grows"

Still will I harvest beauty where it grows:
In coloured fungus and the spotted fog
Surprised on foods forgotten; in ditch and bog
Filmed brilliant with irregular rainbows
Of rust and oil, where half a city throws
Its empty tins; and in some spongy log
Whence headlong leaps the oozy emerald frog. . . .
And a black pupil in the green scum shows.
Her the inhabiter of divers places
Surmising at all doors, I push them all.
Oh, you that fearful of a creaking hinge
Turn back forevermore with craven faces,
I tell you Beauty bears an ultra fringe
Unguessed of you upon her gossamer shawl!

from *Fatal Interview*

II

This beast that rends me in the sight of all,
This love, this longing, this oblivious thing,
That has me under as the last leaves fall,
Will glut, will sicken, will be gone by spring.
The wound will heal, the fever will abate,
The knotted hurt will slacken in the breast;
I shall forget before the flickers mate
Your look that is today my east and west.
Unscathed, however, from a claw so deep
Though I should love again I shall not go:
Along my body, waking while I sleep,
Sharp to the kiss, cold to the hand as snow,
The scar of this encounter like a sword
Will lie between me and my troubled lord.

VII

Night is my sister, and how deep in love,
How drowned in love and weedily washed ashore,
There to be fretted by the drag and shove
At the tide's edge, I lie—these things and more:
Whose arm alone between me and the sand,
Whose voice alone, whose pitiful breath brought near,
Could thaw these nostrils and unlock this hand,
She could advise you, should you care to hear.
Small chance, however, in a storm so black,
A man will leave his friendly fire and snug
For a drowned woman's sake, and bring her back
To drip and scatter shells upon the rug.
No one but Night, with tears on her dark face,
Watches beside me in this windy place.

XX

Think not, nor for a moment let your mind,
Wearied with thinking, doze upon the thought
That the work's done and the long day behind,
And beauty, since 'tis paid for, can be bought.
If in the moonlight from the silent bough
Suddenly with precision speak your name
The nightingale, be not assured that now
His wing is limed and his wild virtue tame.
Beauty beyond all feathers that have flown
Is free; you shall not hood her to your wrist,
Nor sting her eyes, nor have her for your own
In any fashion; beauty billed and kissed
Is not your turtle; tread her like a dove—
She loves you not; she never heard of love.

XXX

Love is not all: it is not meat nor drink
Nor slumber nor a roof against the rain;
Nor yet a floating spar to men that sink
And rise and sink and rise and sink again;
Love can not fill the thickened lung with breath,
Nor clean the blood, nor set the fractured bone;
Yet many a man is making friends with death
Even as I speak, for lack of love alone.
It well may be that in a difficult hour,
Pinned down by pain and moaning for release,
Or nagged by want past resolution's power,
I might be driven to sell your love for peace,
Or trade the memory of this night for food.
It well may be. I do not think I would.

❖ ❖ ❖

"I will put Chaos into fourteen lines"

I will put Chaos into fourteen lines
And keep him there; and let him thence escape
If he be lucky; let him twist, and ape
Flood, fire, and demon—his adroit designs
Will strain to nothing in the strict confines
Of this sweet Order, where, in pious rape,
I hold his essence and amorphous shape,
Till he with Order mingles and combines.
Past are the hours, the years, of our duress,
His arrogance, our awful servitude:
I have him. He is nothing more nor less
Than something simple not yet understood;
I shall not even force him to confess;
Or answer. I will only make him good.

"Read history: so learn your place in Time"

Read history: so learn your place in Time;
And go to sleep: all this was done before;
We do it better, fouling every shore;
We disinfect, we do not probe, the crime.
Our engines plunge into the seas, they climb
Above our atmosphere: we grow not more
Profound as we approach the ocean's floor;
Our flight is lofty, it is not sublime.
Yet long ago this Earth by struggling men
Was scuffed, was scraped by mouths that bubbled mud;
And will be so again, and yet again;
Until we trace our poison to its bud
And root, and there uproot it: until then,
Earth will be warmed each winter by man's blood.

V

When Man is gone and only gods remain
To stride the world, their mighty bodies hung
With golden shields, and golden curls outflung
Above their childish foreheads; when the plain
Round skull of Man is lifted and again
Abandoned by the ebbing wave, among
The sand and pebbles of the beach,—what tongue
Will tell the marvel of the human brain?
Heavy with music once this windy shell,
Heavy with knowledge of the clustered stars;
The one-time tenant of this draughty hall
Himself, in learned pamphlet, did foretell,
After some aeons of study jarred by wars,
This toothy gourd, this head emptied of all.

❖ WILFRED OWEN ❖

ANTHEM FOR DOOMED YOUTH

What passing-bells for these who die as cattle?
    Only the monstrous anger of the guns.
    Only the stuttering rifles' rapid rattle
Can pattern out their hasty orisons.
No mockeries for them; no prayers nor bells,
Nor any voice of mourning save the choirs,—
The shrill, demented choirs of wailing shells;
And bugles calling for them from sad shires.

What candles may be held to speed them all?
    Not in the hands of boys, but in their eyes
Shall shine the holy glimmers of good-byes.
    The pallor of girls' brows shall be their pall;
Their flowers the tenderness of patient minds,
And each slow dusk a drawing-down of blinds.

Bent double, like old beggars under sacks,
Knock-kneed, coughing like hags, we cursed through sludge,
Till on the haunting flares we turned our backs
And towards our distant rest began to trudge.
Men marched asleep. Many had lost their boots
But limped on, blood-shod. All went lame; all blind;
Drunk with fatigue; deaf even to the hoots
Of tired, outstripped Five-Nines that dropped behind.

Gas! GAS! Quick, boys!—An ecstasy of fumbling,
Fitting the clumsy helmets just in time;
But someone still was yelling out and stumbling,
And flound'ring like a man in fire or lime . . .
Dim, through the misty panes and thick green light,
As under a green sea, I saw him drowning.

In all my dreams, before my helpless sight,
He plunges at me, guttering, choking, drowning.

If in smothering dreams you too could pace
Behind the wagon that we flung him in,
And watch the white eyes writhing in his face,
His hanging face, like a devil's sick of sin;
If you could hear, at every jolt, the blood
Come gargling from the froth-corrupted lungs,
Obscene as cancer, bitter as the cud
Of vile, incurable sores on innocent tongues,—
My friend, you would not tell with such high zest
To children ardent for some desperate glory,
The old Lie: Dulce et decorum est
Pro patria mori.

Move him into the sun—
Gently its touch awoke him once,
At home, whispering of fields half-sown.
Always it woke him, even in France,
Until this morning and this snow.
If anything might rouse him now
The kind old sun will know.

Think how it wakes the seeds—
Woke once the clays of a cold star.
Are limbs, so dear achieved, are sides
Full-nerved, still warm, too hard to stir?
Was it for this, the clay grew tall?
—O what made fatuous sunbeams toil
To break earth's sleep at all?

❖ DOROTHY PARKER ❖

"I SHALL COME BACK"

I shall come back without fanfaronade
Of wailing wind and graveyard panoply;
But, trembling, slip from cool Eternity—
A mild and most bewildered little shade.
I shall not make sepulchral midnight raid,
But softly come where I had longed to be
In April twilight's unsung melody,
And I, not you, shall be the one afraid.

Strange, that from lovely dreamings of the dead
I shall come back to you, who hurt me most.
You may not feel my hand upon your head,
I'll be so new and inexpert a ghost.
Perhaps you will not know that I am near,—
And that will break my ghostly heart, my dear.

"when thou hast taken thy last applause, and when"

when thou hast taken thy last applause,and when
the final curtain strikes the world away,
leaving to shadowy silence and dismay
that stage which shall not know thy smile again,
lingering a little while i see thee then
ponder the tinsel part they let thee play;
i see the large lips vivid,the face grey,
and silent smileless eyes of Magdalen.
The lights have laughed their last;without,the street
darkling awaiteth her whose feet have trod
the silly souls of men to golden dust:
she pauses on the lintel of defeat,
her heart breaks in a smile—and she is Lust....

mine also,little painted poem of god

"my girl's tall with hard long eyes"

my girl's tall with hard long eyes
as she stands,with her long hard hands keeping
silence on her dress,good for sleeping
is her long hard body filled with surprise
like a white shocking wire,when she smiles
a hard long smile it sometimes makes
gaily go clean through me tickling aches,
and the weak noise of her eyes easily files
my impatience to an edge—my girl's tall
and taut,with thin legs just like a vine
that's spent all of its life on a garden-wall,
and is going to die.   When we grimly go to bed
with these legs she begins to heave and twine
about me,and to kiss my face and head.

"it is at moments after i have dreamed"

it is at moments after i have dreamed
of the rare entertainment of your eyes,
when(being fool to fancy)i have deemed

with your peculiar mouth my heart made wise;
at moments when the glassy darkness holds

the genuine apparition of your smile
(it was through tears always)and silence moulds
such strangeness as was mine a little while;

moments when my once more illustrious arms
are filled with fascination,when my breast
wears the intolerant brightness of your charms:

one pierced moment whiter than the rest

—turning from the tremendous lie of sleep
i watch the roses of the day grow deep.

"it may not always be so;and i say"

it may not always be so;and i say
that if your lips,which i have loved,should touch
another's,and your dear strong fingers clutch
his heart,as mine in time not far away;
if on another's face your sweet hair lay
in such a silence as i know,or such
great writhing words as,uttering overmuch,
stand helplessly before the spirit at bay;

if this should be,i say if this should be—
you of my heart,send me a little word;
that i may go unto him,and take his hands,
saying,Accept all happiness from me.
Then shall i turn my face,and hear one bird
sing terribly afar in the lost lands.

from *Sonnets—Actualities*

I

when my love comes to see me it's
just a little like music,a
little more like curving colour(say
orange)
         against silence,or darkness....

the coming of my love emits
a wonderful smell in my mind,

you should see when i turn to find
her how my least heart-beat becomes less.
And then all her beauty is a vise

whose stilling lips murder suddenly me,

but of my corpse the tool her smile makes something
suddenly luminous and precise

—and then we are I and She....

what is that the hurdy-gurdy's playing

II

it is funny,you will be dead some day.
By you the mouth hair eyes,and i mean
the unique and nervously obscene

need;it's funny. They will all be dead

knead of lustfulhunched deeplytoplay
lips and stare the gross fuzzy-pash
—dead—and the dark gold delicately smash....
grass,and the stars,of my shoulder in stead.

It is a funny,thing. And you will be

and i and all the days and nights that matter
knocked by sun moon jabbed jerked with ecstasy
.... tremble(not knowing how much better

than me will you like the rain's face and

the rich improbable hands of the Wind)

VII

yours is the music for no instrument
yours the preposterous colour unbeheld

—mine the unbought contemptuous intent
till this our flesh merely shall be excelled
by speaking flower
                    (if i have made songs

it does not greatly matter to the sun,
nor will rain care
                    cautiously who prolongs
unserious twilight)Shadows have begun

the hair's worm huge,ecstatic,rathe....

yours are the poems i do not write.

In this at least we have got a bulge on death,
silence,and the keenly musical light

of sudden nothing.... la bocca mia "he
kissed wholly trembling"

                    or so thought the lady.

    X

a thing most new complete fragile intense,
which wholly trembling memory undertakes
—your kiss,the little pushings of flesh,makes
my body sorry when the minute moon
is a remarkable splinter in the quick
of twilight
                ....or if sunset utters one
unhurried muscled huge chromatic
fist skilfully modeling silence
—to feel how through the stopped entire day
horribly and seriously thrills
the moment of enthusiastic space
is a little wonderful,and say
Perhaps her body touched me;and to face

suddenly the lighted living hills

XII

my love is building a building
around you,a frail slippery
house,a strong fragile house
(beginning at the singular beginning

of your smile)a skilful uncouth
prison,a precise clumsy
prison(building thatandthis into Thus,
Around the reckless magic of your mouth)

my love is building a magic,a discrete
tower of magic and(as i guess)

when Farmer Death(whom fairies hate)shall

crumble the mouth-flower fleet
He'll not my tower,

            laborious,casual

where the surrounded smile

                hangs

                    breathless

❖ ❖ ❖

"i like my body when it is with your"

i like my body when it is with your
body.   It is so quite new a thing.
Muscles better and nerves more.
i like your body.   i like what it does,
i like its hows.   i like to feel the spine
of your body and its bones,and the trembling
-firm-smooth ness and which i will
again and again and again
kiss,   i like kissing this and that of you,
i like,slowly stroking the,shocking fuzz
of your electric fur,and what-is-it comes
over parting flesh.... And eyes big love-crumbs,

and possibly i like the thrill

of under me you so quite new

" 'next to of course god america i"

"next to of course god america i
love you land of the pilgrims' and so forth oh
say can you see by the dawn's early my
country 'tis of centuries come and go
and are no more what of it we should worry
in every language even deafanddumb
thy sons acclaim your glorious name by gorry
by jingo by gee by gosh by gum
why talk of beauty what could be more beaut-
iful than these heroic happy dead
who rushed like lions to the roaring slaughter
they did not stop to think they died instead
then shall the voice of liberty be mute?"

He spoke. And drank rapidly a glass of water

"if i have made,my lady,intricate"

if i have made,my lady,intricate
imperfect various things chiefly which wrong
your eyes(frailer than most deep dreams are frail)
songs less firm than your body's whitest song
upon my mind—if i have failed to snare
the glance too shy—if through my singing slips
the very skilful strangeness of your smile
the keen primeval silence of your hair

—let the world say "his most wise music stole
nothing from death"—
                              you only will create
(who are so perfectly alive)my shame:
lady through whose profound and fragile lips
the sweet small clumsy feet of April came

into the ragged meadow of my soul.

i carry your heart with me(i carry it in
my heart)i am never without it(anywhere
i go you go, my dear;and whatever is done
by only me is your doing,my darling)
                                        i fear
no fate(for you are my fate,my sweet)i want
no world(for beautiful you are my world,my true)
and it's you are whatever a moon has always meant
and whatever a sun will always sing is you

here is the deepest secret nobody knows
(here is the root of the root and the bud of the bud
and the sky of the sky of a tree called life;which grows
higher than soul can hope or mind can hide)
and this is the wonder that's keeping the stars apart

i carry your heart(i carry it in my heart)

❖ JEAN TOOMER ❖

NOVEMBER COTTON FLOWER

Boll-weevil's coming, and the winter's cold,
Made cotton-stalks look rusty, season's old,
And cotton, scarce as any southern snow,
Was vanishing; the branch, so pinched and slow,
Failed in its function as the autumn rake;
Drouth fighting soil had caused the soil to take
All water from the streams; dead birds were found
In wells a hundred feet below the ground—
Such was the season when the flower bloomed.
Old folks were startled, and it soon assumed
Significance. Superstition saw
Something it had never seen before:
Brown eyes that loved without a trace of fear,
Beauty so sudden for that time of year.

❖ ROBERT GRAVES ❖

HISTORY OF THE WORD

The Word that in the beginning was the Word
For two or three, but elsewhere spoke unheard,
Found Words to interpret it, which for a season
Prevailed until ruled out by Law and Reason
Which, by a lax interpretation cursed,
In Laws and Reasons logically dispersed;
These, in their turn, found they could do no better
Than fall to Letters and each claim a letter.
In the beginning then, the Word alone,
But now the various tongue-tied Lexicon
In perfect impotence the day nearing
When every ear shall lose its sense of hearing
And every mind by knowledge be close-shuttered—
But two or three, that hear the Word uttered.

❖ EDMUND BLUNDEN ❖

VLAMERTINGHE: PASSING THE CHATEAU, JULY 1917

"And all her silken flanks with garlands drest"—
But we are coming to the sacrifice.
Must those have flowers who are not yet gone West?
May those have flowers who live with death and lice?
This must be the floweriest place
That earth allows; the queenly face
Of the proud mansion borrows grace for grace
Spite of those brute guns lowing at the skies.

Bold great daisies, golden lights,
Bubbling roses' pinks and whites—
Such a gay carpet! poppies by the million;
Such damask! such vermilion!
But if you ask me, mate, the choice of colour
Is, scarcely right; this red should have been much duller.

FIFTEENTH FAREWELL

I

You may have all things from me, save my breath,
The slight life in my throat will not give pause
For your love, nor your loss, nor any cause.
Shall I be made a panderer to death,
Dig the green ground for darkness underneath,
Let the dust serve me, covering all that was
With all that will be? Better, from time's claws,
The hardened face under the subtle wreath.

Cooler than stones in wells, sweeter, more kind
Than hot, perfidious words, my breathing moves
Close to my plunging blood. Be strong, and hang
Unriven mist over my breast and mind,
My breath! We shall forget the heart that loves,
Though in my body beat its blade, and its fang.

II

I erred, when I thought loneliness the wide
Scent of mown grass over forsaken fields,
Or any shadow isolation yields.
Loneliness was the heart within your side.
Your thought, beyond my touch, was tilted air
Ringed with as many borders as the wind.
How could I judge you gentle or unkind
When all bright flying space was in your care?
Now that I leave you, I shall be made lonely
By simple empty days,—never that chill
Resonant heart to strike between my arms
Again, as though distraught for distance,—only
Levels of evening, now, behind a hill,
Or a late cock-crow from the darkening farms.

SIMPLE AUTUMNAL

The measured blood beats out the year's delay.
The tearless eyes and heart, forbidden grief,
Watch the burned, restless, but abiding leaf,
The brighter branches arming the bright day.

The cone, the curving fruit should fall away,
The vine stem crumble, ripe grain know its sheaf.
Bonded to time, fires should have done, be brief,
But, serfs to sleep, they glitter and they stay.

Because not last nor first, grief in its prime
Wakes in the day, and hears of life's intent.
Sorrow would break the seal stamped over time
And set the baskets where the bough is bent.

Full season's come, yet filled trees keep the sky
And never scent the ground where they must lie.

SONNET

Dark, underground, is furnished with the bone;
The tool's lost, and the counter in the game.
Eaten as though by water or by flame
The elaborate craft built up from wood and stone.

Words made of breath, these also are undone,
And greedy sight abolished in its claim.
Light fails from ruin and from wall the same;
The loud sound and pure silence fall as one.

Worn flesh at last is history and treasure
Unto itself; its scars it still can keep,
Received from love, from memory's false measure,
From pain, from the long dream drawn back in sleep.

Attest, poor body, with what scars you have,
That you left life, to come down to the grave.

SINGLE SONNET

Now, you great stanza, you heroic mould,
Bend to my will, for I must give you love:
The weight in the heart that breathes, but cannot move,
Which to endure flesh only makes so bold.

Take up, take up, as it were lead or gold
The burden; test the dreadful mass thereof.
No stone, slate, metal under or above
Earth, is so ponderous, so dull, so cold.

Too long as ocean bed bears up the ocean,
As earth's core bears the earth, have I borne this;
Too long have lovers, bending for their kiss,
Felt bitter force cohering without motion.

Staunch meter, great song, it is yours, at length,
To prove how stronger you are than my strength.

MUSICIAN

Where have these hands been,
By what delayed,
That so long stayed
Apart from the thin

Strings which they now grace
With their lonely skill?
Music and their cool will
At last interlace.

Now with great ease, and slow,
The thumb, the finger, the strong
Delicate hand plucks the long
String it was born to know.

And, under the palm, the string
Sings as it wished to sing.

❖ HART CRANE ❖

TO EMILY DICKINSON

You who desired so much—in vain to ask—
Yet fed your hunger like an endless task,
Dared dignify the labor, bless the quest—
Achieved that stillness ultimately best,

Being, of all, least sought for: Emily, hear!
O sweet, dead Silencer, most suddenly clear
When singing that Eternity possessed
And plundered momently in every breast;

—Truly no flower yet withers in your hand,
The harvest you descried and understand
Needs more than wit to gather, love to bind.
Some reconcilement of remotest mind—

Leaves Ormus rubyless, and Ophir chill.
Else tears heap all within one clay-cold hill.

❖ ALLEN TATE ❖

from *Sonnets at Christmas*

2

Ah, Christ, I love you rings to the wild sky
And I must think a little of the past:
When I was ten I told a stinking lie
That got a black boy whipped; but now at last
The going years, caught in an accurate glow,
Reverse like balls englished upon green baize—
Let them return, let the round trumpets blow
The ancient crackle of the Christ's deep gaze.
Deafened and blind, with senses yet unfound,
Am I, untutored to the after-wit
Of knowledge, knowing a nightmare has no sound;
Therefore with idle hands and head I sit
In late December before the fire's daze
Punished by crimes of which I would be quit.

❖ YVOR WINTERS ❖

TO EMILY DICKINSON

Dear Emily, my tears would burn your page,
But for the fire-dry line that makes them burn—
Burning my eyes, my fingers, while I turn
Singly the words that crease my heart with age.
If I could make some tortured pilgrimage
Through words or Time or the blank pain of Doom
And kneel before you as you found your tomb,
Then I might rise to face my heritage.

Yours was an empty upland solitude
Bleached to the powder of a dying name;
The mind, lost in a word's lost certitude
That faded as the fading footsteps came
To trace an epilogue to words grown odd
In that hard argument which led to God.

❖ ROY CAMPBELL ❖

LUIS DE CAMÕES

Camões, alone, of all the lyric race,
Born in the angry morning of disaster,
Can look a common soldier in the face:
I find a comrade where I sought a master:
For daily, while the stinking crocodiles
Glide from the mangroves on the swampy shore,
He shares my awning on the dhow, he smiles,
And tells me that he lived it all before.
Through fire and shipwreck, pestilence and loss,
Led by the ignis fatuus of duty
To a dog's death—yet of his sorrows king—
He shouldered high his voluntary Cross,
Wrestled his hardships into forms of beauty,
And taught his gorgon destinies to sing.

YET DO I MARVEL

I doubt not God is good, well-meaning, kind,
And did He stoop to quibble could tell why
The little buried mole continues blind,
Why flesh that mirrors Him must some day die,
Make plain the reason tortured Tantalus
Is baited by the fickle fruit, declare
If merely brute caprice dooms Sisyphus
To struggle up a never-ending stair.
Inscrutable His ways are, and immune
To catechism by a mind too strewn
With petty cares to slightly understand
What awful brain compels His awful hand.
Yet do I marvel at this curious thing:
To make a poet black, and bid him sing!

AT THE WAILING WALL IN JERUSALEM

Of all the grandeur that was Solomon's
High testament of Israel's far pride,
Shedding its lustre like a sun of suns,
This feeble flicker only has not died.
This wall alone reminds a vanquished race,
This brief remembrance still retained in stone,
That sure foundations guard their given place
To rehabilitate the overthrown.

So in the battered temple of the heart,
That grief is harder on than time on stone,
Though three sides crumble, one will stand apart,
Where thought may mourn its past, remembrance groan,
And hands now bare that once were rich with rings
Rebuild upon the ancient site of things.

❖ EDWIN DENBY ❖

AIR

Thin air I breathe and birds use for flying
Over and through trees standing breathing in air
Air insects drop through in insect dying
And deer that use it to listen in, share—

Thickens with mist on the lake, or rain
Cuts it with tasteless water and a grey
Day colours it and it is the thin and plain
Air in my mouth the air for miles away.

So close it feeds me each second, everyone's friend
Hugging outside and inside, I can't get rid
Of air, I know it, till the hateful end
When with it I give up the insanely hid

The airless secret I strangle not to share
With all the others as others share the air.

❖ MERRILL MOORE ❖

THEY ALSO STAND . . .

At midnight, in the garden never planted,
They are unwanted, they were never wanted.

The wanderers in the dark have never come
Upon their use and uses in the kingdom—
The garden with so many in daylight,

With the sun to paint their faces white,
Who were wanted, who were always wanted.

Always asking permission to stand there,
Begging the heel of a loaf, something to wear,
Asking for faggots, fuel, asking for food
(They had none of any), all of them stood,
Standing there as if they were rooted there
Begging, and whether it is fair or unfair,
I, standing apart, have seen them standing there.

❖ PATRICK KAVANAGH ❖

CANAL BANK WALK

Leafy-with-love banks and the green waters of the canal
Pouring redemption for me, that I do
The will of God, wallow in the habitual, the banal,
Grow with nature again as before I grew.
The bright stick trapped, the breeze adding a third
Party to the couple kissing on an old seat,
And a bird gathering materials for the nest for the Word
Eloquently new and abandoned to its delirious beat.
O unworn world enrapture me, encapture me in a web
Of fabulous grass and eternal voices by a beech,
Feed the gaping need of my senses, give me ad lib
To pray unselfconsciously with overflowing speech
For this soul needs to be honoured with a new dress woven
From green and blue things and arguments that cannot be proven.

❖ PHYLLIS McGINLEY ❖

EVENING MUSICALE

Candles. Red tulips, ninety cents the bunch.
  Two lions, Grade B. A newly tuned piano.
No cocktails, but a dubious kind of punch,
  Lukewarm and weak. A harp and a soprano.
The "Lullaby" of Brahms. Somebody's cousin
  From Forest Hills, addicted to the pun.
Two dozen gentlemen; ladies, three dozen,
  Earringed and powdered. Sandwiches at one.

The ash trays few, the ventilation meager.
  Shushes to greet the late-arriving guest
Or quell the punch-bowl group. A young man eager
  To render "Danny Deever" by request.
And sixty people trying to relax
On little rented chairs with gilded backs.

❖ ELLIOTT COLEMAN ❖

from *Oedipus Sonnets*

In a May evening, commuter, king,
On the last platform desperately retching
His purposes. 'O golden bow and string.'
Who locked, unlocked, and locked again the stretching
Corridor of the thorn-dust of the west
Must find a subtler raison d'être hereafter.
Only his love, prevenient now, can wrest
A meaning from his sobs, his brutal laughter.
What he has willed he had better not will again.
Sky and the night unlatch another portal:
Let him ignore it, coolly: last among men
To prove in a gouging of eyes that he is mortal.
There is a legend longer than his race
To scar the beauty of a lover's face.

❖ W. H. AUDEN ❖

WHO'S WHO

A shilling life will give you all the facts:
How Father beat him, how he ran away,
What were the struggles of his youth, what acts
Made him the greatest figure of his day:
Of how he fought, fished, hunted, worked all night,
Though giddy, climbed new mountains; named a sea:
Some of the last researchers even write
Love made him weep his pints like you and me.

With all his honours on, he sighed for one
Who, say astonished critics, lived at home;
Did little jobs about the house with skill
And nothing else; could whistle; would sit still
Or potter round the garden; answered some
Of his long marvellous letters but kept none.

OUR BIAS

The hour-glass whispers to the lion's paw,
The clock-towers tell the gardens day and night,
How many errors Time has patience for,
How wrong they are in being always right.

Yet Time, however loud its chimes or deep,
However fast its falling torrent flows,
Has never put the lion off his leap
Nor shaken the assurance of the rose.

For they, it seems, care only for success:
While we choose words according to their sound
And judge a problem by its awkwardness;

And Time with us was always popular.
When have we not preferred some going round
To going straight to where we are?

MONTAIGNE

Outside his library window he could see
A gentle landscape terrified of grammar,
Cities where lisping was compulsory
And provinces where it was death to stammer.

The hefty lay exhausted. O it took
This donnish undersexed conservative
To start a revolution, and to give
The Flesh its weapons to defeat the Book.

When devils drive the reasonable wild,
They strip their adult century so bare,
Love must be regrown from the sensual child:

To doubt becomes a way of definition,
Even belles lettres legitimate as prayer,
And laziness an act of pure contrition.

RIMBAUD

The nights, the railway-arches, the bad sky,
His horrible companions did not know it;
But in that child the rhetorician's lie
Burst like a pipe: the cold had made a poet.

Drinks bought him by his weak and lyric friend
His senses systematically deranged,
To all accustomed nonsense put an end;
Till he from lyre and weakness was estranged.

Verse was a special illness of the ear;
Integrity was not enough; that seemed
The hell of childhood: he must try again.

Now, galloping through Africa, he dreamed
Of a new self, the son, the engineer,
His truth acceptable to lying men.

BRUSSELS IN WINTER

Wandering the cold streets tangled like old string,
Coming on fountains silent in the frost,
The city still escapes you; it has lost
The qualities that say "I am a Thing."

Only the homeless and the really humbled
Seem to be sure exactly where they are,
And in their misery are all assembled;
The winter holds them like the Opera.

Ridges of rich apartments rise tonight
Where isolated windows glow like farms:
A phrase goes packed with meaning like a van,

A look contains the history of man,
And fifty francs will earn the stranger right
To warm the heartless city in his arms.

from *The Quest: A Sonnet Sequence*

THE DOOR

Out of it steps the future of the poor,
Enigmas, executioners and rules,
Her Majesty in a bad temper or
The red-nosed Fool who makes a fool of fools.

Great persons eye it in the twilight for
A past it might so carelessly let in,
A widow with a missionary grin,
The foaming inundation at a roar.

We pile our all against it when afraid,
And beat upon its panels when we die:
By happening to be open once, it made

Enormous Alice see a wonderland
That waited for her in the sunshine, and,
Simply by being tiny, made her cry.

from *In Time of War*

XII

And the age ended, and the last deliverer died
In bed, grown idle and unhappy; they were safe:
The sudden shadow of the giant's enormous calf
Would fall no more at dusk across the lawn outside.

They slept in peace: in marshes here and there no doubt
A sterile dragon lingered to a natural death,
But in a year the spoor had vanished from the heath;
The kobold's knocking in the mountain petered out.

Only the sculptors and the poets were half sad,
And the pert retinue from the magician's house
Grumbled and went elsewhere. The vanquished powers were glad

To be invisible and free: without remorse
Struck down the sons who strayed into their course,
And ravished the daughters, and drove the fathers mad.

XXVII

Wandering lost upon the mountains of our choice,
Again and again we sigh for an ancient South,
For the warm nude ages of instinctive poise,
For the taste of joy in the innocent mouth.

Asleep in our huts, how we dream of a part
In the glorious balls of the future; each intricate maze
Has a plan, and the disciplined movements of the heart
Can follow for ever and ever its harmless ways.

We envy streams and houses that are sure:
But we are articled to error; we
Were never nude and calm like a great door,

And never will be perfect like the fountains;
We live in freedom by necessity,
A mountain people dwelling among mountains.

❖ LOUIS MacNEICE ❖

SUNDAY MORNING

Down the road someone is practicing scales,
The notes like little fishes vanish with a wink of tails,
Man's heart expands to tinker with his car
For this is Sunday morning, Fate's great bazaar,
Regard these means as ends, concentrate on this Now,
And you may grow to music or drive beyond Hindhead anyhow,
Take corners on two wheels until you go so fast
That you can clutch a fringe or two of the windy past,
That you can abstract this day and make it to the week of time
A small eternity, a sonnet self-contained in rhyme.

But listen, up the road, something gulps, the church spire
Opens its eight bells out, skulls' mouths which will not tire
To tell how there is no music or movement which secures
Escape from the weekday time. Which deadens and endures.

❖ MALCOLM LOWRY ❖

DELIRIUM IN VERA CRUZ

Where has tenderness gone, he asked the mirror
Of the Biltmore Hotel, cuarto 216. Alas,
Can its reflection lean against the glass
Too, wondering where I have gone, into what horror?
Is that it staring at me now with terror
Behind your frail tilted barrier? Tenderness
Was here, in this very bedroom, in this
Place, its form seen, cries heard, by you. What error
Is here? Am I that rashed image?
Is this the ghost of the love you reflected?
Now with a background of tequila, stubs, dirty collars,
Sodium perborate, and a scrawled page
To the dead, telephone off the hook? In rage
He smashed all the glass in the room. (Bill: $50.)

❖ JAMES REEVES ❖

LEAVING TOWN

It was impossible to leave the town.
Bumping across a maze of obsolete rails
Three times we reached the gasworks and reversed.
We could not get away from the canal;
Dead cats, dead hopes, in those grey deeps immersed,
Over our efforts breathed a spectral prayer.
The cattle-market and the gospel-hall
Returned like fictions of our own despair,
And like Hesperides the suburbs seemed,
Shining far off towards the guiltless fields.
We finished in a little cul-de-sac
Where on the pavement sat a ragged girl
Mourning beside a jug-and-bottle entrance.
Once more we turned the car and started back.

"Without that once clear aim, the path of flight"

Without that once clear aim, the path of flight
To follow for a lifetime through white air,
This century chokes me under roots of night
I suffer like history in Dark Ages, where
Truth lies in dungeons, from which drifts no whisper:
We hear of towers long broken off from sight
And tortures and war, in dark and smoky rumor,
But on men's buried lives there falls no light.
Watch me who walk through coiling streets where rain
And fog drown every cry: at corners of day
Road drills explore new areas of pain,
Nor summer nor light may reach down here to play.
The city builds its horror in my brain,
This writing is my only wings away.

THE PRODIGAL

The brown enormous odor he lived by
was too close, with its breathing and thick hair,
for him to judge. The floor was rotten; the sty
was plastered halfway up with glass-smooth dung.
Light-lashed, self-righteous, above moving snouts,
the pigs' eyes followed him, a cheerful stare—
even to the sow that always ate her young—
till, sickening, he leaned to scratch her head.
But sometimes mornings after drinking bouts
(he hid the pints behind a two-by-four),
the sunrise glazed the barnyard mud with red;
the burning puddles seemed to reassure.
And then he thought he almost might endure
his exile yet another year or more.

But evenings the first star came to warn.
The farmer whom he worked for came at dark
to shut the cows and horses in the barn
beneath their overhanging clouds of hay,
with pitchforks, faint forked lightnings, catching light,
safe and companionable as in the Ark.
The pigs stuck out their little feet and snored.
The lantern—like the sun, going away—
laid on the mud a pacing aureole.
Carrying a bucket along a slimy board,
he felt the bats' uncertain staggering flight,
his shuddering insights, beyond his control,
touching him. But it took him a long time
finally to make his mind up to go home.

SONNET

Caught—the bubble
in the spirit-level,
a creature divided;
and the compass needle
wobbling and wavering,
undecided.
Freed—the broken
thermometer's mercury
running away;
and the rainbow-bird
from the narrow bevel
of the empty mirror,
flying wherever
it feels like, gay!

❖ GEORGE BARKER ❖

TO MY MOTHER

Most near, most dear, most loved and most far,
Under the window where I often found her
Sitting as huge as Asia, seismic with laughter,
Gin and chicken helpless in her Irish hand,
Irresistible as Rabelais, but most tender for
The lame dogs and hurt birds that surround her,—
She is a procession no one can follow after
But be like a little dog following a brass band.

She will not glance up at the bomber, or condescend
To drop her gin and scuttle to a cellar,
But leans on the mahogany table like a mountain
Whom only faith can move, and so I send
O all my faith, and all my love to tell her
That she will move from mourning into morning.

THOSE WINTER SUNDAYS

Sundays too my father got up early
and put his clothes on in the blueblack cold,
then with cracked hands that ached
from labor in the weekday weather made
banked fires blaze. No one ever thanked him.

I'd wake and hear the cold splintering, breaking.
When the rooms were warm, he'd call,
and slowly I would rise and dress,
fearing the chronic angers of that house,

Speaking indifferently to him,
who had driven out the cold
and polished my good shoes as well.
What did I know, what did I know
of love's austere and lonely offices.

FREDERICK DOUGLASS

When it is finally ours, this freedom, this liberty, this beautiful
and terrible thing, needful to man as air,
usable as earth; when it belongs at last to all,
when it is truly instinct, brain matter, diastole, systole,
reflex action; when it is finally won; when it is more
than the gaudy mumbo jumbo of politicians:
this man, this Douglass, this former slave, this Negro
beaten to his knees, exiled, visioning a world
where none is lonely, none hunted, alien,
this man, superb in love and logic, this man
shall be remembered. Oh, not with statues' rhetoric,
not with legends and poems and wreaths of bronze alone,
but with the lives grown out of his life, the lives
fleshing his dream of the beautiful, needful thing.

❖ MURIEL RUKEYSER ❖

ON THE DEATH OF HER MOTHER

A seacoast late at night and a wheel of wind.
All those years, Mother, your arms were full of absence
And all the running of arrows could never not once find
Anything but your panic among all that substance,
Until your wide eyes opened forever. Until it all was true.
The fears were true. In that cold country, winter,
The wordless king, went isolate and cruel,
And he alone real. His armies all that entered.

But here is peacock daybreak; thought-yoked and warm, the light,
The cloud-companions and the greenest star.
Starflash on water; the embryo in the foam.
Dives through my body in the waking bright,
Watchmen of birth; I see. You are here, Mother, and you are
Dead, and here is your gift: my life which is my home.

❖ DELMORE SCHWARTZ ❖

THE BEAUTIFUL AMERICAN WORD, SURE

The beautiful American word, Sure,
As I have come into a room, and touch
The lamp's button, and the light blooms with such
Certainty where the darkness loomed before,

As I care for what I do not know, and care
Knowing for little she might not have been,
And for how little she would be unseen,
The intercourse of lives miraculous and dear.

Where the light is, and each thing clear,
Separate from all others, standing in its place,
I drink the time and touch whatever's near,

And hope for day when the whole world has that face:
For what assures her present every year?
In dark accidents the mind's sufficient grace.

❖ JOHN BERRYMAN ❖

from *Berryman's Sonnets*

7

I've found out why, that day, that suicide
From the Empire State falling on someone's car
Troubled you so; and why we quarrelled. War,
Illness, an accident, I can see (you cried)
But not this: what a bastard, not spring wide! . .
I said a man, life in his teeth, could care
Not much just whom he spat it on . . and far
Beyond my laugh we argued either side.

'One has a right not to be fallen on! . . '
(Our second meeting . . yellow you were wearing.)
Voices of our resistance and desire!
Did I divine then I must shortly run
Crazy with need to fall on you, despairing?
Did you bolt so, before it caught, our fire?

15

What was Ashore, then? . . Cargoed with Forget,
My ship runs down a midnight winter storm
Between whirlpool and rock, and my white love's form
Gleams at the wheel, her hair streams. When we met
Seaward, Thought frank & guilty to each oar set
Hands careless of port as of the waters' harm.
Endless a wet wind wears my sail, dark swarm
Endless of sighs and veering hopes, love's fret.

Rain of tears, real, mist of imagined scorn,
No rest accords the fraying shrouds, all thwart
Already with mistakes, foresight so short.
Muffled in capes of waves my clear sighs, torn,
Hitherto most clear,—Loyalty and Art.
And I begin now to despair of port.

(after Petrarch and Wyatt)

36

Keep your eyes open when you kiss: do: when
You kiss. All silly time else, close them to;
Unsleeping, I implore you (dear) pursue
In darkness me, as I do you again
Instantly we part . . only me both then
And when your fingers fall, let there be two
Only, 'in that dream-kingdom': I would have you
Me alone recognize your citizen.

Before who wanted eyes, making love, so?
I do now. However we are driven and hide,
What state we keep all other states condemn,
We see ourselves, we watch the solemn glow
Of empty courts we kiss in . . Open wide!
You do, you do, and I look into them.

107

Darling I wait O in my upstairs box
O for your footfall, O for your footfall
in the extreme heat—I don't mind at all,
it's silence has me and the no of clocks
keeping us isolated longer: rocks
did the first martyr and will do to stall
our enemies, I'll get up on the roof of the hall
and heave freely. The University of Soft Knocks

will headlines in the *Times* make: Fellow goes mad,
crowd panics, rhododendrons injured. Slow
will flow the obituaries while the facts get straight,
almost straight. He was in love and he was had.
That was it: he should have stuck to his own mate,
before he went a-coming across the sea-O.

All we were going strong last night this time,
the *mots* were flying & the frozen daiquiris
were downing, supine on the floor lay Lise
listening to Schubert grievous & sublime,
my head was frantic with a following rime:
it was a good evening, an evening to please,
I kissed her in the kitchen—ecstasies—
among so much good we tamped down the crime.

The weather's changing. This morning was cold,
as I made for the grove, without expectation,
some hundred Sonnets in my pocket, old,
to read her if she came. Presently the sun
yellowed the pines & my lady came not
in blue jeans & a sweater. I sat down & wrote.

❖ WELDON KEES ❖

FOR MY DAUGHTER

Looking into my daughter's eyes I read
Beneath the innocence of morning flesh
Concealed, hintings of death she does not heed.
Coldest of winds have blown this hair, and mesh
Of seaweed snarled these miniatures of hands;
The night's slow poison, tolerant and bland,
Has moved her blood. Parched years that I have seen
That may be hers appear: foul, lingering
Death in certain war, the slim legs green.
Or, fed on hate, she relishes the sting
Of others' agony; perhaps the cruel
Bride of a syphilitic or a fool.
These speculations sour in the sun.
I have no daughter. I desire none.

❖ WILLIAM STAFFORD ❖

TIME

The years to come (empty boxcars
waiting on a siding while someone forgets
and the tall grass tickles their bellies)
will sometime stay, rusted still;
and a little boy who clambers up,
saved by his bare feet, will run
along the top, jump to the last car,
and gaze down at the end into that river
near every town.
           Once when I was a boy
I took that kind of walk,
beyond the last houses, out where the grass
lived, then the tired siding where trains whistled.
The river was choked with old Chevies and Fords.
And that was the day the world ended.

❖ DYLAN THOMAS ❖

AMONG THOSE KILLED IN THE DAWN RAID WAS
A MAN AGED A HUNDRED

When the morning was waking over the war
He put on his clothes and stepped out and he died,
The locks yawned loose and a blast blew them wide,
He dropped where he loved on the burst pavement stone
And the funeral grains of the slaughtered floor.
Tell his street on its back he stopped a sun
And the craters of his eyes grew springshoots and fire
When all the keys shot from the locks, and rang.
Dig no more for the chains of his gray-haired heart.
The heavenly ambulance drawn by a wound
Assembling waits for the spade's ring on the cage.
O keep his bones away from that common cart,
The morning is flying on the wings of his age
And a hundred storks perch on the sun's right hand.

❖ MARGARET WALKER ❖

CHILDHOOD

When I was a child I knew red miners
dressed raggedly and wearing carbide lamps.
I saw them come down red hills to their camps
dyed with red dust from old Ishkooda mines.
Night after night I met them on the roads,
or on the streets in town I caught their glance;
the swing of dinner buckets in their hands,
and grumbling undermining all their words.

I also lived in low cotton country
where moonlight hovered over ripe haystacks,
or stumps of trees, and croppers' rotting shacks
with famine, terror, flood, and plague near by;
where sentiment and hatred still held sway
and only bitter land was washed away.

FOR MALCOLM X

All you violated ones with gentle hearts;
You violent dreamers whose cries shout heartbreak;
Whose voices echo clamors of our cool capers,
And whose black faces have hollowed pits for eyes.
All you gambling sons and hooked children and bowery bums
Hating white devils and black bourgeoisie,
Thumbing your noses at your burning red suns,
Gather round this coffin and mourn your dying swan.

Snow-white moslem head-dress around a dead black face!
Beautiful were your sand-papering words against our skins!
Our blood and water pour from your flowing wounds.
You have cut open our breasts and dug scalpels in our brains.
When and where will another come to take your holy place?
Old man mumbling in his dotage, or crying child, unborn?

from *The Children of the Poor*

I

People who have no children can be hard:
Attain a mail of ice and insolence:
Need not pause in the fire, and in no sense
Hesitate in the hurricane to guard.
And when wide world is bitten and bewarred
They perish purely, waving their spirits hence
Without a trace of grace or of offense
To laugh or fail, diffident, wonder-starred.
While through a throttling dark we others hear
The little lifting helplessness, the queer
Whimper-whine; whose unridiculous
Lost softness softly makes a trap for us.
And makes a curse. And makes a sugar of
The malocclusions, the inconditions of love.

4

First fight. Then fiddle. Ply the slipping string
With feathery sorcery; muzzle the note
With hurting love; the music that they wrote
Bewitch, bewilder. Qualify to sing
Threadwise. Devise no salt, no hempen thing
For the dear instrument to bear. Devote
The bow to silks and honey. Be remote
A while from malice and from murdering.
But first to arms, to armor. Carry hate
In front of you and harmony behind.
Be deaf to music and to beauty blind.
Win war. Rise bloody, maybe not too late
For having first to civilize a space
Wherein to play your violin with grace.

from *Gay Chaps at the Bar*

GAY CHAPS AT THE BAR

. . . and guys I knew in the States, young officers, return from the front crying
and trembling. Gay chaps at the bar in Los Angeles, Chicago, New York . . .
—LIEUTENANT WILLIAM COUCH IN THE SOUTH PACIFIC

We knew how to order. Just the dash
Necessary. The length of gaiety in good taste.
Whether the raillery should be slightly iced
And given green, or served up hot and lush.
And we knew beautifully how to give to women
The summer spread, the tropics, of our love.
When to persist, or hold a hunger off.
Knew white speech. How to make a look an omen.
But nothing ever taught us to be islands.
And smart, athletic language for this hour
Was not in the curriculum. No stout
Lesson showed how to chat with death. We brought
No brass fortissimo, among our talents,
To holler down the lions in this air.

STILL DO I KEEP MY LOOK, MY IDENTITY . . .

Each body has its art, its precious prescribed
Pose, that even in passion's droll contortions, waltzes,
Or push of pain—or when a grief has stabbed,
Or hatred hacked—is its, and nothing else's.
Each body has its pose. No other stock
That is irrevocable, perpetual
And its to keep. In castle or in shack.
With rags or robes. Through good, nothing, or ill.
And even in death a body, like no other
On any hill or plain or crawling cot
Or gentle for the lilyless hasty pall
(Having twisted, gagged, and then sweet-ceased to bother),
Shows the old personal art, the look. Shows what
It showed at baseball. What it showed in school.

MY DREAMS, MY WORKS, MUST WAIT TILL AFTER HELL

I hold my honey and I store my bread
In little jars and cabinets of my will.
I label clearly, and each latch and lid
I bid, Be firm till I return from hell.
I am very hungry. I am incomplete.
And none can tell when I may dine again.
No man can give me any word but Wait,
The puny light. I keep eyes pointed in;
Hoping that, when the devil days of my hurt
Drag out to their last dregs and I resume
On such legs as are left me, in such heart
As I can manage, remember to go home,
My taste will not have turned insensitive
To honey and bread old purity could love.

PIANO AFTER WAR

On a snug evening I shall watch her fingers,
Cleverly ringed, declining to clever pink,
Beg glory from the willing keys. Old hungers
Will break their coffins, rise to eat and thank.
And music, warily, like the golden rose
That sometimes after sunset warms the west,
Will warm that room, persuasively suffuse
That room and me, rejuvenate a past.
But suddenly, across my climbing fever
Of proud delight—a multiplying cry.
A cry of bitter dead men who will never
Attend a gentle maker of musical joy.
Then my thawed eye will go again to ice.
And stone will shove the softness from my face.

THE PROGRESS

And still we wear our uniforms, follow
The cracked cry of the bugles, comb and brush
Our pride and prejudice, doctor the sallow
Initial ardor, wish to keep it fresh.
Still we applaud the President's voice and face.
Still we remark on patriotism, sing,
Salute the flag, thrill heavily, rejoice
For death of men who too saluted, sang.
But inward grows a soberness, an awe,
A fear, a deepening hollow through the cold.
For even if we come out standing up
How shall we smile, congratulate: and how
Settle in chairs? Listen, listen. The step
Of iron feet again. And again wild.

❖ CHARLES CAUSLEY ❖

AUTOBIOGRAPHY

Now that my seagoing self-possession wavers
I sit and write the letter you will not answer.
The razor at my wrist patiently severs
Passion from thought, of which the flesh is censor.
I walk by the deep canal where moody lovers
Find their Nirvana on each other's tongues,
And in my naked bed the usual fevers
Invade the tropic sense, brambling the lungs.
I am drowned to the sound of seven flooding rivers
The distant Bombay drum and the ghazel dancer,
But the English Sunday, monstrous as India, shivers,
And the voice of the muezzin is the voice of the station announcer.
The wet fields blot the bitterness of the cry,
And I turn from the tactful friend to the candid sky.

HISTORY

History has to live with what was here,
clutching and close to fumbling all we had—
it is so dull and gruesome how we die,
unlike writing, life never finishes.
Abel was finished; death is not remote,
a flash-in-the-pan electrifies the skeptic,
his cows crowding like skulls against high-voltage wire,
his baby crying all night like a new machine.
As in our Bibles, white-faced, predatory,
the beautiful, mist-drunken hunter's moon ascends—
a child could give it a face: two holes, two holes,
my eyes, my mouth, between them a skull's no-nose—
O there's a terrifying innocence in my face
drenched with the silver salvage of the mornfrost.

WORDS FOR HART CRANE

"When the Pulitzers showered on some dope
or screw who flushed our dry mouths out with soap,
few people would consider why I took
to stalking sailors, and scattered Uncle Sam's
phony gold-plated laurels to the birds.
Because I knew my Whitman like a book,
stranger in America, tell my country: I,
Catullus redivivus, once the rage
of the Village and Paris, used to play my role
of homosexual, wolfing the stray lambs
who hungered by the Place de la Concorde.
My profit was a pocket with a hole.
Who asks for me, the Shelley of my age,
must lay his heart out for my bed and board."

EZRA POUND

Horizontal in a deckchair on the bleak ward,
some feeble-minded felon in pajamas, clawing
a Social Credit broadside from your table, you saying,
". . . here with a black suit and black briefcase; in the briefcase,
an abomination, Possum's *hommage* to Milton."
Then sprung; Rapallo, and then the decade gone;
then three years, then Eliot dead, you saying,
"And who is left to understand my jokes?
My old Brother in the arts . . . and besides, he was a smash of poet."
He showed us his blotched, bent hands, saying, "Worms.
When I talked that nonsense about Jews on the Rome
wireless, she knew it was shit, and still loved me."
And I, "Who else has been in Purgatory?"
And he, "To begin with a swelled head and end with swelled feet."

ROBERT FROST

Robert Frost at midnight, the audience gone
to vapor, the great act laid on the shelf in mothballs,
his voice is musical and raw—he writes in the flyleaf:
For Robert from Robert, his friend in the art.
"Sometimes I feel too full of myself," I say.
And he, misunderstanding, "When I am low,
I stray away. My son wasn't your kind. The night
we told him Merrill Moore would come to treat him,
he said, 'I'll kill him first.' One of my daughters thought things,
thought every male she met was out to make her;
the way she dressed, she couldn't make a whorehouse."
And I, "Sometimes I'm so happy I can't stand myself."
And he, "When I am too full of joy, I think
how little good my health did anyone near me."

FISHNET

Any clear thing that blinds us with surprise,
your wandering silences and bright trouvailles,
dolphin let loose to catch the flashing fish . . .
saying too little, then too much.
Poets die adolescents, their beat embalms them,
the archetypal voices sing offkey;
the old actor cannot read his friends,
and nevertheless he reads himself aloud,
genius hums the auditorium dead.
The line must terminate.
Yet my heart rises, I know I've gladdened a lifetime
knotting, undoing a fishnet of tarred rope;
the net will hang on the wall when the fish are eaten,
nailed like illegible bronze on the futureless future.

DOLPHIN

My Dolphin, you only guide me by surprise,
captive as Racine, the man of craft,
drawn through his maze of iron composition
by the incomparable wandering voice of Phèdre.
When I was troubled in mind, you made for my body
caught in its hangman's-knot of sinking lines,
the glassy bowing and scraping of my will. . . .
I have sat and listened to too many
words of the collaborating muse,
and plotted perhaps too freely with my life,
not avoiding injury to others,
not avoiding injury to myself—
to ask compassion . . . this book, half fiction,
an eelnet made by man for the eel fighting—

my eyes have seen what my hand did.

❖ WILLIAM MEREDITH ❖

THE ILLITERATE

Touching your goodness, I am like a man
Who turns a letter over in his hand
And you might think this was because the hand
Was unfamiliar but, truth is, the man
Has never had a letter from anyone;
And now he is both afraid of what it means
And ashamed because he has no other means
To find out what it says than to ask someone.

His uncle could have left the farm to him,
Or his parents died before he sent them word,
Or the dark girl changed and want him for beloved.
Afraid and letter-proud, he keeps it with him.
What would you call his feeling for the words
That keep him rich and orphaned and beloved?

❖ AMY CLAMPITT ❖

THE CORMORANT IN ITS ELEMENT

That bony potbellied arrow, wing-pumping along
implacably, with a ramrod's rigid adherence,
airborne, to the horizontal, discloses talents
one would never have guessed at. Plummeting

waterward, big black feet splayed for a landing
gear, slim head turning and turning, vermilion-
strapped, this way and that, with a lightning glance
over the shoulder, the cormorant astounding-

ly, in one sleek involuted arabesque, a vertical
turn on a dime, goes into that inimitable
vanishing-and-emerging-from-under-the-briny-

deep act which, unlike the works of Homo Houdini,
is performed for reasons having nothing at all
to do with ego, guilt, ambition, or even money.

❖ HOWARD NEMEROV ❖

A PRIMER OF THE DAILY ROUND

A peels an apple, while B kneels to God,
C telephones to D, who has a hand
On E's knee, F coughs, G turns up the sod
For H's grave, I do not understand
But J is bringing one clay pigeon down
While K brings down a nightstick on L's head,
And M takes mustard, N drives into town,
O goes to bed with P, and Q drops dead,
R lies to S, but happens to be heard
By T, who tells U not to fire V
For having to give W the word
That X is now deceiving Y with Z,
    Who happens just now to remember A
    Peeling an apple somewhere far away.

❖ HAYDEN CARRUTH ❖

from *Sonnets*

2

How is it, tell me, that this new self can be—
and so quickly? God knows, none is the lord
of his own face or ever was. So what accord
of rearranging nuclei changes me
into this alien now so familiarly
staring from the bathroom mirror? What word
reforms my mind and all its wretched hoard
of worn-out feelings suddenly fresh and free?
Woman, I'm not sure of much. Are you?
More and more I believe the age demands
incertitude. I am no one. Yet your hands,
touching, word-like, can make a person. Who
is the strange new myself? Woman, do we know
the I of love that you in love bestow?

3

Last night, I don't know if from habit or intent,
when we lay together you left the door ajar,
a small light in which to see how you are
very beautiful. I saw. And so we spent
ourselves in this private light; the hours went
in a kind of wisdom, the night in a love far
inward drawn to the hot center of our
compassion, which was a wonderment
to me.
      But today in a cold snow-light,
so public and glaring, I have seen a wrong,
a brutal human wrong, done in my sight
to you, and the world I have tried to put in song
is more ugly to me now than I can say.
Love, we must keep our own light through the day.

4

While you stood talking at the counter, cutting
leftover meat for a casserole, out came
a cruelty done you—yes, almost the same
as others, but of such evil I think nothing
could enter my mind like this and be shut in
forever, black and awful. No tears of shame
secreted from all humanity's self-blame
will ever leach it or cover it. What in
this world or out of it, Christ, you horrid
cadaver, permitted you to permit this
to happen to her? Silly to think a kiss
or a sonnet or anything might help: that coward
did what he did. Evil is more than love.
It is consciousness, whatever we're conscious of.

5

From our very high window at the Sheraton
in Montreal, amazed I stood a long time
gazing at Cosmopolis outward and down
in all its million glitterings, I who am
a countryman temerarious and lost
like our planet in the great galaxy,
one spark, one speck, one instant, yet the most
part of my thought was not displeasing to me,
but rather an excitement, a dare that could
still raise my pulse-rate after these sixty years
to exult in humanity so variable and odd
and burgeoning, so that bewildered tears
stood briefly in my eyes when we went to bed.
For hours we made love and the night sped.

❖   ❖   ❖

SONNET

Well, she told me I had an aura. "What?" I said.
"An aura," she said. "I heered you," I said, "but
you ain't significating." "What I mean, you got
this fuzzy light like, all around your head,
same as Nell the epelectric when she's nigh read-
y to have a fit, only you ain't having no fit."
"Why, that's a fact," I said, "and I ain't about
to neither. I reckon it's more like that dead
rotten fir stump by the edge of the swamp on misty
nights long about cucumber-blossoming time
when the foxfire's flickering round." "I be goddamn
if that's it," she said. "Why, you ain't but sixty-
nine, you ain't a-rotting yet. What I say
is you got a goddamn naura." "Ok," I said. "Ok."

LATE SONNET

For that the sonnet no doubt was my own true
singing and suchlike other song, for that
I gave it up half-coldheartedly to set
my lines in a fashion that proclaimed its virtue
original in young arrogant artificers who
had not my geniality nor voice, and yet
their fashionableness was persuasive to me,—what
shame and sorrow I pay!
                    And that I knew
that beautiful hot old man Sidney Bechet
and heard his music often but not what he
was saying, that tone, phrasing, and free play
of feeling mean more than originality,
these being the actual qualities of song.
Nor is it essential to be young.

❖   MARIE PONSOT   ❖

OUT OF EDEN

Under the May rain over the dug grave
my mother is given canticles and I who believe
in everything watch flowers stiffen to new bloom.

Behind us the rented car fabricates a cave.
My mother nods: Is he? He is. But, is? Nods.
Angels shoo witches from this American tomb.

The nod teaches me. It is something I can save.
He left days ago. We, so that we too may leave,
install his old belongings in a bizarre new room.
I want to kneel indignantly anywhere and rave.

    Well, God help us, now my father's will is God's.
    At games and naming he beat Adam. He loved his Eve.
    I knew him and his wicked tongue. What he had, he gave.

I do not know where to go to do it, but I grieve.

CALL

Child like a candelabra at the head
of my bed, wake in me & watch me as
I sleep; maintain your childlife undistracted
where, at the borders of its light, it has
such dulcet limits it becomes the dark.
Maintain against my hungry selfishness
your simple gaze where fear has left no mark.

Today my dead mother to my distress
said on the dreamphone, "Marie, I'll come read
to you," hung up, & in her usual dress
came & stood here. Cold—though I know I need
her true message—I faced her with tenderness
& said, "This isn't right," & she agreed.

Child, watched by your deeper sleep, I may yet say yes.

❖ RICHARD WILBUR ❖

PRAISE IN SUMMER

Obscurely yet most surely called to praise,
As sometimes summer calls us all, I said
The hills are heavens full of branching ways
Where star-nosed moles fly overhead the dead;
I said the trees are mines in air, I said
See how the sparrow burrows in the sky!
And then I wondered why this mad *instead*
Perverts our praise to uncreation, why
Such savor's in this wrenching things awry.
Does sense so stale that it must needs derange
The world to know it? To a praiseful eye
Should it not be enough of fresh and strange
That trees grow green, and moles can course in clay,
And sparrows sweep the ceiling of our day?

❖ PHILIP LARKIN ❖

"Love, we must part now: do not let it be"

Love, we must part now: do not let it be
Calamitous and bitter. In the past
There has been too much moonlight and self-pity:
Let us have done with it: for now at last
Never has sun more boldly paced the sky,
Never were hearts more eager to be free,
To kick down worlds, lash forests; you and I
No longer hold them; we are husks, that see
The grain going forward to a different use.

There is regret. Always, there is regret.
But it is better that our lives unloose,
As two tall ships, wind-mastered, wet with light,
Break from an estuary with their courses set,
And waving part, and waving drop from sight.

DOUBLE SONNET

I recall everything, but more than all,
Words being nothing now, an ease that ever
Remembers her to my unfailing fever,
How she came forward to me, letting fall
Lamplight upon her dress till every small
Motion made visible seemed no mere endeavor
Of body to articulate its offer,
But more a grace won by the way from all
Striving in what is difficult, from all
Losses, so that she moved but to discover
A practice of the blood, as the gulls hover,
Winged with their life, above the harbor wall,
Tracing inflected silence in the tall
Air with a tilt of mastery and quiver
Against the light, as the light fell to favor
Her coming forth; this chiefly I recall.

It is a part of pride, guiding the hand
At the piano in the splash and passage
Of sacred dolphins, making numbers human
By sheer extravagance that can command
Pythagorean heavens to spell their message
Of some unlooked-for peace, out of the common;
Taking no thought at all that man and woman,
Lost in the trance of lamplight, felt the presage
Of the unbidden terror and bone hand
Of gracelessness, and the unspoken omen
That yet shall render all, by its first usage,
Speechless, inept, and totally unmanned.

THE FEAST OF STEPHEN

I

The coltish horseplay of the locker room,
Moist with the steam of the tiled shower stalls,
With shameless blends of civet, musk and sweat,
Loud with the cap-gun snapping of wet towels
Under the steel-ribbed cages of bare bulbs,
In some such setting of thick basement pipes
And janitorial realities
Boys for the first time frankly eye each other,
Inspect each others' bodies at close range,
And what they see is not so much another
As a strange, possible version of themselves,
And all the sparring dance, adrenal life,
Tense, jubilant nimbleness, is but a vague,
Busy, unfocused ballet of self-love.

II

If the heart has its reasons, perhaps the body
Has its own lumbering sort of carnal spirit,
Felt in the tingling bruises of collision,
And known to captains as *esprit de corps.*
What is this brisk fraternity of timing,
Pivot and lobbing arc, or indirection,
Mens sana in men's sauna, in the flush
Of health and toilets, private and corporal glee,
These fleet caroms, *pliés* and genuflections
Before the salmon-leap, the leaping fountain
All sheathed in glistening light, flexed and alert?
From the vast echo-chamber of the gym,
Among the scumbled shouts and shrill of whistles,
The bounced basketball sound of a leather whip.

III

Think of those barren places where men gather
To act in the terrible name of rectitude,
Of acned shame, punk's pride, muscle or turf,
The bully's thin superiority.
Think of the *Sturm-Abteilungs Kommandant*
Who loves Beethoven and collects Degas,
Or the blond boys in jeans whose narrowed eyes
Are focussed by some hard and smothered lust,
Who lounge in a studied mimicry of ease,
Flick their live butts into the standing weeds,
And comb their hair in the mirror of cracked windows
Of an abandoned warehouse where they keep
In darkened readiness for their occasion
The rope, the chains, handcuffs and gasoline.

IV

Out in the rippled heat of a neighbor's field,
In the kilowatts of noon, they've got one cornered.
The bugs are jumping, and the burly youths
Strip to the waist for the hot work ahead.
They go to arm themselves at the dry-stone wall,
Having flung down their wet and salty garments
At the feet of a young man whose name is Saul.
He watches sharply these superbly tanned
Figures with a swimmer's chest and shoulders,
A miler's thighs, with their self-conscious grace,
And in between their sleek, converging bodies,
Brilliantly oiled and burnished by the sun,
He catches a brief glimpse of bloodied hair
And hears an unintelligible prayer.

PRAISE

But I love this poor earth,
because I have not seen another. . . .
—OSIP MANDELSTAM

Between five and fifty
most people construct a little lifetime:
they fall in love, make kids, they suffer
and pitch the usual tents of understanding.
But I have built a few unexpected bridges.
Out of inert stone, with its longing to embrace inert stone,
I have sent a few vaults into stainless air.
Is this enough—when I love our poor sister earth?
Sister earth, I kneel and ask pardon.
A clod of turf is no less than inert stone.
Nothing is enough!
In this field set free for our play
who could have foretold
I would live to write at fifty?

THE WALL

The walls surrounding them they never saw;
The angels, often. Angels were as common
As birds or butterflies, but looked more human.
As long as the wings were furled, they felt no awe.
Beasts, too, were friendly. They could find no flaw
In all of Eden: this was the first omen.
The second was the dream which woke the woman.
She dreamed she saw the lion sharpen his claw.
As for the fruit, it had no taste at all.
They had been warned of what was bound to happen.
They had been told of something called the world.
They had been told and told about the wall.
They saw it now; the gate was standing open.
As they advanced, the giant wings unfurled.

for John Berryman

MRS. SNOW

Busts of the great composers glimmered in niches,
Pale stars. Poor Mrs. Snow, who could forget her,
Calling the time out in that hushed falsetto?
(How early we begin to grasp what kitsch is!)
But when she loomed above us like an alp,
We little towns below would feel her shadow.
Somehow her nods of approval seemed to matter
More than the stray flakes drifting from her scalp.
Her etchings of ruins, her mass-production Mings
Were our first culture: she put us in awe of things.
And once, with her help, I composed a waltz,
Too innocent to be completely false
Perhaps, but full of marvellous clichés.
She beamed and softened then.
                              Ah, those were the days.

In a hotel room by the sea, the Master
Sits brooding on the continent he has crossed.
Not that he foresees immediate disaster,
Only a sort of freshness being lost—
Or should he go on calling it Innocence?
The sad-faced monsters of the plains are gone;
Wall Street controls the wilderness. There's an immense
Novel in all this waiting to be done,
But not, not—sadly enough—by him. His talents,
Such as they may be, want an older theme,
One rather more civilized than this, on balance.
For him now always the consoling dream
Is just the mild dear light of Lamb House falling
Beautifully down the pages of his calling.

❖ **JAMES K. BAXTER** ❖

from *Jerusalem Sonnets*

The small gray cloudy louse that nests in my beard
Is not, as some have called it, "a pearl of God"—

No, it is a fiery-tormentor
Waking me at two a.m.

Or thereabouts, when the lights are still on
In the houses in the pa, to go across thick grass

Wet with rain, feet cold, to kneel
For an hour or two in front of the red flickering

Tabernacle light—what He sees inside
My meandering mind I can only guess—

A madman, a nobody, a raconteur
Whom He can joke with—"Lord," I ask Him,

"Do You or don't You expect me to put up with lice?"
His silent laugh still shakes the hills at dawn.

❖ JAMES MERRILL ❖

MARSYAS

I used to write in the café sometimes:
Poems on menus, read all over town
Or talked out before ever written down.
One day a girl brought in his latest book.
I opened it—stiff rhythms, gorgeous rhymes—
And made a face. Then crash! my cup upset.
Of twenty upward looks mine only met
His, that gold archaic lion's look

Wherein I saw my wiry person skinned
Of every skill it labored to acquire
And heard the plucked nerve's elemental twang.
They found me dangling where his golden wind
Inflicted so much music on the lyre
That no one could have told you what he sang.

LAST WORDS

My life, your light green eyes
Have lit on me with joy.
There's nothing I don't know
Or shall not know again,
Over and over again.
It's noon, it's dawn, it's night,
I am the dog that dies
In the deep street of Troy
Tomorrow, long ago—
Part of me dims with pain,
Becomes the stinging flies,
The bent head of the boy.
Part looks into your light
And lives to tell you so.

❖ W. D. SNODGRASS ❖

Μή τις . . . Οὖτις

for R. M. Powell

He fed them generously who were his flocks,
Picked, shatterbrained, for food. Passed as a goat
Among his sheep, I cast off. Though hurled rocks
And prayers deranged by torment tossed our boat,
I could not silence, somehow, this defiant
Mind. From my fist into the frothed wake ran
The white eye's gluten of the living giant
I had escaped, by trickery, as no man.

Unseen where all seem stone blind, pure disguise
Has brought me home alone to No Man's land
To look at nothing I dare recognize.
My dead blind guide, you lead me here to claim,
Still waters that will never wash my hand,
To kneel by my old face and know my name.

❖ JOHN ASHBERY ❖

RAIN MOVING IN

The blackboard is erased in the attic
And the wind turns up the light of the stars,
Sinewy now. Someone will find out, someone will know.
And if somewhere on this great planet
The truth is discovered, a patch of it, dried, glazed by the sun,
It will just hang on, in its own infamy, humility. No one
Will be better for it, but things can't get any worse.
Just keep playing, mastering as you do the step
Into disorder this one meant. Don't you see
It's all we can do? Meanwhile, great fires
Arise, as of haystacks aflame. The dial has been set
And that's ominous, but all your graciousness in living
Conspires with it, now that this is our home:
A place to be from, and have people ask about.

❖ W. S. MERWIN ❖

EPITAPH ON CERTAIN SCHISMATICS

These were they whom the body could not please,
Shaded between the shaded lights who rose
Quavering and forsook the arrogant knees,
The bodies death had made incredulous.
They had known, that season, lights in the trees
Moving when none felt wind, whisper of candles,
Pursuit of strange hinds, signs in snarled spindles,
Omens from alien birds, and after these
They descended into Hell. "Suffering is
Measure of nothing, now measure is lost," one said.
They fell to stroking their shyest histories.
Even cool flesh (so gaunt they grew and loveless),
When they could best remember it, only made
A wry shadow between the quick and the dead.

SUBSTANCE

I could see that there was a kind of distance lighted
    behind the face of that time in its very days
as they appeared to me but I could not think of any
    words that spoke of it truly nor point to anything
except what was there at the moment it was beginning
    to be gone and certainly it could not have been proven
nor held however I might reach toward it touching
    the warm lichens the features of the stones the skin
of the river and I could tell then that it was
    the animals themselves that were the weight and place
of the hour as it happened and that the mass of the cow's neck
    the flash of the swallow the trout's flutter were
where it was coming to pass they were bearing the sense of it
    without questions through the speechless cloud of light

❖   JAMES WRIGHT   ❖

SAINT JUDAS

When I went out to kill myself, I caught
A pack of hoodlums beating up a man.
Running to spare his suffering, I forgot
My name, my number, how my day began,
How soldiers milled around the garden stone
And sang amusing songs; how all that day
Their javelins measured crowds; how I alone
Bargained the proper coins, and slipped away.

Banished from heaven, I found this victim beaten,
Stripped, kneed, and left to cry. Dropping my rope
Aside, I ran, ignored the uniforms:
Then I remembered bread my flesh had eaten,
The kiss that ate my flesh. Flayed without hope,
I held the man for nothing in my arms.

MY GRANDMOTHER'S GHOST

She skimmed the yellow water like a moth,
Trailing her feet across the shallow stream;
She saw the berries, paused and sampled them
Where a slight spider cleaned his narrow tooth.
Light in the air, she fluttered up the path,
So delicate to shun the leaves and damp,
Like some young wife, holding a slender lamp
To find her stray child, or the moon, or both.

Even before she reached the empty house,
She beat her wings ever so lightly, rose,
Followed a bee where apples blew like snow;
And then, forgetting what she wanted there,
Too full of blossom and green light to care,
She hurried to the ground, and slipped below.

❖ DONALD HALL ❖

PRESIDENT AND POET

Granted that what we summon is absurd:
Mustaches and the stick, the New York fake
In cowboy costume grinning for the sake
Of cameras that always just occurred;
Granted that his Rough Riders fought a third-
Rate army badly general'd, to make
Headlines for Mr. Hearst: that one can take
Trust-busting not exactly at its word:

Robinson, alcoholic and unread,
Received a letter with a White House frank.
To court the Muse, you'd think T.R.'d've killed her
And had her stuffed, and yet this mountebank
Chose to belaurel Robinson instead
Of famous men like Richard Watson Gilder.

❖ PHILIP LEVINE ❖

LLANTO

for Ernesto Trejo

Plum, almond, cherry have come and gone,
the wisteria has vanished in
the dawn, the blackened roses rusting
along the barbed-wire fence explain

how April passed so quickly into
this hard wind that waited in the west.
Ahead is summer and the full sun
riding at ease above the stunned town

no longer yours. Brother, you are gone,
that which was earth gone back to earth,
that which was human scattered like rain
into the darkened wild eyes of herbs

that see it all, into the valley oak
that will not sing, that will not even talk.

❖ THOM GUNN ❖

FIRST MEETING WITH A POSSIBLE MOTHER-IN-LAW

She thought, without the benefit of knowing,
You, who had been hers, were not any more.
We had locked our love in to leave nothing showing
From the room her handiwork had crammed before;
But—much revealing in its figured sewing—
A piece of stuff hung out, caught in the door.
I caused the same suspicion I watched growing:
Who could not tell what whole the part stood for?

There was small likeness between her and me:
Two strangers left upon a bare top landing,
I for a prudent while, she totally.

But, eyes turned from the bright material hint,
Each shared too long a second's understanding,
Learning the other's terms of banishment.

KEATS AT HIGHGATE

A cheerful youth joined Coleridge on his walk
("Loose," noted Coleridge, "slack, and not well-dressed")
Listening respectfully to the talk talk talk
Of First and Second Consciousness, then pressed
The famous hand with warmth and sauntered back
Homeward in his own state of less dispersed
More passive consciousness—passive, not slack,
Whether of Secondary type or First.

He made his way toward Hampstead so alert
He hardly passed the small grey ponds below
Or watched a sparrow pecking in the dirt
Without some insight swelling the mind's flow
That banks made swift. Everything put to use.
Perhaps not well-dressed but oh no not loose.

from *Powers of Thirteen*

"Just the right number of letters—half the alphabet"

Just the right number of letters—half the alphabet;
Or the number of rows on this monument we both
Have to share in the building of. We start out each course
Now, of dressed stone, with something of me, ending where you
Handle the last block and leave something of you within
Or outside it. So we work and move toward a countdown,
Loving what we have done, what we have left to do. A
Long day's working makes us look up where we started from
And slowly to read down to the end, down to a base,
Not out, to some distant border, the terminal bland
Destructions at their ends that lines of time undergo.
Endings as of blocks of text, unlit by the late sun
Really underlie our lives when all is said and done.

"That other time of day when the chiming of Thirteen"

That other time of day when the chiming of Thirteen
Marks the hour in truth comes after midnight has made
Its unseen appearance. Then the whole trembling house starts
Gathering itself together in sudden fear, creaks
On the stairs grow tacit, and, even outside, the wind
In the lindens has been hushed. Unlike the time beyond
Noon, when your visitations shape that original
Hour, when we pull the shades down in our space between
Moments totally contiguous in the clocked world,
This black gap between days is no place for us: should you
Creep into my bed then you would find me shuddering
As at the opening of a secret whose shadowed
Power unbroken lay in coupling day unto day.

from *The Mad Potter* [CLOSING STANZA]

Clay to clay: Soon I shall indeed become
Dumb as these solid cups of hardened mud
(Dull *terra cruda* colored like our blood);
Meanwhile the slap and thump of palm and thumb
On wet mis-shapenness begins to hum
With meaning that was silent for so long.
The words of my wheel's turning come to ring
Truer than Truth itself does, my great *Ding
Dong-an-sich* that echoes everything
(Against it even lovely bells ring wrong):
Its whole voice gathers up the purest parts
Of all our speech, the vowels of the earth,
The aspirations of our hopeful hearts
Or the prophetic sibillance of song.

❖ ADRIENNE RICH ❖

from *Contradictions: Tracking Poems*

I

Look: this is January   the worst onslaught
is ahead of us   Don't be lured
by these soft grey afternoons   these sunsets cut
from pink and violet tissue-paper   by the thought
the days are lengthening
Don't let the solstice fool you:
our lives will always be
a stew of contradictions
the worst moment of winter can come in April
when the peepers are stubbornly still   and our bodies
plod on without conviction
and our thoughts cramp down before the sheer
arsenal of everything that tries us:
this battering, blunt-edged life

14

Lately in my dreams I hear long sentences
meaningless in ordinary American
like, *Your mother, too, was a missionary of poets*
and in another dream one of my old teachers
shows me a letter of reference
he has written for me, in a language
I know to be English but cannot understand,
telling me it's in "transformational grammar"
and that the student who typed the letter
does not understand this grammar either.
Lately I dreamed about my father,
how I found him, alive, seated on an old chair.
I think what he said to me was,
You don't know how lonely I am.

18

The problem, unstated till now, is how
to live in a damaged body
in a world where pain is meant to be gagged
uncured   un-grieved-over   The problem is
to connect, without hysteria, the pain
of any one's body with the pain of the body's world
For it is the body's world
they are trying to destroy forever
The best world is the body's world
filled with creatures   filled with dread
misshapen so   yet the best we have
our raft among the abstract worlds
and how I longed to live on this earth
walking her boundaries   never counting the cost

❖   ❖   ❖

it will not be simple, it will not be long
it will take little time, it will take all your thought
it will take all your heart, it will take all your breath
it will be short, it will not be simple

it will touch through your ribs, it will take all your heart
it will not be long, it will occupy your thought
as a city is occupied, as a bed is occupied
it will take all your flesh, it will not be simple

You are coming into us who cannot withstand you
you are coming into us who never wanted to withstand you
you are taking parts of us into places never planned
you are going far away with pieces of our lives

it will be short, it will take all your breath
it will not be simple, it will become your will

❖   DEREK WALCOTT   ❖

HOMAGE TO EDWARD THOMAS

Formal, informal, by a country's cast
topography delineates its verse,
erects the classic bulk, for rigid contrast
of sonnet, rectory or this manor house
dourly timbered against these sinuous
Downs, defines the formal and informal prose
of Edward Thomas's poems, which make this garden
return its subtle scent of Edward Thomas
in everything here hedged or loosely grown.
Lines which you once dismissed as tenuous
because they would not howl or overwhelm,
as crookedly grave-bent, or cuckoo-dreaming,
seeming dissoluble as this Sussex down
harden in their indifference, like this elm.

❖ GEOFFREY HILL ❖

SEPTEMBER SONG

born 19.6.32—deported 24.9.42

Undesirable you may have been, untouchable
you were not. Not forgotten
or passed over at the proper time.

As estimated, you died. Things marched,
sufficient, to that end.
Just so much Zyklon and leather, patented
terror, so many routine cries.

(I have made
an elegy for myself it
is true)

September fattens on vines. Roses
flake from the wall. The smoke
of harmless fires drifts to my eyes.

This is plenty. This is more than enough.

FUNERAL MUSIC

William de la Pole, Duke of Suffolk: beheaded 1450
John Tiptoft, Earl of Worcester: beheaded 1470
Anthony Woodville, Earl Rivers: beheaded 1483

1

Processionals in the exemplary cave,
Benediction of shadows. Pomfret. London.
The voice fragrant with mannered humility,
With an equable contempt for this World,
"In honorem Trinitatis." Crash. The head
Struck down into a meaty conduit of blood.
So these dispose themselves to receive each
Pentecostal blow from axe or seraph,
Spattering block-straw with mortal residue.
Psalteries whine through the empyrean. Fire
Flares in the pit, ghosting upon stone
Creatures of such rampant state, vacuous
Ceremony of possession, restless
Habitation, no man's dwelling-place.

2

For whom do we scrape our tribute of pain—
For none but the ritual king? We meditate
A rueful mystery; we are dying
To satisfy fat Caritas, those
Wiped jaws of stone. (Suppose all reconciled
By silent music; imagine the future
Flashed back at us, like steel against sun,
Ultimate recompense.) Recall the cold
Of Towton on Palm Sunday before dawn,
Wakefield, Tewkesbury: fastidious trumpets
Shrilling into the ruck; some trampled
Acres, parched, sodden or blanched by sleet,
Stuck with strange-postured dead. Recall the wind's
Flurrying, darkness over the human mire.

3

They bespoke doomsday and they meant it by
God, their curved metal rimming the low ridge.
But few appearances are like this. Once
Every five hundred years a comet's
Over-riding stillness might reveal men
In such array, livid and featureless,
With England crouched beastwise beneath it all.
"Oh, that old northern business . . . " A field
After battle utters its own sound
Which is like nothing on earth, but is earth.
Blindly the questing snail, vulnerable
Mole emerge, blindly we lie down, blindly
Among carnage the most delicate souls
Tup in their marriage-blood, gasping "Jesus."

4

Let mind be more precious than soul; it will not
Endure. Soul grasps its price, begs its own peace,
Settles with tears and sweat, is possibly
Indestructible. That I can believe.
Though I would scorn the mere instinct of faith,
Expediency of assent, if I dared,
What I dare not is a waste history
Or void rule. Averroes, old heathen,
If only you had been right, if Intellect
Itself were absolute law, sufficient grace,
Our lives could be a myth of captivity
Which we might enter: an unpeopled region
Of ever new-fallen snow, a palace blazing
With perpetual silence as with torches.

5

As with torches we go, at wild Christmas,
When we revel in our atonement
Through thirty feasts of unction and slaughter,
What is that but the soul's winter sleep?
So many things rest under consummate
Justice as though trumpets purified law,
Spikenard were the real essence of remorse.
The sky gathers up darkness. When we chant
"Ora, ora pro nobis" it is not
Seraphs who descend to pity but ourselves.
Those righteously-accused those vengeful
Racked on articulate looms indulge us
With lingering shows of pain, a flagrant
Tenderness of the damned for their own flesh:

6

My little son, when you could command marvels
Without mercy, outstare the wearisome
Dragon of sleep, I rejoiced above all—
A stranger well-received in your kingdom.
On those pristine fields I saw humankind
As it was named by the Father; fabulous
Beasts rearing in stillness to be blessed.
The world's real cries reached there, turbulence
From remote storms, rumour of solitudes,
A composed mystery. And so it ends.
Some parch for what they were; others are made
Blind to all but one vision, their necessity
To be reconciled. I believe in my
Abandonment, since it is what I have.

7

"Prowess, vanity, mutual regard,
It seemed I stared at them, they at me.
That was the gorgon's true and mortal gaze:
Averted conscience turned against itself."
A hawk and a hawk-shadow. "At noon,
As the armies met, each mirrored the other;
Neither was outshone. So they flashed and vanished
And all that survived them was the stark ground
Of this pain. I made no sound, but once
I stiffened as though a remote cry
Had heralded my name. It was nothing . . . "
Reddish ice tinged the reeds; dislodged, a few
Feathers drifted across; carrion birds
Strutted upon the armour of the dead.

8

Not as we are but as we must appear,
Contractual ghosts of pity; not as we
Desire life but as they would have us live,
Set apart in timeless colloquy:
So it is required; so we bear witness,
Despite ourselves, to what is beyond us,
Each distant sphere of harmony forever
Poised, unanswerable. If it is without
Consequence when we vaunt and suffer, or
If it is not, all echoes are the same
In such eternity. Then tell me, love,
How that should comfort us—or anyone
Dragged half-unnerved out of this worldly place,
Crying to the end "I have not finished."

❖ SYLVIA PLATH ❖

MAYFLOWER

Throughout black winter the red haws withstood
Assault of snow-flawed winds from the dour skies
And, bright as blood-drops, proved no brave branch dies
If root's firm-fixed and resolution good.
Now, as green sap ascends the steepled wood,
Each hedge with such white bloom astounds our eyes
As sprang from Joseph's rod, and testifies
How best beauty's born of hardihood.

So when staunch island stock chose forfeiture
Of the homeland hearth to plough their pilgrim way
Across Atlantic furrows, dark, unsure—
Remembering the white, triumphant spray
On hawthorn boughs, with goodwill to endure
They named their ship after the flower of May.

❖ JOHN UPDIKE ❖

ISLAND CITIES

You see them from airplanes, nameless green islands
in the oceanic, rectilinear plains,
twenty or thirty blocks, compact, but with
everything needed visibly in place—
the high-school playing fields, the swatch of park
along the crooked river, the feeder highways,
the main drag like a zipper, outlying malls
sliced from dirt-colored cakes of plowed farmland.

Small lives, we think—pat, flat—in such tight grids.
But, much like brains with every crease CAT-scanned,
these cities keep their secrets: vagaries
of the spirit, groundwater that floods
the nearby quarries and turns them skyey blue,
dewdrops of longing, jewels, boxed in these blocks.

❖ TED BERRIGAN ❖

from *The Sonnets*

III

Stronger than alcohol, more great than song,
deep in whose reeds great elephants decay;
I, an island, sail, and my shores toss
on a fragrant evening, fraught with sadness
bristling hate.
It's true, I weep too much. Dawns break
slow kisses on the eyelids of the sea,
what other men sometimes have thought they've seen.
And since then I've been bathing in the poem
lifting her shadowy flowers up for me,
and hurled by hurricanes to a birdless place
the waving flags, nor pass by prison ships
O let me burst, and I be lost at sea!
and fall on my knees then, womanly.

❖ JEAN VALENTINE ❖

RAIN

Snakes of water and light in the window
snakes that shrug out of their skins and follow
pushing a path with their heads full of light
—heavy trembling mercury headlights—
leaving trails of clear grass, and rocks,
nests where they half live, half sleep,
above ground:
Snake where do you come from?
who leave your grass path
and follow me wordless
into our glass
water and light house,
earth wet on your mouth,
you the ground of my underground.

❖ ROBERT MEZEY ❖

HARDY

Thrown away at birth, he was recovered,
Plucked from the swaddling-shroud, and chafed and slapped,
The crone implacable. At last he shivered,
Drew the first breath, and howled, and lay there, trapped
In a world from which there is but one escape
And that forestalled now almost ninety years.
In such a scene as he himself might shape,
The maker of a thousand songs appears.

From this it follows, all the ironies
Life plays on one whose fate it is to follow
The way of things, the suffering one sees,
The many cups of bitterness he must swallow
Before he is permitted to be gone
Where he was headed in that early dawn.

❖ GRACE SCHULMAN ❖

THE ABBESS OF WHITBY

There must have been an angel at his ear
When Caedmon gathered up his praise and sang,
Trembling in a barn, of the beginning,
Startled at words he never knew were there.

I heard a voice strike thunder in the air:
Of many kings, only one god is king!
There must have been an angel at his ear
When Caedmon gathered up his praise and sang.

When Caedmon turned in fear from songs of war,
Gleemen who sang the glories of the king
And holy men wondered that so great a power
Could whirl in darkness and force up his song;
There must have been an angel at his ear
When Caedmon gathered up his praise and sang.

COMPOSITION IN GREY AND PINK

The souls of the day's dead fly up like birds, big sister,
The sky shutters and casts loose.
And faster than stars the body goes to the earth.

Heat hangs like a mist from the trees.
Butterflies pump through the banked fires of late afternoon.
The rose continues its sure rise to the self.

Ashes, trampled garlands . . .

I dream of an incandescent space
                              where nothing distinct exists,
And where nothing ends, the days sliding like warm milk through
          the clouds,
Everyone's name in chalk letters once and for all,

The dogstar descending with its pestilent breath . . .

Fatherless, stiller than still water,
I want to complete my flesh
                              and sit in a quiet corner
Untied from God, where the dead don't sing in their sleep.

❖ JUNE JORDAN ❖

SUNFLOWER SONNET NUMBER TWO

Supposing we could just go on and on as two
voracious in the days apart as well as when
we side by side (the many ways we do
that) well! I would consider then
perfection possible, or else worthwhile
to think about. Which is to say
I guess the costs of long term tend to pile
up, block and complicate, erase away
the accidental, temporary, near
thing/pulsebeat promises one makes
because the chance, the easy new, is there
in front of you. But still, perfection takes
some sacrifice of falling stars for rare.
And there are stars, but none of you, to spare.

❖ JUDITH RODRIGUEZ ❖

IN-FLIGHT NOTE

Kitten, writes the mousy boy in his neat
fawn casuals sitting beside me on the flight,
neatly, *I can't give up everything just like that.*
Everything, how much was it, and just like what?
Did she cool it or walk out? Loosen her hand from his tight
white-knuckled hand, or not meet him, just as he thought
*You mean far too much to me. I can't forget
the four months we've known each other.* No, he won't eat,
finally he pays—pale, careful, distraught—
for a beer, turns over the page he wrote
and sleeps a bit. Or dreams of his Sydney cat.
The pad cost one dollar twenty. He wakes to write
It's naïve to think we could just be good friends.
Pages and pages. And so the whole world ends.

❖ FREDERICK SEIDEL ❖

ELMS

It sang without a sound: music that
The naive elm trees loved. They were alive.
Oh silky music no elm tree could survive.
The head low slither of a stalking cat,
Black panther darkness pouring to the kill,
Entered every elm—they drank it in.
Drank silence. Then the silence drank. Wet chin,
Hot, whiskered darkness. Every elm was ill.
What else is there to give but joy? Disease.
And trauma. Lightning, or as slow as lava.
Darkness drinking from a pool in Java,
Black panther drinking from a dream. The trees
Around the edge are elms. Below, above,
Man-eater drinking its reflection: love.

❖ JOHN FULLER ❖

from *Lily and Violin*

6

Afterwards we may not speak: piled chords
Are broken open with changes of key;
Logs in settling shoot a surprising flame;
A petal folds more slowly than night falls;
A face is lifted to catch the last
Ache of struggling body or air.

Afterwards we may not speak, since
Everything hastens towards its end
With an enlarging beauty. May not,
Need not, will not, we say, obsessed
Like vagrant creatures with consummation.
But it is all our dear illusion
Belonging to the experience itself
Which must not speak of afterwards.

from *from The School of Eloquence*

ON NOT BEING MILTON

for Sergio Vieira & Armando Guebuza (Frelimo)

Read and committed to the flames, I call
these sixteen lines that go back to my roots
my *Cahier d'un retour au pays natal,*
my growing black enough to fit my boots.

The stutter of the scold out of the branks
of condescension, class and counter-class
thickens with glottals to a lumpen mass
of Ludding morphemes closing up their ranks.
Each swung cast-iron Enoch of Leeds stress
clangs a forged music on the frames of Art,
the looms of owned language smashed apart!

Three cheers for mute ingloriousness!

Articulation is the tongue-tied's fighting.
In the silence round all poetry we quote
Tidd the Cato Street conspirator who wrote:

Sir, I Ham a very Bad Hand at Righting.

❖ LES MURRAY ❖

COMETE

Uphill in Melbourne on a beautiful day
a woman was walking ahead of her hair.
Like teak oiled soft to fracture and sway
it hung to her heels and seconded her
as a pencilled retinue, an unscrolling title
to ploughland, edged with ripe rows of dress,
a sheathed wing that couldn't fly her at all,
only itself, loosely, and her spirits.
                              A largesse
of life and self, brushed all calm and out,
its abstracted attempts on her mouth weren't seen,
nor its showering, its tenting. Just the detail
that swam in its flow-lines, glossing about—
as she paced on, comet-like, face to the sun.

❖ CHARLES SIMIC ❖

HISTORY

On a gray evening
Of a gray century,
I ate an apple
While no one was looking.

A small, sour apple
The color of woodfire,
Which I first wiped
On my sleeve.

Then I stretched my legs
As far as they'd go,
Said to myself
Why not close my eyes now

Before the Late
World News and Weather.

❖ DICK ALLEN ❖

LOST LOVE

You're in the city, somewhere. I suppose if I stood
On Times Square a year or two I'd find you,
Face pleasant and older, coming out of the subway crowd,
Or studying poinsettias in a florist's window.
A flicker—that would be all. Both of us
Looked so much like others, which of us could be sure
We were not others? Once, we met in a glance.
So, too, in a glance, should both of us disappear.

But I'm lying. Often, on West Coast or East,
I'll be at a movie before the lights go down
And Beauty flees through the meadows from the Beast
Or the boy steps out of a throng to claim his crown
When far down the aisles and rows I'll see you there,
Your body still young, your eyes, your taffeta hair!

❖ FRANK BIDART ❖

SELF-PORTRAIT, 1969

He's *still* young—; thirty, but looks younger—
or does he? . . . In the eyes and cheeks, tonight,
turning in the mirror, he saw his mother,—
puffy; angry; bewildered . . . Many nights
now, when he stares there, he gets angry:—
something *unfulfilled* there, something dead
to what he once thought he surely could be—
Now, just the glamour of habits . . .

                              Once, instead,
he thought insight would remake him, he'd reach
—what? The thrill, the exhilaration
unravelling disaster, that seemed to teach
necessary knowledge . . . became just jargon.

Sick of being decent, he craves another
crash. What *reaches* him except disaster?

❖ SEAMUS HEANEY ❖

THE FORGE

All I know is a door into the dark.
Outside, old axles and iron hoops rusting;
Inside, the hammered anvil's short-pitched ring,
The unpredictable fantail of sparks
Or hiss when a new shoe toughens in water.
The anvil must be somewhere in the centre,
Horned as a unicorn, at one end square,
Set there immoveable: an altar
Where he expends himself in shape and music.
Sometimes, leather-aproned, hairs in his nose,
He leans out on the jamb, recalls a clatter
Of hoofs where traffic is flashing in rows;
Then grunts and goes in, with a slam and flick
To beat real iron out, to work the bellows.

ACT OF UNION

I

Tonight, a first movement, a pulse,
As if the rain in bogland gathered head
To slip and flood: a bog-burst,
A gash breaking open the ferny bed.
Your back is a firm line of eastern coast
And arms and legs are thrown
Beyond your gradual hills. I caress
The heaving province where our past has grown.
I am the tall kingdom over your shoulder
That you would neither cajole nor ignore.
Conquest is a lie. I grow older
Conceding your half-independent shore
Within whose borders now my legacy
Culminates inexorably.

II

And I am still imperially
Male, leaving you with the pain,
The rending process in the colony,
The battering ram, the boom burst from within.
The act sprouted an obstinate fifth column
Whose stance is growing unilateral.
His heart beneath your heart is a wardrum
Mustering force. His parasitical
And ignorant little fists already
Beat at your borders and I know they're cocked
At me across the water. No treaty
I foresee will salve completely your tracked
And stretchmarked body, the big pain
That leaves you raw, like opened ground, again.

THE SEED CUTTERS

They seem hundreds of years away. Brueghel,
You'll know them if I can get them true.
They kneel under the hedge in a half-circle
Behind a windbreak wind is breaking through.
They are the seed cutters. The tuck and frill
Of leaf-sprout is on the seed potatoes
Buried under that straw. With time to kill,
They are taking their time. Each sharp knife goes
Lazily halving each root that falls apart
In the palm of the hand: a milky gleam,
And, at the centre, a dark watermark.
Oh, calendar customs! Under the broom
Yellowing over them, compose the frieze
With all of us there, our anonymities.

A DREAM OF JEALOUSY

Walking with you and another lady
In wooded parkland, the whispering grass
Ran its fingers through our guessing silence
And the trees opened into a shady
Unexpected clearing where we sat down.
I think the candour of the light dismayed us.
We talked about desire and being jealous,
Our conversation a loose single gown
Or a white picnic tablecloth spread out
Like a book of manners in the wilderness.
'Show me,' I said to our companion, 'what
I have much coveted, your breast's mauve star.'
And she consented. Oh neither these verses
Nor my prudence, love, can heal your wounded stare.

from *Clearances*

II

Polished linoleum shone there. Brass taps shone.
The china cups were very white and big—
An unchipped set with sugar bowl and jug.
The kettle whistled. Sandwich and tea scone
Were present and correct. In case it run,
The butter must be kept out of the sun.
And don't be dropping crumbs. Don't tilt your chair.
Don't reach. Don't point. Don't make noise when you stir.

It is Number 5, New Row, Land of the Dead,
Where grandfather is rising from his place
With spectacles pushed back on a clean bald head
To welcome a bewildered homing daughter
Before she even knocks. 'What's this? What's this?'
And they sit down in the shining room together.

III

When all the others were away at Mass
I was all hers as we peeled potatoes.
They broke the silence, let fall one by one
Like solder weeping off the soldering iron:
Cold comforts set between us, things to share
Gleaming in a bucket of clean water.
And again let fall. Little pleasant splashes
From each other's work would bring us to our senses.

So while the parish priest at her bedside
Went hammer and tongs at the prayers for the dying
And some were responding and some crying
I remembered her head bent towards my head,
Her breath in mine, our fluent dipping knives—
Never closer the whole rest of our lives.

from *Boy on the Step*

I

He's out of breath only halfway up the hill,
which is brickwalk, awkward, and just steep enough
his mother's letting him rest but all the while
coaxing—there's like a climber's rope gone slack
between them, the thing you trip when your eye goes
from her face to his and then his arm, the left
one, off at the elbow, wrapped in heavy gauze.
This is none of your business yet intimate,
the way surprise is open, vulnerable,
the way the woman who came up to you was
anyone, pretty, so innocent of guile
you thought she was lost until she got too close
and the child in her turned hard, scared, her hand thrust
out for change, anything, wounds in the air, rest.

5

None of us dies entirely—some of us, all
of us sometimes come back sapling, seedling, cell,
like second growth, slowly, imperceptibly,
in the imprint of rings that wind like music
written down, in notes and bars, scale and silence.
Even the child, who was immortal, becomes
purity, anonymity inside us.
Which is why to watch a tree turn into fire
or fall is like a second death, like the grace
in stillness gone, exploded, fatal, final,
as someone loved, within whose face we confused
the infinite with the intimate, is last
a name, the point of a green leaf drawn across
the heart, whose loss is felt, though invisible.

AMERICAN SONNET

We do not speak like Petrarch or wear a hat like Spenser
and it is not fourteen lines
like furrows in a small, carefully plowed field

but the picture postcard, a poem on vacation,
that forces us to sing our songs in little rooms
or pour our sentiments into measuring cups.

We write on the back of a waterfall or lake,
adding to the view a caption as conventional
as an Elizabethan woman's heliocentric eyes.

We locate an adjective for the weather.
We announce that we are having a wonderful time.
We express the wish that you were here

and hide the wish that we were where you are,
walking back from the mailbox, your head lowered
as you read and turn the thin message in your hands.

A slice of this place, a length of white beach,
a piazza or carved spires of a cathedral
will pierce the familiar place where you remain,

and you will toss on the table this reversible display:
a few square inches of where we have strayed
and a compression of what we feel.

DUCK / RABBIT

The lamb may lie down with the lion,
But they will never be as close as this pair
Who share the very lines
Of their existence, whose overlapping is their raison d'etre.
How strange and symbiotic the binds
That make one disappear
Whenever the other is spied.
Throw the duck a stare,
And the rabbit hops down his hole.
Give the rabbit the eye,
And the duck waddles off the folio.
Say, these could be our mascots, you and I—
    I could look at you forever
    And never see the two of us together.

SONNET

All we need is fourteen lines, well, thirteen now,
and after this next one just a dozen
to launch a little ship on love's storm-tossed seas,
then only ten more left like rows of beans.
How easily it goes unless you get Elizabethan
and insist the iambic bongos must be played
and rhymes positioned at the ends of lines,
one for every station of the cross.
But hang on here while we make the turn
into the final six where all will be resolved,
where longing and heartache will find an end,
where Laura will tell Petrarch to put down his pen,
take off those crazy medieval tights,
blow out the lights, and come at last to bed.

❖ DOUGLAS DUNN ❖

FRANCE

A dozen sparrows scuttled on the frost.
We watched them play. We stood at the window,
And, if you saw us, then you saw a ghost
In duplicate. I tied her nightgown's bow.
She watched and recognized the passers-by.
Had they looked up, they'd know that she was ill—
"Please, do not draw the curtains when I die"—
From all the flowers on the windowsill.

"It's such a shame," she said. "Too ill, too quick."
"I would have liked us to have gone away."
We closed our eyes together, dreaming France,
Its meadows, rivers, woods and *jouissance*.
I counted summers, our love's arithmetic.
"Some other day, my love. Some other day."

❖ MARILYN HACKER ❖

SONNET

Love drives its rackety blue caravan
right to the edge. The valley lies below,
unseasonable leaves shading the so-
seemly houses from the sun. We can
climb down. Cornflowers push from crevices
and little purple star-blooms with no name
we know. Look up. I didn't think we came
this far. Look down. No, don't. I think there is
a path between those rocks. Steady. Don't hold
my sleeve, you'll trip me. Oh, Jesus, I've turned
my ankle. Let me just sit down. . . .
Predictably, it's dark. No lights go on
below. There is a dull red glow of burn-
ing at the edge. Predictably, it's cold.

from *Love, Death, and the Changing of the Seasons*

Did you love well what very soon you left?
Come home and take me in your arms and take
away this stomach ache, headache, heartache.
Never so full, I never was bereft
so utterly. The winter evenings drift
dark to the window. Not one word will make
you, where you are, turn in your day, or wake
from your night toward me. The only gift
I got to keep or give is what I've cried,
floodgates let down to mourning for the dead
chances, for the end of being young,
for everyone I loved who really died.
I drank our one year out in brine instead
of honey from the seasons of your tongue.

from *Cancer Winter*

for Rafael Campo and Hayden Carruth

Syllables shaped around the darkening day's
contours. Next to armchairs, on desks, lamps
were switched on. Tires hissed softly on the damp
tar. In my room, a flute concerto played.
Slate roofs glistened in the rain's thin glaze.
I peered out from a cave like a warm bear.
Halls lights flicked on as someone climbed the stairs
across the street, blinked out: a key, a phrase
turned in a lock, and something flew open.
I watched a young man at his window write
at a plank table, one pooled halogen
light on his book, dim shelves behind him, night
falling fraternal on the flux between
the odd and even numbers of the street.

I woke up, and the surgeon said, "You're cured."
Strapped to the gurney, in the cotton gown
and pants I was wearing when they slid me down
onto the table, made new straps secure
while I stared at the hydra-headed O.R.
lamp, I took in the tall, confident, brown-
skinned man, and the ache I couldn't quite call pain
from where my right breast wasn't anymore
to my armpit. A not-yet-talking head,
I bit dry lips. What else could he have said?
And then my love was there in a hospital coat;
then my old love, still young and very scared.
Then I, alone, graphed clock hands' asymptote
to noon, when I would be wheeled back upstairs.

The odd and even numbers of the street
I live on are four thousand miles away
from an Ohio February day
snow-blanketed, roads iced over, with sleet
expected later, where I'm incomplete
as my abbreviated chest. I weigh
less—one breast less—since the Paris-gray
December evening, when a neighbor's feet
coming up ancient stairs, the feet I counted
on paper were the company I craved.
My calm right breast seethed with a grasping tumor.
The certainty of my returns amounted
to nothing. After terror, being brave
became another form of gallows humor.

At noon, an orderly wheeled me upstairs
via an elevator hung with Season's
Greetings streamers, bright and false as treason.
The single room the surgeon let us share
the night before the knife was scrubbed and bare
except for blush-pink roses in a vase on
the dresser. Veering through a morphine haze on
the cranked bed, I was avidly aware
of my own breathing, my thirst, that it was over—
the week that ended on this New Year's Eve.
A known hand held, while I sipped, icewater,
afloat between ache, sleep, lover and lover.
The one who stayed would stay; the one would leave.
The hand that held the cup next was my daughter's.

❖ DAVID HUDDLE ❖

from *Tour of Duty*

WORDS

What did those girls say when you walked the strip
of tin-shack bars, gewgaw stores, barber shops,
laundries, and restaurants, most all of which
had beds in back, those girls who had to get up
in Saigon before dawn to catch their rides to Cu Chi,
packed ten to a Lambretta, chattering, happy
in their own lovely tongue, on the dusty
circus road to work, but then what did they say?

Come here, talk to me, you handsome, GI,
I miss you, I love you too much, you want
short time, go in back, I don't care, I want
your baby, sorry about that, GI,
you number ten. A history away
I translate dumbly what those girls would say.

from *Album*

CODA

Sons grown and gone, they adopt a mutt
that comes, stays ten years, and learns their ways.
On slow walks that good dog leads my parents
a hundred yards out the gravel driveway
until a gunshot rips through one day's silence.
My mother and father break into a trot,
though they are old now, too old to run like
this to the curve of the road and the sight
of fat old Daisy's neck a bloody spout,
one spent shell a step away, smoke still spooling,
the backs of two running boys, the one not
carrying the gun looking back and laughing.
They are not strong enough to lift the weight
of their dog. They turn back to the empty house.

Through the hundreds of miles between my house
and theirs, my daughters, my wife, and I
take turns talking with my parents in our
twice-a-month phone call. In our talk we try
to pretend it won't be long before our
visit next summer. I hardly hear how
their words sound; I've lost them and they've lost me,
this is just habit, blood, and memory.
They pause, then they tell us about Daisy,
how she must have walked right up to those boys
before they shot her down. . . . And yes, I am
seeing just how it was. My mother's voice
breaks. I am with you, I want to tell them,
but I manage to say only that I see.

APERTURE

It does not come as hairline fractures
Mapping plaster with brittle rivers
Nor with the unmeasured gait
Of a tulip's averting grace
(Lathed to half-rhyme with death)
While these others, these anemones,
Peel back Padua's choir of angels
Plummeting and stayed, frescoes of disbelief
That came only by faith, never by description
Which cannot save despite its comforts
As we might say: touch me here,
Put your hand here where it hurts. Where
Is it? What is the unimaginable source of it?
This transparent stain left on the air where was is.

❖ CHARLES MARTIN ❖

EASTER SUNDAY, 1985

*To take steps toward the reappearance alive of the disappeared is a subversive
act, and measures will be adopted to deal with it.*

—GENERAL OSCAR MEJIA VICTORES,
PRESIDENT OF GUATEMALA

In the Palace of the President this morning,
The General is gripped by the suspicion
That those who were disappeared will be returning
In a subversive act of resurrection.

Why do you worry? The disappeared can never
Be brought back from wherever they were taken;
The age of miracles is gone forever;
These are not sleeping, nor will they awaken.

And if some tell you Christ once reappeared
Alive, one Easter morning, that he was seen—
Give them the lie, for who today can find him?

He is perhaps with those who were disappeared,
Broken and killed, flung into some ravine
With his arms safely wired up behind him.

from *Making Faces*

II   THE END OF THE WORLD

We've practiced it too often in our age
To see it merely as the subtraction
Of bird from tree, of tree from earth, of earth from space,
As one erases letters from a page.
Yet we still think of it as an abstraction,
Something that isn't likely to take place—
Although it's taken place at places called
Guernica, Hiroshima, Buchenwald.
We think of the unthinkable with ease,
We've had such practice of it for so long;
And speak of it in ways which help conceal
From ourselves the dark realities
That numb the mind and paralyze the tongue.
And now in the parade there comes a skel-

etal figure on a skeletal horse,
Made of raw strips of pine lashed together.
Its attitude is distant yet familiar,
As though it were confident that in the course
Of time we'd get to know each other better.
It knows this in its bones, as we in ours.
(And so if Death should ever wave at you,
You may wave back, for you have manners too;
You needn't ask it to slow down or stop.)
It's followed by a Dragon, belching smoke;
One Demon drives it, another one attends
To the Great Devourer who sits on top,
Quietly enjoying some huge cosmic joke—
And that is the way The End Of The World ends.

❖   ❖   ❖

THE PHILOSOPHER'S BALLOON

Whether the Laws that govern us were fashioned
For our benefit (who otherwise
Might find ourselves in the breathless stratosphere)
Or were meant to keep us from our rightful station
Remains unsettled, open to surmise—
But that there *are* Laws is absolutely clear.
We derive the existence of these Laws
Not from the necessity of a First Cause,
Some creator inflating us until we squeal,
But from the strings to which we are attached,
Which represent the Laws and those who make them;
That the strings attached to us are really real,
And not, as some say, just a figure of speech,
Becomes apparent only when we break them.

❖   WILLIAM MATTHEWS   ❖

VERMIN

"What do you want to be when you grow up?"
What child cries out, "An exterminator!"?
One diligent student in Mrs. Taylor's
class will get an ant farm for Christmas, but
he'll not see industry; he'll see dither.
"The ant sets an example for us all,"
wrote Max Beerbohm, a master of dawdle,
"but it is not a good one." These children
don't hope to outlast the doldrums of school
only to heft great weights and work in squads
and die for their queen. Well neither did we.
And we knew what we didn't want to be:
the ones we looked down on, the lambs of God,
blander than snow and slow to be cruel.

❖ HENRY TAYLOR ❖

GREEN SPRINGS THE TREE

My young son lurches halfway down the stair
or shrieks and totters midway through a climb
from the wobbling bookcase to the rocking chair.
I freeze and hold my breath. Most of the time
I am too far away to break the fall
that seldom comes. Instead, I stoop and bend
with him, as if threads of remote control
could reel out and connect him to my hand
that strains against his fall, against my leap
to rescue him. My twisting body prays
for skill in this, the high wire he will keep
both of us on as we rehearse the ways
to braid these strands of our inheritance
and teach poor body english how to dance.

❖ LOUISE GLÜCK ❖

SNOWDROPS

Do you know what I was, how I lived? You know
what despair is; then
winter should have meaning for you.

I did not expect to survive,
earth suppressing me. I didn't expect
to waken again, to feel
in damp earth my body
able to respond again, remembering
after so long how to open again
in the cold light
of earliest spring—

afraid, yes, but among you again
crying yes risk joy

in the raw wind of the new world.

from *Kyrie*

"Dear Mattie, You're sweet to write me every day"

Dear Mattie, You're sweet to write me every day.
The train was not so bad, I found a seat,
watched the landscape flatten until dark,
ate the lunch you packed, your good chess pie.
I've made a friend, a Carolina man
who looks like Emmett Cocke, same big grin,
square teeth. Curses hard but he can shoot.
Sergeant calls him Pug I don't know why.
It's hot here but we're not here for long.
Most all we do is march and shine our boots.
In the drills they keep us 20 feet apart
on account of sickness in the camp.
In case you think to send more pie, send two.
I'll try to bring you back some French perfume.

"When does a childhood end? Mothers"

When does a childhood end? Mothers
sew a piece of money inside a sock,
fathers unfold the map of the world, and boys
go off to war—that's an end, whether
they come back wrapped in the flag or waving it.
Sister and I were what they kissed goodbye,
complicitous in the long dream left behind.
On one page, willful innocence,
                            on the next
an Army Captain writing from the ward
with few details and much regret—a kindness
she wouldn't forgive, and wouldn't be reconciled
to her soldier lost, or me in my luck, or the petals
strewn on the grass, or the boys still on the playground
routing evil with their little sticks.

"This is the double bed where she'd been born"

This is the double bed where she'd been born,
bed of her mother's marriage and decline,
bed her sisters also ripened in,
bed that drew her husband to her side,
bed of her one child lost and five delivered,
bed indifferent to the many bodies,
bed around which all of them were gathered,
watery shapes in the shadows of the room,
and the bed frail abroad the violent ocean,
the frightened beasts so clumsy and pathetic,
heaving their wet breath against her neck,
she threw off the pile of quilts—white face like a moon—
and then entered straightway into heaven.

"Once the world had had its fill of war"

Once the world had had its fill of war,
in a secret wood, as the countryside lay stunned,
at the hour of the wolf and the vole, in a railroad car,
the generals met and put their weapons down.
Like spring it was, as word passed over all
the pocked and riven ground, and underground;
now the nations sat in a gilded hall,
dividing what they'd keep of what they'd won.

And so the armies could be done with war,
and soldiers trickled home to study peace.
But the old gardens grew a tough new weed,
and the old lives didn't fit as they had before,
and where there'd been the dream, a stranger's face,
and where there'd been the war, an empty sleeve.

❖ EAVAN BOLAND ❖

YEATS IN CIVIL WAR

In middle age you exchanged the sandals
Of a pilgrim for a Norman keep
in Galway. Civil war started. Vandals
Sacked your country, made off with your sleep.

Somehow you arranged your escape
Aboard a spirit ship which every day
Hoisted sail out of fire and rape.
On that ship your mind was stowaway.

The sun mounted on a wasted place.
But the wind at every door and turn
Blew the smell of honey in your face
Where there was none.
                              Whatever I may learn
You are its sum, struggling to survive—
A fantasy of honey your reprieve.

THE SINGERS

for M.R.

The women who were singers in the West
lived on an unforgiving coast.
I want to ask was there ever one
moment when all of it relented,
when rain and ocean and their own
sense of home were revealed to them
as one and the same?
                                        After which
every day was still shaped by weather,
but every night their mouths filled with
Atlantic storms and clouded-over stars
and exhausted birds.
                                        And only when the danger
was plain in the music could you know
their true measure of rejoicing in

finding a voice where they found a vision.

HEROIC

Sex and history. And skin and bone.
And the oppression of Sunday afternoon.
Bells called the faithful to devotion.

I was still at school and on my own.
And walked and walked and sheltered from the rain.

The patriot was made of drenched stone.
His lips were still speaking. The gun
he held had just killed someone.

I looked up. And looked at him again.
He stared past me without recognition.

I moved my lips and wondered how the rain
would taste if my tongue were made of stone.
And wished it was. And whispered so that no one
could hear it but him: *make me a heroine.*

❖ J. D. McCLATCHY ❖

MY MAMMOGRAM

I

In the shower, at the shaving mirror or beach,
For years I'd led . . . the unexamined life?
When all along and so easily within reach
(Closer even than the nonexistent wife)

Lay the trouble—naturally enough
Lurking in a useless, overlooked
Mass of fat and old newspaper stuff
About matters I regularly mistook

As a horror story for the opposite sex,
Nothing to do with what at my downtown gym
Are furtively ogled as The Guy's Pecs.

But one side is swollen, the too tender skin
Discolored. So the doctor orders an X-
Ray, and nervously frowns at my nervous grin.

II

Mammography's on the basement floor.
The nurse has an executioner's gentle eyes.
I start to unbutton my shirt. She shuts the door.
Fifty, male, already embarrassed by the size

Of my "breasts," I'm told to put the left one
Up on a smudged, cold, Plexiglas shelf,
Part of a robot half menacing, half glum,
Like a three-dimensional model of the Freudian self.

Angles are calculated. The computer beeps.
Saucers close on a flatness further compressed.
There's an ache near the heart neither dull nor sharp.

The room gets lethal. Casually the nurse retreats
Behind her shield. Anxiety as blithely suggests
I joke about a snapshot for my Christmas card.

III

"No sign of cancer," the radiologist swans
In to say—with just a hint in his tone
That he's done me a personal favor—whereupon
His look darkens. "But what these pictures show . . .

Here, look, you'll notice the gland on the left's
Enlarged. See?" I see an aerial shot
Of Iraq, and nod. "We'll need further tests,
Of course, but I'd bet that what *you've* got

Is a liver problem. Trouble with your estrogen
Levels. It's time, my friend, to take stock.
It happens more often than you'd think to men."

Reeling from its millionth scotch on the rocks,
In other words, my liver's sensed the end.
Why does it come as something less than a shock?

IV

The end of life as I've known it, that is to say—
Testosterone sported like a power tie,
The matching set of drives and dreads that may
Now soon be plumped to whatever new designs

My apparently resentful, androgynous
Inner life has on me. Blind seer?
The Bearded Lady in some provincial circus?
Something that others both desire and fear.

Still, doesn't everyone *long* to be changed,
Transformed to, no matter, a higher or lower state,
To know the leathery D-Day hero's strange

Detachment, the queen bee's dreamy loll?
Yes, but the future each of us blankly awaits
Was long ago written on the genetic wall.

V

So suppose the breasts fill out until I look
Like my own mother . . . ready to nurse a son,
A version of myself, the infant understood
In the end as the way my own death had come.

Or will I in a decade be back here again,
The diagnosis this time not freakish but fatal?
The changes in one's later years all tend,
Until the last one, toward the farcical,

Each of us slowly turned into something that hurts,
Someone we no longer recognize.
If soul is the final shape I shall assume,

(—*A knock at the door. Time to button my shirt*
And head back out into the waiting room.)
Which of my bodies will have been the best disguise?

❖ LEON STOKESBURY ❖

TO HIS BOOK

Wafer; thin and hard and bitter pill I
   Take from time to time; pillow I have lain
      Too long on; holding the brief dreams, the styled
Dreams, the nightmares, shadows, red flames high
   High up on mountains; wilted zinnias, rain
      On dust, and great weight, the dead dog, and wild
Onions; mastodonic woman who knows how,—
   I'm tired of you, tired of your insane
      Acid eating in the brain. Sharp stones, piled
Particularly, I let you go. Sink, or float, or fly now,
      Bad child.

RILKE'S LETTER FROM ROME

Certainly you've missed this on your reading list,
or have you? do you truly agree with Rilke's dark
equality, that women should be set free to be who
they are? are you that committed to this anguished

apartness? after all, we're no longer young, hello?
The phone's ringing once again, Housman calling,
the cherry blossoms fall. Frost, hunched upon
the old farm, is gazing at white spiders. Jarrell

is gone, his love for Mary—"Change me, change me"—
is all that is left of him, his beloved semesters,
his street crossings, his crooning essays, and, yes,
each woman misses him as I miss you, immediately,

so, let the letter from Rome go. You've read it. I've
read it. It's a good letter. Not as good as you, though.

PERSONALS

Approximate and unfulfilled, a devilish nymph
in the underworld seeks huge black swan for fiery
twills in cranium's caverns, gray-matter indifference
preferred, although will take sensitivity, as well,

if inexperience in hell is available, for long-term
committed one-flight stand with ensuing consequences
such as bestial transformations and showering soot.
Nymph will attempt to run, as required, from

dark thwunking destiny. Nymph will not be easy
to acquire, though promised to succumb to aerial fury.
Various disguises necessary, drop chute appreciated.

Do not send photograph, please; visuals confusing,
element of surprise essential, fact of advertisement
accidental. Pretend you don't read and never will.

BALANCE

He watch her like a coonhound watch a tree.
What might explain the metamorphosis
he underwent when she paraded by
with tea-cakes, in her fresh and shabby dress?
(As one would carry water from a well—
straight-backed, high-headed, like a diadem,
with careful grace so that no drop will spill—
she balanced, almost brimming, her one name.)

She thinks she something, stuck-up island bitch.
Chopping wood, hanging laundry on the line,
and tantalizingly within his reach,
she honed his body's yearning to a keen,
sharp point. And on that point she balanced life.
That hoe Diverne think she Marse Tyler's wife.

CHOSEN

Diverne wanted to die, that August night
his face hung over hers, a sweating moon.
She wished so hard, she killed part of her heart.

If she had died, her one begotten son,
her life's one light, would never have been born.
Pomp Atwood might have been another man:

born with a single race, another name.
Diverne might not have known the starburst joy
her son would give her. And the man who came

out of a twelve-room house and ran to her
close shack across three yards that night, to leap
onto her cornshuck pallet. Pomp was their

share of the future. And it wasn't rape.
In spite of her raw terror. And his whip.

CHOPIN

It's Sunday evening. Pomp holds the receipts
of all the colored families on the Hill
in his wide lap, and shows which white store cheats
these patrons, who can't read a weekly bill.
His parlor's full of men holding their hats
and women who admire his girls' good hair.
Pomp warns them not to trust the Democrats,
controlling half of Hickman from his chair.
The varying degrees of cheating seen,
he nods toward the piano. Slender, tall,
a Fisk girl passing-white, almost nineteen,
his Blanche folds the piano's paisley shawl
and plays Chopin. And blessed are the meek
who have to buy in white men's stores next week.

❖ BRUCE SMITH ❖

from *In My Father's House*

O MY INVISIBLE ESTATE

—Vaughan

Where the afternoon sun blears the city.
Where the high-numbered streets zero
their dignity, we live without irony.
No house but a shadow
of a house, but when we need a shadow
this shadow is ours. The shadow
of a man and his two arms, tenderness
and some hunger that I was rocked in.
And whatever house has been in me since then,
a flesh made and unmade since then,
I find that every churchyard has a stone
that bears our name, Father. Imagine
the monuments to a name so common,
imagine that dark land is what we own.

❖ MOLLY PEACOCK ❖

THE LULL

The possum lay on the tracks fully dead.
I'm the kind of person who stops to look.
It was big and white with flies on its head,
a thick healthy hairless tail, and strong, hooked
nails on its racoon-like feet. It was a full-
grown possum. It was sturdy and adult.
Only its head was smashed. In the lull
that it took to look, you took the time to insult
the corpse, the flies, the world, the fact that we were
traipsing in our dress shoes down the railroad tracks.
"That's disgusting." You said that. Dreams, brains, fur
and guts: what we are. That's my bargain, the Pax
Peacock, with the world. Look hard, life's soft. Life's cache
is flesh, flesh, and flesh.

DESIRE

It doesn't speak and it isn't schooled,
like a small foetal animal with wettened fur.
It is the blind instinct for life unruled,
visceral frankincense and animal myrrh.
It is what babies bring to kings,
an eyes-shut, ears-shut medicine of the heart
that smells and touches endings and beginnings
without the details of time's experienced *part-
fit-into-part-fit-into-part*. Like a paw,
it is blunt; like a pet who knows you
and nudges your knee with its snout—but more raw
and blinder and younger and more divine, too,
than the tamed wild—it's the drive for what is real,
deeper than the brain's detail: the drive to feel.

INSTEAD OF HER OWN

Instead of her own, my grandmother washed my hair.
The porcelain was cold at the back of my neck,
my fragile neck. Altogether it was cold there.

She did it so my hair would smell sweet.
What else is like the moist mouse straw
of a girl's head? Why, the feeling of complete

peace the smell brings to a room whose window
off oily Lake Erie is rimmed with snow.
Knuckles rasping at young temples know,

in the involuntary way a body knows,
that as old is, so young grows. Completion
drives us: substitution is our mission.

Thin little head below thin little head grown old.
Water almost warm in a room almost cold.

THE PURR

As you stand still in the hall thinking what
to do next and I approach you from behind,
I think behind must be best: your naked
rump scalloped beneath the plumb

line of your spine's furred tree. But
as I catch the concentration in the kind
angling of your head toward the cats and tread
catlike myself behind you, your scrotum

hung like an oriole's nest, I cut
beneath your outstretched arm and find
I'm hungry for your face instead,
hungry for my future. The mysterious thrum

that science can't yet explain awakes a hum
in me, the sound something numb come alive makes.

THE HUNT

The stubby black-jowled dog inside me growls
and drools and warns and plants its crooked feet,
legs quivering, brindle chest staunched, and howls
until approachers back off in defeat,
although a brilliant poacher sometimes cows
my dog, my heart, its bitten hope, with meat,
flung viscera my tamed dog mauls
and then protects, well guarding what I eat
while poacher raises rifle: he follows
my deer into my wood, calling me dear, fleet
beauty, and I run, wholly my wild soul,
while the dumb, bristled dog I too am prowls,
guarding empty gate and empty street
till hunter becomes me, and we repeat.

❖ HUGH SEIDMAN ❖

14 FIRST SENTENCES

He had never kept a journal.
Sometimes he wanted to write prose about first love.
Once he heard Auden lecture: Don't falsify history.
He used to feel better if people in novels were rich.
Williams wrote: Old woman, all this was for you.
He was going to type: The form of a life changes little.
Reich said the Eskimos say: Don't thwart a child.
Zukofsky taught: The poet makes one long poem.
Mathematicians say: Notation is notion.
The dream voice said: Imagination fails the dream.
He read in the paper: The poor, mired in poverty.
Sometimes he remembered the books forgotten in libraries.
Do we sleep only because night falls?
How shall one speak how another suffers?

❖ FLOYD SKLOOT ❖

MY DAUGHTER CONSIDERS HER BODY

She examines her hand, fingers spread wide.
Seated, she bends over her crossed legs
to search for specks or scars and cannot hide
her awe when any mark is found. She begs
me to look, twisting before her mirror,
at some tiny bruise on her hucklebone.
Barely awake, she studies creases her
arm developed as she slept. She has grown
entranced with blemish, begun to know
her body's facility for being
flawed. She does not trust its will to grow
whole again, but may learn that too, freeing
herself to accept the body's deep thirst
for risk. Learning to touch her wounds comes first.

❖ RACHEL HADAS ❖

MOMENTS OF SUMMER

I

Let gleaming motes of hayseed in the barn
be asterisks embedded in the text
of ever after. Over by the lawn
let the hammock be an ampersand
skewed to the horizontal, loosely slung
between an evergreen and larch whose sap
sometimes bedews the dreamer in suspension.
Let the book left open on her lap
and on whose margins scattered symbols mark
tempo as slow, as slower, as quite still,
guide her between this twilight and the next.
The swinging stops. Behind the pine-treed hill
Venus appears to herald in the green
slumber of gardens growing in the dark.

II

June's supple weavings covered up the dry
tank winter had just drained. So did it fill?
Not yet. The least green gesture halted me.
A sundial blandly bedded among flowers
foreshadows a beginning or an end,
silently tells the passing of the hours:
that promise, that futility, that beauty.
Each summer points to picnics on the hill.
What if what falters is the sheer desire
to scale even our modest little mound,
look over treetops, steeples, see the whole?
Somewhere invisible a chainsaw roars.
Precisely where pines creak and sway and fall
is muffled in imagination's veil.

III

The horizontal tugs me more and more.
Childhood hours spent reading with my father
rise in a kind procession once again.
Disparate gravities of our two ages
dissolve as we lie back and let the pages
take us, float us, sail us out to sea.
What special spell (not always narrative;
the winter we read "De Senectute"
I was fifteen; you had two years to live)
braided our endless differences to one?
Today a mother reading to my son,
I savor freshly that sweet nourishment,
timeless hours reading motionless together,
especially if we are lying down.

❖ DAVID LEHMAN ❖

SONNET

No roof so poor it does not shelter
The memory of the death of at least one man
In at least one septic room,
No wind so light it dare not dislodge
From their neglected home beneath the house
The bones of a discarded belief.

Yet the buyer cannot bear to look, keeps
A lock on the cellar door, and prays
For the well-behaved past to stay in place
As if, like the date on the blackboard,
It existed only to be ignored and erased
But threatens nevertheless to endure
Beyond the hour of its chalk, suspected
If not seen, like the smudge of a star.

❖ TIMOTHY STEELE ❖

SUMMER

Voluptuous in plenty, summer is
Neglectful of the earnest ones who've sought her.
She best resides with what she images:
Lakes windless with profound sun-shafted water;
Dense orchards in which high-grassed heat grows thick;
The one-lane country road where, on his knees,
A boy initials soft tar with a stick;
Slow creeks which bear flecked light through depths of trees.

And he alone is summer's who relents
In his poor enterprisings; who can sense,
In alleys petal-blown, the wealth of chance;
Or can, supine in a deep meadow, pass
Warm hours beneath a moving sky's expanse,
Chewing the sweetness from long stalks of grass.

❖ AGHA SHAHID ALI ❖

from *I Dream I Am the Only Passenger on Flight 423 to Srinagar,*

and when we—as if from ashes—ascend
into the cold where the heart must defend

its wings of terror and even pity
and below us the haze of New Delhi

grays, *In your eyes I look for my wounds' deep sea.*
But five hundred years waved with history?

It is to song that one must turn for flight.
But with what measure will I shed sunlight

on pain? *In your eyes—Was her sari turquoise?—*
I look for the deep sea . . . That is her voice—

Begum Akhtar's. "You were the last, we know,
to see her in Delhi, Desperado

in search of catastrophe." Heartbreak of perfume
is mine again. The pilot turns up the volume:

Attar—of jasmine? What was it she wore
that late morning in October '74

when we were driven (it was the sunniest
day) from Connaught Place to Palam Airport? She pressed

a note—Rs. 100—into my palm:
"Take it or, on my life, I will perish."

They announced DEPARTURE. I touched her arm.
Her sari *was* turquoise! She turned to vanish,

but then turned to wave. (*My silk is stained,*
How will I face my Lord? she'd set in Pain—

her chosen raga that July in Srinagar.)
A week later: GHAZAL QUEEN BEGUM AKHTAR

IS DEAD. She had claimed her right-to-die:
She had sung "Everyone Will Be Here But I"

SWAY

Since I find you will no longer love,
from bar to bar in terror I shall move
past Forty-third and Halsted, Twenty-fourth
and Roosevelt where fire-gutted cars,
their bones the bones of coyote and hyena,
suffer the light from the wrestling arena
to fall all over them. And what they say
blends in the tarantellasmic sway
of all of us between the two of these:
harmony and divergence,
their sad story of harmony and divergence,
the story that begins
I did not know who she was
and ends *I did not know who she was.*

PASSENGERS

The world will burst like an intestine in the sun,
the dark turn to granite and the granite to a name,
but there will always be somebody riding the bus
through these intersections strewn with broken glass
among speechless women beating their little ones,
always a slow alphabet of rain
speaking of drifting and perishing to the air,
always these definite jails of light in the sky
at the wedding of this clarity and this storm
and a woman's turning—her languid flight of hair
traveling through frame after frame of memory
where the past turns, its face sparkling like emery,
to open its grace and incredible harm
over my life, and I will never die.

MARRIED LOVE

As they sat and talked beneath the boundary trees
In the abandoned park, neither one mentioning
Her husband, or his wife, it seemed as though
Their summer shadows had detached themselves
In the confusion of those thousand leaves: but no more
Than they could call those shadows back from the air,
Could they ignore the lives they had undone,
And would undo once more, that afternoon,
Before giving in to what they knew, had always known.
And yet, in turning away, what they would say was not
That thing, but something else, that mild excuse
That lovers use of how things might have been
Had they met somewhere else, or in some better time,
Were they less like themselves than what they are.

❖ JULIA ALVAREZ ❖

from *33*

"Where are the girls who were so beautiful?"

Where are the girls who were so beautiful?
I don't mean back in the olden days either,
I mean yesterday and the day before
yesterday? Tell me, if you can, where will
I find breathless Vivien or Marilyn,
her skirt blown up? Certainly Natalie,
struggling in the cold waves, deserved to be
fished out when the crew finished and given
her monogrammed beach towel and a hot drink.
How many times didn't we pay good money
to see them saved from worse catastrophes
as they trembled in swimsuits on the brink
of death, Rita and Jean, Lana and Joan,
Frances, Marlene—their names sound like our own.

"Let's make a modern primer for our kids"

Let's make a modern primer for our kids:
A is for Auschwitz; B for Biafra;
Chile; Dachau; El Salvador; F is
the Falklands; Grenada; Hiroshima
stands for H; Northern Ireland for I;
J is for Jonestown; K for Korea;
L for massacres in Lidice; My Lai;
N, Nicaragua; O, Okinawa;
P is the Persian Gulf and Qatar, Q;
Rwanda; Sarajevo—this year's hell;
T is Treblinka and Uganda U;
Vietnam and Wounded Knee. What's left to spell?
An X to name the countless disappeared
when they are dust in Yemen or Zaire.

"Ever have an older lover say: God"

Ever have an older lover say: God!
I once thought I used to love so and so
so much, but now that I love you, I know
that wasn't love. Even though it feels good
at our age to be flattered with being
the first woman a man has ever loved,
it burns my blood thinking of those I loved
with my whole soul (small as it was back then)
quibble if what they felt for me was love
now that they've had a taste of the real stuff.
I say, Don't trust those men with better,
bigger versions of love if they refuse
the small, shabby sample they gave others
the tribute of believing it was true.

Secretly I am building in the heart
a delicate structure like one of those
cardhouses or Popsicle palaces
kids build, patiently piecing each part
together, fingers pinching a small tube
of glue, eyes straining to perceive what new
thing I am making that takes so much time
to finish if there's finish in these things.
And making it out of nothing but what
are ruins from an earlier effort
and tempted constantly to believe that
a readymade is better, and yet I've
labored with my heart to outlast the heart
with this thing I'm creating out of love.

❖ DANA GIOIA ❖

SUNDAY NIGHT IN SANTA ROSA

The carnival is over. The high tents,
the palaces of light, are folded flat
and trucked away. A three-time loser yanks
the Wheel of Fortune off the wall. Mice
pick through the garbage by the popcorn stand.
A drunken giant falls asleep beside
the juggler, and the Dog-Faced Boy sneaks off
to join the Serpent Lady for the night.
Wind sweeps ticket stubs along the walk.
The Dead Man loads his coffin on a truck.
Off in a trailer by the parking lot
the radio predicts tomorrow's weather
while a clown stares in a dressing mirror,
takes out a box, and peels away his face.

❖ T. R. HUMMER ❖

THE RURAL CARRIER STOPS TO KILL
A NINE-FOOT COTTONMOUTH

Lord God, I saw the son-of-a-bitch uncoil
In the road ahead of me, uncoil and squirm
For the ditch, squirm a hell of a long time.
Missed him with the car. When I got back to him, he was all
But gone, nothing left on the road but the tip-end
Of his tail, and that disappearing into Johnson grass.
I leaned over the ditch and saw him, balled up now, hiss.
I aimed for the mouth and shot him. And shot him again.

Then I got a good strong stick and dragged him out.
He was long and evil, thick as the top of my arm.
There are things in this world a man can't look at without
Wanting to kill. Don't ask me why. I was calm
Enough, I thought. But I felt my spine
Squirm suddenly. I admit it. It was mine.

❖ MEDBH McGUCKIAN ❖

STILL LIFE OF EGGS

for Sylvia Kelly

You are almost kneeling, a diagonal shoreline
between two harbours, in the house-fostered darkness.
The tilt of your head reflects the arc
of the tablecloth, the curve of the sea.
And if the weather could fling its reds,
greens, blues, and purples across table-tops
(thought upon the unthinking) the blue might stay
a river or a lake, the fraying edges fog.
Like the beginning of a painting you have been
so watched: like an additional storey squeezed
into a steep roof, you freeze
the forever ripening shadows under
your eyebrows and neck into younger stone.
Contained, containing—perfectly alone.

WHY BROWNLEE LEFT

Why Brownlee left, and where he went,
Is a mystery even now.
For if a man should have been content
It was him; two acres of barley,
One of potatoes, four bullocks,
A milker, a slated farmhouse.
He was last seen going out to plough
On a March morning, bright and early.

By noon Brownlee was famous;
They had found all abandoned, with
The last rig unbroken, his pair of black
Horses, like man and wife,
Shifting their weight from foot to
Foot, and gazing into the future.

HOLY THURSDAY

They're kindly here, to let us linger so late,
Long after the shutters are up.
A waiter glides from the kitchen with a plate
Of stew, or some thick soup,

And settles himself at the next table but one.
We know, you and I, that it's over,
That something or other has come between
Us, whatever we are, or were.

The waiter swabs his plate with bread
And drains what's left of his wine,
Then rearranges, one by one,
The knife, the fork, the spoon, the napkin,
The table itself, the chair he's simply borrowed,
And smiles, and bows to his own absence.

Whatever it is, it all comes down to this;
My father's cock
Between my mother's thighs.
Might he have forgotten to wind the clock?

Cookers and eaters, Fuck the Pope,
Wow and flutter, a one-legged howl,
My sly quadroon, the way home from the pub—
Anything wild or wonderful—

Whatever it is, it goes back to this night,
To a chance remark
In a room at the top of the stairs;
To an open field, as like as not,
Under the little stars.
Whatever it is, it leaves me in the dark.

❖ RITA DOVE ❖

HADES' PITCH

If I could just touch your ankle, he whispers, *there*
on the inside, above the bone—leans closer,
breath of lime and peppers—*I know I could*
make love to you. She considers
this, secretly thrilled, though she wasn't quite
sure what he meant. He was good
with words, words that went straight to the liver.
Was she falling for him out of sheer boredom—
cooped up in this anything-but-humble dive, stone
gargoyles leering and brocade drapes licked with fire?
Her ankle burns where he described it. She sighs
just as her mother aboveground stumbles, is caught
by the fetlock—bereft in an instant—
while the Great Man drives home his desire.

This is for the woman with one black wing
perched over her eyes: lovely Frida, erect
among parrots, in the stern petticoats of the peasant,
who painted herself a present—
wildflowers entwining the plaster corset
her spine resides in, that flaming pillar—
this priestess in the romance of mirrors.

Each night she lay down in pain and rose
to the celluloid butterflies of her Beloved Dead,
Lenin and Marx and Stalin arrayed at the footstead.
And rose to her easel, the hundred dogs panting
like children along the graveled walks of the garden, Diego's
love a skull in the circular window
of the thumbprint searing her immutable brow.

❖ MARK JARMAN ❖

from *Unholy Sonnets*

2

Which is the one, which of the imps inside
Unglues itself from the yin-yang embrace
Of its good twin or its bad twin and plays
The angel advocate, the devil's guide?
Which blob of conscience, like a germicide,
Catches and kills the impulse when it strays?
Which impulse with light playing on its face,
Its fright mask, leads to the dark outside?

All of them shapeless feelings given form
By words which they in turn give substance to.
As particle and wave make light, they swarm
Together with their names. And we do, too,
Praying that God knows each of us and cares
About the things we speak of in our prayers.

9

Someone is always praying as the plane
Breaks up, and smoke and cold and darkness blow
Into the cabin. Praying as it happens,
Praying before it happens that it won't.
Someone was praying that it never happen
Before the first window on Kristallnacht
Broke like a wine glass wrapped in bridal linen.
Before it was imagined, someone was praying
That it be unimaginable. And then,
The bolts blew off and people fell like bombs
Out of their names, out of the living sky.
Surely, someone was praying. And the prayer
Struck the blank face of earth, the ocean's face,
The rockhard, rippled face of facelessness.

14   *In via est cisterna*

All she remembers from her Latin class
Is a phrase she echoes for her granddaughter.
Lately I hear in everything she says
A depth that she covers up with laughter.
In the road is a well. But in her mind
It fills with blanks, like a shaft of sand and pebbles.
A well is in the road. It is profound,
I'm sure, it is a phrase with many levels.
And then, I see one: the woman with five husbands
Met Jesus there. But my mother had only one—
Unless now having lost him she understands
That he was never who she thought, but someone
Who was different men with different women through the years.
In the road is a well. It fills with tears.

❖ ELIZABETH MACKLIN ❖

I FAIL TO SPEAK TO MY EARTH, MY DESIRE

Having set my heart on you, I remove it
and set it aside. You my desire,
my table, my solid ground, my own true
surface. A mouse in any corner may try
to come out. A wind may cool and blow
us askew. You my desire are not my
property. You may not ever be so.

You my love, my world. Now, have I set my heart on
you? A trace, a kiss, a print, a small brown
scratch: Do you have a clue? Kind as you are,
I am proud or— Nothing in the whole great house
will show where the heart is now. Nor
will the mouse find comforting crumbs. As if, my ground,
I were still waiting to be shown what it is I am for.

FOOLISHLY HALVED, I SEE YOU

The white-green wheel of a sliced lime
after a day: so naturally dry,

and so protective of all its remaining
juice. This is the quick thought so sly
of the classic survivor. But you have survived

the living! the only in doubt,
for now, the only in danger.

Now the foolish attempt to—*wait*—not think
about the cut fruit. No, don't cry,

not yet, over its unspilled half-green
milk. It dries hard overnight. I
am you. And the dying hasn't died

yet. In fact, is perhaps not dying,
although—you do too love him—he is in danger.

THE VERY END

for my grandmother

My eyes are strange to the print tonight;
Nero, Caligula, their crimes disappear.
Instead, a pair of button-shoes you wore,
False teeth, a veil, a monogrammed bracelet,
Blot the Roman sun with their antiquity;
And risen in its place, you dust or cook,
Read the latest in child psychology,
Your gloved voice threatening, "Wouldn't you like . . . "
Yes, it is miraculous to think of you
At all, what with history droning names
Pricked by the triumvirate, Oblivion,
Epitaph, Farewell. Even to see you
Surface above your facts, the dates marked for birth,
Marriage, death, asks that I float you on my breath.

ECLIPSE

for my mother

When from among the dead the faces
Of her mother and father turn to her,
At first bright and blank as ice, then melting
To flow to see their only daughter

Miraculously restored, then the living
She loved and who loved her
Fade like fog and are forgotten;
Blank as a wall, her mind registers

The mutual play of light off those long-dead faces
Which, as her parents move to embrace her,
Glow blindingly bright—my final glimpse
Of her face eclipsed by the other dead coming near:

Stepping from every shadow to surround her
They lock hands in an unbreakable chain.

from *The Work*

4. THE GOD

a dream

A warming pulsing flood like blood surging through
Veins, and now the god stirs in my hands
Dull as stone in this gravity-less Nowhere.
Sensation shivering through me, deliberate and sure,

I cradle you, I sponge you clean
As if you were *my* son, the emptiness you
Drink like heavy black milk erasing
Your wrinkles and gouged lines of pain.

The god bends me to the work, my fingers driven
By the god, blinded by the god's
Neutrality, until I pull apart the threads
In this place the god commands:

Face wholly unwoven, without heart, mind, you
Are nothing in my hands but my hands moving.

❖ ROSANNA WARREN ❖

NECROPHILIAC

More marrow to suck, more elegies
to whistle through the digestive track. So help
me God to another dollop of death,
come on strong with the gravy and black-eyed peas,
slop it all in the transcendental stew
whose vapors rise and shine in the nostrils of heaven.
Distill the belches, preserve the drool as ink:
Death, since you nourish me, I'll flatter you
inordinately. Consumers both, with claws
cocked and molars prompt at the fresh-dug grave,
reaper and elegist, we collaborate
and batten in this strictest of intimacies,
my throat an open sepulchre, my tongue
forever groping grief forever young.

❖ DAVID WOJAHN ❖

from *Mystery Train: A Sequence*

I.

HOMAGE: LIGHT FROM THE HALL

It is Soul Brother Number One, James Brown,
Chanting. "It wouldn't be nothing, noth-iiiiinnnnnggg. . . ."
Dismembering the notes until everything hangs
On his mystical half-screech, notes skidding 'round
Your brain as you listen, rapt, thirteen,
Transistor and its single earphone tucked
With you beneath the midnight covers, station WKED,
Big Daddy Armand, The Ragin' Cajun,
"Spinning out the *bossest* platters for you all,"
Golden Age trance, when New Orleans stations
Traveling two thousand miles shaped distance
Into alchemy. Beneath the door, a light from the hall
Bathing the bedroom in its stammering glow:
Cooke and Redding risen, James Brown quaking the Apollo.

BUDDY HOLLY WATCHING
REBEL WITHOUT A CAUSE,
LUBBOCK, TEXAS, 1956

He's played hookey to see the flick again,
Though it's only showing at The Alhambra,

The run-down joint in the barrio. Spanish version,
Tawdry trashed marquee: *Rebelde Sin Causa.*

Dean staggers into Juvey, playing a credible drunk,
Though his dubbed voice squeaks like Mickey Mouse.

Me llamo Jaime Stark. But Dean's trademark smirk
Obliterates the dialogue. Buddy studies every gesture,

Hornrims sliding the bridge of his nose,
Though the smirk doesn't save that punk in the car,

Crashing to some stock-footage ocean, doesn't save Sal Mineo's
Benighted life. But Buddy, walking home, wants a *trademark.*

In shop window reflections, he practices the Jim Dean strut.
Some of us, he thinks, will never get it right.

❖ DAVID BAKER ❖

TOP OF THE STOVE

And then she would lift her griddle
tool from the kindling bin, hooking one
end through a hole in the cast-iron disk
to pry it up with a turn of her wrist.

Our faces pinked over to watch coal
chunks churn and fizz. This was before
I had language to say so, the flatiron
hot all day by the kettle, fragrance

of coffee and coal smoke over
the kitchen in a mist. What did I know?
Now they've gone. Language remains.
I hear her voice like a lick of flame

to a bone-cold day. Careful, she says.
I hold my head close to see what she means.

❖ BRUCE BOND ❖

ISAAC

There are mountains, ask any believer,
where to wake suddenly is to risk
your life, where the spirit cold and fevered
would burn like rope in the body's fist,
so when I woke under the winter sky
last night, startled by the copper bell
of a goat above me, the way its eye
met mine I took it for a man or angel
or some such frightened thing. Like me it
darted backwards, tightening the thread
of sight between us. And so I slipped
a little farther out of sleep, my head
aching, my father mumbling where he lay,
one wakeful star above us like a blade.

❖ PHILLIS LEVIN ❖

FINAL REQUEST

If I die I will need a cross
To carry me to the next world,
The one I do not believe in.
But a cross will carry me
Anyway. When I meet the dory
That overturns despair—
When he who could not
Let love carry him over

Weeps, finally weeps there,
Where he does not believe
He will go—my arms will be
So cruel. Whether or not
They hold him, whether or not
I want to they will want to.

❖ JAMES McCORKLE ❖

DEER AT THE CORNER OF THE HOUSE

Sight takes place at the edge, around corners, along snow-sagged
Fences, cutting across spirea flattened under a mat of white.
Looking straight ahead is dangerous for what can be
Missed, not that answers slide along this corridor of hedge and pine,
Coming to us by luck, not that answers even move
In the snow-stirred air, as though someone had passed by, as they have
Before, in the early morning before light, here and elsewhere,
Never to arrive again, like deer at the corner
Of the empty white house above the ravine, caught sight of
By the luck of passing by not too quickly that day—they must come
Out of hunger, the snow too deep to paw out shoots,
The branches ringed like a shell's suture with new buds,
Maroon and hard—then they turn, as though the short nights
Of August were already here, the gardens full, and no one on this path.

❖ JOHN BURNSIDE ❖

THE MYTH OF THE TWIN

Say it moved when you moved:
a softness that rose in the ground
when you walked, or a give in your step,
the substance that Virgil saw
in the shadows under our feet;

and say it was out there, out in the snow,
meshed with the birdsong and light
the way things are real: a blackbird, a scribble of thorns,
a quickening into the moment, the present tense,

and the way that a stumbling or sudden
rooting in authenticity is not
the revelation of a foreign place,
but emptiness, a stillness in the frost,
the silence that stands in the birchwoods, the common soul.

PRAYER

Some days, although we cannot pray, a prayer
utters itself. So, a woman will lift
her head from the sieve of her hands and stare
at the minims sung by a tree, a sudden gift.

Some nights, although we are faithless, the truth
enters our hearts, that small familiar pain;
then a man will stand stock-still, hearing his youth
in the distant Latin chanting of a train.

Pray for us now. Grade I piano scales
console the lodger looking out across
a Midlands town. Then dusk, and someone calls
a child's name as though they named their loss.

Darkness outside. Inside, the radio's prayer—
Rockall. Malin. Dogger. Finisterre.

❖ ROBIN ROBERTSON ❖

WEDDING THE LOCKSMITH'S DAUGHTER

The slow-grained slide to embed the blade
of the key is a sheathing,
a gliding on graphite, pushing inside
to find the ribs of the lock.

Sunk home, the true key slots to its matrix;
geared, tight-fitting, they turn
together, shooting the spring-lock,
throwing the bolt. Dactyls, iambics—

the clinch of words—the hidden couplings
in the cased machine. A chime of sound
on sound: the way the sung note snibs on meaning

and holds. The lines engage and marry now,
their bells are keeping time;
the church doors close and open underground.

❖ APRIL BERNARD ❖

SONNET IN E

The diction of the dispossessed, clattering.
Is there nothing that will glide, or is all to be caught
like a woollen sock on the nail in the floorboard,
caught and ripped and cursed and caught again?
For these are the alternatives: to inhale the world
into the magnificent misery of the solitary,
who feeds and grows thereby, or else, or else—
to fling the particles of person wide, awash on the blue.
Explosion: tiny feathered hands that touch cheeks,
and rush past, streaming chloroplasts, golden green
and living, is this too much to ask, that it glide
and swell in the sacrament of self-possession?
I am no longer obliged to sit like a china dog
on a table in the corner of the room.

CHIFFON MORNING

I

I am lying in bed with my mother,
where my father seldom lay. Little poem,
help me to say all I need to say, better.
Hair dyed, combed; nails polished; necklace-like scar
ear-to-ear; stocky peasant's bulk hidden
under an unfeminine nightgown; sour-milk
breaths rehearsing death, she faces me, her room
a pill museum where orange teabags
draining on napkins almost pass for art.
Even the Christmas amaryllis sags
under the weight of its blood red
petals, unfolding like a handkerchief.
From the television screen, a beauty-
pageant queen waves serenely at me.

II

In the oily black barbecue smoke,
in our blue Chevrolet station wagon,
in a cottage at the sea, no one spoke
but me to the nerveless God
who never once stopped their loveless act:
the cursing mouths, the shoving and choking,
the violent pulse, the wrecked hair, the hunchbacked
reprisal, the suddenly inverted sky,
the fiendish gasping, the blade that cuts all
understanding, the white knuckles, the fly
remarkably poised on a blue throat.
I try to pity them. Perhaps God did
on those occasions when battle was a prelude
to sex, and peace, like an arrow, found us.

III

How many nights did I throw my arms around
our black dog's neck and listen to Mother,
on her knees, retching supper? The love hound
licked my face again and again like fur.
Far off, the weirdly ethereal bells
of an ice cream truck, hypnotic in contrast,
calmed me like tapers burning steadily.
Near dawn, when she was pregnant with her last-
born, there were complications. The long path
to the ambulance was splashed with what came
from inside her, a floating purplish wax
our neighbor, a cheerful woman, mopped up.
When Mother came home thin again, the sun crowned
whom she cradled. Father was out of town.

IV

On the mowed grass, I once posed in black tie;
now a neighbor's labradors sow lawn-burn.
Pink dogwoods Mother and I transplanted
throw off their sentimental silks.
If squirrels nest in a tree too close by,
she hires a colonel's son to oust them.
No one calls except born-again women.
"Must you tell everyone what you are?"
she protests, during each of our visits;
I rake leaves and burn them like a corpse,
wondering if I'm better off without her—
like Father when he was a GI
and their trailer-park love got coffined up
in a suburban dream house, for sale now.

V

As the cuckoo clock crows in the kitchen,
on her nightstand others as bluntly chime,
but cannot break her drugged oblivion.
Please wake up, Mother, and wet your cottonmouth.
"She was agitated," nurses whispered
when we found her tied to the bed, knocked out.
Demerol blocked the pain, entering through the eyes,
while the mind, crushed like a wineglass, healed.
"I'll bury you all," she gloated, at home again.
Months later, they stitched her throat in surgery.
The voice that had been on the radio
when the war was on, plunged a tragic octave.
More pills crowded her daily glass of milk.
My guilt seemed vain compared to what she felt.

VI

Mother is naked and holding me up
above her as soap streams from my face
(I'm wearing a dumb ape's frown) into the tub
where she is seated: the mind replays
what nurtures it. The black months when she
would lie assassinated like our Siamese cat
are still far off. Yet, tranced by a lush light,
which no one else sees, like a leaden bee
shackled to a poppy, I am not free.
Each time I am dunked in the green, green
sacramental water, I glare shamelessly
as she shrieks and kisses me, gripped in air;
I do not know if she loves me or cares,
if it's suffering or joy behind her tears.

❖ ANNIE FINCH ❖

MY RAPTOR

My mind hovered over my baby, like
a raptor, and froze everything it saw.
I looked through my own pregnant belly's raw
perimeters and found his heart to strike
attentive until, helpless with the pound
of still more blood, he seemed to settle down.
It was my loss to feel like god alone
for a new one always listening, to reach
inside for his ears to share the flying speech
I heard so constantly. Within my grown
silence, my sounding, my loud body where
the baby turned, my mind learned not to care
whether thoughts I felt he noticed with no fear
were mine alone—or whether he could hear.

❖ KARL KIRCHWEY ❖

ZOO STORY

It *could* have been the soul of my dead mother
I recognized quite accidentally
in the eyes of an Asian elephant cow.
That body shrugged toward me like a boulder
set to run downhill. The trunk idled with a listless
delicacy over dirty straw,
pinkly inquisitive. I heard a sigh.
I do not believe in metempsychosis;
yet, in a temple lobed and domed most strangely,
I mourned again, and worshiped after her,
buried in this landslide of a creature,
its crushing, dreamlike step, its slack repose,
its gaze, deep as the past or the hereafter,
swaying through counts of years, steady on me.

"Sandals more interwoven and complete
To fit the naked foot of poesy. . . . "
I look up, on this now-midmorning ride:
there, angled dozing in a dove-gray seat,
a ginger-haired girl's anonymous beauty
has caught my eye, the usual distraction.
And then, a brick wall on the urban hillside
beyond, sent past at the appropriate
moment in this private itinerary,
is the hospital where my father died.
Forever beyond pity or contrition,
I am fixed, unmoving. I sweat at how
slowly the wheel of my regard moves on.
I will not recall her an hour from now.

❖ DEBORAH LASER ❖

from *Between Two Gardens*

Night shares this day with me, is the rumpled
air about me. All day I go about dressed
in a stubborn dress, pink broadcloth
creased and starched and scented by night.

When I feel its scratch I think of night.
When I smell its slow drying I remember
the distant moon, cat across the yard,
my arms suspended, towels, and it

underneath the maple's stars. On days I want
to hold the dark. I dig in the garden,
tear up dandelions, long to enter the earth.

This is no death wish: I want to blossom
into a maple or an oak. Come, sit between
my shallow roots, lean; but do not pull me up.

❖ JACQUELINE OSHEROW ❖

SONNET FOR A SINGLE DAY IN AUTUMN

What was it payment for, the trove of gold
That landed on the lawn outside my door?
And what turned it instantly to oracle:
A heady vision of my study floor
Completely covered over as leaves of gold
Came flying off my printer, singing odes
Obliquely tuned to an improvident God's
Unwillingness to stint His taste for miracle
Despite our constant failure at belief.
This was what the angels use—gold leaf—
To plug the hairline fractures in their halos.
If only they'd gathered some before the snow's
Extravagantly surreptitious siege
Hushed them with its supple empty page.

YOM KIPPUR SONNET, WITH A LINE FROM LAMENTATIONS

Can a person atone for pure bewilderment?
For hyperbole? for being wrong
In a thousand categorical opinions?
For never opening her mouth, except too soon?
For ignoring, all week long, the waning moon
Retreating from its haunt above the local canyons,
Signaling her season to repent,
Then deflecting her repentance with a song?
Because the rest is just too difficult to face—
What we are—I mean—in all its meagerness—
The way we stint on any modicum of kindness—
What we allow ourselves—what we don't learn—
How each lapsed, unchanging year resigns us—
Return us, Lord, to you, and we'll return.

❖ JAMES LASDUN ❖

POWDER COMPACT

Twenties, machine-age cloisonné, steel lines
Shimmying through the enamel plaque,
Priced voluptuously—as I wrote the check
My new love surged on its own extravagance—
Nocturnal, businesslike, here was your brisk
Sinuous walk, your pagan/Puritan air—
It was like buying you in miniature . . .
I didn't look inside. A stifling musk
Burst on us as you opened it: the past;
The original owner's scented powder puff—
That's all. I didn't catch *memento mori*
Whispered in her spilt, too intimate dust
Till now, or read in hers, love's epitaph
Still pink and scut-soft in its reliquary.

PLAGUE YEARS

*There is, it would seem, in the dimensional scale of the world, a kind of delicate
meeting place between imagination and knowledge, a point, arrived at by dimin-
ishing large things and enlarging small ones, that is intrinsically artistic.*
—VLADIMIR NABOKOV, *SPEAK MEMORY*

Sore throat, persistent cough . . . The campus doctor
Tells me "just to be safe" to take the test.
The clinic protocol seems to insist
On an ironic calm. I hold my fear.
He draws a vial of blood for the City Lab,
I have to take it there, but first I teach
A class on Nabokov. Midway I reach
Into my bag for *Speak Memory,* and grab
The hot bright vial instead. I seem at once
Wrenched from the quizzical faces of my class
Into some silent anteroom of hell:
The "delicate meeting place"; I feel it pounce;
Terror—my life impacted in the glass
My death enormous in its scarlet grail.

READING SOMEONE ELSE'S LOVE POEMS

is, after all, all we've ever done
for centuries—except write them—but what
a strange thing it is, after all, rose-cheeks and sun-
hair and lips, and underarms, and that little gut
I love to nuzzle on, soft underbelly—oops—
that wasn't what I meant to talk about;
ever since handkerchiefs fell, and hoop-
skirts around ankles swirled
and smiled, lovers have dreamed their loves upon
the pages, courted and schemed and twirled
and styled, hoping that once they'd unfurled their down-
deep longing, they would have their prize—
not the songs of love, but love beneath disguise.

YOUR UNCONSCIOUS SPEAKS TO MY UNCONSCIOUS

Your unconscious speaks to my unconscious
like subtitles of another language, saying:
Why? Why did you do this
to me? So while we are laughing and playing,
my unconscious, hearing, says, *What did I*
do? Now yours is crying, weeping, saying,
Why are you doing this? Why
do you leave me? Aren't you staying?
And mine, astonished, says, *Sweetheart, I*
am right here. I am here. Your eyes
looking into mine. Your fingers in my hair.
But as our spines bend, something unties
in me, and I *am* no longer there.
For I have already watched you go,
in the movie, in the darkness, through the snow.

AND THEN THERE IS THAT INCREDIBLE MOMENT,

when you realize what you're reading,
what's being revealed to you, how it is not
what you expected, what you thought
you were reading, where you thought you were heading.
Then there is that incredible knowing
that surges up in you, speeding
your heart; and you swear you will keep on reading,
keep on writing until you find another not going
where you thought—and until *you* have taken
someone on that ride, so that *they* take in
their breath, so that *they* let out their
sigh, so that they will swear
they will not rest until they too
have taken someone the way they were taken by you.

for Agha Shahid Ali

❖ JOE BOLTON ❖

from *Style*

II

I was surprised to find how light I felt
With most of the back of my head missing.
I recall, when I was twelve, French kissing
A girl named Star in the dark of a half-built
Duplex at the edge of our subdivision.
It was twilight. I hear my mother's voice,
My name. Women loved me like licorice.
It took me years to find a decision
I could make; now I want to change my mind.
I want to stand up and say "It's all right"
To the mirror. I want to fall crying
Into my father's arms, ask what happened.
At least I looked good, walking down the street
With all the well-dressed dead, the chic dying.

❖ SASCHA FEINSTEIN ❖

from *Sonnets for Stan Gage (1945–1992)*

Floodlight shadow. Your shoes are stroking
  The platform's edge. Two hours before the gig—
    The drums HAVE to be intimidating!—
And because you think they're not you take a swig
  Of J.D. from a shiny flask. But they were.
    This was pain: each platinum strike drove nails
Into my head. ("STAN!") I'm still caught there,
  Pressed against the auditorium wall,
    Twitching as warm-up shots detonated
My chest. ("STAN! You've made the clock jump
  Forward!") *Yeah, but did they INTIMIDATE?*
    Sticks on the drum kit rug, you walk to the front
Of the stage, fingers slicing the air,
    Flicking blood across rows of empty chairs.

With young people the heart keeps beating even
  After other organs decay, your mother told me
    In the hours when tubes of pure oxygen
Failed to purify your liver, your kidneys—
  Just days after being admitted, amused,
    Almost, that you'd finally quit smoking. (And what
Hipster wrote, "Drummers and poets are used
  Like ashtrays YES"?) I loved how with cigarettes
    You'd sketch Emily Remler's guitar solos
At Fat Tuesday's, and you wanted every note
  She played. *Can you believe it? Thirty-two!*
    ("Was it a heart attack? Someone wrote—")
No, speedball. Impish smile. *But okay, sure—*
  I mean, you know—EVERYONE dies of heart failure.

❖ RAFAEL CAMPO ❖

THE MENTAL STATUS EXAM

What is the color of the mind? Beneath
The cranium it's pinkish grey, with flecks
Of white mixed in. What is the mind's motif?
Depends on what you mean: it's either sex
Or it's a box, release or pessimism.
Remember these three things: ball, sorrow, red.
Count backwards, from one-hundred down by sevens.
What is the color of the mind? It's said
That love can conquer all—interpret, please.
And who's the President? What year is it?
The mind is timeless, dizzy, unscrupulous;
The mind is sometimes only dimly lit.
Just two more silly questions: Can you sing
For us? Do you remember those three things?

❖ MIKE NELSON ❖

LIGHT SONNET FOR THE LOVER OF A DARK

I was not much more than a boy in those
days, and of all the half-witted ideas
I had, the one that a woman could mean
everything has come back to haunt me.

She and I went walking and arguing
about her face. Though it was night, the dark
brushed its hair aside, as she brushed her hair
aside, and I clearly saw it. It was

what happened in a planetarium
when the lights faded out and the stars came on
and were set turning. Way back. Way back. Fooled
by the illusion so the mystery

could take place. Squinting to make the ceiling
vault again. Just try and forget it.

❖ DANIEL GUTSTEIN ❖

WHAT CAN DISAPPEAR

"The very structure of it," said Warren, "the very idea. Now, think.
Rhyme—yes. Meter—yes. The number of lines—yes, yes, yes,—"
he said, as I got it, it seemed, an eight and a six, an eight and two less,
the sestet as an octave minus two. We smiled a moment, then drank
down our drafts, and more, and more after those. The dull clinks
our glasses left on the table, in toast, until we slurred—"less and loss,
lesson lost." We gave up laughing. Warren went to pay, then to piss.
Then I thought: two lines gone—the genius of the sonnet—in a blink.

We would never meet again. I would sit at our table and conjure
the very structure of it, the very idea. Meter—yes, yes, and rhyme.
The sestet as an octave minus two—or, *what can disappear.* I mull
the table's quiet grain, my draft (a couple sips short), and I figure
how the loss of a person grows beyond form, magnitude, and time.
How there used to be two glasses rising and falling. Now, the lull—

❖ BETH ANN FENNELLY ❖

POEM NOT TO BE READ AT YOUR WEDDING

You ask me for a poem about love
in place of a wedding present, trying to save me
money. For three nights I've lain under
glow-in-the-dark stars I've stuck to the ceiling
over my bed. I've listened to the songs
of the galaxy. Well, Carmen, I would rather
give you your third set of steak knives
than tell you what I know. Let me find you
some other store-bought present. Don't
make me warn you of stars, how they see us
from that distance as miniature and breakable,
from the bride who tops the wedding cake
to the Mary on Pinto dashboards
holding her ripe red heart in her hands.

THE DISEASE COLLECTOR

Odd word: culture, as though this swab cared
About art and music, loved the opera,
Saw the Ballet Russe when Nijinsky still bared
His chest, could quote the illuminata
In the original Italian. As though this petri dish
Were a center of learning, and parents wished
For their children to go there, like Harvard or Yale,
As though a positive answer would not pale
My cheeks, or force me to wholly rearrange
My life around pills and doctor's visits;
Force me to find old lovers and tricks,
Warn that their bodies may too grow strange;
To play the old game of who gave it to whom,
Gently lowering voices, alone in one's room.

Appendix: The Architecture of a Sonnet

GLOSSARY AND TRANSLATION OF TERMS

douzain: a twelve-line stanza

heroic couplet: a rhyming pair of iambic pentameter lines

rima baciata: Italian for "kissing rhyme"; "envelope rhyme" in English (abba)

rima alternata: Italian for "alternating rhyme"; any rhyme scheme that goes back and forth between two rhymes (abab . . .)

rima incatenata: Italian for "chained rhyme" or "linking rhyme"; an interlacing pattern, with many variations possible (abcabc, abcacb, etc.)

Sicilian stanza: any stanza in *rima alternata*

SONNETS OF THE SICILIAN COURT OF FREDERICK II

RHYME SCHEME

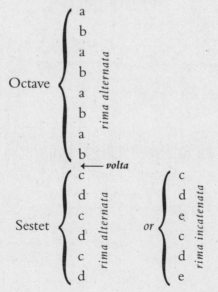

The first sonnets appeared in the Sicilian court of Emperor Frederick II. In the earliest sonnets, the exact same words repeat where the rhymes later occurred.

THE ITALIAN/PETRARCHAN SONNET

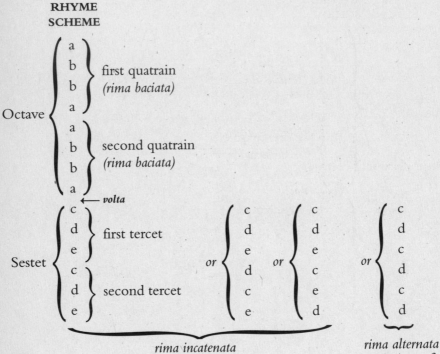

**RHYME
SCHEME**

Octave
{
a
b — first quatrain
b — *(rima baciata)*
a
a
b — second quatrain
b — *(rima baciata)*
a
}

← *volta*

Sestet
{
c
d — first tercet
e
c
d — second tercet
e
}

or
{
c
d
e
d
c
e
}

or
{
c
d
e
c
e
d
}

or
{
c
d
c
d
c
d
}

rima incatenata
variations of the sestet

rima alternata
variation of
the sestet
(Sicilian)

THE FRENCH SONNET

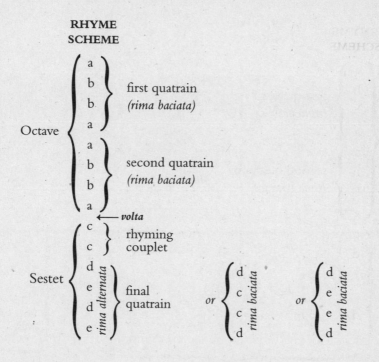

**RHYME
SCHEME**

Octave
- a
- b ⎫ first quatrain
- b ⎬ *(rima baciata)*
- a ⎭
- a
- b ⎫ second quatrain
- b ⎬ *(rima baciata)*
- a ⎭

← *volta*

Sestet
- c ⎫ rhyming
- c ⎭ couplet
- d ⎫ final
- e ⎬ quatrain *(rima alternata)*
- d
- e

or
- d
- c ⎬ *rima baciata*
- c
- d

or
- d
- e ⎬ *rima baciata*
- e
- d

The French sonnet follows the same pattern as the Italian/Petrarchan sonnet in its octave, but consistently begins the sestet with a rhyming couplet.

THE ENGLISH/SHAKESPEAREAN SONNET

**RHYME
SCHEME**

a ⎫
b ⎬ first quatrain
a ⎬ *(Sicilian)*
b ⎭

c ⎫
d ⎬ second quatrain
c ⎬ *(Sicilian)*
d ⎭

←— **shift**
e ⎫
f ⎬ third quatrain
e ⎬ *(Sicilian)*
f ⎭

←— **turn**
g ⎫ heroic
g ⎭ couplet

The English sonnet allows itself to gel into a variety of thematic or rhetorical groupings. The poem can flow as (12+2) or [(8+4)+2] or [8+(4+2)] or [(4+4+4)+2]. The most common oscillation in the English sonnet is between octave/sestet and douzain/couplet.

THE SPENSERIAN SONNET

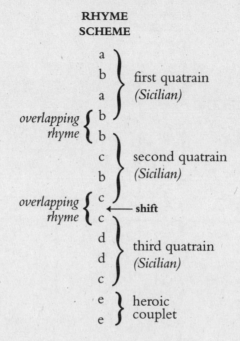

**RHYME
SCHEME**

a ⎫
b ⎬ first quatrain
a ⎭ *(Sicilian)*

overlapping ⎰ b
rhyme ⎱ b

c ⎫
b ⎬ second quatrain
⎭ *(Sicilian)*

overlapping ⎰ c
rhyme ⎱ c ←— **shift**

d ⎫
d ⎬ third quatrain
c ⎭ *(Sicilian)*

e ⎫ heroic
e ⎭ couplet

The Spenserian sonnet consists of three interlocking Sicilian quatrains followed by a heroic couplet.

THE CAUDATED SONNET

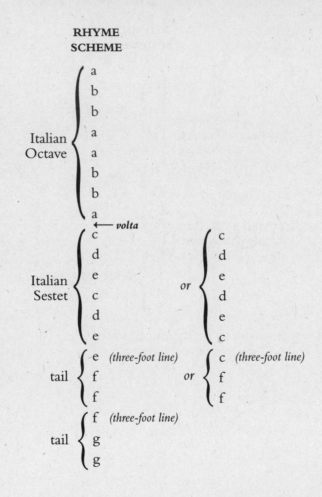

**RHYME
SCHEME**

Italian
Octave
{
a
b
b
a
a
b
b
a

← *volta*

Italian
Sestet
{
c
d
e
c
d
e

or
{
c
d
e
d
e
c

tail
{
e *(three-foot line)*
f
f

or
{
c *(three-foot line)*
f
f

tail
{
f *(three-foot line)*
g
g

Milton developed the caudated sonnet form in English, basing it on a fifteenth-century Italian Renaissance model. The rhyme scheme of the sestet can be substituted with any of the variations found in the Italian sonnet. The first line of the first "tail" picks up the rhyme of the last line of the sestet.

THE CURTAL SONNET

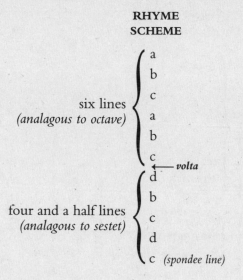

**RHYME
SCHEME**

six lines
(analagous to octave)
— a
— b
— c
— a
— b
— c

←— *volta*

four and a half lines
(analagous to sestet)
— d
— b
— c
— d
— c *(spondee line)*

Gerard Manley Hopkins invented the curtal sonnet.

THE PUSHKIN SONNET STANZA

The Pushkin sonnet may be the most extreme example of the sonnet's ability to function as a stable object and an endlessly fluctuating set of possibilities. Pushkin invented the form for his novel in verse, *Evgeny Onegin*, which is composed of 365 sonnets in iambic tetrameter. Due to its hybrid nature, the Pushkin sonnet can behave like an Italian sonnet or an English sonnet while its rhyme scheme remains constant:

RHYME SCHEME	ITALIAN *reading*	ENGLISH *reading*
a	a ⎫	a ⎫
b	b ⎬ first quatrain	b ⎬ first quatrain
a	a ⎪ *(alternating rhyme)*	a ⎪ *(alternating rhyme)*
b	b ⎭	b ⎭
c	c ⎫	c ⎫
c	c ⎬ second quatrain	c ⎬ second quatrain
d	d ⎪ *(two rhyming couplets)*	d ⎪ *(two rhyming couplets)*
d	d ⎭	d ⎭
	← **shift or volta**	
e	e ⎫	e ⎫
f	f ⎬ tercet	f ⎬ third quatrain
f	f ⎭	f ⎪ *(envelope rhyme)*
e	e ⎫	e ⎭
		← **shift or volta**
g	g ⎬ tercet	g ⎫ closing couplet
g	g ⎭	g ⎭

The sestet can be read either as two tercets or as a four-line envelope quatrain and a couplet. As A. D. P. Briggs notes in his introduction to *Evgeny Onegin* (Bristol Classical Press), Pushkin "invented a 'sonnet' form which can go either way; it can become Italian or English at the flick of a switch in mid-stanza. . . . The Onegin stanza is a mettlesome creature; when it starts out you can never tell where it will take you, or by what route. Similarly, when you look back on a stanza it will not remind you of its predecessor or of any other stanza; each one will seem to be what it is, a unique little lyric in its own right. . . . One famous critic [Nabokov] has likened this movement to that of a painted ball; you see the pattern clearly at the beginning and at the end of its movement, but in mid-spin all you get is a colorful blur." Vikram Seth's novel in verse, *The Golden Gate,* is written entirely in the Pushkin sonnet stanza.

ADDITIONAL SONNET FORMS

Couplet Sonnet: a sonnet made of seven rhyming couplets (aabbccddeeffgg)

Corona or **Crown:** a sequence of seven to fourteen sonnets in which the last line of each sonnet becomes the first line of the next sonnet; the first line of the first sonnet becomes the last line of the last sonnet, closing the circle

Double Sonnet: a sonnet that either doubles a fourteen-line rhyme scheme or repeats the octave pattern and then the sestet pattern (a double Italian sonnet: abbaabbaabbaabba cdecdecdecde), a twenty-eight-line sonnet. Also, two sonnets on a related theme functioning as a single poem

Envelope Sonnet: a variant of the Italian sonnet that adds two more rhymes to the octave (abbacddc), resulting in two separate quatrains of *rima baciata*; the sestet remains variable, as in the Italian sonnet

Heroic Sonnet: a variant of the English sonnet form, adding a fourth Sicilian quatrain before the closing couplet (ababcdcdefefghghii); or an eighteen-line sonnet composed of two heroic octaves (rhyming ababababcc) and a heroic couplet

Rondel Prime: a variant of the complicated thirteen-line rondel, a French form; the rondel prime has a fourteenth line and can sometimes act as a sonnet

Sonnet Redoublé: a sequence of fifteen sonnets in which each of the fourteen lines of the first sonnet becomes, in order, the final line in each of the succeeding sonnets

Terza Rima **Sonnet:** a sonnet in *terza rima* (aba bcb cdc ded ee), ending in a rhyming couplet

lxxviii Petrarch: Poem 132 in Petrarch's *Canzoniere*, a collection of 366 poems (including 317 sonnets) also known as the *Rime sparse* or *Rime*. Petrarch gave no specific title to his collection of verse, which he referred to as *Rerum vulgarium fragmenta*. The rhyme pattern is abba abba cde dce, with no two succeeding lines rhyming with each other in the sestet, as is typical in the Italian (Petrarchan) rhyme scheme; the last two lines of the sonnet, however, end with the same long "o" ("voglio"/ "verno"). The cde dce rhyme pattern in the sestet is one of the most common variations on the cde cde sestet pattern. *Rime sparse* means "scattered rhymes."

lxxix Chaucer: A translation (three stanzas of rhyme royal) of Petrarch's sonnet, *Rime*, 132, embedded in *Troilus and Criseyde*; from *The Works of Geoffrey Chaucer*, edited by F. N. Robinson. In Chaucer's version, the words are uttered by Troilus upon seeing Criseyde (lines 400–420).

3–5 Sir Thomas Wyatt: "The longe love, that in my thought doeth harbar" is after the Italian of Petrarch, *Rime*, 140; "Who so list to hounte I know where is an hynde" is after *Rime*, 190; "My galy chargèd with forgetfulnes," after *Rime*, 189, sometimes appears under the title "The lover compareth his state to a ship in perilous storm tossed on the sea" (the trope of the poet/lover whose "craft" is caught in a storm recurs throughout the sonnet tradition); "I find no peace, and all my war is done" is after *Rime*, 134, which Thomas Lodge also translated (see Sonnet 35 in his sequence entitled *Phillis*).

5–7 Henry Howard, Earl of Surrey: "The soote season, that bud and blome furth bringes" is an adaptation of Petrarch, *Rime*, 310; "Alas, so all things nowe doe holde their peace" is an adaptation of Petrarch, *Rime*, 164; "Love that liveth and reigneth in my thought" is an adaptation of *Rime*, 140, which Sir Thomas Wyatt also imitated, producing a very different poem. The translations, adaptations, and imitations of Petrarch done by Wyatt and Surrey first appeared in print in *Tottel's Miscellany* (1557), an anthology that circulated widely throughout the second half of the sixteenth century and went into many editions.

8 Anne Locke (also known as Anne Vaughan Lock): *A Meditation of a Penitent Sinner: Written in maner of a Paraphrase upon the 51 Psalme of David* (1560) is the earliest known sonnet sequence in the English language. The sonnets are all written in the rhyme scheme developed by Henry Howard, Earl of Surrey (abab cdcd efef gg). In this sequence of twenty-six sonnets, the first five form an introduction to the following twenty-one, which are keyed to the nineteen verses of Psalm 51. The words printed to the right of each sonnet are Locke's own prose translation of the particular verse of the psalm to which that sonnet is keyed. Each sonnet is keyed to one verse, except for verses 1 and 4, which are split into two. Though the sequence functions as an autonomous work, it appeared at the end of a volume that also included Locke's translation of John Calvin's sermons "upon the songe that Ezechias made after he had bene sicke, and afflicted by the hand of God . . ." and an epistle to the Duchess of Suffolk, to whom the book is dedicated. During her two years in Geneva among a community of English Protestant exiles, Locke must have acquired the transcript of sermons she heard John Calvin preach, which she then translated from French into English. Michael R. G. Spiller speculates very convincingly that Locke probably discovered the sonnet form not in *Tottel's Miscellany* (1557), but in her reading of Sir Thomas Wyatt's *terza rima* translation of the penitential psalms of David, published in 1549 with a prefatory sonnet written by Surrey. Since the majority of Locke's sonnets do not register a significant change after the eighth line, Spiller concludes that this sonnet of Surrey's was most likely Locke's model for the sonnet as a new type of stanza pattern: as Spiller points out, that prefatory sonnet *"is actually one of the very few sonnets by Surrey to obliterate the octave break.* Wyatt's text would thus have introduced her both to the meditation/translation form and to the sonnet form in the way in which she uses it, even if she could not name it." After the death of Mary Tudor in 1558, and Elizabeth's accession to the throne, Anne Locke decided it was safe to return to England. She arrived in London in June 1559, and in January 1560 published her first volume. As Susan Felch explains in her introduction to *The Collected Works of Anne Vaughan Lock* (Arizona Center for Medieval and Renaissance Studies, 1999), Anne Locke's first book "begins with a short discourse on the diagnosis and cure of spiritual illness. . . . The book holds out the hope that through repentance and faith England and her new queen, Elizabeth, may be restored to spiritual health." Kel Morin Parsons edited the first modern edition of Anne Locke's sequence and epistle (North Waterloo Academic Press, 1997).

10–17 Edmund Spenser: *Amoretti* is a sequence of eighty-nine sonnets published in 1595 along with "Epithalamion"; the poems were written to Spenser's bride-to-be, Elizabeth Boyle, his second wife. Spenser also composed a number of unrhymed sonnets, translations from the French poet du Bellay, which he later rewrote as rhymed sonnets and published in *Complaints*.

19–27 Sir Philip Sidney: My selection of Sidney's sonnets is taken from *Elizabethan Sonnets*, edited by Maurice Evans, who uses the 1598 Folio as his text, with minor emendations. *Astrophel and Stella*, composed around 1582, circulated in manuscript and first appeared in print in 1591 in pirated editions, "two incomplete and unauthorized quartos (Q1, Q2). The complete text was printed at the end of the 1598 Folio of the *Arcadia*, apparently under the supervision of the Countess of Pembroke herself" (Evans). The 1591 publication of Sidney's sequence precipitated the fashion in sonneteering, introducing a theory of poetry based on an Aristotelian model of imitation of action rather than the copying of literary models. The poet Sidney has created a character named Astrophel (Starlover; Stella means Star). The sequence deploys many Petrarchan conventions. In Sonnet 57 Sidney puns on the word "rich," alluding to his platonic relationship with Penelope Devereux (Lady Rich), who married Lord Robert Rich in 1581. "Leave me, O Love, which reachest but to dust" is the last poem in a collection of songs and sonnets entitled *Certaine Sonnets written by Sir Philip Sidney: Never Before Printed*.

27–28 Sir Walter Ralegh: "A vision upon This Conceipt of the Faery Queene" appeared in both the 1590 and 1596 editions of Spenser's *The Faerie Queene*.

29 Thomas Lodge: "I hope and feare, I pray and hould my peace" is after Petrarch, *Rime,* 134 (see Wyatt, "I find no peace, and all my war is done"). This is sonnet 33 in the sequence.

29 George Chapman: "A Coronet for his Mistress Philosophy" is a crown of sonnets. This is the first sonnet in the sequence.

30 Henry Constable: The first edition of Constable's sonnet cycle known as *Diana* was published in 1592 under the title *Diana, The praises of his Mistres in certaine sweete sonnets*. "Needs must I leave and yet needs must I love," which does not appear in that edition, is from the 1594 version of *Diana,* commonly known as the Todd mauscript, which Jane Grundy, who edited *The Poems of Henry Constable* (English Texts and Studies, Liverpool University Press, 1960), believes was arranged and supervised by Constable. The 1594 edition of the sequence, entitled *Diana. or, The excellent conceitful Sonnets of* H. C. *Augmented with diverse Quatorzains of honorable and learned personages*, is arranged around the mystical numbers seven and three. Constable explains "The order of the booke" in his preface: "The sonets following are divided into 3 parts, each parte contayning 3 severall arguments, and every argument 7 sonets"(there are three sections, each including three sets of seven poems). "Needs must I leave and yet needs must I love" is "Sonet 2" in the last set of seven sonnets entitled "The last 7 of the end and death of his love." Grundy's edition also includes Constable's seventeen devotional sonnets (from Harleian MS. 7553), which appear under the heading *Spirituall Sonnettes: To the honour of God and hys saints.*

31–32 Samuel Daniel: *To Delia* is a sequence of fifty-five sonnets; an earlier version of this sequence, fifty sonnets entitled *Delia*, appeared in 1592. Delia is depicted as blond in the 1592 edition, and dark-haired in the revised edition of 1601. These sonnets are from the 1594 text.

32–35 Michael Drayton: *Idea in Sixtie Three Sonnets* (1619 text) first appeared as *Ideas Mirrour, Amours in quatorzaines* (1594); in the prologue (which itself is a sonnet), Drayton gives a warning to his readers: "Into these Loves, who but for Passion lookes, / At this first sight, here let him lay them by, / And seeke else-where, in turning other Bookes."

35–36 John Davies of Hereford: "Some blaze the precious beauties of their loves" is from *Wit's Pilgrimage* (1695?); "Although we do not all the good we love" is from *The Holy Rood* (1609); "The author loving these homely meats specially . . . " is from *The Scourge of Folly* (1611?).

37–53 William Shakespeare: Shakespeare's 154 sonnets break into two main groups: the first 126 are addressed to a fair friend, a young man of higher social station who is the apotheosis of perfection, as unattainable as a Petrarchan mistress—his form and character an object of total devotion; and sonnets 127 to 152, addressed to a Dark Lady, whose form and character elicit a more ambiguous, contradictory response—the extreme polarities of erotic love and loathing, carnal desire and despair, that we find in Catullus's poems to his Lesbia. The last poem in the group addressed to the beautiful young man is a douzain (twelve-line poem) in rhyming couplets. The authenticity of the last two sonnets in the second group has been questioned: they do not participate in the same metaphysical quest. None of Shakespeare's sonnets can be dated. They were published together in 1609 in a quarto entitled "SHAKE-SPEARES SONNETS. Never before Imprinted," a paperback volume that also included Shakespeare's long poem (forty-seven stanzas in rhyme royal) *A Lover's Complaint,* which was influenced in theme and form by Spenser's poem *The Ruines of Time* (1591), which in turn had been influenced strongly by du Bellay's *Antiquitez de Rome.* The prologues to Act I and Act II of *Romeo and Juliet* are also written in sonnet form.

55 Sir John Davies: "Mine Eye, myne eare, my will . . . " is a parody of the blazon (a catalogue of celebrated virtues), from a satiric sequence. *Gullinge Sonnets,* written around 1594, was not published until 1873. This is sonnet 5 in the sequence.

55–63 John Donne: "La Corona" belongs to a group of "Divine" poems that Donne entitled *Holy Sonnets. Holy Sonnets,* first published in 1633, is the title given to a group of nineteen sonnets whose order was not arranged by Donne but by later editors. "Sonnet. The Token" is written in the form of a heroic sonnet, which has an extra Sicilian quatrain before the closing couplet. It was first printed in 1649.

66–72 Lady Mary Wroth: "A crowne of Sonetts dedicated to Love" falls at the end of *Pamphilia to Amphilanthus,* a sequence of eighty-three sonnets and nineteen songs in her single published work, *Urania* (1621).

76–77 George Herbert: In *The Temple,* Herbert's posthumously published volume of verse, the sonnet "Love (I)" is followed by a sonnet entitled "Love (II)." Herbert's poem "Love (III)," one of the most well-known devotional lyrics in English, is not a sonnet, but the rhyme pattern in each of its three stanzas seems to have evolved from the rhyme scheme of "Love (I)" and "Love (II)": the ababcc pattern in "Love (III)" combines a Sicilian quatrain with a rhyming couplet.

81–82 John Milton: "On the Late Massacre in Piedmont" commemorates a massacre that occurred on Easter Sunday of 1655, when the Duke of Savoy's forces attacked members of a Protestant sect in the Piedmont region of Italy, killing more than seventeen hundred people. "When I consider how my light is spent" was written c. 1652, by which point Milton was completely blind; in the same year, his first wife, Mary Powell, with whom he had three children, died in childbirth. The "late espousèd Saint" in "Methought I saw" (c. 1658) probably refers to Katherine Woodcock, whom Milton married in 1655, and who died in 1658, three months after giving birth; but some critics argue that the sonnet refers to Mary Powell, who returned to Milton in 1645, after their marriage had failed three years before.

84 Thomas Gray: "On the Death of Mr. Richard West." Richard West was a childhood friend of Thomas Gray's. They met at Eton and were friends until West's death at the age of twenty-six. This is the only sonnet written by Gray, who is most known for his "Elegy Written in a Country Churchyard."

89 Elizabeth Cobbold: In "Sonnets of Laura," Cobbold imagines the discovery of a sonnet sequence by Petrarch's Laura in a manuscript that has just been disinterred from her grave.

89–94 William Wordsworth: "To Toussaint L'Ouverture" and "London, 1802" are part of a group of twenty-six sonnets entitled "Sonnets Dedicated to Liberty." Toussaint L'Ouverture (1743–1803), born François Dominique Toussaint, added L'Ouverture (or Louverture) to his name in 1793. The leader of the Haitian independence movement during the French Revolution, he emancipated the slaves and briefly established Haiti as a black-governed French protectorate. A devout Catholic, Toussaint L'Ouverture changed from fighting with the Spanish against the French and British when France freed the slaves. Shortly after retiring he was arrested under suspicion of starting an uprising, and brought to the French Alps for questioning. He died after repeated interrogation.

"It is no Spirit who from heaven hath flown" is a tailed sonnet, with a three-line "tail" after the fourteenth line; Wordsworth would have found this type of sonnet, also called a caudated sonnet, in Milton, who first introduced its pattern into English after reading caudated sonnets written by fifteenth-century Italian Renaissance poets.

The River Duddon is a series of thirty-three sonnets; *Ecclesiastical Sonnets* is a long sequence praising the Anglican Church.

Regarding his relationship to the sonnet, Wordsworth wrote: "My admiration of some of the Sonnets of Milton first tempted me to write in that form. The fact is not mentioned from a notion that it will be deemed of any importance by the reader, but merely as a public acknowledgement of one of the innumerable obligations, which, as a Poet and a man, I am under to our great fellow-countryman."

Years later, he added:

In the cottage of Town-End, one afternoon in 1801 [1802], my sister read to me the sonnets of Milton. I had long been well acquainted with them, but I was particularly struck on that occasion with the dignified simplicity and majestic harmony that runs through most of them—in character so totally different from the Italian, and still more so from Shakespeare's fine sonnets. I took fire, if I may be allowed to say so, and produced three sonnets the same afternoon—the first I ever wrote, except an irregular one at school. Of these three, the only one I distinctly remember is "I grieved for Bounaparté," &c. One was never written down; the third, which was I believe preserved, I cannot particularise.

In 1833, asked for "specimens of the best sonnet writers" in English, he answered as follows:

Do you mean to have a short preface upon the Construction of the Sonnet? Though I have written so many, I have scarcely made up my own mind upon the subject. It should seem that the Sonnet, like every other legitimate composition, ought to have a beginning, a middle, and an end—in other words, to consist of three parts, like the three propositions of a syllogism, if such an illustration may be used. But the frame of metre adopted by the Italians does not accord with this view, and, as adhered to by them, it seems to be, if not arbitrary, best fitted to a division of the sense into two parts, of eight and six lines each. Milton, however, has not submitted to this. In the better half of his sonnets the sense does not close with the rhyme at the eighth line, but overflows into the second portion of the metre. Now it has struck me, that this is not done merely to gratify the ear by variety and freedom of sound, but also to aid in giving that pervading sense of intense Unity in which the excellence of the Sonnet has always seemed to me to consist. Instead of looking at this composition as a piece of architecture, making a whole out of three parts, I have been much in the habit of preferring the image of an orbicular body,—a sphere—or a dew-drop. All this will appear to you a little fanciful; and I am well aware that a Sonnet will often be found excellent, where the beginning, the middle, and the end are distinctly marked, and also where it is distinctly separated into *two* parts, to which as I before observed the strict Italian model, as they write it, is favorable. Of this last construction of Sonnet, Russell's upon Philoctetes is a fine specimen; the first eight lines give the hardship of the case, the six last the consolation, or the *per-contra*.

97 Robert Southey: "Poems on the Slave Trade" is a series of six sonnets.

98 Joseph Blanco White: "To Night" is dedicated to White's friend Samuel Taylor Coleridge.

99 Horace Smith: "Ozymandias" was written by Smith in a competition with his friend Percy Shelley.

101 Leigh Hunt: This sonnet was written by Hunt in a competition with his friend John Keats. The date of the contest was December 30, 1816; the poems, written by the poets in a period of fifteen minutes, appeared together in the *Examiner* on September 21, 1817.

102 George Gordon, Lord Byron: "Rousseau—Voltaire—our Gibbon—and de Staël" is also called "Sonnet to Lac Leman."

104–106 Percy Bysshe Shelley: "Ode to the West Wind," written in *terza rima*, invokes Dante in its rhyme pattern, making the source of creation (inspiration, divine breath) the object of praise.

109-14 John Keats: Unable to read Greek, Keats knew Homer's poetry first through translations done by Alexander Pope, and later from those of George Chapman, who was the first to translate Homer into English. The "Great spirits" is a reference to three of Keats's friends, William Wordsworth, Leigh Hunt, and the painter Benjamin Robert Haydon (1786–1846). "On the Grasshopper and Cricket" was written in a competition with Leigh Hunt, Keats's friend. "Bright star" was revised by Keats on board the ship taking him to Italy. "I cry your mercy—pity—love!—aye, love" was dedicated to Fanny Brawne, to whom he was betrothed.

117–19 Elizabeth Barrett Browning: *Sonnets from the Portuguese* (1850) is a sequence of forty-three sonnets. Elizabeth Barrett invented the title for this sequence to protect her privacy; she wrote the sonnets while she was conducting a secret love affair with the man she eventually married, Robert Browning. The sequence was written between 1845, when she first met Browning, and 1846, when they married. In an earlier poem, "Catrina to Camoëns," Barrett Browning had assumed the persona of the girl who was loved by Camões, the sixteenth-century Portuguese poet who was the author of an epic and of numerous sonnets, and whom Wordsworth praises in "Scorn Not the Sonnet."

130–33 George Meredith: *Modern Love* (1862) is a sequence of fifty sonnets, each one sixteen lines long.

134–36 Dante Gabriel Rossetti: *The House of Life* is a sequence of 102 sonnets that Rossetti wrote between 1841 and 1881. Many of the poems included in that work were written after his wife's suicide and buried by him in 1862, in his wife's tomb. Rossetti disinterred those poems in 1870, when they were published; within a year, they were attacked as pornographic by Robert Buchanan (1841–1901).

138 Christina Rossetti: "The Thread of Life" is a sequence of three sonnets on solitude that Christina Rossetti wrote before 1882 and published in 1890; this is the second in the sequence.

140–42 Thomas Hardy: "She, to Him (I)" and "She, to Him (II)" are from a sequence of five sonnets, each with the same title and succeeding Roman numerals; "Over the Coffin" is from *Satires of Circumstance in Fifteen Glimpses*, number 14.

146–51 Gerard Manley Hopkins: "Pied Beauty" and "Peace" are curtal sonnets; "That Nature is a Heraclitean Fire and of the comfort of the Resurrection" is a caudated sonnet. "Thou art indeed just, Lord . . .": The first three lines of this untitled sonnet are a translation of the Latin epigraph that appears above it. The epigraph is from the Vulgate version of Jeremiah 12:1. Hopkins makes allusions to the rest of the Biblical passage throughout this sonnet. "To R. B." is dedicated to Robert Bridges, a friend of Hopkins's, who collected his poems after his death.

152 Eugene Lee-Hamilton: "Luther to a Bluebottle Fly (1540)" is from *Imaginary Sonnets* (1888).

153 Emma Lazarus: "The New Colossus" is engraved on a plaque attached to the base of the Statue of Liberty; Lazarus wrote this sonnet as part of a project to raise money for the base of the statue. Lazarus also wrote a sonnet entitled "1492."

155–58 W. B. Yeats: "The Fascination of What's Difficult," a sonnet in thirteen lines, speaks of the fascination of what's difficult, pulling out the bolt by pulling out a line. "While I, from that reed-throated whisperer" is the epilogue to Yeats's collection *Responsibilities* (1914), where it is often printed in italics. "Leda and the Swan" is a hybrid of the Italian and the

Shakesperean sonnet. "High Talk" is in hexameter meter. Helen Vendler's essay "Yeats at Sonnets" is extraordinarily insightful, asking us to consider, among other things, how "The Second Coming" can be read as a monstrous sonnet about a monstrous birth.

167 Rupert Brooke: "The Soldier" is number 5 in a sonnet sequence entitled "1914" in a volume entitled *Nineteen-Fourteen and Other Poems*.

168–73 Robert Frost: Frost experimented with the sonnet throughout his career; he opened his first volume, *A Boy's Will* (1913), with a sonnet entitled "Into My Own." "Hyla Brook" is a fifteen-line sonnet, whose extra line causes the poem to constantly reconfigure itself; "Acquainted with the Night" is written in *terza rima*. In his essay "The Constant Symbol, " Frost discusses his complex relationship to the sonnet form.

175 Elinor Wylie: "Wild Peaches" is a sequence of four sonnets.

178 Siegfried Sassoon: In his poem "On Passing the New Menin Gate," published in 1928, Sassoon creates a bitter verbal memorial in response to the New Menin Gate, on which the names of 54,889 men who died in the First World War are engraved.

179 Marianne Moore: "No Swan So Fine" invokes the formal movement of the sonnet in the way it meditates on an image and then makes a sudden break with the past in terms of both subject and strategy; the abrupt change of course in the last line owes a debt to the sonnet.

180 T. S. Eliot: The first fourteen lines of "The Dry Salvages," from Eliot's *The Four Quartets*, allude to the tradition of river sonnets, which has an antecedent in the Romantic Movement, but also in Petrarch and Dante. In a prose passage of *La Vita Nuova*, Dante describes how the opening line of the first poem he was able to compose after deciding to take as his theme the praise of Beatrice's "gracious being" came to him when he passed by a flowing stream: "Ladies who know by insight what love is" (in Barbara Reynolds's translation). In the second of six visions recalled in poem 323 of Petrarch's *Canzoniere*, a fountain of murmuring water springs from a rock inside a grove.

181 Claude McKay: "If We Must Die" was written by McKay in response to the Harlem race riots of 1919; during the Second World War, to mobilize public sentiment in favor of entering the war, the poem was read by Winston Churchill in an address to the House of Commons. It was also read into the *Congressional Record* by U.S. senator Henry Cabot Lodge.

183 Archibald MacLeish: The title "Aeterna Poetae Memoria" may be translated as "In Everlasting Remembrance of a Poet."

183–91 Edna St. Vincent Millay: *Collected Sonnets of Edna St. Vincent Millay* draws on sonnets from Millay's entire career, from her first book, *Renascence*, to "Epitaph for the Race of Man." "When Man is gone and only gods remain" is the fifth sonnet in "Epitaph for the Race of Man," a sequence of eighteen sonnets published in Millay's collection *Wine from These Grapes* (1934). *Fatal Interview* (1931) is a sequence of fifty-two sonnets. "Sonnets from an Ungrafted Tree," a sequence of seventeen sonnets, is one of Millay's major achievements as a poet but is not represented here because excerpting poems from it would distort its narrative context and disrupt the integrity of its psychological complexity. In her revised and expanded edition of Millay's *Collected Sonnets*, Elizabeth Barnett quotes Millay's notes on sonnets and sonneteers from an unpublished draft that Millay wrote for the first edition of her collected sonnets, which was published in 1941. This is what Millay had to say after reading Wordsworth's sonnet "Composed upon Westminster Bridge, September 3, 1802":

> It was so beautiful that I did not know until after I had finished it whether it was a sonnet or a chant royal. Then I read it for a second time. Then I read them, all of them, over and over. Some of them *were* funny. There was the stuffed owl, of course, and a few other incredible pieces of awkwardness and utter absence of any sensitive foreknowledge of the possible reaction of the reader. But the sonnet, like a sharp-tongued wife, pulled Wordsworth together, made him pull up his socks, told him to shut up, when he had finished what he had to say, et cet.—et cet.

192 Wilfred Owen: "Dulce et Decorum Est" was written between 1917 and 1918. It is a double sonnet composed of seven Sicilian quatrains; the second half of the poem begins with a couplet that is not "heroic."

194–200 E. E. Cummings: The sonnets are taken from various collections published by Cummings and appear together in his *Collected Poems*, edited by George J. Firmage. They are identified here by first line rather than by number because Cummings often renumbered the same sonnet for publication in different editions, and sometimes he gave different sequences the same title. These poems are from the following sequences or individual volumes: "Sonnets-Realities," "Sonnets-Unrealities," "Sonnets-Actualities" (from *Tulips and Chimneys*), "Sonnets-Actualities" (from *&*), *is 5*, and *95 Poems*. "My true love hath my hart, and I have his," Sir Philip Sidney's sonnet in *The Countess of Pembroke's Arcadia*, is echoed in Cummings's "i carry your heart . . ."

206 Roy Campbell: Luis Vaz de Camões (1524?–1580), also known as Camoëns (as Wordsworth refers to him in "Scorn not the sonnet"), a major poet of Portugal, wrote 196 sonnets as well as a national epic.

208 Edwin Denby: Most of Denby's sonnets belong to extensive sequences; "Air" is an exception.

210 Elliott Coleman: "Oedipus Sonnets" is a sequence of three sonnets; this is the third.

213–14 W. H. Auden: "The Quest" comprises twenty sonnets (although the third "sonnet" is twenty-one lines long); it is subtitled "A Sonnet Sequence." "In Time of War" comprises twenty-seven sonnets and is subtitled "A Sonnet Sequence with a Verse Commentary."

217–18 Elizabeth Bishop: Her first sonnet, called "Sonnet," was written in 1928; "The Prodigal" in 1955; and her last sonnet, also entitled "Sonnet," in 1979.

219 Robert Hayden: In addition to invoking the Petrarchan motif of freezing and burning, "Those Winter Sundays" contains an acoustical quotation of the first three words in line four of Shakespeare's Sonnet 73: "banked fires blaze" (the first three words of line five in Hayden's sonnet) mimics the stress pattern of Shakespeare's phrase, "Bare ruined choirs." Hayden seems not only to be writing an elegiac sonnet for his father—and on the "austere and lonely offices" of parental love—but to be claiming both Petrarch and Shakespeare as his literary forebears, making himself one of their descendants.

221–23 John Berryman: The book-length sequence that Berryman himself titled *Berryman's Sonnets* (1967) contains 115 sonnets.

224 Dylan Thomas: "Alterwise by Owl-Light," Thomas's sequence of ten sonnets, is not included here because it is difficult to excerpt due to the many cross-references and allusions within the sequence.

226–29 Gwendolyn Brooks: "The Children of the Poor" is a sequence of five sonnets comprising part 1 of a long poem entitled *The Womanhood*; "Gay Chaps at the Bar" is a sequence of twelve sonnets.

234–36 Hayden Carruth: The set of four sonnets are from Carruth's book-length sequence entitled *Sonnets* (1989).

243 Jane Cooper: "Praise." About her own poem, "Praise," Jane Cooper writes in an author's note at the end of *The Flashboat*:

> The image of stone as the poet's building material and the phrase about the world's being set free for our play during the two thousand years of Christian civilization are both taken from Osip Mandelstam, as reported by Nadezhda Mandelstam in *Hope Against Hope*, Chapter 56, "The Earth and Its Concerns." The chapter begins: "A woman who has come back after many years in the forced-labor camps tells me that she and her companions in misfortune always found comfort in the poetry which, luckily, she knew by heart and was able to recite to them. They were particularly moved by some lines M. wrote as a young man: *But I love this poor earth, because I have not seen another*."

245 Donald Justice: "Henry James by the Pacific." In California, James stayed at the famous Hotel del Coronado near San Diego.

245 James K. Baxter: "Jerusalem Sonnets" refers to a Maori village, Jerusalem, where Baxter lived.

246 James Merrill: Marsyas was tied to a tree and flayed alive after losing a competition judged by the Muses, in which he had challenged Apollo. Merrill also wrote a number of sonnet sequences, including "The Broken Home" and "Matinees."

247 W. D. Snodgrass: The Greek title means "not any man . . . nobody," the words spoken by Odysseus to the Cyclops in Homer's *Odyssey*. Lines 408–414, in the translation by Robert Fagles, follow:

> 'So, you ask me the name I'm known by Cyclops?
> I will tell you. But you must give me a guest gift

as you've promised. Nobody—that's my name. Nobody—
so my mother and father call me, all my friends.'

But he boomed back at me from his ruthless heart,
'*Nobody?* I'll eat Nobody last of all his friends—
I'll eat the others first! That's my gift to *you!*'

250 Donald Hall: "President and Poet" was originally published under the title "T. R." (Theodore Roosevelt).

251 Philip Levine: "Llanto," a word that the poet García Lorca also preferred to "elegy," means "a pouring forth of tears" in Spanish. Ernesto Trejo, a poet who published books both in Mexico and the United States, was born in Fresnillo, Mexico, and educated at California State University, Fresno, where he took an advanced degree in economics. He worked for some years as an economist for the Mexican federal government, and after taking an M.F.A. in poetry at Iowa, settled in Fresno, where he taught at the city college until his death a few days after his fortieth birthday.

253–54 John Hollander: "Thirteen" is a sequence of eleven sonnets in *Powers of Thirteen*, a number that represents the total of eight and five, whose proportions approximate the Golden Section, a mathematical expression of the ratios that bring the world soul into harmony, as explained in Plato's *Timaeus*. Hollander plays with "thirteen" in relation to how we mark time: the thirteenth hour of the day is represented by the number one, thus the end of the poem is also a beginning. The last section of "The Mad Potter" is a sonnet.

256 Adrienne Rich: "Final Notations" is the closing poem in Rich's collection *An Atlas of the Difficult World*, a book whose poet-speaker takes on the role of both mapmaker and Atlas, who takes on the burden of holding up the world; the beloved "object" is nothing less than the earth itself. Rich plays on the ambiguous meaning of "will" in English, where it means both "purpose" and "desire," and also on its grammatical ambiguity as both a noun and a verb. The poem celebrates the union of one's purpose with one's desire in a tradition whose obsession has often been the irreconcilable conflict between the two. Shakespeare often puns on the meaning of "will" in relation to his own name.

264 Grace Schulman: "The Abbess of Whitby" is written in the form of a rondel prime. Caedmon is the name of the first English poet.

268 Tony Harrison: In "On Not Being Milton," line 3 is the title of a work by Aimé Césaire. Harrison's sequence, *from The School of Eloquence*, was published in 1978.

270 Frank Bidart: In his book of poems entitled *Desire*, Bidart includes his translation of a sonnet from Dante's *Vita Nuova*, to which Bidart gives the title "Love Incarnate."

273–74 Seamus Heaney: "The Seedcutters" is the second part of "Mossbawn: Two Poems in Dedication." "Clearances" is a sequence of eight sonnets.

275 Stanley Plumly: The pieces in this volume are from a fourteen-part sonnet sequence entitled "Boy on the Step," the title poem of the collection in which this sequence appears.

279–81 Marilyn Hacker: *Love, Death, and the Changing of the Seasons* (1986) is a book-length sonnet sequence whose most obvious precedent is Shakespeare, with a twist; Hacker joins the longing for an ideal, unrequited love and the desire for a lover who no longer reciprocates. "Cancer Winter" is a crown of fourteen sonnets; these are the first four.

281 David Huddle: "Tour of Duty" is a sonnet sequence reflecting on Huddle's experience in Vietnam.

284–85 Charles Martin: "Easter Sunday, 1985," in addition to commemorating "the disappeared," invokes Milton's sonnet "On the Late Massacre in Piedmont." The double sonnet entitled "The End of the World" is part of the sonnet sequence "Making Faces" about the parade of the Bread and Puppet Theater that takes place in Barton, Vermont, every summer.

288–89 Ellen Bryant Voigt: In an author's note at the end of *Kyrie* (1995), Voigt discusses the extent to which the influenza epidemic of 1918 devastated entire populations, with most fatalities occurring among young adults. In the tradition of the sonnet sequence, *Kyrie* is a requiem for the dead and an ode to the survivors, a verbal monument expressing the poet's ethical desire—to commemorate a tragedy that has almost disappeared from national memory.

> In March 1918, what the Germans would call "Flanders Fever" was
> first recorded at Camp Funston, Kansas. By March 1919, "Spanish"

influenza had killed, by conservative estimate, more than twenty-five million world-wide. . . . The U.S. toll was half a million dead: as many servicemen killed by influenza as in combat, and ten times that many civilians.

294 Leon Stokesbury: "To His Book" is a curtal sonnet.

304 Agha Shahid Ali: "I Dream I Am the Only Passenger on Flight 423 to Srinagar" is a sonnet sequence in five parts. The author explains in his note to the poem that Begum Akhtar was "one of the Indian subcontinent's greatest singers and certainly the greatest ghazal singer of all time. She died in 1974." The "ghazal" is a poetic form.

306–308 Julia Alvarez: "33" is a sequence of forty-six sonnets that explore, in an episodic fashion, the nature of love, passion, and friendship, the crisis of facing mortality (of turning thirty-three), and the process of rebuilding the self.

310–11 Paul Muldoon: "Holy Thursday" creates an ironic double exposure of a last supper, with all the rituals of the sacrament, "absence" being the one word without a mate, without a rhyme; in "October 1950" Muldoon locates the site of his own conception in a sonnet, suggesting the form as a seminal moment in his development (his surrealism owes a debt to the rupture generated by the *volta*).

311–12 Rita Dove: "Hades' Pitch" is one of a number of sonnets in Dove's collection, *Mother Love*, that meditates on the triangular relationship of Demeter, Persephone, and Hades. In a brief essay on the sonnet and her own attraction to its potential energies, Rita Dove refers to the sonnet as "an intact world where everything is in synch, from the stars down to the tiniest mite on a blade of grass." "If the 'true' sonnet reflects the music of the spheres, it then follows that any variation from the strictly Petrarchan or Shakespearean forms represents a world gone awry." (From "An Intact World," published in *A Formal Feeling Comes*, edited by Annie Finch, Story Line Press, 1994.)

312–13 Mark Jarman: *Unholy Sonnets* (2000) is a book-length sequence of sixty-four sonnets.

316 Tom Sleigh: "The God" is from a sonnet sequence entitled "The Work."

317–18 David Wojahn: "Mystery Train: A Sequence" contains thirty-five poems, all but one of which are sonnets.

323 Robin Robertson: "The locksmith's daughter" is Victorian slang for a key.

328 Karl Kirchwey: The first two lines of "In Transit" quote lines five and six of Keats's sonnet "If by dull rhymes our English must be chain'd." Imitating Keats's extremely complicated rhyme pattern (abcabdcabcdede), a weave of rhymes so subtle they seem as unconstricting as a Greek sandal, Kirchwey invokes Keats as a poetic master, gentle father, and liberator.

330 James Lasdun: "Plague Years" alludes to Daniel Defoe's novel *Journal of the Plague Year*, and more immediately to the anxiety of living in the years of the HIV virus/AIDS epidemic.

332 Joe Bolton: "Style" is a two-part sequence.

333 Sascha Feinstein: "Sonnets for Stan Gage" is a four-part sequence. These two sonnets are the second and third.

336 Jason Schneiderman: "The Disease Collector" is in the rhyme pattern of the Pushkin sonnet stanza.

SUGGESTIONS FOR FURTHER READING

Abutafia, David. *Frederick II: A Medieval Emperor*. New York and London: Oxford University Press, 1992.

Achinstein, Sharon. *Milton and the Revolutionary Reader*. Princeton, NJ: Princeton University Press, 1994.

Ackerman, James. *The Architecture of Michelangelo*. Second edition. London: Penguin Books, 1995.

————. *Distance Points: Essays in Theory and Renaissance Art and Architecture*. Cambridge, MA: MIT Press, 1991.

Altieri, Charles. "Rhetorics, Rhetoricity and the Sonnet as Performance." *Tennessee Studies in Literature* 25 (1980): 1–23.

Auden, W. H. "Shakespeare's Sonnets." In *Forewords and Afterwards*. New York: Random House, 1973; Vintage, 1989.

Barkin, Leonard. *Unearthing the Past: Archaeology and Aesthetics in the Making of Renaissance Culture*. New Haven, CT: Yale University Press, 1999.

Baudelaire, Charles. *Les Fleurs du Mal*. Translated by Richard Howard. Boston: Godine, 1982.

Bermann, Sandra L. *The Sonnet Over Time: A Study in the Sonnets of Petrarch, Shakespeare, and Baudelaire*. Chapel Hill: University of North Carolina Press, 1988.

Berry, Edward. *The Making of Sir Philip Sidney*. Toronto and Buffalo: University of Toronto Press, 1998.

Bloom, Harold. *Shakespeare: The Invention of the Human*. New York: Penguin Putnam, 1998.

————, editor. *William Shakespeare's Sonnets*. Modern Critical Interpretations. New York: Chelsea House Publishers, 1992.

Booth, Stephen. *Shakespeare's Sonnets*. New Haven, CT: Yale University Press, 1985.

Brewer, Derek. "Reading, Writing, and Individualism." In *The New Pelican Guide to English Literature*. 1. Medieval Literature. Middlesex, England, and New York: Penguin, 1997.

Browne, Sir Thomas. *Religio Medici*. Cambridge: Cambridge University Press, 1963.

Bullock, Walter L. "The Genesis of the English Sonnet Form." *PMLA* 38 (1923): 729–44.

Carlin, Patricia. *Shakespeare's Mortal Men*. New York: Peter Lang, 1993.

Carruth, Hayden. "Cummings and the Sonnet." *The Journal of the E. E. Cummings Society* 4 (Fall 1995): 8–13.

Cassirer, Ernst, Paul Oscar Kristeller, and John H. Randall, Jr., editors. *The Renaissance Philosophy of Man*. Chicago: University of Chicago Press, 1990.

Chaucer, Geoffrey. *Chaucer's Dream Poetry: Longman's Annotated Text*. Edited by Helen Phillips and Nick Havely. New York: Longman's Publishing Group, 1998.

———. *The Works of Geoffrey Chaucer*. Edited by F. N. Robinson. Boston: Houghton Mifflin, 1957.

Corrigan, Beatrice. "Petrarch in English." *Italica* 50 (1973): 400–407.

Craft, William. *Labyrinth of Desire: Invention and Culture in the Work of Sir Philip Sidney*. Newark: University of Delaware Press; London and Cranbury, NJ: Associated University Press, 1994.

Curran, Stuart. *Poetic Form and British Romanticism*. New York: Oxford University Press, 1986.

Dante Alighieri. *Dante's "Vita Nuova": A Translation and an Essay*. Translated by Mark Musa. Bloomington, IN: Indiana University Press, 1973.

———. *La Vita Nuova*. Translated by Barbara Reynolds. New York and London: Penguin, 1978.

Dubrow, Heather. *Captive Victors: Shakespeare's Narrative Poems and Sonnets.* Ithaca, NY: Cornell University Press, 1987.

————. *Echoes of Desire: English Petrarchism and Its Counterdiscourses.* Ithaca, NY: Cornell University Press, 1995.

————. *Shakespeare and Domestic Loss: Forms of Deprivation, Mourning, and Recuperation.* Cambridge, UK, and New York: Cambridge University Press, 1999.

Evans, Maurice, editor. *Elizabethan Sonnets.* London: J. M. Dent & Sons; Totowa, NJ: Rowman and Littlefield Library, Everyman's University Library, 1977; Rutland, VT: Charles E. Tuttle Co., 1977.

Feldman, Paula R., and Daniel Robinson, editors. *A Century of Sonnets: The Romantic-Era Revival.* New York: Oxford University Press, 1999.

Ferry, Anne. *The "Inward" Language: Sonnets of Wyatt, Sidney, Shakespeare, and Donne.* Chicago: University of Chicago Press, 1983.

Fineman, Joel. *Shakespeare's Perjured Eye. The Invention of Poetic Subjectivity in the Sonnets.* Berkeley, CA: University of California Press, 1986.

Fowler, Alastair, editor. *Silent Poetry: Essay in Numerological Analysis.* London: Routledge & Kegan Paul, 1970.

————. *Triumphal Forms: Structural Patterns in Elizabethan Poetry.* Cambridge, UK: Cambridge University Press, 1970.

Fuller, John. *The Sonnet.* London: Methuen, 1972.

Fussell, Paul. *Poetic Meter and Poetic Form.* Revised edition. New York: Random House, 1979.

Greenblatt, Stephen. *Renaissance Self-Fashioning: From More to Shakespeare.* Chicago: University of Chicago Press, 1980.

Greene, Thomas M. *The Light in Troy: Imitation and Discovery in Renaissance Poetry.* New Haven, CT: Yale University Press, 1982.

Grossman, Marshall. "Literary Forms and Historical Consciousness in Renaissance Theory." *Exemplaria: A Journal of Theory in Medieval and Renaissance Studies* 1, no. 2 (Fall 1989): 247–264.

————. *The Story of All Things: Writing the Self in English Renaissance Narrative*. Durham, NC: Duke University Press, 1998.

Hardison, O. B., Jr. *The Enduring Monument: A Study of the Idea of Praise in Renaissance Literary Theory and Practice*. Chapel Hill: University of North Carolina Press, 1962.

Heale, Elizabeth. *Wyatt, Surrey, and Early Tudor Poetry*. New York: Longman, 1988.

Hedley, Jane. *Power in Verse: Metaphor and Metonymy in the Renaissance Lyric*. University Park, PA: Pennsylvania State University Press, 1988.

Heninger, S. K., Jr. "Sequences, Systems, Models: Sidney and the Secularization of Sonnets." In *Poems in Their Place: The Intertextuality and Order of Poetic Collections*. Edited by Neil Fraistat. Chapel Hill and London: University of North Carolina Press, 1986.

————. *The Subtext of Form in the English Renaissance: Proportion Poetical*. University Park, PA: Pennsylvania State Press, 1994.

Hollander, John. *Melodious Guile: Fictive Pattern in Poetic Language*. New Haven, CT: Yale University Press, 1990.

Hopkins, Gerard Manley. *Gerard Manley Hopkins: A Critical Edition of the Major Works*. Edited by Catherine Phillips. Oxford and New York: Oxford University Press, 1986.

Kerrigan, John. "Wordsworth and the Sonnet: Building, Dwelling, Thinking." *Essays in Criticism* 35 (1985): 45–71.

Kitchin, Laurence. *Love Sonnets of the Renaissance*. Translated from the Italian, French, Spanish, and Portuguese. London: Forest Books, 1990.

Klein, Lisa M. *The Exemplary Sidney and the Elizabethan Sonneteer*. Newark, DE: University of Delaware Press; London; Cranbury, NJ: Associated University Presses, 1998.

Kuin, Roger. *Chamber Music: Elizabethan Sonnet-Sequences and the Pleasure of Criticism*. Toronto: University of Toronto Press, 1997.

Lever, J. W. *The Elizabethan Love Sonnet*. London: Methuen, 1956.

McFarland, Thomas. *Romanticism and the Forms of Ruin: Wordsworth, Coleridge, and Modalities of Fragmentation*. Princeton, NJ: Princeton University Press, 1981.

Martz, Louis. *The Poetry of Meditation*. New Haven, CT: Yale University Press, 1962.

Matthews, G. M. "Sex and the Sonnet." In *Essays in Criticism* 2 (1952).

Mazzaro, Jerome. "Tapping God's Other Book: Wordsworth at Sonnets." *Studies in Romanticism* 33, no. 3 (Fall 1994): 337–54.

Mazzotta, Giuseppe. "The *Canzoniere* and the Language of the Self." *Studies in Philology* 75, no. 3 (Summer 1978).

Millay, Edna St. Vincent. *Collected Sonnets*. Revised and expanded edition. New York: Harper & Row, 1988.

Neruda, Pablo. *100 Love Sonnets*. Translated by Stephen Tapscott. Austin, TX: University of Texas Press, 1986.

Norbrook, David. *Poetry and Politics in the English Renaissance*. London and Boston: Routledge & Kegan Paul, 1984.

Oppenheimer, Paul. *The Birth of the Modern Mind: Self, Consciousness, and the Invention of the Sonnet*. New York: Oxford University Press, 1989.

———. "The Origin of the Sonnet." *Comparative Literature* 34, no. 4 (Fall 1982): 289–304.

Parker, Tom W. *Proportional Form in the Sonnets of the Sidney Circle: Loving in Truth*. New York and London: Oxford University Press, 1998.

Petrarch, Francesco. *Canzoniere, or, Rerum Vulgarium Fragmenta*. Translated with notes and commentary by Mark Musa. Introduction by Mark Musa with Barbara Manfredi. Bloomington, IN: Indiana University Press, 1996.

———. *Petrarch's Lyric Poems: The "Rime sparse" and Other Lyrics*. Edited and translated by Robert M. Durling. Cambridge, MA, and London, England: Harvard University Press, 1990.

————. *Selections from the Canzoniere and Other Works.* Translated by Mark Musa. New York: Oxford University Press, 1985.

Pico della Mirandola, Conte Giovanni. *Oration on the Dignity of Man.* Translated by Robert A. Caponigri. Introduction by Russell Kirk. Chicago: H. Regnery Publishing, 1956; 1967; 1996.

Praz, Mario. *The Flaming Heart: Essays on Crashaw, Machiavelli, and Other Studies of the Relations Between Italian and English Literature from Chaucer to T. S. Eliot.* New York: Norton, 1973.

Prince, F. T. "The Sonnet from Wyatt to Shakespeare." In *Elizabethan Poetry.* London: E. Arnold, Stratford-Upon-Avon-Studies, 1960.

Quillen, Carol E. *Rereading the Renaissance: Petrarch, Augustine, and the Language of Humanism.* Ann Arbor, MI: University of Michigan Press, 1998.

Rilke, Rainer Maria. *The Sonnets to Orpheus.* Translated by Stephen Mitchell. New York: Simon & Schuster, 1985.

————. *The Sonnets to Orpheus.* Translated by David Young. Middletown, CT: Weslyan University Press, 1987.

Roche, Thomas P., Jr. *Petrarch and the English Sonnet Sequences.* New York: AMS Press, 1989.

————. "Shakespeare and the Sonnet Sequence." In *New History of Literature, II: English Poetry and Prose 1540–1674.* Edited by Christopher Ricks. New York: Peter Bedrick, 1987.

Rougemont, Denis de. *Love in the Western World.* Translated by Montgomery Belgion. Princeton, NJ: Princeton University Press, 1983.

Rylestone, Ann L. *Prophetic Memory in Wordsworth's "Ecclesiastical Sonnets."* Carbondale, IL: Southern Illinois University Press, 1991.

Saintsbury, George. *A History of English Prosody.* London: Macmillan & Co., 1906–1910.

Scaglione, Aldo. "Classical Heritage and Petrarchan Self-Consciousness in the Literary Emergence of the Interior 'I.'" In *Alto Polo.* Fredrick May Foundation for Italian Studies, University of Sydney, 1984.

Seth, Vikram. *The Golden Gate*. New York: Random House, 1986.

Shakespeare, William. *The Sonnets and A Lover's Complaint*. Edited by John Kerrigan. New York: Penguin, 1999.

———. *The Sonnets and A Lover's Complaint*. Edited by Stanley Wells. New York and London: Oxford University Press, 1989.

———. *The Sonnets and Narrative Poems: The Complete Non-Dramatic Poetry*. Edited by William Burto. New York: New American Library, 1986.

Sidney, Sir Philip. *The Countess of Pembroke's Arcadia*. Edited by Maurice Evans. New York: Viking Penguin, 1997.

———. *The Defense of Poesie, Astrophel and Stella, and Other Writings*. Edited by Elizabeth Porges Watson. Boston: Charles E. Tuttle Co., 1997.

Singleton, Charles S. *An Essay on the "Vita Nuova."* Reprinted edition. Baltimore: Johns Hopkins University Press, 1977.

Smith, Barbara Hernnstein. *Poetic Closure: A Study of How Poems End*. Chicago: University of Chicago Press, 1968.

Smith, G. Gregory, ed. *Elizabethan Critical Essays*. Oxford: Clarendon Press, 1904.

Spiller, Michael R. G. *The Development of the Sonnet: An Introduction*. London and New York: Routledge, 1992.

———. "A Literary 'First': The Sonnet Sequence of Anne Locke (1560)." *Renaissance Studies* 11, no. 1 (March 1997): 41–55.

———. *The Sonnet Sequence: A Study of Its Strategies*. New York and London: Twayne Publishers, Prentice Hall International, 1997.

Vendler, Helen. *The Art of Shakespeare's Sonnets*. Cambridge, MA, and London, England: Harvard University Press, 1999.

———. "Yeats at Sonnets." The Parnell Lecture, Magdalene College, Cambridge University, 1995. Published in *Magdalene College Occasional Papers*, 1995.

Wagner, Jennifer Ann. *A Moment's Monument: Revisionary Poetics and the Nineteenth-Century English Sonnet*. Madison, WI, and Teaneck, NJ: Fairleigh Dickinson University Press, 1996.

Watkins, Renee Neu. "Petrarch and the Black Death: From Fear to Monuments." *Studies in the Renaissance* 19 (1972): 196–223.

Weir, Alison. *The Life of Elizabeth I*. London: J. Cape, 1998; New York: Ballantine, 1998.

Wilkins, Ernest Hatch. *The Invention of the Sonnet and Other Studies in Italian Literature*. Rome: Edizione di Storia e Letteratura, 1959.

Wind, Edgar. *Pagan Mysteries in the Renaissance*. Revised edition. New York and Oxford: Oxford University Press, 1980.

Wittkower, Rudolf. *Architectural Principles in the Age of Humanism*. New York: W. W. Norton, 1971.

Wolfson, Susan J. *Formal Changes: The Shaping of Poetry in British Romanticism*. Stanford, CA: Stanford University Press, 1997.

Woodhuysen, H. R., editor. *The Penguin Book of Renaissance Verse: 1509–1659*. Selected and with an Introduction by David Norbrook. London; New York: Allen Lane/Penguin Press, 1992.

AGHA SHAHID ALI (b. 1949), a Kashmiri-American, has taught at Hamilton College, the University of Massachusetts at Amherst, and the University of Utah, and held visiting appointments at New York University and Princeton. His collections of poetry include *A Nostalgist's Map of America*, *The Half-Inch Himalayas*, and *The Country Without a Post Office*. He is also the translator of *The Rebel's Silhouette: Selected Poems* by the fabled Urdu poet Faiz Ahmed Faiz.

DICK ALLEN's (b. 1939) poetry collections include *Ode to the Cold War: Poems New and Selected*. He was one of fifteen American writers chosen for the NEA-sponsored National Millennium Survey Project, recording American culture in the final year of the twentieth century. Allen has received grants from the National Endowment for the Arts and the Ingram Merrill Foundation; his poems have appeared in several annual editions of *The Best American Poetry*.

JULIA ALVAREZ (b. 1950) was born in the Dominican Republic and migrated with her family to the United States in 1960. Her novels include *How the Garcia Girls Lost Their Accents* and *In the Time of the Butterflies* (nominated for the 1995 National Book Critics Circle Award). Her poetry collections include *The Other Side* and *Homecoming*. She lives in Middlebury, Vermont.

MATTHEW ARNOLD (1822–1888) was born in Laleham-on-Thames, England, and was educated at Rugby and at Balliol College, Oxford. In 1844, he returned to Rugby as a teacher of classics. After marrying in 1851, he began work as a government school inspector, a position he held for thirty-five years. His reputation as a poet was established with the publication of *Empedocles on Etna* (1852) and *Poems* (1853). Arnold was elected professor of poetry at Oxford in 1858, but his subsequent work was in prose, except for the publication of his *New Poems* in 1867.

JOHN ASHBERY (b. 1927) was born in Rochester, New York, raised on a farm near Lake Ontario, and graduated from Harvard and Columbia. He went to Paris on a Fulbright grant in 1955 and settled there for ten years, working as an art reviewer; later he was poetry editor of the *Partisan Review* and an art critic for *New York* and *Newsweek* magazines. Ashbery is the author of numerous collections, including *Self-Portrait in a Convex Mirror*, which won the Pulitzer Prize, *A Wave*, *April Galleons*, and *Girls on the Run*. He has lived in New York City since 1965

W[YSTAN] H[UGH] AUDEN (1907–1973) was born in York, England, and educated at Christ Church College, Oxford. He traveled widely, and in 1939 emigrated to the United States, becoming an American citizen in 1946. A prolific poet throughout his life, Auden also published several collections of essays, including *The Dyer's Hand*, and collaborated with Christopher Isherwood and Louis MacNeice on verse plays, and on librettos with Chester Kallman, an American poet and close friend with whom he lived for more than twenty years. He was professor of poetry at Oxford from 1956 to 1961, and received the National Medal for Literature in 1967. He translated *The Collected Poems of Saint-John Perse* (1972) and in his later years revised and collected his poems in two volumes, *Collected Shorter Poems 1927–1957* (1967) and *Collected Longer Poems* (1969). His *Lectures on Shakespeare*, reconstructed and edited by Arthur Kirsch, was published posthumously in December 2000.

DAVID BAKER (b. 1954) is the author of a number of books, including *The Truth about Small Towns*, a collection of poems, and *Heresy and the Ideal: On Contemporary Poetry*, a book of essays. He holds the Thomas B. Fordham Chair of Poetry at Denison University and also teaches in the M.F.A. program for writers at Warren Wilson College. He is the poetry editor of *The Kenyon Review* and the recipient of a Guggenheim Fellowship.

GEORGE BARKER (1913–1991) was born in Loughton, Essex, England. He studied in London until the age of fourteen, and then worked at a series of odd jobs. His first novel and first poetry collection were both published in 1933; his long poem, *Calamiterror*, was inspired by the Spanish Civil War. Barker spent a year in Japan as professor of English literature at the Imperial Tohoku University, and in 1941 he came to the United States, where he stayed until 1943. After returning to England, he continued teaching literature until 1974. His later volumes include *Villa Stellar* and *Anno Domini*.

JAMES K. BAXTER (1926–1972) was born in Dunedin, New Zealand, and educated at Quaker schools in New Zealand and England, the University of Otago, and the University of Victoria at Wellington. He worked as a laborer, journalist, teacher, and literary editor. After becoming a Roman Catholic in 1958, following a long struggle with alcoholism, Baxter founded a religious commune and actively participated in social welfare programs. His collection *Jerusalem Sonnets* is a sequence of poems based on his experiences in a Maori village called Jerusalem.

THOMAS LOVELL BEDDOES (1803–1849), the son of a famous physician, was educated at Charterhouse, Oxford. He abandoned his medical studies at the University at Göttingen, but completed his degree in medicine later in life. His play *The Bride's Tragedy* appeared in 1822 and was an overnight success; *Death's Jest-Book* (1850) is considered his greatest work. He took his own life in Basel, Switzerland.

APRIL BERNARD (b. 1956) is the author of several poetry collections, including *Blackbird Bye Bye* and *Psalms*, and a novel, *Pirate Jenny*. Her essays have appeared in *The New York Review of Books*, *The New Republic*, and *Parnassus*. She teaches at Mount Holyoke College in Massachusetts.

TED BERRIGAN (1934–1983) was born Edmund Joseph Michael in Providence, Rhode Island. He served in the army from 1954 to 1957, then attended the University of Tulsa. In the early 1960s, after moving to New York City, he immersed himself in the world of poetry and the visual arts and became established as an art critic and book reviewer. His cycle of lyric poems written in 1963 was published the following year as *The Sonnets*. Berrigan's collection of sonnets was reprinted by Penguin in 2000.

JOHN BERRYMAN (1914–1972), born John Smith, Jr., in rural Oklahoma, moved to Florida at the age of ten, where his parents opened a restaurant in Tampa. His father committed suicide, shooting himself outside his son's window; his mother later married John Berryman, who adopted her sons. Berryman studied at South Kent School and Columbia, and earned a scholarship to Clare College, Cambridge University. He taught at Princeton, Harvard, Iowa, and the University of Minnesota. His works include *77 Dream Songs* (1964), which was awarded a Pulitzer Prize, *Berryman's Sonnets* (1967), and *Love and Fame* (1970). He leaped to his death from a bridge over the Mississippi River.

CHARLES BEST (15??–1602) All that is known of Charles Best is his sonnet "Of the Moon," which appears in the volume *Elizabethan Lyrics*. Norman Ault, who edited a reprint edition of the book, explains in a note that the original text of the poem appeared in the unique complete copy of the original volume of 1602 (now in the United States). In the Bodleian copy of 1602, the poem appeared on a leaf that is now missing.

FRANK BIDART (b. 1939) grew up in Bakersfield, California, and attended Harvard University, where he formed friendships with Elizabeth Bishop and Robert Lowell. Bidart teaches at Wellesley College and Brandeis University. His collections of poetry include *Golden State*, *The Sacrifice*, *In the Western Night: Collected Poems 1965–1990*, and *Desire*, in which appears "Love Incarnate," Bidart's translation of one of Dante's sonnets in *La Vita Nuova*. With poet David Gewanter he edited the definitive edition of Robert Lowell's *Collected Poems* (2001).

ELIZABETH BISHOP (1911–1979) was born in Worcester, Massachusetts. After her father's death when she was eight months old, her mother had a series of breakdowns, leading to her permanent hospitalization. From the age of five, Bishop lived with her maternal grandparents in Nova Scotia, then with her father's relatives in Massachusetts. She was educated at Vassar College, where she met Marianne Moore, who became her mentor. Bishop traveled widely and in 1951 settled near Rio de Janeiro, where she lived for many years. After returning to the United States she taught at the University of Washington in Seattle, and then at Harvard from 1970 to 1979. Her work is collected in *The Complete Poems 1927–1979* and *The Collected Prose*, and her letters in *One Art* (1994). She also wrote a travel book, *Brazil*, and translated poetry and prose from the Portuguese.

STAR BLACK (b. 1946) was born in Coronado, California, and raised in Hawaii and Washington, D.C. She holds degrees from Wellesley College and Brooklyn College and works as a photographer and visual artist based in New York City, where she co-directs the KGB Bar Poetry Reading Series and serves as an associate editor for *Parnassus: Poetry in Review* and for *American Letters & Commentary*. She is the author of *Double Time, Waterworn, October for Idas*, and *Balefire*. Her collages have been shown in various galleries in New York, and her photographs are housed in the permanent collections of the Library of Congress and the New York Public Library.

WILLIAM BLAKE (1757–1827) was born in London and educated at the Royal Academy. At fourteen he was apprenticed for seven years to James Basire, a well-known engraver. His collections of poetry were illustrated with his own etchings. In his sixties he abandoned poetry to concentrate on pictorial art. A major painter and a major poet, Blake transformed eighteenth-century diction and prosody into a vehicle of visionary experience. In addition to his lyrics, he wrote a number of long prophetic poems, revising biblical motifs and creating his own complex mythology.

EDMUND BLUNDEN (1896–1974) was born in London and raised in Yalding, Kent. From 1916 to 1918, he served in the army, fighting at the front in France and receiving the Military Cross. He then attended Queen's College, Oxford. In 1922 he won the Hawthornden Prize for *The Shepherd*. The following year he traveled to South America to recuperate from the lingering effects of the war. He continued to travel widely before returning to England in 1964. He taught at Tokyo University, the University of Hong Kong, and Oxford University, was a writer for the *Times Literary Supplement*, and edited poetry collections by John Clare and Wilfred Owen.

LOUISE BOGAN (1897–1970) was born in Livermore Falls, Maine. She attended the Girls' Latin School in Boston, and then Boston University for one year before she left school to marry. In 1919, after separating from her husband, Bogan moved to New York City. She became the poetry editor for *The New Yorker* in 1931, a position she held until her retirement in 1969. She was Poetry Consultant to the Library of Congress from 1945 to 1946. Bogan published translations and several important critical studies, including *Achievement in American Poetry 1900–1950*; her poems are collected in *The Blue Estuaries: Poems 1923–1968*.

EAVAN BOLAND (b. 1944), daughter of the painter Frances Kelly and the Irish diplomat F. H. Boland, was born in Dublin, but spent most of her youth outside of Ireland due to her father's diplomatic service as the Irish ambassador to England and as a representative at the United Nations in New York. She graduated from Trinity College, Dublin, and lectured there until 1968. A member of the Irish Academy of Letters, Boland is also a noted critic and radio broadcaster. She directs the writing program at Stanford University, but lives part of each year in Dublin. Her collections of poetry include *An Origin Like Water: Collected Poems 1967–1987*, *In a Time of Violence*, and *The Lost Land*; she is also the author of *Object Lessons: The Life of the Woman and the Poet in Our Time*.

JOE BOLTON (1961–1990) is the author of *Days of Summer Gone: Poems* and a posthumously published collection, *The Last Nostalgia*, edited by Donald Justice. He committed suicide in 1990.

BRUCE BOND (b. 1954) is director of the creative writing program at the University of North Texas and poetry editor for *The American Poetry Review*. His award-winning poetry has been published in major literary journals, including *The Paris Review*. He is the author of a number of collections, including *Independence Days*, *The Anteroom of Paradise*, *Radiography*, and *The Throats of Narcissus*.

MARK ALEXANDER BOYD (1563–1601), born and educated in Scotland, was a soldier and Latin scholar. Most of his work is written in Latin. He traveled widely in France and the Netherlands, publishing his poems and letters at Bordeaux in 1590 and another collection in Belgium in 1592.

ROBERT SEYMOUR BRIDGES (1844–1930) attended Eton and Corpus Christi College, Oxford. He was financially independent, but after a period of travel he decided to study medicine at St. Bartholomew's Hospital and became a practicing physician. His sonnet sequence, *The Growth of Love*, was published anonymously in 1876; two more volumes of poems appeared in 1879 and 1880. In 1881, after living in Italy for a year to recuperate from pneumonia, he retired from medical practice; several years later, he married. In 1913, he was made poet laureate and in 1929 he received the Order of Merit.

RUPERT BROOKE (1875–1915) was born in Rugby, England. He was educated at Rugby, where his father was a housemaster, and won a scholarship to King's College, Cambridge. After an unhappy love affair he traveled to France and Germany in 1912; the following year he went to the United States, Canada, and the South Seas. He returned to England at the outbreak of the war and joined the Royal Navy. He participated in the retreat from Antwerp in 1914, and composed his war sonnets in the winter of 1914-15 in Dorset. He died of dysentery and blood poisoning on a troopship bound for Gallipoli.

GWENDOLYN BROOKS (1917–2000) was born in Topeka, Kansas, and raised in Chicago. At the age of sixteen she met Langston Hughes, who encouraged her in her writing. She graduated from Wilson Junior College. She ran workshops for underprivileged youths, taught poetry at a number of universities, including City College of New York and served as Poetry Consultant to the Library of Congress from 1985 to 1986. She published a novel, *Maud Martha* (1953); a book for children, *Bronzeville Boys and Girls* (1956); and many poetry collections, including *The Bean Eaters* (1960), *In the Mecca* (1968), and *Children Coming Home* (1991).

ELIZABETH BARRETT BROWNING (1806–1861) was born Elizabeth Barrett and raised in Herefordshire, England. She studied Greek and Latin at home. In 1846, without her father's knowledge, she married the poet Robert Browning, an admirer of her work, and eloped with him to Italy. Though she had been an invalid in England, in Italy her health returned, and she became active in Italian politics. *Sonnets from the Portuguese* (1850), well received when it first appeared, continues to be one of the most popular sonnet sequences. Barrett Browning also wrote a verse novel, *Aurora Leigh* (1857).

ROBERT BROWNING (1812–1889) was born in Camberwell, a suburb of London. He attended London University. Due to family circumstances, he was financially independent. In 1846 he eloped with the poet Elizabeth Barrett, and they lived together in Florence, Italy. After her death in 1861, he returned to London. His early work in poetry and drama was received poorly by the general public, but after the publication of *Dramatis Personae* (1861) and *The Ring and The Book* (1864) his reputation grew; he is best known for his work in the dramatic monologue.

ROBERT BURNS (1759–1796) was born into a farming family in Ayreshire, Scotland, and attended the school established by his father and neighbors. His first book, *Poems, Chiefly in the Scottish Dialect* (1786), was a great success, and gained him entry into high society in Edinburgh. He returned home in 1788 to marry and to accept a sinecure in the Excise Office and continue farming. In 1791, he gave up his land and moved to Dunfries to become a tax collector. Burns wrote, collected, and edited Scottish folk songs as part of a project to preserve Scottish culture and national identity.

JOHN BURNSIDE (b. 1955) was born in Dunfermline, Fife, and educated at Cambridge College of Arts and Technology. He received a Scottish Arts Council Literary Award for his first volume of poems, *The Hoop*, in 1988. His other collections include *Feast Days* and *Knowledge*. He lives in Bramley, Surrey.

GEORGE GORDON, LORD BYRON (1788–1824) was born near Aberdeen, Scotland. His father died when he was three, at which point his mother's fortune had been dissipated. At ten, Byron inherited his great uncle's title and land. After graduating from Trinity College, Cambridge, Byron traveled for two years in Portugal, Spain, Malta, Greece, and Asia Minor. With the publication of the first two cantos of *Childe Harold* (1812) he became well known throughout Europe and Russia. He left England in 1816 after a scandal. Sections of *Don Juan*, Byron's epic satire, began to appear in 1819. Galvanized by the Greek and Italian independence movements, Byron led Greek troops against the Turks. During a training exercise he died from a fever; Greece mourned him as a national hero.

ROY CAMPBELL (1902–1957) was born Ignatius Roy Dunnachie Campbell in Durban, South Africa. He traveled widely throughout his life and followed a variety of occupations, including bullfighting. He fought with the Nationalists in the Spanish Civil War, and during World War II served in East and North Africa until he was disabled. Campbell lived in France and Spain, and settled in Portugal five years before his death in an automobile crash. His works include a long poem, *The Flaming Terrapin* (1924), which gained him immediate recognition; *The Wayzgoose* (1928), a satire on South African intellectuals; and *The Georgiad* (1931), an attack on the Bloomsbury group in England. His lyrical works include *Adamastor* (1930), *Flowering Reeds* (1933), and *Talking Bronco* (1946); he also published two autobiographical books and many translations.

RAFAEL CAMPO (b. 1964) teaches and practices medicine at Beth Israel Deaconess Medical Center and Harvard Medical School. His volumes of poetry include *The Other Man Was Me: A Voyage to the New World*, *What the Body Told* (winner of a Lambda Literary Award), and *Diva*. His collection of essays, *The Poetry of Healing: A Doctor's Education*, also won a Lambda Literary Award.

HAYDEN CARRUTH (b. 1921) was born in Waterbury, Connecticut, and for many years lived in northern Vermont. He lives now in upstate New York, retired from teaching in the Graduate Creative Writing Program at Syracuse University. His numerous books of poetry include *Beside the Shadblow Tree* and *Reluctantly*, as well as the *Collected Shorter Poems 1946–1991* and *Collected Longer Poems*; he has also published a novel, four books of criticism, and two anthologies. He has been editor of *Poetry*, the poetry editor of *Harper's*, and for more than twenty-five years was an advisory editor of *The Hudson Review*. He has received fellowships from the Bollingen Foundation, the Guggenheim Foundation, and the National Endowment for the Arts. In 1998, he was appointed a senior fellow by the National Endowment for the Arts.

CHARLES CAUSLEY (b. 1917) was born in Launceston, Cornwall. His father, who returned as an invalid from the First World War, later died from the residual effects of nerve gas. Causley was educated at a local grammar school and published two plays in 1936 and 1937. He served in the Royal Navy from 1940 to 1946, and worked as a teacher after the war. His first volume of poems, *Farewell, Aggie Weston*, appeared in 1951. He left teaching in 1965 to write full-time, but has periodically taught at various universities outside England. His other collections include *A Field of Vision* and *The Young Man of Cury*.

GEORGE CHAPMAN (1559?–1634) was born in or near Hitchin, Herefordshire. He is thought to have been educated at Oxford, although he claimed to have been self-taught. His first published poem was *In the Shadow of the Night* (1594); *Ovid's banquet of sense* appeared in 1595. He published a poem in praise of Sir Walter Ralegh, *De Guiana, Carmen Epicum* ("An Epic Poem about Guiana"). In 1598, Chapman began to translate from Homer under the patronage of Prince Henry, son of James I. He published the first books of his translation of the *Iliad* in 1598, completing the entire work by 1611. His translation of the *Odyssey* appeared in 1615. After Prince Henry's death and James I's accession to the throne in 1603, Chapman was imprisoned with his friend Ben Jonson and John Marston for staging *Eastward Ho*. He died in poverty and was buried in St. Giles-in-the-Fields, London, where Inigo Jones provided a monument.

GEOFFREY CHAUCER (1343?–1400) was born in London into a middle-class merchant family. At about fifteen he became a page to the Countess of Ulster, who was married to the second son of King Edward III. Chaucer began his life as a poet by translating the opening passage of *Le Roman de la Rose*, an allegorical poem of courtly love written in medieval French. He wrote his early poem *The Book of the Duchess* for John of Gaunt, uncle and advisor of Richard II, and whose sister-in-law he later married. In 1367 Chaucer was granted an annuity in the royal household. His travels to the Continent on diplomatic missions began in 1366, and he spent much of the 1370s in Italy. In the 1380s, a time of great personal and political anxiety for him, Chaucer wrote the *Parliament of Fowles*, a dream vision for St. Valentine's Day; with this poem of 699 lines he introduced rhyme royal into English. After completing his prose translation of *The Consolation of Philosophy*, written by the Roman philosopher Boethius in the early sixth century, Chaucer wrote *Troilus and Criseyde*, taking the basic plot for this 8,239-line poem (also written in rhyme royal) from Boccaccio's *Filostrato*. In 1386, Chaucer began writing his *Canterbury Tales*, which were never completed. He held a succession of public offices, including MP and a justice of the peace in Kent. Though most of his English contemporaries were writing in Latin or French, Chaucer chose to write in English: his use of the vernacular helped to establish English as a viable medium for poetry.

AMY CLAMPITT (1920–1994) was born and raised in the small farming village of New Providence, Iowa, and educated at Grinnell College and Columbia University. She worked as an editor and for many years was a reference librarian at the National Audubon Society. In 1983 she published her first book of poetry, *The Kingfisher*; she then became a visiting professor at a number of universities. Her last collection, *A Silence Opens*, appeared in 1994. *The Collected Poems of Amy Clampitt* brings together the work of her five volumes; she also wrote a play and a collection of essays.

JOHN CLARE (1793–1864) left school at the age of twelve and worked on the English land as a gardener and field hand. In 1820, he published his first book, *Poems Descriptive of Rural Life and Scenery*, a collection marketed as the work of a young "Northamptonshire Peasant." The book was so successful that it changed his life, resulting in a move from the rural village of his birthplace, Helpstone, in Northamptonshire, England, to a cottage provided by a patron in a village four miles away. Uprooted from the place he knew and loved, Clare never regained his mental stability. He was declared insane in 1836 and sent to an asylum in southeast England, from which he escaped; he was recommitted to Northampton General Asylum, where he remained until his death. But he never ceased writing. His poem *The Parish*, a satire on social injustice, was published long after his death. Recent editions of his poetry, prose, and letters have helped bring his work out of relative obscurity.

ELIZABETH COBBOLD (1767–1824), born Eliza Knipe, published her first poetry collection at the age of nineteen, gaining critical success four years later with *Six Narrative Poems*, dedicated to her friend Sir Joshua Reynolds. She published a novel in 1791 and the next year married John Cobbold, an Ipswich brewer who already had fourteen children; they eventually had seven children together. Cobbold became an amateur naturalist and continued to publish. In 1812, she founded the Society for Clothing the Infant Poor. Her collected poems appeared in 1825.

HENRI COLE (b. 1956) was born in Fukuoka, Japan. His books of poetry include *The Look of Things* and *The Visible Man*. He is the recipient of the Rome Fellowship in Literature from the American Academy of Arts and Letters and a fellowship to the American Academy in Berlin. Cole was executive director of the Academy of American Poets from 1982 to 1988, and he has since taught at Columbia University, Reed College, Yale University, the University of Maryland, and Brandeis University. He was the Briggs-Copeland Lecturer in Poetry at Harvard University. He lives in Cambridge, Massachusetts.

ELLIOTT COLEMAN (1906–1980) graduated from Princeton University and taught for twelve years before starting The Writing Seminars at The Johns Hopkins University. He taught for thirty years at Johns Hopkins, and after retiring spent two years as poet-in-residence at Oxford University in England. Ill health brought him back to Baltimore, where he died after two strokes. He is one of the most prolific sonneteers of the twentieth century.

HARTLEY COLERIDGE (1796–1849), the eldest son of Samuel Taylor Coleridge, entered Oxford, but after gaining an Oriel fellowship in 1819 was dismissed a year later for intemperance and lack of application. After an attempt to support himself in London in the 1820s, when he did literary work and contributed to the *London Magazine*, he retired to the Lake District in 1833, where he lived mostly at Grasmere. His collected poems appeared in 1851.

SAMUEL TAYLOR COLERIDGE (1772–1834) was born in Ottery St. Mary, a rural village in Devon, the son of a clergyman. He was raised in London and educated at Jesus College, Cambridge, where he met Robert Southey, with whom he planned to start a utopian community in Pennsylvania, and whose sister he married. In 1798 he and his friend William Wordsworth published *Lyrical Ballads*, a work that represents a turning point in the history of English literature. From the age of thirty, Coleridge turned his energies to philosophy and criticism, developing a theory of "organic form," an antimechanistic approach to the creative process that profoundly affected the way we talk about poetry. Coleridge became addicted to opium, which had been prescribed to relieve extreme physical pain. He spent his last years in the care of a clergyman.

BILLY COLLINS (b. 1941) was born in New York City. His books include *Questions About Angels, The Art of Drowning, Picnic, Lightning*, and *The Best Cigarette*. Winner of five of *Poetry* magazine's annual prizes and a recipient of grants from the Guggenheim Foundation and the National Endowment for the Arts, he is a professor of English at Lehman College and a visiting writer at Sarah Lawrence College. In 2001 he was named poet laureate of the United States.

HENRY CONSTABLE (1562–1613) was educated at St. John's College, Cambridge, and Lincoln's Inn. In 1583 he went to Paris as a diplomatic emissary to Sir Francis Walsingham, which placed him in an atmosphere sympathetic to Catholicism. He dedicated much of his lyric poetry to Penelope Rich. By 1590 he had converted to Roman Catholicism and his poetry became mystical. His collection *Diana* was written in Paris, and later printed in 1592; he published an enlarged edition in 1594, dividing the volume into eight "decades." Constable lived in Paris and Rome, and returned to England in 1603, where he was imprisoned and lived in poverty until he returned to Paris seven years later. He was one of the first Elizabethan sonneteers. His *Spirituall Sonnette* were not published until 1815.

JANE COOPER (b. 1924) was born in Atlantic City, New Jersey, and educated at Vassar College, the University of Wisconsin, and the University of Iowa; at Iowa, she was a student of John Berryman and a classmate of Donald Justice, Philip Levine, and W. D. Snodgrass. From 1950 to 1987, she taught at Sarah Lawrence College. Her books include *Scaffolding, Green Notebook, Winter Road*, and *The Flashboat: Poems Collected and Reclaimed*. She lives in New York City.

CHARLES COTTON (1630–1687), of Beresford, Staffordshire, is chiefly known for Part II of *The Compleat Angler*, "Being Instructions how to angle for a Trout or Grayling in a clear stream" (1676). He translated Montaigne's *Essays* and wrote burlesques of Lucian and Vergil.

HART CRANE (1899–1932) was born in Garrettsville, Ohio, and published his first poem in a New York magazine at the age of sixteen. He moved to New York in 1917, after the divorce of his parents, but returned to Ohio to work for his father, whose candy company invented the Life Saver; he also wrote copy for various advertising agencies both in Cleveland and New York. Crane settled in New York in 1923, continuing to publish poetry and critical reviews. His first collection of poems, *White Buildings*, appeared in 1926. He received a Guggenheim Fellowship in 1930, following the publication of *The Bridge*, and traveled to Mexico, where he planned to write a poem about the Spanish Conquest. On his return voyage to New York, he jumped over the stern of the ship; his body was not recovered.

COUNTEE CULLEN (1903–1946) was born in Louisville, Kentucky, and at the age of fifteen was adopted by an Episcopal minister from New York City. He received his undergraduate degree from New York University and his M.A. in

English from Harvard University. A major writer of the Harlem Renaissance, Cullen modeled his poetic style on Keats. He published five volumes of poetry, including *Copper Sun*, *The Ballad of the Brown Girl*, and *On These I Stand*, edited an anthology of African-American poetry, *Caroling Dusk*, and translated Euripides. After living in Paris on a fellowship, he returned to New York, where he taught English and French in the public schools.

E[DWARD] E[STLIN] CUMMINGS (1894–1962) was born in Cambridge, Massachusetts, and educated at Harvard University. In 1916, he went to France to serve as a volunteer with a Red Cross ambulance corps on the Western Front, but was imprisoned for criticizing the military—an experience explored in *The Enormous Room*, an account of his four-month confinement, deprivation, and journey to spiritual freedom. In the early 1920s, he lived both in Paris, where he studied art, and in New York City, where he eventually settled. A classicist and serious painter, Cummings wrote hundreds of sonnets, combining traditional rhyme schemes with experimental syntax and typography, intermingling Elizabethan and contemporary diction.

SAMUEL DANIEL (1563–1619) was born in Somerset and educated at Magdalen Hall, Oxford. He mastered a variety of literary genres, from the sonnet sequence to tragedy to the historical poem; his critical essay *The Defence of Rhyme* (1603) is an important treatise of the Elizabethan era. In 1592, Daniel printed his own edition of *Delia*, dedicating the book of fifty sonnets to Mary Sidney, the Countess of Pembroke, Sir Philip Sidney's sister and later Daniel's patron (Daniel was her son's tutor); the sequence was reprinted many times, with numerous revisions, omissions, and additions. Daniel came under suspicion early in the reign of King James I, and never fully regained favor, though the queen still patronized him; he had to defend himself against a charge of sympathizing with the Earl of Essex in *The Tragedie of Philotas*, acted in 1604 (published in 1605). He spent the rest of his life working on a prose history, *The Collection of the Historie of England* (1612–18), through the reign of Edward III.

SIR JOHN DAVIES (1569–1626) was born in Wiltshire, educated at Oxford, and also studied on the Continent. He was one of the "university wits" at the Middle Temple. Expelled in 1598 for assault, he began to write didactic and panegyric verse. In 1603, he was made solicitor-general for Ireland. He was appointed Lord Chief Justice of England, but died before taking office.

JOHN DAVIES OF HEREFORD (1563?–1618) moved to London around 1600 after teaching at Oxford. He primarily wrote religious and philosophical verse. His collections include *Micro-cosmos* (1603), *The Holy Rood* (1609), *Wit's Pilgrimage* (1605), and a book of epigrams, *The Scourge of Folly* (1610?).

EDWIN DENBY (1903–1983) was born in Tientsin, China, where his father was the American consul, and raised in China, Austria, and the United States. He entered Harvard University, but left to go to Europe. He studied dance in Vienna, and during the twenties and thirties worked as a dancer, choreographer, and librettist in Austria, Germany, and France. After returning to New York in 1935 he focused on writing and became one of the most important dance critics of his time. He composed a number of long sonnet sequences, devoting his life in poetry to that form.

AUBREY THOMAS DE VERE (1814–1902), son of the poet Sir Aubrey de Vere, was born in Curragh Chase, County Limerick, Ireland, and educated at Trinity College, Dublin, where he studied metaphysics. He was a friend of Alfred, Lord Tennyson and Robert Browning. He converted to Catholicism in 1851.

SYDNEY DOBELL (1824–1874), who wrote under the pseudonym "Sydney Yendys," was born in Cranbrook, Kent. He worked with his father as a wine merchant in London and Cheltenham, then lived in the Scottish Highlands, and also spent time abroad. His long dramatic poem *The Roman* (1850), celebrating the revolutionary year of 1848, was praised by critics and resulted in Dobell's making the acquaintance of many notable figures in liberal politics and in literature. With Alexander Smith, Dobell wrote a sonnet sequence on the Crimean War. In his life and work, he advocated the cause of the oppressed.

JOHN DONNE (1572–1631) was the son of a London ironmonger, a prosperous merchant; his mother, a lifelong Catholic, was the daughter of John Heywood and a lineal descendent of Sir Thomas More. He was educated at Hart Hall, Oxford, and Lincoln's Inn, but was not allowed to take a degree because as a Roman Catholic he could not swear the required oath of allegiance to the Protestant queen, Elizabeth I. He entered the service of Sir Thomas Egerton, the Lord Keeper, but was dismissed when his secret marriage to Anne More, Lady Egerton's niece, was revealed. Finally, Donne entered the Church of England, and was ordained deacon and priest in 1615; two years later, his wife died at the age of thirty-three, after giving birth to a stillborn child. In 1621 he was made dean of St. Paul's Cathedral, turned fully to his vocation as an Anglican divine, and became the foremost preacher in England of his time, a favorite of King James I and Charles I. Donne's devotional prose was published in 1624; most of his poetry circulated in manuscript, remaining unprinted until after his death. In the second edition of his collected poems, published in 1635, his poetic work is divided into nine genres, including the *Elegies*; the secular love poems of the *Songs and Sonnets*, some of the greatest erotic poems in the English language; and the *Holy Sonnets*, which contains the crown of sonnets entitled "La Corona" and an untitled group of nineteen meditative sonnets arranged later by Donne's editors and known by the name *Holy Sonnets*.

RITA DOVE (b. 1952) served as poet laureate of the United States from 1993 to 1995. Among her honors are the Pulitzer Prize and the National Humanities Medal. Her poetry collections include *Thomas and Beulah*, *Grace Notes*, *Mother Love*, and *On the Bus with Rosa Parks*; her verse play *The Darker Face of the Earth* has been staged at the Royal National Theatre in London, the Guthrie in Minneapolis, and other major theaters. She is Commonwealth Professor of English at the University of Virginia.

ERNEST DOWSON (1867–1900) was born in Kent, England, and attended Queen's College, Oxford, but left to go to London. He studied Latin poetry, traveled widely, and was familiar with French literature. Along with Lionel Johnson, Arthur Symons, and W. B. Yeats, he was a member of the Rhymer's Club and contributed to *The Yellow Book* and *The Savoy*. In 1891, he fell in love with a twelve-year-old girl who became a symbol of innocence in his work. In 1895, his parents committed suicide within months of each other. Dowson is associated with the Decadent movement. He suffered from poverty and died of alcoholism.

MICHAEL DRAYTON (1563–1631) was born in Warwickshire and lived most of his adult life in London, where he is thought to have been friends with Shakespeare and Ben Jonson. His career as a poet spanned forty years, starting with *Harmony of the Church* (1591), a translation of scripture into metrical verse. He also wrote for the public stage. *Endymion and Phoebe* (1595), an erotically charged mythological narrative, is one of the sources for Keats's *Endymion*. His sonnet sequence *Ideas Mirrour: Amours in quatorzains* was published in 1594, and the last of a succession of revisions was published in 1619 in an edition called *Idea in Sixtie Three Sonnets*.

WILLIAM DRUMMOND OF HAWTHORNDEN (1585–1649) was born in Hawthornden, Midlothian, and educated at Edinburgh University. His mother was the sister of the Scottish court poet William Fowler. After graduation, Drummon traveled the Continent and studied law. He was friends with Michael Drayton and Ben Jonson. He tried to avoid political involvement, and rarely left his estate. *Flowers of Sion* (1623) is considered the finest collection of seventeenth-century Scottish religious poetry. He left his extensive library to Edinburgh University upon his death.

CAROL ANN DUFFY (b. 1955) was born in Glasgow and spent her childhood in Staffordshire. She graduated in philosophy from the University of Liverpool, and has enjoyed success as a playwright. Her volumes of poetry include *Standing Female Nude*, *Selling Manhattan*, *Mean Time*, which won both the Forward Prize and the Whitbread Prize, and *The World's Wife*. Duffy is a Fellow of the Royal Society of Literature. She lives in Manchester, England, where she lectures on poetry for the Writing School at Manchester Metropolitan University.

PAUL LAURENCE DUNBAR (1872–1906) was born in Dayton, Ohio, the son of former slaves; his father had escaped to Canada but returned to America to fight in the Civil War. Dunbar graduated from a white high school, where his classmates included Orville and Wilbur Wright; he published his first poems at the age of seventeen in an African-American newspaper. He was unable to pursue his hope to become a law clerk and went to work as an elevator operator. He self-published his first collection, *Oak and Ivy* (1892), and by the age of twenty-four had become the first African-American poet to garner a national reputation. Frederick Douglass secured a job for him at the Columbian Exposition in Chicago. From 1897 to 1898, Dunbar worked as an assistant in the reading room of the Library of Congress. He later published and lectured in the United States and England. He died an early death of tuberculosis.

ALICE DUNBAR-NELSON (1875–1935) was born Alice Ruth Moore in New Orleans and received her master's degree from Cornell University. She married Paul Laurence Dunbar after an epistolary courtship that began when he saw her photograph and read her poems in a newspaper; they separated in 1902. She taught in New York City and later in Washington, D.C., and Delaware, and was active in the National Association of Colored Women. In 1916, she married Robert John Nelson, with whom she co-edited the *Wilmington Advocate*. "Sonnet" appears in Countee Cullen's anthology *Caroling Dusk* (1927).

DOUGLAS DUNN (b. 1942) was born and raised in Renfrewshire and educated at the Scottish School of Librarianship and the University of Hull. He worked for many years as a librarian. His collections of poetry include *Elegies*, *Northlight*, and *Dante's Drum-Kit*; he is also the author of several volumes of short stories and the editor of *The Oxford Book of Scottish Short Stories* and *The Faber Book of Twentieth-Century Scottish Verse*

GEORGE ELIOT (1819–1880) was born Mary Ann (or Marian) Evans in Warwickshire, near Nuneaton. After her father died in 1849, she traveled through Europe before settling in London and becoming an assistant editor at *The Westminster Review*. She lived with the writer George Henry Lewes from 1854 until his death in 1878. In 1857 she began to publish short stories under the name George Eliot in *Blackwood's*; the stories were collected later that year in *Scenes of Clerical Life*. Best known as the author of such major novels as *Adam Bede*, *Silas*

Marner, *The Mill on the Floss*, *Daniel Deronda*, and *Middlemarch*, Eliot was also a poet and a translator. In May of 1880, she married John Walter Cross, the banker who had handled her investments. Eliot died in December of that year.

T[HOMAS] S[TEARNS] ELIOT (1888–1965) was born and raised in St. Louis, Missouri, and educated at Harvard, where he studied philosophy, and also at the Sorbonne and Oxford. In his late twenties he moved to England permanently; in 1927 he became a British citizen and an Anglican. Towards the end of the First World War, he began working in the International Department at Lloyd's Bank. He left banking after eight years to work at the book publisher Faber and Faber, where he remained for the rest of his life. In 1948, he was awarded the Nobel Prize for Literature. In addition to his poetry and verse drama, collected in *The Complete Poems and Plays*, Eliot published a number of highly influential books of essays and literary criticism.

EBENEZER ELLIOTT (1781–1849), called the "Corn Law Rhymer," urged the repeal of excessive taxes on bread in his collection entitled *Corn Law Rhymes* (1830). Elliott was a Sheffield iron foundry master for many years and a crusader for social justice in his poetic works.

SASCHA FEINSTEIN (b. 1963) won the 1999 Hayden Carruth Award for his poetry collection *Misterioso*. Individual poems have appeared in publications such as *American Poetry Review, North American Review, Ploughshares*, and *New England Review*. He is the author of two critical books, including *Jazz Poetry: From the 1920s to the Present*, and co-editor (with Yusef Komunyakaa) of *The Jazz Poetry Anthology* and its companion volume, *The Second Set*. He teaches poetry at Lycoming College and edits *Brilliant Corners: A Journal of Jazz & Literature*.

BETH ANN FENNELLY (b. 1971) received her B.A. from the University of Notre Dame and her M.F.A. from the University of Arkansas. She was the 1998–1999 Diane Middlebrook Fellow at the University of Wisconsin, and currently she teaches at Knox College in Galesburg, Illinois. Her poems have been published in *The Kenyon Review, Shenandoah*, and *TriQuarterly*, and have also appeared in *The Best American Poetry 1996* and the writing textbook *13 Ways of Looking for a Poem*.

ANNIE FINCH (b. 1956) was educated at Yale University, the University of Houston Creative Writing Program, and Stanford University. She is the author of *The Ghost of Meter: Culture and Prosody in American Free Verse* and the editor of *A Formal Feeling Comes: Poems in Form by Contemporary American Women*. Her volumes of poetry include *Catching the Mermother, The Encyclopedia of Scotland* (a book-length poem), and *Eve*. She teaches on the creative writing faculty at Miami University in Ohio.

GILES FLETCHER THE ELDER (1549?–1611) was born in Watford and educated at Eton and Cambridge, earning a degree in law. He went on diplomatic missions to Scotland and Germany. Later he traveled to Russia to secure concessions for English merchants, an experience he recounted in *The Russe Commonwealth* (1591). *Licia* (1593) is one of the earliest sonnet cycles.

ROBERT FROST (1875–1963), the son of two schoolteachers, a father from New Hampshire and a mother originally from Scotland, was born and raised in San Francisco. After his father's death in 1885, he moved with his mother to Massachusetts. In high school he wrote poetry and excelled as a student of classics. He briefly attended Dartmouth on a scholarship, then Harvard (his father's alma mater), before he withdrew to move to a farm in New Hampshire that his grandfather had bought him. For ten years, Frost struggled with financial difficulties until he found a teaching job at Pinkerton Academy. In 1911 he sold the farm, and from 1912 to 1915 he lived with his wife and children in London, where he began to establish his reputation as poet, receiving strong support from Ezra Pound and Edward Thomas. His two early collections, *A Boy's Will* (1913) and *North of Boston* (1914), were first published in England; on his return to the United States, which was necessitated by the First World War, the American publisher Henry Holt published those two volumes and all subsequent collections. Frost held a number of teaching appointments, the most enduring being at Amherst College. In 1961, John F. Kennedy invited him to read a poem at the presidential inauguration ceremony.

JOHN FULLER (b. 1937) was born in Ashford, Kent, the son of the poet Roy Fuller. He was educated at St. Paul's School and New College, Oxford, and in 1966 became a fellow of Magdalen College, Oxford. His poetry collections include his *Selected Poems*; he is also the author of *W. H. Auden: A Commentary*. Fuller's critical study *The Sonnet* is essential reading for anyone interested in the form.

GEORGE GASCOIGNE (1539–1578) probably attended Trinity College, Cambridge, and Gray's Inn. He served as a member in Queen Mary's last Parliament. In 1561 he married Elizabeth Breton, a wealthy widow, but her fortune was lost in a legal battle. He wrote a court masque performed at Kenilworth for Queen Elizabeth I. After a time in debtors' prison, he volunteered in 1572 for military service in the Netherlands, where he surrendered to the Spanish. His first published work, *A Hundredth Sundrie Flowers* (1573), a collection of amatory verse and prose that contained groups of linked sonnets, was censored while Gascoigne was a prisoner of the Spanish; after returning to England he revised and republished the collection as *The Posies*, but it was again banned. Gascoigne wrote the first treatise on prosody in English, "Certayne notes of Instruction," the first translation of a Greek play into English, and the first English poem in blank verse.

DANA GIOIA (b. 1950) is the author of the collections of poetry *Daily Horoscope* and *The Gods of Winter*. His critical book *Can Poetry Matter?* was a finalist for the 1992 National Book Critics Circle Award. Gioia is the editor of several best-selling literary anthologies and a frequent commentator for the BBC. He lives in California.

LOUISE GLÜCK (b. 1943) was born in New York, raised on Long Island, and lived for many years in Plainfield, Vermont. She has taught at various American colleges and universities, including Columbia University, the University of Iowa, and Williams College. Her collections of poetry include *The Triumph of Achilles, Ararat, The Wild Iris*, for which she received the Pulitzer Prize in 1992, and *Vita Nova*; she is also the author of *Proofs and Theories: Essays on Poetry*.

ROBERT GRAVES (1895–1985) was born in Wimbledon, England, and attended Charterhouse School, which he left to fight in the First World War with the Royal Welsh Fusiliers. He served at the front in France, where he met Siegfried Sassoon; in 1916 he was sent back to English after being seriously injured at the Battle of the Somme. His education resumed at St. John's College, Oxford, and in 1926 he began teaching English. He cofounded the Seizin Press (London) with the poet Laura Riding, and they lived together in Majorca until the beginning of the Spanish Civil War. In 1961 he became a professor of poetry at Oxford. In addition to his collections of poetry, Graves published novels, essays, translations, biography, autobiography, and criticism, including *Goodybe to All That*, an account of his wartime experiences, *Homer's Daughter, The White Goddess: A Historical Grammar of Poetic Myth*, and *I, Claudius*.

THOMAS GRAY (1716–1771) was born in Cornhill, London, and educated at Eton and Peterhouse College, Cambridge. Though his family was prosperous, he was the only child of twelve to survive infancy. At Cambridge he studied classics, early English poetry, and ancient Welsh and Norse literature. After graduating he traveled to France, Switzerland, and Italy with his friend Horace Walpole. His first poem, "Ode on a Distant Prospect of Eton College," was published in 1747. In 1751 Gray received immense attention after the publication of "Elegy Written in a Country Churchyard." His celebrity had little impact on his shy and studious nature; he rarely left Cambridge. He developed a romantic devotion to a young Swiss nobleman named Charles Victor de Bonstetten, whose studies he directed in 1769. Gray's monument in Westminister Abbey is next to Spenser's.

FULKE GREVILLE, LORD BROOKE (1554–1628) was born to a prosperous family and educated at Shrewsbury School and Jesus College, Cambridge. He came to court with Philip Sidney, where they quickly became favorites of Queen Elizabeth I. Greville's devotion to Sidney can be seen in his *The life of the renowned Sir Philip Sidney*, which was published posthumously (1652). He patronized and helped many writers, including John Davies, John Speed, and Samuel Daniel. He wrote philosophical verse and closet dramas in addition to his poetry. Greville was stabbed to death by a servant.

THOM GUNN (b. 1929) was born in Kent, England, and attended Trinity College, Cambridge, after serving in the army for a year and then living for a time in Paris and then in Rome. He moved to California in 1954, doing graduate work at Stanford University, where he studied with the poet Yvor Winters. That same year, his first collection, *Fighting Terms*, was published. He is the author of many volumes of poetry, including *The Passages of Joy, The Man with Night Sweats, Collected Poems* (1994), and *Boss Cupid* (2000); he has also published several works of prose, including *The Occasions of Poetry: Essays in Criticism and Autobiography*.

DANIEL GUTSTEIN's (b. 1968) work has appeared in *Ploughshares, Fiction, The Journal, Poet Lore, Third Coast*, and *Cream City Review*. A former economist, farmhand, Tae Kwon Do instructor, arts educator, and editor, he currently teaches English at George Washington University. He has held two work-study scholarships to the Bread Loaf Writers' Conference.

MARILYN HACKER (b. 1942) was born in New York City and educated at the Bronx High School of Science, New York University, and the Art Students League. She has published many volumes of poetry, including *Presentation Piece*, which received the National Book Award in 1975, *Love, Death, and the Changing of the Seasons*, a book-length sonnet sequence, *Winter Numbers*, and *Squares and Courtyards*. She was editor of the feminist literary magazine *13th Moon* from 1982 to 1986, and of *The Kenyon Review* from 1990 to 1994. Hacker lives in New York and Paris, and is director of the M.A. program in English and creative writing at the City College of New York.

RACHEL HADAS (b. 1948) is the author of more than a dozen books of poetry, essays, and translations, including *Halfway Down the Hall: New and Selected Poems*. Her honors include a Guggenheim Fellowship in Poetry and an American

Academy–Institute of Arts and Letters Award in Literature. Hadas lives in New York City and teaches English at Rutgers (Newark campus).

DONALD HALL (b. 1928) was born in Connecticut and since 1975 has lived in New Hampshire on an old family farm. He has published many books of essays, a memoir, and numerous books of poetry, including *Old and New Poems, The Museum of Clear Ideas*, and *Without*. He was married to the poet Jane Kenyon until her death in 1995.

MARTHA HANSON (fl. 1809) spent her childhood near Hurstpierpoint, Sussex, and wrote her poems at Bellevue House. She published a two-volume poetry collection entitled *Sonnets and Other Poems* (1809).

THOMAS HARDY (1840–1928) was born in a village in Dorset, England, and was apprenticed to an architect there. In 1867, after spending seven years in London, he returned to Dorset, where he wrote most of his work. Hardy considered himself primarily a poet, but it was his fiction that gained him success and for which he is best known. He is the author of many novels, including *Far From the Madding Crowd, The Return of the Native*, and *Tess of the D'Ubervilles*. After the poor critical reception of *Jude the Obscure* (1895), Hardy abandoned fiction and dedicated the last thirty years of his life to writing poetry, publishing *Wessex Poems* in 1898, and many collections therafter, including *The Dynasts*, his epic drama on the Napoleonic era, *Satires of Circumstance*, and *Late Lyrics and Earlier* (1922).

TONY HARRISON (b. 1937) was born in Leeds, England, and educated at Leeds Grammar School and Leeds University, where he studied classics and linguistics. He has lectured in English at Ahmadu Bello University, Nigeria, and at Charles University, Prague; in 1977–1978 he was resident dramatist at the National Theatre. He is the author of a long lyric sequence entitled *from The School of Eloquence;* his other works include *V. and Other Poems, Dramatic Verse: 1973–1985, A Cold Coming: Gulf War Poems*, and *The Shadow of Hiroshima and Other Film Poems*.

ROBERT HAYDEN (1913–1980) was born Asa Bundy Sheffey in Detroit, Michigan, and educated at Detroit City College (now Wayne State University) and the University of Michigan at Ann Arbor, where he studied with W. H. Auden. As an infant he was abandoned by his biological parents and taken in by neighbors, who renamed him Robert Hayden. In 1936 he began research on the Underground Railroad as part of the Writers' Project of the WPA. In 1940 Hayden published his first collection of poems, *Heart-Shape in the Dust*; he gained prominence when *A Ballad of Remembrance* (1962) won a grand prize at the First World Festival of Negro Arts in Dakar, Senegal. In 1976 he became the first African American to be appointed Poetry Consultant to the Library of Congress. His other works include his long poem, "Middle Passage," *American Journal* (1980), and *Angle of Ascent: New and Selected Poems* (1985).

SEAMUS HEANEY (b. 1939) was born in Mossbawn, County Derry, Northern Ireland, and educated at St. Columb's College, and Queen's University, Belfast. He was the oldest of nine children in a Catholic family. In 1966 he published his first book of poems, *Death of a Naturalist*, and six years later he moved to Belfast. Since 1984 he has been Boylston Professor of Rhetoric and Oratory at Harvard; he has also been professor of poetry at Oxford since 1989. Heaney received the Nobel Prize for Literature in 1995. He has published several volumes of essays as well as numerous books of poetry, including *Field Work*, *Station Island*, *Seeing Things*, and *Opened Ground*, his collected poems. He has also published *The Cure at Troy* (a version of Sophocles's *Philoctetes*), and a new verse translation of *Beowulf*.

ANTHONY HECHT (b. 1923) was born in New York City. After graduating from Bard College in 1944, he entered the army, serving in Europe and Japan. His collections of poetry include *The Hard Hours*, which won a Pulitzer Prize, *The Transparent Man*, and *Flight Among the Tombs*. He has also published criticism, including *The Hidden Law*, a major study of the poetry of W. H. Auden, and written an introduction to an edition of Shakespeare's sonnets. Hecht has been awarded fellowships from the Ford, Guggenheim, and Rockefeller foundations, as well as the Bollingen Prize, the Eugenio Montale Award, and the Tanning Prize. He taught for many years at Georgetown University, and lives in Washington, D.C.

EDWARD HERBERT, LORD HERBERT OF CHERBURY (1583–1648) was born in Eyton, Shropshire, and educated at University College, Oxford. Under James I, he was made a knight of the Bath, an ambassador to Paris, and a peer of the realm. In 1624 he published *De Veritate* ("On Truth"), in which he explored his skeptical views on religion. He was unable to remain neutral in the Civil War, and ultimately sided with Parliament to save his lands. His poems and autobiography were published after his death. He also wrote several historical works, including *The Life and Raigne of King Henry the Eighth* (1649).

GEORGE HERBERT (1593–1633), a family friend of John Donne, was educated at home and at Westminster School and Trinity College, Cambridge, where he became public orator in 1620. In 1624 he was elected to Parliament; by 1625 his sponsors at court were dead or out of favor. In 1630 he became rector of Bemerton near Salisbury, a position endowed by William Herbert, third Earl of Pembroke. He died three years later. His close friend Nicholas Ferrar published his poems with the title *The Temple: Sacred Poems and Private Ejaculations* in 1633.

ROBERT HERRICK (1591–1674) was apprenticed as a goldsmith, attended St John's College, Cambridge, and in 1623 was ordained a priest. Four years later, he served as chaplain to the Duke of Buckingham on his Isle of Rhé expedition. In 1629, Herrick was made dean prior in Devonshire. In 1647, on being ousted from his post by the Puritans, he went to London, and the following year he published his collection of secular verse, *Hesperides*, and his religious poems, *The Noble Numbers*. He returned to Devon in 1660, after the monarchy had been restored.

GEOFFREY HILL (b. 1932) was born in Bromsgrove, Worcestershire, England, and educated at Keble College, Oxford. He taught at the University of Leeds and then at Cambridge, before moving to the United States in 1988 to teach at Boston University. His stage version of Ibsen's *Brand* was commissioned and performed by The National Theatre, London in 1978. His books of poetry include *New and Collected Poems 1952–1992*, *Canaan*, and *The Triumph of Love*; he has also published two volumes of critical essays.

JOHN HOLLANDER (b. 1929) was born in New York City and educated at Columbia University and Indiana University at Bloomington. He has taught at Harvard University, Connecticut College, and Hunter College, and for many years has taught at Yale University, where he is the Sterling Professor of English. In addition to numerous volumes of poetry, including *Figurehead and Other Poems*, Hollander has published plays, children's verse, and is the author of many major scholarly studies, including *Vision and Resonance: Two Senses of Poetic Form*, *The Figure of Echo: A Mode of Allusion in Milton and After*, and *The Work of Poetry*; he has also edited a number of anthologies and written an important handbook, *Rhyme's Reason: A Guide to English Verse*.

GERARD MANLEY HOPKINS (1844–1889) was born in Stratford, Essex, and educated at Highgate and Balliol College, Oxford. Hopkins studied with Walter Pater, whose sensibility resonated with his own. In 1855 he converted to Catholicism, which estranged him from his parents; he became a novitiate of the Society of Jesus, and was ordained in 1877. Hopkins had stopped writing poetry in 1868, believing it incompatible with his religious vocation; in 1875 the Church urged him to continue writing. He served as a parish priest, and in 1884 was appointed professor of Greek at University College, Dublin. He developed "sprung rhythm," a stress-based metrical system rooted in Old English poetry. His poems were transcribed and collected after his death by his friend and literary executor, the poet Robert Bridges, who released them for publication in 1918.

HENRY HOWARD, EARL OF SURREY (1517?–1547), the eldest son of Thomas Howard (who became Duke of Norfolk), was raised at Windsor. He was descended from kings, and the Surrey family embodied the old Catholic aristoc-racy. After talk of marriage with the Princess Mary, daughter of Henry VIII and Catherine of Aragon, in 1523 he married Lady Frances de Vere, the fourteen-year-old daughter of the Earl of Oxford, but they did not live together until 1535. Between 1537 and 1539 Surrey was confined at Windsor after being charged with having secretly favored the Roman Catholics in the rebellion of 1530, when in fact he had joined his father against the insurgents. He was a champion in court jousts in 1540 and served in the campaigns in Scotland, France, and Flanders. Shortly after his return to England in 1546, he and his fa-ther were both accused of treason. Surrey was beheaded on Tomb Hill; his fa-ther was saved because Henry VIII died before he too could be executed. Most of Surrey's poetry was probably written during the time of his confinement at Windsor; it was published ten years after his death in the anthology that came to be known as *Tottel's Miscellany*.

DAVID HUDDLE (b. 1942) was born in Ivanhoe, Virginia, and for many years has lived in Vermont, where he teaches at the University of Vermont and the Bread Loaf School of Writing. In 1999, he published *Summer Lake: New and Se-lected Poems*, as well as his first novel, *The Story of a Million Years*. Among his other books are *The Writing Habit*, *Paper Boy*, and *Only the Little Bone*.

T. R. HUMMER (b. 1950) was born and raised in Macon, Mississippi. He received a B.A. and M.A. in English literature from the University of Southern Missis-sippi in Hattiesburg, and later a Ph.D. in English and creative writing from the University of Utah. He has served as editor of several literary periodicals, and currently is a professor of creative writing and literature at Middlebury College in Vermont. His collections of poetry include *Lower-Class Heresy* and *Walt Whitman in Hell*.

LEIGH HUNT (1784–1859) was born in Southgate, Middlesex, and educated at Christ's Hospital. In 1813, Hunt and his brother were imprisoned for two years for criticizing the Prince Regent in their journal, *The Examiner*; Hunt contin-ued to edit the journal from prison. Hunt later traveled to Italy with Lord By-ron and Percy Bysshe Shelley, where together they published *The Liberal*.

JAMES I OF ENGLAND (1566–1625), King James VI of Scotland, wrote on a vari-ety of subjects, including tobacco, witchcraft, and religion. He wrote most of his verse before acceding to the English throne in 1603.

MARK JARMAN (b. 1952) teaches at Vanderbilt University. His collections of poetry include *Questions for Ecclesiastes*, which won the Lenore Marshall Poetry Prize for 1998, and *Unholy Sonnets*. He is co-editor (with David Mason) of *Rebel Angels: 25 Poets of the New Formalism*, co-author (with Robert McDowell) of *The Reaper Essays*, and author of a book of essays entitled *The Secret of Poetry*.

ROBINSON JEFFERS (1887–1962) was born in Pittsburgh, Pennsylvania, and educated at the University of Pittsburgh and Occidental College, as well as in Germany and Switzerland. He did advanced studies in medicine. His work appears in three volumes edited by Tim Hunt, *The Collected Poetry of Robinson Jeffers: 1920–1928, The Collected Poetry of Robinson Jeffers: 1928–1938*, and *The Collected Poetry of Robinson Jeffers: 1939–1962*.

DENIS JOHNSON (b. 1949) was born in 1949 in Munich, Germany, and raised in Tokyo, Manila, and Washington. His many awards include a Lannan Fellowship in Fiction and a Whiting Writer's Award. He has published a number of books of fiction, including *Angels, Fiskadoro*, and *Jesus' Son*. His books of poetry include *The Incognito Lounge* and *The Throne of the Third Heaven of the Nations Millennium General Assembly: Poems Collected and New*. He lives in northern Idaho.

JAMES WELDON JOHNSON (1871–1938) was born in Jacksonville, Florida, and educated at Atlanta University and Columbia University. He was the first African-American lawyer in Florida. He moved to New York City, where he became a successful songwriter. Johnson was a founding member and then secretary of the National Association for the Advancement of Colored People. While in South America as a U.S. consul, he published his first novel, *The Autobiography of an Ex-Colored Man* (1912), anonymously; he claimed authorship in subsequent printings. His first collection of poetry appeared five years later. He is perhaps best known for his anthem, "Lift Every Voice and Sing."

MARY F. JOHNSON (fl. 1810, d. 1863) is the author of *Original Sonnets and Other Poems* (1810), which she wrote at Wroxhall Farm, Isle of Wight. The volume also contains a number of odes. She later married George Moncrieff, younger brother of Sir Harry Moncrieff.

BEN JONSON (1572?–1637), was born in London a month after his father died, and was educated at Westminster School. He was apprenticed to his stepfather as a bricklayer; he left his trade to join the military and distinguished himself in battle in the Netherlands. He returned to London and became one of the most important playwrights of his age. In 1598, Jonson killed a fellow actor in a duel, but escaped execution. He converted to Catholicism that same year, but returned to the Anglican Church in 1610. Under James I he wrote a series of court masques and received patronage from the third Earl of Pembroke and other nobles. The publication of his *Workes* (1616) helped establish the respectability of the professional writer.

JUNE JORDAN (b. 1936) was born in New York, the only child of Jamaican immigrants, and attended Barnard College. She has taught at the City College of New York, Sarah Lawrence, Yale, and the State University of New York at Stony Brook. She has been a Fellow at the American Academy in Rome. Her collections of poetry include *Things I Do in the Dark*, *Passion*, *Civil Wars*, and *Kissing God Goodbye: Poems 1991–1996*. She teaches African-American studies at the University of California, Berkeley.

DONALD JUSTICE (b. 1925) was born in Miami, Florida, and studied music composition before turning to poetry. In 1980, he received the Pulitzer Prize for his *Selected Poems*; his *New and Selected Poems* appeared in 1995. Justice is also the author of a book of essays, *Oblivion: On Writers and Writing*, and he has edited the work of a number of poets, including Weldon Kees and Joe Bolton. He is married to the short-story writer Jean Ross Justice and lives in Iowa City.

PATRICK KAVANAGH (1904–1967) was born in Monaghan, Ireland, and left school at the age of twelve. Like his father, he supported himself by farming. In 1939 he moved to Dublin. After selling his land in 1949 he became a full-time writer. His works include *Complete Poems* (1972) and *By Night Unstarred: An Autobiographical Novel* (1977).

JOHN KEATS (1795–1821) was born in London to a livery stableman, and educated at Guy's Hospital, London, after an apprenticeship to an apothecary surgeon. Keats lost both of his parents while young, his father to a riding accident, his mother to tuberculosis. He left medicine to concentrate on poetry, and was encouraged by Leigh Hunt. He began publishing poetry in 1816, and by 1818 had published his epic poem *Endymion*. In 1819 he composed some of his finest poems, including "The Fall of Hyperion," his odes, and many sonnets. He helplessly watched his brother Tom die of tuberculosis; shortly thereafter, Keats himself became ill with the disease. He journeyed to Italy in an attempt to recover, but died in Rome, where he is buried.

WELDON KEES (1914–1955) was born in Nebraska and grew up during the Depression. He published his first story at the age of sixteen, considered himself a Trotskyite, and made a living as a librarian and by writing for *Time*, *The New Yorker*, and *The Nation*. Kees was also a jazz pianist, a composer, a filmmaker, and a painter. On July 15, 1955, his automobile was discovered parked near the Golden Gate Bridge, with the keys left inside; his disappearance has been treated as a suicide.

KARL KIRCHWEY (b. 1956) was born in Boston, educated at Yale and Columbia, and has lived in this country and abroad. He is the author of *A Wandering Island*, which received the Poetry Society of America's Norma Farber First Book Award for 1990, *Those I Guard*, and *The Engrafted Word*. His work has been anthologized in *The Best of the Best American Poetry*, *Walk on the Wild Side: Urban American Poetry Since 1975*, *After Ovid: New Metamorphoses*, *Twentieth Century Poems on the Gospels: An Anthology*, and elsewhere. His work-in-progress, based on the *Alcestis* of Euripides, received *The Paris Review*'s Prize for Poetic Drama in 1997. He lives in New York City, where for many years he served as director of the Unterberg Poetry Center of the Ninety-second Street Y. Currently he is Director of Creative Writing and Senior Lecturer in the Arts at Bryn Mawr College.

CHARLES LAMB (1775–1834) was born in London and educated at Christ's Hospital, where he met Samuel Taylor Coleridge. Lamb and Coleridge published their early poems together in a volume called *Poems* (1796). After leaving school at fifteen, he worked as a clerk in the East India Company for thirty-five years. He was part of a circle of writers sympathetic to political reform, a group including Shelley, Hazlett, Byron, and Hunt. His sister, Mary Lamb, murdered their mother, and was later released into his custody; he cared for her until her death. Together they adapted Shakespeare's plays into a collection of stories for children called *Tales from Shakespeare* (1807).

PHILIP LARKIN (1922–1985) was born in Coventry and educated at King Henry VIII School and St. John's College, Oxford. He worked as a librarian at the University of Hull for most of his life, and published many articles on jazz. In addition to his collections of poetry he published two novels and several collections of essays, including *All What Jazz: A Record Diary 1961–1971*. In 1984 he refused the post of poet laureate. His *Collected Poems* appeared in 1989.

JAMES LASDUN (b. 1958) was born and educated in England. He has published collections of short stories as well as several volumes of poetry, including *A Jump Start* and *Woman Police Officer in Elevator*. With Michael Hofmann, he co-edited the anthology *After Ovid: New Metamorphoses*. He has taught in the poetry and fiction writing programs at Princeton, New York University, and Columbia, and is the recipient of a Guggenheim Fellowship in Poetry.

DEBRA LASER (b. 1956), who was born in Maryland and grew up there and in Brazil, worked for many years as a librarian. She received her M.F.A. from the University of Maryland, College Park, in 1997, and is the recipient of an Associated Writing Programs award. Laser has completed the manuscript of her first book, *Part & Parcel*. She lives in Rockville, Maryland.

ANN LAUTERBACH (b. 1942) is the author of *Before Recollection*, *Clamor*, *On a Stair*, *If In Time*, and other poetry collections; she has also published essays about art. In 1993 she was awarded a MacArthur Fellowship. She lives in New York City, where she is a professor at the City College and Graduate Center; she is also head of the writing faculty in the M.F.A. program at Bard College.

EMMA LAZARUS (1849–1887) was born in New York city to a prominent family of Portuguese Jewish descent. She was educated at home, and by the age of eighteen had published a book of verse translations. In her thirties, Lazarus became increasingly interested in her Jewish identity, translating medieval Hebrew poets and writing essays supporting the establishment of a Jewish homeland. In her poems and essays, she also argued for the rights of Jewish immigrants fleeing European persecution. Her sonnet "The New Colossus" (1883) is inscribed on a plaque attached to the pedestal of the Statue of Liberty, which was dedicated on October 28, 1886. Her works include *Admetus* and *Spagnoletto: A Drama in Verse*, and *Dance Till Death*, a play about a plague in fourteenth-century Germany. Her translations include *Poems and Ballads of Heinrich Heine*.

EUGENE LEE-HAMILTON (1845–1907) was born in London and educated in France and Germany before attending Oxford. He became a diplomat, but in 1875, incapacitated by illness, he resigned from these duties and concentrated on poetry. In 1896 he regained his health, and two years later he married.

DAVID LEHMAN (b. 1948) was born in New York City. His books of poetry include *An Alternative to Speech*, *Operation Memory*, *Valentine Place*, and *The Daily Mirror*. He has also written a number of nonfiction books, including *Signs of the Times: Deconstruction and the Fall of Paul de Man* and *The Last Avant-Garde: The Making of the New York School of Poets*. In 1988 Lehman launched *The Best American Poetry*, an annually published anthology for which he serves as series editor. He teaches in the graduate writing programs of Bennington College and the New School, and offers a "great poems" course for honors undergraduates at New York University.

PHILLIS LEVIN (b. 1954) was born in Paterson, New Jersey, and educated at Sarah Lawrence College and The Johns Hopkins University. She is the author of *Temples and Fields*, which received the Poetry Society of America's Norma Farber First Book Award for 1988, *The Afterimage*, and *Mercury*; she is also the editor of this anthology. Her other awards include a Fulbright Fellowship to Slovenia and the Amy Lowell Poetry Travelling Scholarship. Levin has taught at the University of Maryland, College Park, and the Unterberg Poetry Center of the Ninety-second Street Y. She lives in New York City and currently teaches in the M.A. Program in English and Creative Writing at Hofstra University.

PHILIP LEVINE (b. 1928) was born in Detroit and educated in the public schools, at Wayne University, and at Iowa, where he studied with Robert Lowell and John Berryman. He taught for twenty-two years at Fresno State. His first book, *On the Edge*, appeared in 1963, and he has published numerous other collections, including *They Feed They Lion* and *The Mercy*; he is also the author of a memoir, *The Bread of Time*. He has received two National Book Awards (for *Ashes* and *What Work Is*), and won the Pulitzer Prize in 1995 for *The Simple Truth*.

KATE LIGHT (b. 1960) has published her poetry in *The Paris Review*, *Western Humanities Review*, *The Washington Post*, *Feminist Studies*, *The Formalist*, *Sparrow*, *Barrow Street*, and *Carolina Quarterly*. Her first collection, *The Laws of Falling Bodies*, was co-recipient of the 1997 Nicholas Roerich Prize. She has been a fellow at Yaddo and at the Sewanee Writers' Conference. She lives in New York City and is a violinist with the New York City Opera.

ANNE LOCKE (1533?–1595), also known as Anne Vaughan Lock, was born in London to a successful merchant and a seamstress in the Tudor court. Around 1551 she married Henry Lock(e). Anne Locke's correspondence with John Knox began in 1556; only his letters survived, but they are one of the primary sources of information about her life. In 1557 Locke joined the exiled Protestant community in Geneva, returning to England after Elizabeth's accession to the throne. In January 1560 she published her first volume, comprising an epistle to the Duchess of Suffolk, her translation of John Calvin's sermons, and "A Meditation of a Penitent Sinner," a series of twenty-six sonnets. In 1572, after the death of Henry Locke, she married Edward Dering (1540?–1576), also a devoted Calvinist. Anne Locke was the great-great-great aunt of John Locke.

THOMAS LODGE (1558–1625), was the son of a lord mayor of London; he was educated at Merchant Taylors' School, at Oxford. He gave up the study of law for writing, and wrote a number of prose romances. After several journeys to the New World, Lodge studied medicine and became a prominent physician. He converted to Catholicism in 1600, after which he translated Josephus and Seneca.

HENRY WADSWORTH LONGFELLOW (1807–1882) was born in Portland, Maine, and was educated at Bowdoin College, where he was a classmate of Nathaniel Hawthorne, and where he was appointed professor of modern languages after studying in Europe. From 1835 to 1854 he taught at Harvard, and thereafter he devoted himself fully to writing. Throughout his career Longfellow wrote poetry, verse drama, and fiction, and translated the work of many poets, including Dante. In 1843 he became partially blind. In 1861, in a tragic house fire, his second wife died and he was severely burned. "The Cross of Snow" was found among his papers after his death.

AMY LOWELL (1874–1925) was born in Brookline, Massachusetts, and educated privately. She traveled extensively, and published her first collection of poems, *A Dome of Many Colored Glass*, in 1912. In 1913 she went to England, where she met Ezra Pound and other poets of the Imagist circle; she later became a major figure in the Imagist movement, influencing its direction. Lowell supported many struggling artists. In addition to her volumes of poetry— the posthumously published *What's O'Clock* (1925) received the Pulitzer Prize —she wrote several critical studies, including *Six French Poets* (1915), *Tendencies in Modern American Poetry* (1917), and a two-volume biography of the poet John Keats.

JAMES RUSSELL LOWELL (1819–1891) was born in Cambridge, Massachusetts, into a distinguished New England family. He graduated from Harvard in 1838 and took a degree in law in 1840. In 1844 he married the poet Maria White, who had inspired the poems in his collection *A Year's Life* (1841). His collection of critical essays, *Conversations on Some of the Old Poets* (1845), which included pleas for the abolition of slavery, was followed by the publication of many of his antislavery articles in various periodicals. In his *Bigelow Papers,* a series of satirical verses, he expressed his opposition to the Mexican War. With the publication of *The Vision of Sir Launfal*, a long poem celebrating the brotherhood of man, and *A Fable for Critics*, an evaluation of contemporary American authors, Lowell became a popular figure in American literature. In 1853 the deaths of three of his four children were followed by the death of his wife. In 1857 he married Frances Dunlap, who had cared for his only remaining child. Lowell taught modern languages at Harvard, and was an editor of the *Atlantic Monthly*; with Charles Eliot Norton he became an editor of the *North American Review*, during which time he began publishing a series of essays on major literary figures. President Rutherford B. Hayes appointed him minister to Spain (1877–80) and ambassador to Great Britain (1880–85).

ROBERT LOWELL (1917–1977) was born in Boston, Massachusetts. He attended Harvard University, but under the advice of the psychiatrist who treated him for the first of a series of breakdowns, he transferred to Kenyon College. During the Second World War he was imprisoned as a conscientious objector. In his sonnets, Lowell explored the failures and accomplishments of his own life, as well as the destiny of historical figures in the ancient and modern world. He died in a taxi in New York. His books of poetry include *The Dolphin, Notebook*, and *Day by Day*; his essays and reviews appear in his *Collected Prose*.

MALCOLM LOWRY (1909–1957) was born in Birkenhead, Cheshire, England, and attended St. Catherine's College, Cambridge, after working as a crew member on a freighter bound for China. In his early twenties, he lived in London and Paris, and in 1935 moved to Hollywood, California, and then to Cuernavaca, Mexico. He continued to explore different ways of being in the world—living in a primitive cabin in Dollarton, British Columbia, from 1940 to 1954, and spending the last few years of his life in Italy and then in England. Lowry is most known for his novel *Under the Volcano* (1947); in addition to works of fiction, plays, and film scripts, Lowry wrote a large number of poems, most of which were unpublished at the time of his death and which now are at the University of British Columbia.

ELIZABETH MACKLIN (b. 1952) was born in Poughkeepsie, New York. She is the author of *A Woman Kneeling in the Big City* and *You've Just Been Told*. Her poems have appeared in *The Nation, The New Republic, The New Yorker, The Threepenny Review*, and elsewhere; she has also published a number of essays. She was a 1994 Guggenheim Fellow in Poetry, and spent 1999–2000 on an Amy Lowell Poetry Travelling Scholarship in Bilbao, Spain. She now lives in New York City.

ARCHIBALD MACLEISH (1892–1983) was born and raised in Glencoe, Illinois, and educated at Yale University. In 1917 he enlisted in the army, volunteering to serve at the front. He attended Harvard Law School after the war bur abandoned the law in 1923 and went to Paris to focus on his poetry. He returned to America in 1928, where he later became an editor at *Fortune* magazine. MacLeish was appointed Librarian of Congress in 1939 and was an advisor to Franklin Delano Roosevelt. He was Assistant Secretary of State from 1944 to 1945. He was later Boylston Professor at Harvard. In addition to many volumes of poetry, he also wrote essays, verse plays, and radio plays. He received three Pulitzer Prizes for his verse, and won an Oscar for his screenplay, *The Eleanor Roosevelt Story*.

LOUIS MACNEICE (1907–1963) was born in Belfast and educated at Marlborough and Merton College, Oxford, where he studied classics and philosophy. He taught Greek before becoming a writer and producer for BBC radio. His collections of poetry include *The Earth Compels, Autumn Journal*, and *Solstices*.

CHARLES MARTIN (b. 1942) was born in New York City. He is the author of several collections of poetry, including *Steal the Bacon* and *What the Darkness Proposes*, and has published a new verse translation of the *Metamorphoses* of Ovid. He has also translated the poems of Catullus, and his critical introduction to the Latin poet's work appears in the Yale University Press's Hermes Series. Martin is the recipient of a Bess Hokin Award from *Poetry* and grants from the

Ingram Merrill Foundation and the National Endowment for the Arts. He is a professor at Queensborough Community College of the City University of New York and has taught poetry workshops at the Sewanee Writers Conference and the Unterberg Poetry Center of the Ninety-second Street Y.

WILLIAM MATTHEWS (1942–1997) was born in Cincinnati, Ohio, and educated at Yale University, where he studied classics. While working toward a Ph.D. at the University of North Carolina, Matthews founded, with Newton Smith and Russell Banks, the magazine *Lillabulero*. Matthews also served as a member of the literature panel of the National Endowment for the Arts and as president of the Poetry Society of America. He published translations, several volumes of essays, and many books of poetry, including *Blues If You Want, Time & Money*, which won the 1996 National Book Critics Circle Award, and *After All: Last Poems*. He lived in New York City and taught in the graduate writing program at City College.

J. D. McCLATCHY (b. 1945) is the author of collections of poems that include *Scenes from Another Life, Stars Prinicipal, The Rest of the Way*, and *Ten Commandments*. His essays are collected in *White Paper* and *Twenty Questions*. He has edited several anthologies, and has published both fiction and translations. He has taught at Princeton, Yale, Columbia, Johns Hopkins, and other universities. He is an increasingly prominent librettist, and holds many honors, including chancellor of the Academy of American Poets, fellow of the American Academy of Arts and Sciences, and membership in the American Academy of Arts and Letters. He has received grants from the Guggenheim Foundation and the National Endowment for the Arts.

JAMES McCORKLE (b. 1954), born in St. Petersburg, Florida, is the author of *The Still Performance*, a study of postmodern American poetry, and the editor of *Conversant Essays: Contemporary Poets on Poetry*. He has been awarded fellowships from the National Endowment for the Arts and the Ingram Merrill Foundation, as well as the Campbell Corner Poetry Prize. His poems have been widely published and are included in several editions of *The Best American Poetry*. He lives in upstate New York.

PHYLLIS McGINLEY (1905–1978) was born in Oregon and educated at the universities of Utah and California. She won the Pulitzer Prize for Poetry in 1960, and was a frequent contributor to *The New Yorker*.

MEDBH McGUCKIAN (b. 1950) was born in Belfast, Ireland. She began to write in the 1970s, and her collections include *Marconi's Cottage, The Flower Master*, and *Captain Lavender*.

CLAUDE MCKAY (1890–1948) was born in Sunny Ville, Jamaica, to a family of farm workers, went to live with his older brother at the age of six, and under his brother's influence became acquainted with major works of history and philosophy. He emigrated to the United States and studied at the Tuskegee Institute and at Kansas State College. In 1914 he moved to Harlem and was among the most important writers of the Harlem Renaissance. He worked as an editor for *The Liberator* and *The Masses*. His poetry collections include *Harlem Shadows* (1922); he also wrote a number of novels. McKay traveled widely and was active in radical causes, visiting Moscow in 1922 to meet Lenin and Trotsky, then living for a time in France and Morocco. After the success of his novel *Home to Harlem* in 1928 he remained in the United States for the rest of his life. Eventually he moved away from his commitment to Communism, and in 1942 he converted to Catholicism. He died in Chicago.

GEORGE MEREDITH (1828–1909) was born in Portsmouth, England. For two years, he attened a Moravian academy in Germany. At the age of seventeen he was apprenticed to a lawyer, but he left to write articles and poems. Unable to support himself as a novelist, he took a job reading manuscripts for a publishing company. *Modern Love* (1862), a cycle of fifty sixteen-line sonnets in iambic pentameter, is loosely based on the breakdown of his nine-year marriage to Thomas Love Peacock's daughter, who left him in 1857 and died in 1861.

WILLIAM MEREDITH (b. 1919) was born in New York City and educated at Princeton University. He worked as a reporter for *The New York Times* and served in the Second World War as a naval aviator in the Pacific. His first collection, *Love Letter from an Impossible Land* (1944), won the Yale Series of Younger Poets Award and contained the war poems that brought him to prominence. He received the Pulitzer Prize in 1988 for *Partial Accounts: New and Selected Poems*. He was poetry consultant to the Library of Congress, and was named a chancellor of the Academy of American Poets.

JAMES INGRAM MERRILL (1926–1995) was born and raised in New York City and educated at Amherst College. During the Second World War, he took a year off from his studies to serve in the United States Army. His father, Charles Merrill, was a founding partner of the Merrill Lynch investment firm; Merrill's financial independence made it possible for him to devote himself fully to writing. He received the National Book Award for *Nights and Days* (1966) and the Pulitzer Prize for *Divine Comedies* (1977). In addition to many collections of poetry, including *Water Street* (1962), *Braving the Elements* (1972), and his trilogy, *The Changing Light at Sandover*, he also published novels, plays, literary criticism, and a memoir entitled *A Different Person*. His fifteenth and last book of poetry, *A Scattering of Salts*, appeared posthumously in 1995.

W[ILLIAM] S[TANLEY] MERWIN (b. 1927) was born in New York City, raised in New Jersey and Pennsylvania, and educated at Princeton University, where he studied with John Berryman and R. P. Blackmur. From 1949 to 1956 he traveled through Europe, working first as a tutor and later as a translator for the BBC. He published his first book, *A Mask for Janus*, in 1952. From 1951 until 1953 he was poetry editor at *The Nation*. Merwin's translations from Latin, Greek, French, Russian, Spanish, Chinese, and Japanese are highly regarded. He was awarded the Pulitzer Prize in 1971 for *The Carrier of Ladders*. His other poetry collections include *The Rain in the Trees*, *The Vixen*, and *The River Sound*. He lives in Hawaii.

ALICE CHRISTINA MEYNELL (1847–1922) was born Alice Christina Gertrude Thompson in London and was educated by her father, a convert to Catholicism. She was an active suffragist and edited numerous journals with her husband, Wilfrid Meynell. In addition to poetry, Alice Meynell also wrote art criticism, essays, and biographies.

ROBERT MEZEY (b. 1935) was born in Philadelphia and educated at Kenyon College, the University of Iowa, and Stanford University, where he was a Stegner Fellow. He interrupted his studies to serve in the army for two years. His poetry collection *The Lovemaker* (1960) won the Lamont Award. He has translated Hebrew poetry, and his other volumes of poetry include *Evening Wind* (1987) and *Collected Poems 1952–1999*.

EDNA ST. VINCENT MILLAY (1892–1950) was born in Rockland, Maine, and educated at Vassar College. While still at Vassar, her poem "Renascence" was published in an anthology, *The Lyric Year*, bringing her immediate critical acclaim. In 1917 she moved to Greenwich Village, where she became politically active. She joined the Provincetown Players and wrote a number of verse plays. In 1923 Millay married, and in 1925 she settled with her husband in Austerlitz, New York, where she lived for the rest of her life. In addition to her many volumes of poetry, Millay also published a number of plays and translations. Her poetry collections include *Second April*, *The Harp-Weaver*, which received the Pulitzer Prize in 1923, *Fatal Interview*, *Mine the Harvest*, and her *Collected Sonnets*. Her last two volumes of poetry, *Make Bright the Arrows* (1940) and *The Murder of Lidice* (1942), were a response to the Second World War.

JOHN MILTON (1608–1674) was educated at St Paul's School and Christ's College, Cambridge. He had planned to enter the Church, but instead, supported by his father, undertook a long period of private study. He received a commission for the court masque known as *Comus* (1634). In 1639 he traveled in Italy and on his return began to earn his living as a private tutor. In 1641 he published the first of a series of tracts calling for political and religious reforms. Milton supported Cromwell's republic; in 1649 he was appointed secretary for foreign tongues and his pamphlets defending the republic brought him international fame. By 1652, he had gone completely blind. He published *The readie and easy way to establish a free commonwealth* just before the Restoration and was briefly imprisoned, but released through the intervention of the poet Andrew Marvell, who was foreign secretary. *Paradise lost* appeared in 1667, *Paradise regained* and *Samson agonistes* in 1671.

MARIANNE MOORE (1887–1972) was born in Kirkwood, Missouri, raised in Carlisle, Pennsylvania, and educated at Bryn Mawr College, where she studied biology. Her mother supported the family by teaching; her father had been institutionalized. Moore taught typing and business after graduating, and moved to Greenwich Village with her mother after she placed her first poem in a British journal. She worked as a librarian and later became an editor of *Dial* magazine. She published a translation of Jean de la Fontaine's *Fables*; her poetry collections include *Marriage* (1923), *The Pangolin* (1936), *What Are Years?* (1941), and *O, To Be a Dragon* (1959). T. S. Eliot wrote the introduction to *The Complete Poems of Marianne Moore* (1967); Moore dedicated the collection to her mother.

MERRILL MOORE (1903–1957) was born in Columbia, Tennessee, and educated at Vanderbilt, where he studied medicine and joined the Fugitive group of poets. He specialized in treating alcoholism and wrote a prodigious number of sonnets.

EDWIN MUIR (1887–1959) was born in the Orkney Islands and raised in Glasgow, where he held a number of jobs. His parents and two of his brothers died before he was fifteen; their deaths were related to the poor conditions of the slums and sweatshops. In 1919 he married Willa Anderson and they moved to London, where Muir began his literary career. His first book of poems, *First Poems*, appeared in 1925, after the Muirs had moved to Europe. The husband and wife team translated from German and are well known for their translations of Kafka. *The Collected Poems* appeared in 1960.

PAUL MULDOON (b. 1951), born in Northern Ireland, is the author of many collections of poetry, including *Hay* and *The Annals of Chile*, which won the T. S. Eliot Prize in 1994. His *New and Selected Poems 1968–94* won the 1997 Irish Times Prize for Poetry. Muldoon is Howard G. B. Clark '21 Professor in the Humanities at Princeton University and professor of poetry at Oxford University.

LES MURRAY (b. 1938) was born Leslie Allan Murray in Nabiac, New South Wales, and educated at Sydney University. He is the only son of a dairy farmer.

After studying languages, he worked at the Australian National University as a translator. Murray left the university in 1971 to write full time. His poetry collections include *The Rabbiter's Bounty: Collected Poems*, *Subhuman Redneck Poems*, and *Learning Human: Selected Poems*; he is also the author of a novel in verse, *Fredy Neptune*.

MARILYN NELSON (b. 1946) was a finalist for the 1991 National Book Award with her third book, *The Homeplace*, and won the 1992 Annisfield-Wolf Award. Her other collections include *The Fields of Praise: New and Selected Poems*, which was a finalist for the 1997 National Book Award and won the Poet's Prize, and *Carver*. She teaches at the University of Connecticut at Storrs.

MIKE NELSON (b. 1967) was born in Springfield, Oregon. He grew up mostly in Powell, Tennessee, but also lived in North Dakota, Wisconsin, and Colorado. He has earned degrees from the University of Tennessee (B.A.) and the University of Maryland (M.F.A.), and he currently lives in Kalamazoo, Michigan, where he is a Ph.D. candidate at Western Michigan University.

HOWARD NEMEROV (1920–1991) was born and raised in New York City and educated at The Fieldston School and Harvard University. During the Second World War he served in the Canadian Air Force and the United States Air Force. His first book of poems, *The Image and the Law*, appeared when he was twenty-seven. He worked as an editor and taught at many schools, including Bennington College and Brandeis University. He was named Poetry Consultant to the Library of Congress in 1963 and was poet laureate from 1988 to 1990. His works include *Guide to the Ruins* (1950), *Mirrors and Windows* (1958), *The Collected Poems of Howard Nemerov* (1977), and *Inside the Onion* (1984).

JACQUELINE OSHEROW (b. 1956) is the author of several poetry collections, including *Conversations with Survivors*, *With a Moon in Transit*, and *Dead Men's Praise*. She has received fellowships from the John Simon Guggenheim Foundation, the National Endowment for the Arts, and the Ingram Merrill Foundation; been awarded the Witter Bynner Prize by the American Academy of Arts and Letters; and received a number of awards from the Poetry Society of America. She directs the Creative Writing Program at the University of Utah.

WILFRED OWEN (1893–1918) was born in Oswestry, Shropshire, England. He withdrew from the University of London in 1911 because he had no money for fees and served as an assistant to a vicar in Oxfordshire. Deciding not to become a clergyman, in 1913 he left this post and taught English in Bordeaux. In 1915 he returned to England to enlist in the army and was sent to the front in France. While fighting in the Battle of the Somme he suffered from shell shock and was sent to Craiglockhart War Hospital, where he met Siegfried Sassooon and Robert Graves. He returned to the western front and in October 1918 was awarded the Military Cross. On November 4, 1918, seven days before the war ended, Owen was killed by the machine-gun fire at Sambre Canal, near Ors. He traced the birth of his "poethood" to his intense experience of nature at Broxton by the Hill, where his mother had taken him on a holiday trip when he was ten. Shortly before his death he expressed his burgeoning confidence in a letter to his mother. "I feel the great swelling of the open sea taking my galleon." Siegfried Sassoon and Edith Sitwell published the first edition of his poems in 1920.

DOROTHY PARKER (1893–1967) was born in New Jersey and educated in public schools. She moved to New York, where her acerbic wit earned her positions at *The New Yorker* and *Vanity Fair*; she was the only woman at the famed Algonquin Roundtable. In the 1930s, she and her husband moved to California to write screenplays; she founded the Screen Writers' Guild with Lillian Hellman and Dashiell Hammett. Parker was blacklisted for her role in leftist politics. She attempted suicide many times and took her own life in a New York City hotel room.

MOLLY PEACOCK (b. 1947), born in Buffalo, New York, is the author of *Raw Heaven, Take Heart, Original Love,* and other collections of poetry, as well as a memoir, *Paradise Piece by Piece,* and a book of criticism, *How to Read a Poem & Start a Poetry Circle.* One of the originators of Poetry in Motion on public transportation, she is President Emerita of the Poetry Society of America, poet-in-residence at the Cathedral of St. John the Divine, and contributing writer for *House & Garden.* She lives in Toronto and in New York City with her husband, James Joyce scholar Michael Groden.

FRANCESCO PETRARCA (1304–1374), known in English as Petrarch, was the son of a Florentine notary. Brought up in Provence, where his father was living in political exile, he studied law at Montpellier and Bologna, returning to Avignon to resume literary studies after the death of his father in 1326. In 1330, he entered the service of Cardinal Giovanni Colonna, becoming a consultant to popes, emperors, and kings. Petrarch is best known for his two major works in Italian, the *Canzoniere* and *I Trionfi (The Triumphs)*, both of which are dedicated to the praise and glorification of Laura. Petrarch composed *I Trionfi* after most of the lyrics in the *Canzoniere* were completed, and he dedicated the rest of his life to this unfinished work, which he began around 1352; it is divided into six sections, each part representing a different triumph—of love, of modesty, of death, of fame, of time, and of eternity. After climbing Mount Ventoux in 1336, he wrote the letter known as "The Ascent of Mount Ventoux." Petrarch met

Laura in Avignon in 1327, and began composing his love lyrics in Italian soon after. His coronation with laurels, the highest honor bestowed on a living poet, took place in Rome on Easter Sunday 1341. Laura died in 1348, during the Black Death. In 1350, on his way to Rome to celebrate the Jubilee Year, Petrarch met Boccaccio in Florence, a city that had lost more than half its population to the plague in a period of less than three months. Most of Petrarch's other work is written in Latin, including his unfinished work *Africa*, an epic glorifying Scipio Africanus, for which he was awarded the laurel, and the *Secretum (The Secret)*, based on Saint Augustine's *Confessions*. In 1369 he moved to Arquà, where he lived with his daughter, who cared for him until his death five years later.

SYLVIA PLATH (1932–1963) was born in Boston, Massachusetts, and educated at Smith College and Cambridge University. Her father died when she was eight. By the time she was eighteen, national magazines had already published her stories, poetry, and art. She won numerous prizes, and while in England on a Fulbright Fellowship met the poet Ted Hughes, whom she married. Back in America, she became a student of Robert Lowell, in whose class she met Anne Sexton. Her first book of poems, *The Colossus*, was published in London in 1960 and in the United States in 1962. *Winter Trees* and *Ariel* (published posthumously) followed. In 1963, she took her own life. A highly prolific poet, Plath also wrote a novel, *The Bell Jar*; Ted Hughes edited her *Collected Poems*.

STANLEY PLUMLY (b. 1939) was born and raised in Ohio. His collections of poetry include *Out-of-the-Body Travel*, *Summer Celestial*, *Boy on the Step*, and *Now That My Father Lies Down Beside Me: New and Selected Poems 1970–2000*. Plumly is a Distinguished University Professor at the University of Maryland. His honors include an Ingram Merrill Foundation Fellowship, a Guggenheim Fellowship, and a grant from the National Endowment for the Arts.

EDGAR ALLAN POE (1809–1849) was born in Boston and raised in Virginia. He was orphaned at the age of three and adopted by John Allan, a wealthy tobacco merchant, but the arrangement was unhappy. He ran up gambling debts in his first year at the University of Virginia, and Mr. Allan then refused to pay for his education. Poe joined the army and attended West Point, but was expelled; his adoptive father disowned him. His stories were well received, but he failed to earn enough money. In 1845 his young wife died of tuberculosis. Poe is credited with having invented the detective story.

MARIE PONSOT's (b. 1921) first book of poems, *True Minds* (1957), was followed by *Admit Impediment*, *The Green Dark*, and *The Bird Catcher*, which won the National Book Critics Circle Award. She is a native New Yorker who has taught in graduate programs at Queens College, Beijing United University, Columbia University, and the Unterberg Poetry Center of the Ninety-second Street Y in New York. Her awards include a National Endowment for the Arts grant and the Shaughnessy Medal of the Modern Language Association.

EZRA POUND (1885–1972) was born in Hailey, Idaho, and raised in a suburb of Philadelphia. He was educated at Hamilton College and at the University of Pennsylvania, where he studied Romance languages and became a lifelong friend of William Carlos Williams. In 1908 Pound moved to London, where he met many of the leading artists and writers of his day, including Yeats, for whom he worked as a secretary. He also championed the careers of Frost, Eliot, and Joyce. Pound moved to Paris in 1920; in 1924 he moved to Rapallo, Italy, and in 1930, after meeting the Italian dictator Benito Mussolini, he began to write on economics and politics. During the Second World War, he made a series of pro-Fascist and anti-Semitic radio broadcasts that resulted in an indictment for treason. After standing trial in the United States, he was adjudged mentally unfit and sentenced to St. Elizabeth's Hospital for the Criminally Insane in Washington, D.C. Upon his release in 1958, he returned to Italy.

SIR WALTER RALEGH (1554?–1618) was educated at Oriel College, Oxford, and began his career as a soldier. A favorite of Queen Elizabeth, he was given a royal patent for colonization in North America and traveled to Virginia and Guiana. In 1592, he was imprisoned for marrying Elizabeth Throckmorton, a royal maid of honor, against the queen's will. James I imprisoned him in 1603, accusing Ralegh of conspiring against his succession. While in prison Ralegh wrote poetry as well as *The history of the world*, which was published in 1614. He was released briefly for an expedition to Orinoco in 1616, but the mission failed and he broke a promise not to attack the Spanish. In 1618 he was executed. In addition to his literary accomplishments, Ralegh introduced the potato to Ireland and tobacco to Europe.

JOHN CROWE RANSOM (1888–1974) was born in Pulaski, Tennessee, and educated at Vanderbilt University and Christ Church College, Oxford. He fought in France during the First World War, then returned to Vanderbilt as a member of the faculty. In addition to poetry, he published influential works of literary criticism, including *God Without Thunder* (1930) and *The New Criticism* (1941).

JAMES REEVES (1909–1978) was born in Middlesex, England, and educated at Stowe and Jesus College, Cambridge. He taught for many years, then began to write and edit full-time. His first book, *The Natural Need* (1936), was published by the Seizin Press. His collections include *Subsong* (1969) and *Collected Poems 1929–1974*.

ADRIENNE RICH (b. 1929) was born in Baltimore, Maryland, and educated at Radcliffe College. In 1951, W. H. Auden selected her first book, *A Change of World*, for the Yale Series of Younger Poets Award. In the 1960s she was active in radical politics and the antiwar movement. Rich was an early leader in the feminist movement, and her work has been critical in the redefinition of patriarchy and motherhood. She has taught at, among other schools, Douglass College and Stanford University, and now lives in California. Rich has published several books of essays, including *Of Woman Born: Motherhood As Experience and Institution*, and numerous volumes of poetry, including *Diving into the Wreck, An Atlas of the Difficult World, Dark Fields of the Republic: Poems 1991–1995*, and *Midnight Salvage: Poems 1995–1998*.

ROBIN ROBERTSON (b. 1955) was born on the northeast coast of Scotland. His work appears regularly in the *London Review of Books* and *The New Yorker. A Painted Field* was published in 1997; it won the Forward Prize for Best First Collection and the Saltire Scottish First Book of the Year Award.

EDWIN ARLINGTON ROBINSON (1869–1935) was born and raised in Maine, and educated at Harvard, which he had to leave after two years due to financial problems. In New York City, he worked as a subway-construction inspector. President Theodore Roosevelt admired his poetry, and arranged a position for Robinson in the Customs House. His first of three Pulitzer Prizes brought him financial security, and by the time of his death he had become one of America's most highly regarded poets.

JUDITH RODRIGUEZ (b. 1936) has won national prizes for her poetry, and it has been translated into several languages. In print is her *New and Selected Poems*. Her libretto *Lindy* was commissioned by the Australian Opera, and she has also written a play, *Poor Johanna*. She has edited anthologies, Jennifer Rankin's *Collected Poems*, and a modern poetry series for Penguin Books, Australia. Rodriguez teaches writing at Deakin University, Melbourne.

CHRISTINA ROSSETTI (1830–1894), sister of Dante Gabriel Rossetti, was born in London and was educated at home. In her youth a volume of her poems was privately printed. Her first book, *Goblin Market and Other Poems*, appeared in 1862. Rossetti was a deeply committed Anglican. She was a master of poetic forms, including the sonnet sequence, in which she chronicled the journey of romantic and religious longing. She contributed to the Pre-Raphaelite periodical *The Germ*. After 1871 she became more reclusive, due to a prolonged illness that eventually took her life.

DANTE GABRIEL ROSSETTI (1828–1882), brother of Christina Rossetti, was born in London and educated at King's College School and the Royal Academy Antique School. A painter as well as a poet, in 1848 he, along with William Holman Hunt, John Waterhouse, and others, formed the short-lived Pre-Raphaelite Brotherhood, an influential movement finding its aesthetic ideal in the art of the *quattrocento*, the early Italian Renaissance. His translation of Dante's *Vita Nuova* helped shape the Pre-Raphaelite sensibility. He wrote an early sonnet sequence, *Sonnets for Pictures*. He married his model, Elizabeth Siddal, in 1860; she killed herself two years later. Rossetti buried a number of his poems with her. The poems were later exhumed and published in a volume titled *The House of Life* (1870).

MURIEL RUKEYSER (1913–1980) was born in New York and educated at Vassar and Columbia University. At an early age she trained as an aviator, and this experience informs her first book, *Theory of Flight*, published in the Yale Series of Younger Poets. She was concerned with social injustice and with the atrocities of the Second World War. Rukeyser taught at the California School of Labor, and later at Sarah Lawrence College. In addition to poetry, she published biographies and criticism and translated the work of Brecht, Paz, and Ekelof.

THOMAS RUSSELL (1762–1788) was born in Dorset, England, and educated at New College, Oxford. He was ordained in 1786. Wordsworth, Bowles, and Coleridge were among his admirers. His *Sonnets and Miscellaneous Poems* were published a year after his early death.

SHEROD SANTOS (b. 1949) was born in Greenville, South Carolina, and educated at the University of California and the University of Utah, where he received a Ph.D. His awards include the Delmore Schwartz Memorial Award, a Pushcart Prize, the Ingram Merrill Award, *The Nation*'s Discovery Award, and a Guggenheim Foundation grant. His poetry collections include *Accidental Weather*, *The Southern Reaches*, *The City of Women*, and *The Pilot Star Elegies*. He is a professor of English at the University of Missouri, Columbia.

SIEGFRIED SASSOON (1886–1967) was born in Kent, England and attended Clare College, Cambridge. He divided his time between London's fashionable literary circles and his family's country estate. At the outbreak of the First World War, he enlisted and went to the front with the Royal Welsh Fusiliers; he was awarded the Military Cross. By 1917 he was disillusioned with the war and publicly protested; his actions landed him in the Craiglockhart War Hospital, where he met Wilfred Owen, whose poems he would publish after Owen's death. Clare College made him an honorary fellow in 1953.

JASON SCHNEIDERMAN (b. 1976) was born in San Antonio, Texas, and spent his early childhood in Thetford, England. Owing to his father's military service, he then moved around in Europe and the continental United States with some frequency. He has attended the University of Maryland, the Herzen Institute (St. Petersburg, Russia), and New York University.

GRACE SCHULMAN (b. 1935) was born in New York City. Her collections of poetry include *For That Day Only*, *Hemispheres*, *Burn Down the Icons*, and *The Paintings of Our Lives*. She is the recipient of New York University's Delmore Schwartz Award for Poetry and of a Poetry Fellowship from the New York Foundation of the Arts. Her poems have been anthologized in *The Best American Poetry* and *The Best of the Best American Poetry 1988–1998*, and she is the winner of two Pushcart Prizes. She is also the author of *Marianne Moore: The Poetry of Engagement*. *Days of Wonder: New and Selected Poems* is forthcoming in 2002.

DELMORE SCHWARTZ (1913–1966) was born in Brooklyn, New York, and educated at New York University. From 1943 to 1955, he was an editor of *Partisan Review*. He received the Bollingen Prize for his 1959 volume *Summer Knowledge*. Schwarz also wrote short fiction, including *In Dreams Begin Responsibilities*. He died of alcoholism. His friend Saul Bellow modeled his title character in *Humboldt's Gift* on Schwartz.

FREDERICK SEIDEL (b. 1936) was born in St. Louis, Missouri, and educated at Harvard University. His poetry collection *Sunrise* won the Lamont Award for 1979 and the National Book Critics Circle Award for 1980. Seidel's other books of poetry include *Going Fast: Poems*, *My Tokyo*, and *The Cosmos Poems*.

HUGH SEIDMAN (b. 1947) was born in Brooklyn, New York. He has won two New York State and three NEA grants, and the Yale Younger Poets Prize (1969). In 1995, his *Selected Poems: 1965–1995* was cited by the *Village Voice* and by *The Critics' Choice* as one of the best books of the year. He has taught writing at the University of Wisconsin, Yale University, Columbia University, and elsewhere.

ANNA SEWARD (1747–1809) was born in Eyam, Derbyshire, England. A poet and the author of a novel, *Louisa* (1784), Seward was popular in her day, and became a member of a literary circle in Litchfield that included William Hayley, Erasmus Darwin, and Richard Lovell Edgeworth. She corresponded with Sir Walter Scott and eventually made him her literary executor, something he was not pleased about. She was known for the cult of sentiment.

WILLIAM SHAKESPEARE (1564–1616) was born in Stratford-upon-Avon and most likely attended the free grammar school in Stratford, where he would have been educated in Latin and the classics. His father, a successful glove maker and landowner, later suffered a reversal of fortune, possibly because of adherence to the Catholic faith. Shakespeare married Anne Hathaway in 1582 and had three children with her. Toward the end of the 1580s he left Stratford and may have joined a group of traveling players or worked as a country schoolteacher. He began to emerge as a playwright in London around 1592; in 1594 he began his career as a playwright, actor, and eventually a leading shareholder in the Lord Chamberlain's Men, the company that became the King's Men in the reign of James I. His first published works were two narrative poems, *Venus and Adonis* (1593) and *The Rape of Lucrece* (1594), both of which he dedicated to Henry Wriothesley, Earl of Southampton, who may also be the patron to whom Shakespeare dedicated his *Sonnets*. Shakespeare's sonnets had circulated in manuscript in the 1590s; they were first published in 1609 in a paperback volume, a quarto containing one hundred and fifty-four sonnets and a long poem in rhyme royal, *A Lover's Complaint*, the lament of a young woman abandoned by her lover. The folio collection of his plays, published posthumously in 1623, was dedicated to William Herbert, third Earl of Pembroke, and his brother Philip, the future fourth Earl.

PERCY BYSSHE SHELLEY (1792–1822) was born to a prosperous, aristocratic family in Sussex, England. He attended Eton and University College, Oxford, but was expelled for refusing to repudiate *The Necessity of Atheism*, a pamphlet he and a fellow student had published. In 1811 he married the sixteen-year-old Harriet Westbrook. In 1813 he published *Queen Mab: A Philosophical Poem*. That same year he abandoned Harriet and moved to London, where he met the social philosopher William Godwin, whose work he greatly admired. Shelley fell in love with Mary Wollstonecraft Godwin, the daughter of William Godwin and Mary Wollstonecraft (who had died soon after giving birth to her). He eloped with her to France in 1814, they were married in 1816, following Harriet's suicide. Byron also joined them that year, and Shelley completed *Alastor: or, The Spirit of Solitude* and "Mont Blanc"; he wrote *The Revolt of Islam* and "Ozymandias" in 1817, and the following year translated Plato's *Symposium*. In 1818 Percy and Mary Shelley moved with Byron to Italy, and Shelley turned to verse drama, composing *Prometheus Unbound* and *The Cenci*. In his essay *The Defence of Poetry* (1821), Shelley claimed a central role for the "poetic faculty," calling the poet "the unacknowledged legislator of mankind." He wrote his great elegy, *Adonais*, after the death of John Keats in 1821. Shelley drowned when his sailboat, the *Don Juan*, capsized during a storm on the Gulf of Spezia.

SIR PHILIP SIDNEY (1554–1586) was born at Penshurst, Kent, the eldest son of Sir Henry Sidney and his wife, Mary, the sister of Robert Dudley, Earl of Leicester.

Educated at Shewsbury Grammar School in Shropshire with his friend Fulke Greville, and at Corpus Christi College, Oxford, Sidney toured Europe from 1572 to 1575, and in 1576 participated in a military campaign in Ireland. In the following years he wrote two versions of his epic romance, *Arcadia*, which his sister the Countess of Pembroke edited and published in 1593; his sonnet sequence, *Astrophel and Stella*; and his treatise *A defence of poetry*. In 1583 he was knighted; that same year he married Frances, daughter of Sir Francis Walsingham. In 1585, he went to the Netherlands as part of a military expedition against the Spanish and was made governor of Flushing. He died of wounds suffered at Zutphen.

CHARLES SIMIC (b. 1938) is a poet, essayist, and translator. He teaches American literature and creative writing at the University of New Hampshire. His many books of poetry include *The Book of Gods and Devils*, *Hotel Insomnia*, *Walking the Black Cat*, and *Jackstraws*; he is also the author of several collections of essays and memoirs, including *Orphan Factory* and *The Unemployed Fortune-Teller*. Simic has published a translation of *The Selected Poems of Tomaž Šalamun*, and co-edited (with Mark Strand) *Another Republic: 17 European and South American Writers*. He is the recipient of the MacArthur Fellowship, the Pulitzer Prize, and numerous other literary awards.

FLOYD SKLOOT (b. 1947) lives in Amity, Oregon. His collections of poetry include *The Open Door* and *Summer Blue*. He has also published books of prose and nonfiction, and reviews current fiction for *The Oregonian*.

TOM SLEIGH's (b. 1953) books of poetry include *After One* (Houghton Mifflin New Poetry Prize), *Waking*, *The Chain* (nominated for the Lenore Marshall Poetry Prize), and *The Dreamhouse*. He has also translated Euripides' *The Madness of Herakles*. Among his many awards are the Shelley Memorial Award from the Poetry Society of America, the Lila Wallace/Reader's Digest Award, and grants from the Guggenheim Foundation, the National Endowment for the Arts, the Ingram Merrill Foundation, and the Fine Arts Work Center in Provincetown, where he is a Writing Committee member. He teaches at Dartmouth College and is a visiting professor at Johns Hopkins University.

BRUCE SMITH (b. 1946) was born in Pennsylvania and educated at Bucknell University, and for many years he taught at Phillips Andover Academy. His books include *Silver and Information*, *Mercy Seat*, and *The Other Lover*. He is on the writing faculty at the University of Alabama at Tuscaloosa.

CHARLOTTE SMITH (1749–1806), was born Charlotte Turner in London and educated at schools in Sussex and London. Her husband was sent to jail for debt and later fled England; in his absence she supported twelve children with her writing. In addition to poetry, Smith also wrote numerous novels and children's books. Her first collection, *Elegiac Sonnets and Other Essays* (1784), influenced many Romantic writers, including Keats. The volume, which she continued to expand throughout her life, was translated into French and Italian. She was admired by Sir Walter Scott and Leigh Hunt, among others.

HORACE SMITH (1779–1849), a successful stockbroker, was a friend of Shelley. In the literary parody *Rejected Addresses* (1812), he lampooned Southey, Wordsworth, and Scott. Smith was also the author of a popular novel, *Brambletye House* (1826).

W[ILLIAM] D[EWITT] SNODGRASS (b. 1926) was born in Wilkinsburg, Pennsylvania, and educated at Geneva College. At the end of the Second World War he served in the United States Navy and was stationed in the Pacific. He studied with Robert Lowell at the University of Iowa and is often considered one of the confessional poets. His collections include *Heart's Needle* (1959), which won the Pulitzer Prize for poetry, *After Experience, The Führer Bunker: A Cycle of Poems in Progress*, and *Selected Poems: 1957–1987*. He has also published a book of criticism, *In Radical Pursuit*, and a number of volumes of translation, including the sonnets by Vivaldi from *The Four Seasons*. He has received an Ingram Merrill Award, a fellowship from the Academy of American Poets, and many other honors.

ROBERT SOUTHEY (1774–1843) was educated at Westminster School and at Oxford, where he met Coleridge. The French Revolution inspired one of a number of epics, *Joan of Arc* (1796); but his revolutionary fervor was not sustained. In 1813 he succeeded H. J. Pye as poet laureate.

SIR STEPHEN (HAROLD) SPENDER (1909–1995) was born in London and educated at University College School, Hampstead, and at Oxford, where he met Auden, Isherwood, MacNeice and C. Day Lewis. He traveled to Germany with Isherwood after graduating; he later went to Spain to work on propaganda for the Republican cause in the Spanish Civil War. During the Second World War he refused to take part in combat and served in the National Fire Service in London. He worked as an editor and also for UNESCO. His last volume of poetry, *Dolphins*, appeared in 1994.

EDMUND SPENSER (1552?–1599) was educated at Merchant Taylors' School and Pembroke Hall, Cambridge. He published *The shepheardes calender* in 1579 with a dedication to Sir Philip Sidney, with whom he shared an interest in promoting a new English poetry. In 1580 he went to Ireland as secretary to Arthur, Lord Grey of Wilton; he continued to live in Ireland, employed as a civil servant for most of his adult life and acquiring extensive Irish lands. He published the first three books of *The Faerie Queene* in 1590 and was granted an official pension. In 1595 *Amoretti and Epithalamion* and *Colin Clouts come home againe* were published, followed the next year by the second part of *The Faerie Queene*, the *Fowre hymnes*, and *Prothalamion*. Increasingly disillusioned by the way his government conducted Irish affairs, Spencer wrote *A view of the present state of Ireland*, which was not published until 1633. In 1598, rebels burned down his castle at Kilcolman, and he was forced to flee to London. He died there, and the Earl of Essex paid for his funeral.

WILLIAM STAFFORD (1914–1993) was born and raised in rural Kansas and educated at the University of Kansas and the University of Iowa. He was a conscientious objector during the Second World War. He began teaching at Lewis and Clark College in 1948; his first book of poems, *West of Your City*, appeared in 1960. His collections include *Stories That Could Be True* (1977) and *The Way It Is: New and Selected Poems* (1998). Stafford also wrote a memoir, *Down in my Heart* (1947).

TIMOTHY STEELE's (b. 1948) collections of verse include *The Color Wheel* and *Sapphics and Uncertaintines: Poems 1970–1986*. He also has published two books of literary criticism, *Missing Measures: Modern Poetry and the Revolt Against Meter* and *All the Fun's in How You Say a Thing: An Explanation of Meter and Versification*, and is the editor of *The Poems of J. V. Cunningham*.

TRUMBULL STICKNEY (1874–1904) was born in Geneva, Switzerland, and educated at Harvard University and the Sorbonne, where he was the first American to receive a *Doctorat des Lettres*. His father had tutored him in classics at an early age, and he taught Greek at Harvard before dying suddenly of a brain tumor.

LEON STOKESBURY (b. 1945) teaches in the creative writing program at Georgia State University in Atlanta. His collection *Autumn Rhythm: New and Selected Poems* was awarded the Poet's Prize in 1998. He edited *The Made Thing: An Anthology of Contemporary Poetry*, 2nd edition, in 1999.

ALGERNON CHARLES SWINBURNE (1837–1909) was born in London and attended Balliol College, Oxford, where he became a friend of Dante Gabriel Rossetti, the artist Edward Burne-Jones, and the designer and poet William Morris. In an 1862 review of the French poet Charles Baudelaire's *Les Fleurs du Mal*, Swinburne coined the phrase "art for art's sake."

ALLEN TATE (1899–1979) was born in Winchester, Clarke County, Kentucky. He attended Vanderbilt University, where he was a student of John Crowe

Ransom and a roommate of Robert Penn Warren, together with whom he edited *The Fugitive*. After Tate married, he and his wife, writer Caroline Gordon, moved to New York City. Tate published a number of volumes of essays and edited the *Sewanee Review* from 1944 to 1946. In 1950 he became a Catholic. He was Poetry Consultant to the Library of Congress from 1943 to 1944, and received the Bollingen Prize in 1956. His *Collected Poems* appeared in 1977.

HENRY TAYLOR (b. 1942) is professor of literature at American University. He has held visiting appointments at Hollins College and Randolph-Macon Woman's College. His books of poetry include *An Afternoon of Pocket Billiards*; *The Flying Change*, which won the Pulitzer Prize in 1986 and *Understanding Fiction: Poems 1986–1996*. His criticism and translations are widely published.

ALFRED, LORD TENNYSON (1809–1892), was born in Somersby, Lincolnshire, England, and was educated at Trinity College, Cambridge, where he met Arthur Henry Hallam. He published *Poems by Two Brothers* with his brother Charles in 1827 and *Poems, Chiefly Lyrical* in 1830. In 1843 he began receiving an annual government pension to support his writing. After Hallam died in 1833 Tennyson began writing *In Memoriam*, which he worked on for seventeen years; it was published in 1850, the year he was made poet laureate. Having finally achieved financial stability, in 1850 he married Emily Sellwood, whom he had courted for many years. *Idylls of the King* was his last major work.

DYLAN THOMAS (1914–1953) was born in the Welsh seaport of Swansea and educated at Swansea Grammar School. Ignoring his father's advice to attend university, he left school in 1931 to embark on a literary career. After working at the local newspaper, he went to London in 1934, publishing his first volume that same year. He worked as a broadcaster, wrote radio plays and stories, and gave lectures and poetry readings throughout the United Kingdom, Europe, and the United States. He died from alcoholism after a bout of drinking during a reading tour in New York City.

EDWARD THOMAS (1878–1917) was born in the London suburb of Lambeth and educated at Lincoln College, Oxford. His demanding work as a biographer, critic, and reviewer took a toll on his health, but he had to support a growing family. He began writing poetry in 1914 with the encouragment of his friend Robert Frost, to whom Thomas himself had given crucial literary support. He joined the army in 1915, and was killed in battle in France. A copy of Shakespeare's sonnets was in his pocket.

FRANCIS THOMPSON (1859–1907), the son of Roman Catholic converts, attended Ushaw College, where his religious faith was encouraged. After an unsuccessful attempt at studying medicine he went to London, where he failed to earn a living and through illness and dependency on opium was reduced to utter poverty. In 1888 he sent two poems to *Merry England*, a magazine edited by Wilfrid Meynell. With the aid of Meynell, who recognized his literary talent, Thompson was rescued from opium addiction and began to publish his work. His first collection appeared in 1893; he is best known for his ode "The Hound of Heaven."

JEAN TOOMER (1894–1967) was born Nathan Pinchback Toomer in Washington, D.C., and educated at a number of unversities; he never received a degree. He was raised by his maternal grandfather and divorced mother, who remarried in 1907 and died in 1909. His masterpiece, *Cane*, was published in 1923 at the dawn of the Harlem Renaissance. In the last years of his life, Toomer became a Quaker, moved to Pennsylvania, and wrote on religious and philosophical matters.

FREDERICK GODDARD TUCKERMAN (1821–1873) was born in Boston and was educated at Harvard University and Harvard Law School. After briefly practicing law in his early twenties, he returned to his family estate in Greenfield, Massachusetts, to devote himself to literature, botany, and astronomy.

CHARLES TENNYSON TURNER (1808–1879), and his older brother Alfred, Lord Tennyson, collected their early work in a volume entitled *Poems by Two Brothers* (1827). Charles Tennyson later began to publish as Charles Turner in honor of an uncle who left him a considerable fortune. He published hundreds of sonnets during his career.

JOHN UPDIKE (b. 1932) was born in Shillington, Pennsylvania. He graduated from Harvard College in 1954, and spent a year at the Ruskin School of Drawing and Fine Art in Oxford, England. He has contributed poems, short stories, essays, and book reviews to major publications, most notably *The New Yorker*. For many years, he has lived in Massachusetts. Known primarily as a novelist, Updike has written poetry throughout his career.

JEAN VALENTINE (b. 1934) was educated at Radcliffe College. She is the author of *Pilgrims, Ordinary Things, The Cradle of the Real Life*, and other poetry collections. She teaches in the graduate writing program at New York University, Sarah Lawrence College, and the Unterberg Poetry Center of the Ninety-second Street Y. She lives in New York City.

JONES VERY (1813–1880) was born in Salem, Massachusetts. He was the son of a ship captain. He graduated from Harvard University in 1836 and was appointed a tutor in Greek. In 1837 he experienced a mystical revelation and began writing sonnets which he declared were "communicated" to him by his Lord. In 1838 he was asked to resign from Harvard and entered an asylum. His *Essays and Poems* (1839) was praised by Emerson, Channing, and Bryant. The latter part of his life was spent in retirement.

ELLEN BRYANT VOIGT (b. 1943) is the author of a number of poetry collections, including *Claiming Kin, The Forces of Plenty, The Lotus Flowers, Two Trees*, and *Kyrie*. A National Book Critics Circle Award finalist, she has also published *The Flexible Lyric*, a collection of essays on craft. In addition to her long association with Warren Wilson College and the low-residency program for writers she pioneered, she has taught in the Aspen, Bread Loaf, Indiana, Napa, and Ropewalk writers' conferences. A recipient of grants from the NEA, Guggenheim, and Lila Wallace foundations, Voigt is currently the Vermont state poet.

DEREK WALCOTT (b. 1930) was born on the West Indian island of Saint Lucia and educated at the University of the West Indies, Jamaica. His father died when Walcott was very young. He has worked as a theatrical reviewer and throughout his life has been actively involved in the theater as both playwright and artistic director. He self-published his first book, *Twenty-Five Poems*, at the age of eighteen. He received the Nobel Prize for literature in 1992. His many collections include *The Fortunate Traveller, Collected Poems: 1948–1984, Omeros, The Bounty*, and *Tiepolo's Hound*. A painter as well as a poet, Walcott has also published verse drama, *What the Twilight Says: Essays*, and *The Antilles: Fragments of Epic Memory* (the Nobel Lecture). He currently teaches at Boston University.

MARGARET WALKER (1915–1998) was born in Birmingham, Alabama, and educated at Northwestern University and the University of Iowa, where she received a Ph.D. She worked for three years in the Writers' Project of the WPA in Iowa, where she met Gwendolyn Brooks and Richard Wright. She later worked as a social worker, reporter, and magazine editor. Walker began teaching in the 1940s, and in 1949 joined the faculty of Jackson State College (now Jackson State University) in Mississippi, where in 1968 she founded the Institute for the Study of the History, Life and Culture of Black People. Her poetry collections include *For My People* (1942), *Prophets for a New Day* (1970), and *This Is My Century* (1989). She is also the author of *Richard Wright: Daemonic Genius* (1988).

ROSANNA WARREN (b. 1953) teaches at Boston University. Among other awards, she has received the Witter Bynner Prize, the Lila Wallace Reader's Digest Award, the 1994 Lamont Poetry Prize, the Ingram Merrill Grant for Poetry, the Lavan Younger Poets Prize, and a Guggenheim Fellowship. Her collections include *Each Leaf Shines Separate* and *Stained Glass*.

THOMAS WARTON, THE YOUNGER (1728–1790), like his father Thomas Warton, the Elder, taught poetry at Oxford University. His poetry influenced Charlotte Smith, William Lisle Bowles, and William Wordsworth, among others. His three-volume study, *The History of English Poetry* (1774–81), was the first significant work of its kind. He was appointed poet laureate in 1785; that same year he brought out an edition of Milton's poetry.

JOSEPH BLANCO WHITE (1775–1841) was born in Seville, Spain, where he was ordained as a priest in 1800. After leaving the Catholic priesthood he went to England in 1810. He studied at Oxford and became an Anglican clergyman. His sonnet "To Night," one of the few poems that he wrote, was first published under the title "Night and Death" and dedicated to Samuel Taylor Coleridge, who was a friend of his. The poem was praised highly by Coleridge and was popular for many years. White also wrote a number of religious tracts.

RICHARD WILBUR (b. 1921) was born in New York City, raised in New Jersey, and educated at Amherst College and Harvard University. His father was a painter. He joined the army in 1942 and served as a cryptographer during the Second World War. Wilbur has taught at many schools, including Harvard, and Wellesley College. A renowned translator of Spanish and French poetry, he received the Bollingen Prize in 1963 for his translation of Molière's *Tartuffe*. He again received the Bollingen Prize for Poetry in 1969 for *Walking to Sleep: New Poems and Translations*. Wilbur also writes children's books and literary essays. His numerous collections include *The Beautiful Changes* (1947), *Things of This World* (1956), *Advice to a Prophet* (1961), and *The Mind Reader* (1976).

OSCAR WILDE (1856–1900), the son of an eminent surgeon, studied at Trinity College, Dublin, and graduated from Oxford, where as a disciple of Walter Pater he founded the Aesthetic Movement. He soon became a public figure, making a lecture tour of the United States in 1882, publishing *The Picture of Dorian Gray* in 1891, and writing a series of brilliant comedies performed on the London stage. *An Ideal Husband* and *The Importance of Being Ernest* appeared in 1895, the year that scandal and imprisonment ended Wilde's career. After his release from Reading Gaol in 1897 he moved to Paris, his health severely damaged by the conditions he endured in prison.

YVOR WINTERS (1900–1968) was born in Chicago and spent his childhood in California and Oregon. He studied at the University of Chicago, the University of Colorado, and Stanford University, where he taught for many years. An important critic of poetry, he published a number of highly influential, controversial studies, including *Primitivism and Decadence: A Study of Experimental American Poetry* (1937). In 1961 he received the Bollingen Prize for his *Collected Poems*.

DAVID WOJAHN (b. 1953) is the author of collections of poetry that include *The Falling Hour* (1997), *Late Empire* (1994), and *Mystery Train* (1990). He has received two fellowships in poetry from the National Endowment for the Arts; the William Carlos Williams Book Award; the Yale Series of Younger Poets Award for his first collection, *Icehouse Lights*; two poetry fellowships from the Fine Arts Work Center in Provincetown; and the Amy Lowell Traveling Poetry Scholarship. He teaches in the graduate writing program at Indiana University.

WILLIAM WORDSWORTH (1770–1850) was born in Cockermouth, Cumberland, in the north of England's Lake District, and at eight was sent to school at Hawkshead, a region that became central to his imagination. Orphaned, but with the help of his two uncles, Wordsworth continued his studies and attended St. John's College, Cambridge. During summer vacation in 1790 he took a walking tour of Switzerland and France, where he experienced the euphoria of the early stages of the French Revolution, whose ideals he supported until the onset of the Terror. After graduating from Cambridge he took a walking tour of Wales, and then returned to France. There he fell in love with Annette Vallon, whom he intended to marry, but shortly after their daughter was born lack of funds forced him to return to England. The outbreak of war between England and France prevented his return until years later, when they had grown apart. In 1795, he received a legacy from a friend, which enabled him to settle in Racedown, Dorset, with his beloved sister, Dorothy. In the same year he met Samuel Taylor Coleridge, and moved two years later to Alfoxdon House to be closer to him. In 1798 Wordsworth and Coleridge published *Lyrical Ballads* and Wordsworth began composing his autobiographical epic, which he completed in 1805 but revised throughout his life; it was published posthumously in 1850 under the title *The Prelude*. In the winter of 1798-99 Wordsworth went to Germany with his sister and Coleridge; after his return he moved with Dorothy to Dove Cottage, Grasmere. In 1800 he published his groundbreaking Preface to the second edition of the *Lyrical Ballads*; in 1802 he came into his inheritance and, after a settlement with Vallon, married Mary Hutchinson. Wordsworth was appointed distributor of stamps for Westmoreland in 1813 and became poet laureate in 1843.

CHARLES WRIGHT (b. 1935) was born in Pickwick Dam, Tennessee, and educated at Davidson College and the University of Iowa. He served in the Army

Intelligence Unit, which brought him to Verona, Italy, where he began writing poetry. He returned to Italy as a Fulbright lecturer at the University of Padua and has studied in Rome. His collections include *The Southern Cross*, *Appalachia*, *Black Zodiac*, and *Native Blue: Selected Later Poems*; he has also published *Quarter Notes: Improvisations and Interviews*. He teaches at the University of Virginia.

JAMES WRIGHT (1927–1980) was born and raised in Martin's Ferry, Ohio. Upon graduation from high school in 1946, he joined the army and was stationed in occupied Japan. After his military service, he attended Kenyon College on the G.I. Bill, and studied with John Crowe Ransom. He traveled to Austria on a Fulbright Fellowship, and then earned master's and doctoral degrees at the University of Washington, where he studied with Theodore Roethke. He later taught at the University of Minnesota and Hunter College in New York. He published several volumes of translation; his poetry collections include *The Green Wall*, *Saint Judas*, *The Branch Will Not Break*, and his *Collected Poems*, which won the Pulitzer Prize.

LADY MARY WROTH (1587?–1652?) was the eldest daughter of Robert Sidney, Sir Philip Sidney's younger brother, and the niece of Mary Sidney Herbert, Countess of Pembroke. She was raised and educated at Penshurst, the Sidney family house. Her marriage to Sir Robert Wroth was arranged, and after her husband's death Mary had two children with her first cousin, William Herbert, third Earl of Pembroke. Her sonnet sequence *Pamphilia to Amphilanthus* is appended to her romance, *The Countesse of Mountgomeries Urania*, which appeared in 1621 and was considered scandalous because of its allusions to affairs in the Jacobean court. The second part of the *Urania* was not published. Wroth also wrote the pastoral drama *Love's Victorie*.

SIR THOMAS WYATT (1503–1542) was born at Allingham Castle in Kent, England and educated at St. John's College, Cambridge. He married Elizabeth Brooke in 1520, but separated from her a few years later, charging her with adultery. He was part of a dipomatic mission to France in 1526, accompanied Sir John Russell to the papal court in Rome in 1527, served Henry VIII as Marshall of Calais from 1528 to 1530, and was a member of the Privy Council. His diplomatic service brought him in contact with contemporary writing on the Continent. In June of 1533 he served in the coronation of Anne Boleyn, second queen of Henry VIII (and mother of Elizabeth I), and was knighted in 1535. Wyatt was imprisoned in 1534 on charges of brawling, and in 1536 was arrested and imprisoned in the Tower of London for quarreling with the Duke of Suffolk and possibly because he was suspected of being one of Boleyn's lovers; he witnessed Anne Boleyn's execution through a grate from his cell in Bell Tower, but was released soon after. From 1537 to 1539 he was ambassador to the court of Charles V in Spain. In 1541, accused of high treason, he fell out of royal favor again, but only temporarily. In 1528 Wyatt published *The quyete of mynde*, a translation from Plutarch. His poems, including his translations of Petrarch, through which he introduced the sonnet form into English, had circulated in manuscript in the 1520s and 1530s. Wyatt's translation of *Certayne Psalmes . . . drawen into Englyshe meter* appeared in 1549 and ninety-seven poems attributed to him were published alongside the poems of Surrey by the printer Richard Tottel in *Songes and Sonettes* (1557), an anthology that came to be known as *Tottel's Miscellany*. Wyatt died of a fever.

ELINOR WYLIE (1885–1928), was born in Somerville, New Jersey, to a prominent family. She was educated primarily at home, learning French and German and being taught to draw. She lived for a while in England with her second husband, Horace Wylie, whom she divorced in 1923. From 1922 until her death, she lived in Greenwich Village. Wylie became highly popular in the 1920s with the publication of *Nets to Catch the Wind* (1921) and *Black Armour* (1923). Her *Selected Poems* appeared in 1932.

WILLIAM BUTLER YEATS (1865–1939), was born in Dublin and educated at the Dublin Metropolitan School of Art, where he studied painting. His family went to London in 1868, returning to Dublin when Yeats was sixteen. He published his first poem in 1885 in *The Dublin University Review*. A major force in his life was his relationship with Maud Gonne, the Irish patriot and actress, under whose influence Yeats was drawn into Irish politics, although he eventually rejected her ideals. His many collections of poetry include *The Wind Among the Reeds* (1899), *In the Seven Woods* (1904), *The Green Helmet and Other Poems* (1910), *The Wild Swans at Coole* (1919), *The Tower* (1928), and *The Winding Stair and Other Poems* (1933). He also published many verse plays, translations, and a memoir entitled *A Vision* (1925).

INDEX OF POETS

INDEX OF TITLES AND FIRST LINES

CREDITS

Grace Schulman, "The Abbess of Whitby." Reprinted with permission of the author.

Delmore Schwartz, "The Beautiful American Word, Sure" from *In Dreams Begin Responsibilities*. Copyright © 1959 by Delmore Schwartz. Reprinted with permission of New Directions Publishing Corporation.

Frederick Seidel, "Elms" from *These Days*. Copyright © 1989 by Frederick Seidel. Reprinted with permission of Alfred A. Knopf, a division of Random House, Inc.

Hugh Seidman, "14 First Sentences" from *People Live, They Have Lives* (Columbus: The Ohio State University Press, 1993). Reprinted with permission of the author.

Charles Simic, "History" from *Austerities* (New York: George Braziller, 1982). Copyright © 1982 by Charles Simic. Reprinted with permission of the author.

Floyd Skloot, "My Daughter Considers Her Body" from *Music Appreciation* (Gainesville: University Press of Florida, 1944). Reprinted with permission of the author.

Tom Sleigh, "The Very End" from *After One*. Copyright © 1983 by Thomas R. Sleigh. Reprinted with permission of Houghton Mifflin Company. All rights reserved. "Eclipse" and "The God" from "The Work" from *The Chain* (Chicago: The University of Chicago Press, 1996). Copyright © 1996 by Tom Sleigh. Reprinted with permission of the author.

Bruce Smith, "O My Invisible Estate" from "In My Father's House" from *Silver and Information*. Copyright © 1985 by Bruce Smith. Reprinted with permission of The University of Georgia Press.

W. D. Snodgrass, "Μή τις . . . Οὖτις (Not any man . . . No Man)" from *Heart's Needle*. Copyright © 1959 by W. D. Snodgrass. Reprinted with permission of Alfred A. Knopf, a division of Random House, Inc. and The Marvell Press, London.

Stephen Spender, "Without that once clear aim, the path of flight" from *Collected Poems 1928–1953*. Copyright 1948 and renewed © 1976 by Stephen Spender. Reprinted with permission of Random House, Inc. and Faber & Faber Ltd.

William Stafford, "Time" from *Stories That Could be True* (New York: Harper & Row, Publishers, 1977). Copyright © 1977 by William Stafford. Reprinted with permission of the Estate of William Stafford.

Timothy Steele, "Summer" from *Sapphics and Uncertainties: Poems 1970–1986*. Copyright © 1995 by Timothy Steele. Reprinted with permission of the University of Arkansas Press.

Leon Stokesbury, "To His Book" from *Autumn Rhythm: New and Selected Poems*. Copyright © 1996 by Leon Stokesbury. Reprinted with permission of the University of Arkansas Press.

Allen Tate, 2 (" 'Ah, Christ, I love rings to the wild sky' ") from "Sonnets at Christmas" from *The Collected Poems 1919–1976*. Copyright © 1960 by Allen Tate. Reprinted with permission of Farrar, Straus & Giroux, LLC.

Henry Taylor, "Green Springs the Tree" from *The Flying Change*. Copyright © 1985 by Henry Taylor. Reprinted with permission of Louisiana State University Press.

Dylan Thomas, "Among Those Killed in the Dawn Raid Was a Man Aged a Hundred" from *Selected Poems*. Copyright 1943 by New Directions Publishing Corporation. Reprinted with permission of New Directions Publishing Corporation and David Higham Associates, Ltd.

Jean Toomer, "November Cotton Flower" from *Cane*. Copyright 1923 by Boni & Liveright, renewed 1951 by Jean Toomer. Reprinted with permission of Liveright Publishing Corporation.

John Updike, "Island Cities," published in *The New Yorker* (July 20, 1998). Copyright © 1998 by John Updike. Reprinted with permission of Condé Nast Publications, Inc.

Jean Valentine, "Rain" from *Growing Darkness, Growing Light* (Pittsburgh: Carnegie Mellon University Press, 1997). Copyright © 1997 by Jean Valentine. Reprinted with permission of the author.

Ellen Bryant Voigt, "Dear Mattie, You're sweet to write me every day," "When does childhood end? Mothers," "This is the double bed where she'd been born," and "Once the world had had its fill of war" from *Kyrie*. Copyright © 1995 by Ellen Bryant Voigt. Reprinted with permission of W. W. Norton & Company, Inc.